PENGUIN BOOKS

IN IT TOGETHER

Matthew d'Ancona is the award-winning political columnist for the *Sunday Telegraph*, *Evening Standard*, *The New York Times* and *GQ*. Previously, he was Editor of *The Spectator*, steering the magazine to record circulation. In 2007 he was named Editor of the Year (Current Affairs) at the BSME Awards, and in 2011 won the award for 'Commentariat of the Year', the highest honour at the Comment Awards. He is a Visiting Research Fellow at Queen Mary University of London and was elected a Fellow of All Souls College, Oxford, in 1989. He lives in east London.

D1081482

In It Together

The Inside Story of the Coalition Government

MATTHEW D'ANCONA

PENGUIN BOOKS

PENGUIN BOOKS

Penguin Group (USA) Inc., 375 Hudson Street, New York, New York 10014, USA
Penguin Group (Canada), 90 Eglinton Avenue East, Suite 700, Toronto, Ontario, Canada M4P 2Y3
(a division of Pearson Penguin Canada Inc.)
Penguin Ireland, 25 St Stephen's Green, Dublin 2, Ireland (a division of Penguin Books Ltd)
Penguin Group (Australia), 707 Collins Street, Melbourne, Victoria 3008, Australia
(a division of Pearson Australia Group Pty Ltd)
Penguin Books India Pvt Ltd, 11 Community Centre, Panchsheel Park, New Delhi – 110 017, India
Penguin Group (NZ), 67 Apollo Drive, Rosedale, Auckland 0632, New Zealand
(a division of Pearson New Zealand Ltd)
Penguin Books (South Africa) (Pty) Ltd, Block D, Rosebank Office Park,
181 Jan Smuts Avenue, Parktown North, Gauteng 2193, South Africa

Penguin Books Ltd, Registered Offices: 80 Strand, London WC2R 0RL, England

www.penguin.com

First published by Viking 2013
Published in Penguin Books 2014, with the addition of chapters 22–24
to cover the most recent events of 2013–14
001

Copyright © Matthew d'Ancona, 2013, 2014

The moral right of the author has been asserted

Typeset by Jouve (UK), Milton Keynes
Printed in Great Britain by Clays Ltd, St Ives plc

A CIP catalogue record for this book is available from the British Library

ISBN: 978-0-670-91995-6

www.greenpenguin.co.uk

MIX
Paper from
responsible sources
FSC
www.fsc.org   FSC™ C018179

Penguin Books is committed to a sustainable
future for our business, our readers and our planet.
This book is made from Forest Stewardship
Council™ certified paper.

For Mum and Dad

Great and glorious events which dazzle the beholder are represented by politicians as the outcome of grand designs, whereas they are usually products of temperaments and passions.

François, duc de La Rochefoucauld, *Maxims*, 1665

Contents

Preface: In it together

We hope, no doubt, for tangible profits from every Inner Ring we
penetrate: power, money, liberty to break rules, avoidance of routine
duties, evasion of discipline. But all these would not satisfy us if we
did not get in addition the delicious sense of secret intimacy.

C. S. Lewis, *The Inner Ring* (1944)

When I started writing this book, I assumed I was embarking upon
a portrait of a marriage: namely, the partnership between David
Cameron and Nick Clegg that began with the Rose Garden nuptials
in May 2010. But I quickly realized that the metaphor wasn't quite
right, or at least not quite sufficient. This is not just the story of a
relationship between two people, struggling to make it work and to do
the right thing by the people for whom they were responsible. There
were many people in this marriage.

This book is not a biography of Cameron, or a statistical tract on
the economy, worthy as such undertakings might be. What makes
the Coalition so compelling as a subject is its collective identity; what
makes it so politically strange is the fact that it exists at all. Since 1979,
this country has been edging towards a quasi-presidential political
culture, and politics has been dominated by the cult of personality.
Yet the most singular feature of this Government is not David Cameron's character and political identity – interesting as those subjects
are – but the bipartisanship of the administration he heads. It is a
coalition of two parties or, more truthfully, a partnership of two
party elites – elites that have often struggled to keep their respective
tribes signed up to the arrangement.

The very survival of that arrangement is remarkable. This
Government took the division between two parties as its starting

point and sought to make a virtue of that difference at a time of national crisis. In the Blair–Brown years, division was the problem, pathologically so at times. In the Coalition era, it has been the exo-skeleton and – at the beginning, at least – the claim to strength. There has never been a pretence of comprehensive, cross-Government unity: on a host of issues, Tories and Lib Dems positively advertised their differences. What mattered was agreement on the reforms that counted: notably, economic recovery, but also education, welfare and localism. In the past, 'split stories' were the stock-in-trade of political journalism. In this case, however, the guilty secret has often been that the two party leaders privately agree (on Libya, for example – as we shall see).

What attracted me to this approach was not only the interaction of the two parties, but the very specific origins of the Cameroon elite: they are a social grouping which chanced upon a political project, rather than a regular political faction like New Labour that quite naturally acquired a social dimension along the way. The ori-ginal Blair–Brown–Mandelson team formed around an ideological crusade – the salvation, by any means necessary, of a centre-Left party that had seemed incapable of winning. The people behind New Labour became friends in the process of pursuing that political objective.

In the case of David Cameron's set, the connections almost all predate the emergence of a distinct political mission. The gang came before the faction: indeed my first real contact with it was not through journalism at all, but on a group holiday in Tuscany in my twenties. I had known of Michael Gove and Ed Vaizey at university and later came into contact with George Osborne for the first time through a mutual college friend when I was assistant editor at *The Times*.

The pizza nights, in other words, came before the project and – had the other David (Davis) become leader in 2005 – would probably still be going, along with the bridge evenings, group holidays and children's play dates. After the Tories' third successive defeat, I thought Davis, the tough council estate boy raised by a single mother, would win the leadership, and initially wrote supportively of his candidacy in my columns. It seemed to me that he was a more substantial figure than was claimed by the Cameroons – for whom 'DD' was simply a right-wing Voldemort intent on destroying their beloved boy wizard. The Cameron campaign – though espousing the modernizing principles I had been arguing for myself – struck me as a bunch of talented friends establishing themselves as a powerful faction within the party. In the September of 2005, one of Cameron's campaign lieutenants – now a very senior figure in the Government – asked me when they should throw the towel in, and how. Even at the party conference in October, Osborne was saying that what really mattered was to show the movement and the media that the Cameron caucus was more than 'Michael Howard's boys' and had become a serious force in its own right. But the remarkable speech the young candidate gave in Blackpool transformed his prospects and – of necessity – turned his team from a group of postcode friends into the nucleus of a leader's office.

To add to the eccentricity of the new governing Tory elite in 2010, its ranks were suddenly swollen with the leading figures from a party that, for many years, and in many ways, had treated the Conservative Party as the deadly enemy it shared with Labour, and had explored the possibility of entrenching a 'progressive majority' or a 'realignment of politics' by altering the electoral system. It is one of the great jokes played by fate upon modern politicians – one that the gods of antiquity would have relished – that when the Lib Dems did finally enter government it was with the Tories at their side.

This brings me to an important analytical issue. Too often, the Coalition has been scrutinized through the dusty prism of the New Labour era. That period was utterly dominated by the rivalry between Tony Blair and Gordon Brown and the clashes between their respective supporters. Between 1997 when the Tories limped wretchedly off the pitch and Michael Howard's acclamation as leader in 2003 (the moment when the Conservatives rediscovered a measure of discipline), politics was defined by the conflict between two Labour giants, two mafia families and two irreconcilable sub-parties. Blair and Brown were figures from Shakespearean tragedy, doomed by their respective flaws, fighting to the political death.

Like generals, we journalists find it easier to re-fight the last war. To some extent, Cameron invited this by posturing as the 'heir to Blair' and insisting that only the modernized Conservative Party could complete New Labour's conspicuously incomplete programme of public service and welfare reform. He and Osborne called Blair 'the Master' with a combination of mirth and filial piety. To the extent that the Coalition was seeking to do the work that Blair could not or would not finish, the precedent was valuable. In other areas, Cameron was trying to make a break with the Labour past: in foreign policy, for instance, and public spending (not enough of a break in the latter case, his Conservative critics objected).

But those looking for literary templates for the Coalition are better advised to read, say, Mary McCarthy's *The Group* or Anthony Powell's *A Dance to the Music of Time* than the ever-expanding library of books about, or by, New Labour's prime movers. This is less a story of individuals than of groups – the 'Notting Hill Set', the 'Orange Book' Lib Dems, the Bullingdon Club, Old Etonians, modernizing Tories, Whitehall mandarins and querulous backbenchers.

The Cameroons had prepared well for government – even, as shall be seen, for coalition. But there was no meaningful precedent to hand. Robert Armstrong's recently declassified account of the failed coalition talks in 1974 between Edward Heath and Jeremy Thorpe was fascinating but scarcely a blueprint for 2010. While Blair made quite explicit use of the Thatcher play-book, Cameron was denied the opportunity to model himself on either quasi-presidential predecessor. The Coalition required a quite different and completely new approach to decision-taking and departmental management. With no manual to follow, he and his colleagues were writing their own as they went; and, sometimes, it showed. The New Labour years had often resembled *The Sopranos*. The early days of the Cameron–Clegg partnership were often closer to an episode of *Lost*.

The story told in this book begins on the first night of the new Government and ends (for now) in July 2013. What struck me as I went back to explore relatively recent events was how quickly many of them – even wars and riots – had almost faded from general memory and, more intriguingly, how often they already seemed like episodes from the remote past to those who had been involved in them. We no longer live in the age of 24/7 media, but in the Twit-terverse, where a news cycle can last no more than a couple of hours. A tweet is a long time in politics.

That makes the task of those writing the first draft of history all the more important. In researching this book, I have drawn on more than 130 interviews and countless less formal conversations with the main participants in the Coalition, and some outside its perimeter fence. I took an early decision to conduct all these interviews on a background basis. The Government was too young for on-the-record rumination and reflection, though the time for that will come. Proceeding on this basis, I was able to speak to everyone I needed to, in many cases several times. I am grateful to all who gave up their time to elucidate and explain the inner life of the Coalition. They had a story to tell, one which, at the time of writing, has not yet concluded. Part of its appeal is that (in my view) the ending is genu-inely unpredictable. The failure of the economy to recover with anything like the speed required (by the Tories and Lib Dems, at any rate) has made for many desperate hours on the Coalition side. But Labour's lead in the polls has not yet hardened into a winning pos-ition. With apologies to the *auteur*-director Peter Weir, the players in *The Cameron Show* should indeed be wearing badges asking: 'How will it end?'

Where a thought, opinion or feeling is attributed to an individual, it should not be assumed that the person in question was the source, or the primary source. Often, I am reporting what they said to others contemporaneously. There is no code in this book, either. When I say 'friends', I mean friends. This Coalition is social in every sense of the word.

I have arranged the story around broad themes rather than accord-ing to pure chronology. I hope this is helpful to readers. It certainly helped me: if I were dictator for a day I would outlaw all reference to Harold Macmillan's banal line 'events, dear boy, events' (which he may not even have uttered). The only possible excuse for mentioning it again here is to disown it; an inventory of a government's deeds day after day, week after week, would be very dull work for reader and writer alike. What counts are the patterns and the themes that are to be detected in the political mosaic.

This matters disproportionately because the Coalition has been so bad at public diplomacy – not 'spin', or even day-to-day communications, but the more subtle work of explaining what it is doing, and why. There are no natural teacher-politicians in its ranks. The nostalgia many felt on learning of Margaret Thatcher's death in April 2013 was partly a yearning for clarity and definition. As if by instinct, the late Baroness framed policies and political arguments in rhetoric and metaphor that cut through to the country's cerebral cortex, its heart and its guts. She provoked love and hate – and not much in between – precisely because everyone knew what she was up to. The difference between revenue and expenditure is not the only deficit which afflicts this Government. It also suffers from the gap between political action and popular understanding: the great cognitive deficit between what it is trying to do and what it is thought to be doing. The chronicler of the Coalition has to try and fill in the blanks.

Looking back on the past three years in Westminster and Whitehall, I was surprised by the sheer mass of material. What cannot be denied – even if it is rarely acknowledged – is that the Cameron–Clegg Government has done an awful lot already, with plenty more to come. It will never again be possible to argue, as the Conservative Party always has in the past, that coalitions are invariably paralysed. The mass of Government activity between 2010 and 2013 is another reason why the book, though broadly chronological in shape, is mostly partitioned by theme.

As the full implications of the financial crash became clear in the course of 2008, Cameron (and Osborne) adopted the mantra that 'we are all in this together'. This was the self-conscious language of emergency at a time of national trial. But it was not a Churchillian demand – 'blood, toil, tears and sweat' – nor a Thatcheresque claim of personal destiny amidst faint hearts – 'the lady's not for turning'. As so often, Cameron was making a point about 'fairness' and the distribution of pain. Those with the broadest shoulders would bear the heaviest burden. The vulnerable would be protected – or so the Tory leader claimed.

It was partly a defensive reflex. David Cameron was acutely conscious of his privileged background and frictionless rise – prep school, Eton, Oxford, politics – and his consequent vulnerability to the old charge that the Tory Party is the political face of power, wealth and the status quo. But it also echoed the question that had dominated the politics of post-Thatcher Britain. Like a theorem awaiting proof by mathematicians, the objective had never been in doubt: a political settlement that combined the vigour of free market economics with a sense of social justice and social responsibility. New Labour's answer was the 'Third Way': something old, something new, something borrowed, something blue. Blair promised to reconcile aspiration with community, personal ambition with social solidarity. Brown's more Faustian approach was to set the financial sector free and spend the revenue bounty (and more besides) on public services. The Tory Right still argued that a strong society is one weaned off government and nurtured by tax cuts, by the spread of home- and share-ownership, and by the shrinkage of the 'unproductive part of the economy'.

Cameron sought to do something quite different. His objective was semantic: to insist that the words 'society' and 'state' were not interchangeable, and to show that 'community' and 'government' were not the same thing.[1] That was a bold project in a country as politically ambiguous as this one. This is a land of self-reliance and privacy, a great engine of personal aspiration and dignity.[2] But it is also the country that spawned the NHS and the BBC, the two great institutional creations of the British twentieth century. The people of these islands want to be left alone, to pay lower taxes than their continental counterparts and to enjoy their ancestral liberties. But, to an extent some find hard to accept, they also expect a huge amount from government.

When Cameron talked about the 'Big Society', he aspired to fill the great no-man's-land between the individual citizen and the Goliath of government. That was always going to be the work of decades, unpopular in a culture geared increasingly to instant gratification. It pleased neither the Right, who wanted him to get on with the work of shrinking government, nor the Left, who assumed that dismantling the welfare state was what he was secretly doing anyway.[3]

Yet here was the ultimate product of C. S. Lewis's 'Inner Ring' (see the epigraph above) suggesting that there was indeed a social bond between us all, one that comes into its own in times of adversity. Was this patrician Tory leader serious when he said he wanted to 'spread privilege'? Or was that just another one of the ingenious ways that established power has of reasserting itself? I remember once discussing this with Billy Bragg in a BBC green room. I was explaining to him that Cameron and Osborne really did know the lyrics to songs by the Smiths – and probably some of his own. The great folksinger, writer of such classics of lyrical protest as 'Between the Wars' and 'Waiting for the Great Leap Forwards', shook his head: 'Amazing, innit? They always find a way. The Tories. They absorb everything. In the end.'

It is an irresistible subject: a bunch of well-heeled Tories joining forces with a bunch of middle-class Lib Dems and asserting that they felt our pain. Cameron's true audacity – or bare-faced cheek – lay in his claim to be in the same boat as the electorate. Clegg's courage inspired him to clamber aboard, too. Was boldness their friend or their enemy? Were they really in it together? And – for that matter – were we? In the answers to those questions lies the true story of the Coalition.

London, 2013

1. 'How the hell did *this* happen?'

It felt like a break-in. On the evening of Tuesday, 11 May 2010, David Cameron, George Osborne and William Hague prowled the corridors of Number Ten, as the endorphins of newly acquired power battled with the unavoidable sense of imposture that afflicts any new Government. Exhaustion vied with exhilaration, fatigue with adrenaline. The 'fierce urgency of now', a phrase annexed from Martin Luther King by President Obama, competed with reflections upon the long journey that had brought the Conservative Party back to power.

After five days of nerve-shredding negotiation – on top of months on the campaign trail – the party and the Liberal Democrats were signing off a deal that, depending upon your perspective, was a political master-stroke; or nonsense on stilts, swaying precariously on a foundation of sand; or, perhaps, both. The path from general election to the formation of this Government had been unconventional, to say the least, and the warm embrace of power still seemed conditional and probationary. But power it most certainly was, however acquired.

The moment was captured by Andy Parsons, Cameron's court photographer, in a picture of the three men with their arms round each other's shoulders: weary, elated, like exhausted marathon runners who have finally crossed the line. Copies of the photo now stand by Osborne's desk at the Treasury, in Hague's cavernous office in King Charles Street and in the PM's Downing Street flat.

Down a long corridor to the left of the famous hallway leading to Number 12, they found the L-shaped suite of offices that Gordon Brown had used as his 'war room'. Here, the Labour Prime Minister had sat with Peter Mandelson, Alastair Campbell and other key aides. The 'horseshoe' of work stations, with Brown's at the centre, was meant to encourage a sense of urgency, to symbolize the supposedly military speed and discipline of the Number Ten command centre. Osborne reflected that it was less a war room than a newsroom, with Brown trying to 'edit the nation'. In its dying days, Labour had become a parody of the media with which it felt itself to be at war, fighting off every bad headline, governing by spin, seeking what the party's master-strategist, Philip Gould, had once called the 'daily mandate'. The new leaders of the Coalition were determined not to make the same mistakes in their handling of the media – little suspecting in these first heady hours the toxic role that their relationship with the press was to play in the months to come.

In the British system, power is transferred instantly and without delicacy. Brown's command centre was still littered with empty pizza boxes and coffee cups, last remnants of the fallen regime. Cameron took one look at the shabby scene and gave his verdict: 'Well, no one can work here!' Then he led the way back to the more salubrious rooms of Number Ten.

This was indeed a moment to savour for the new Prime Minister and the 38-year-old lieutenant who would shortly become the youngest Chancellor of the Exchequer since Randolph Churchill in 1886: two young men who, five years previously, had defied the early odds to seize control of the Tory Party and now, with fleet footwork, had turned a disappointing election result into a bipartisan national government.

For the first time in thirty-one years, a Conservative Prime Minister had replaced a Labour incumbent; for the first time in eighteen, Labour had lost an election. Cameron, born in 1966, was the first 'Generation X' premier, a politician raised in quite different circumstances from those of his Baby Boom predecessors. He was also Eton's nineteenth Prime Minister, a graduate of Oxford University and – like Osborne and the Mayor of London, Boris Johnson – a former member of the Bullingdon, an undergraduate dining society so infamous that it had been satirized as the 'Bollinger Club' in Evelyn Waugh's *Decline and Fall* and, more recently, as the 'Riot Club' in Laura Wade's savagely funny play *Posh*.

The son of a successful stockbroker and a magistrate, Cameron was a One Nation Tory by temperament and background. His intellect had secured him a First Class degree, but his politics were visceral rather than deductive. Like Margaret Thatcher, he believed that the facts of life were Conservative and that the country was better off when governed by the Tory Party. More specifically, he argued that his father, Ian, who was disabled, had given him an unquenchable sense of optimism – 'that no matter how bad things are, you can overcome them'. From his mother, Mary, he claimed to have inherited 'an enduring sense of community, responsibility, obligation'.[1]

Osborne, though heir to a baronetcy, had emerged from a much more metropolitan background, a day-boy at St Paul's whose mother was firmly of the Left. Had he not applied for a job at Conservative Central Office in 1994 at the suggestion of a friend, it is probable that he would have become a journalist.[2] Instead, sixteen years after choosing the path of politics, he was the second most powerful man in the country.

And Hague? Though still in his forties, he was the undisputed elder statesman of the Cameron kindergarten, the third voice in the room and, as a former leader of the party, a man who knew where all the potholes and pitfalls lay. His presence in Downing Street that evening was an apt recognition of past service and his success alongside Osborne in the coalition negotiations; but it was also prophetic. 'Few people realize,' as one Cabinet minister put it, 'that the most powerful decision-making body in the Coalition is the Cameron–Osborne–Hague triangle.'[3]

As the Cameron team gathered in the Cabinet Room, the excitement was palpable. But Osborne's emotions were still governed by straightforward relief: after days of anxiety and brinkmanship, they were through the door. Others came and went: Patrick McLoughlin, the Conservative Chief Whip and a confidant of the new Prime Minister; Jeremy Heywood, Brown's Downing Street Permanent Secretary, effortlessly adjusting to the new regime; Steve Hilton, Cameron's strategy director; and Andy Coulson, communications director. Ed Llewellyn, the PM's chief of staff, assumed immediate charge of Cabinet appointments, taking as his text a provisional list that had been drawn up on polling day at Hilton's Oxfordshire home. That plan would now have to be significantly amended to accommodate the Lib Dems.

The politicians' instinct was to err on the side of generosity and appoint more Cabinet ministers. Sue Gray, the head of propriety and ethics at the Cabinet Office, impressed Osborne by her refusal to let them have their way on a night when most officials were testing the water and behaving deferentially around their new political masters. 'There's a limit to how many Cabinet ministers you can have,' she told Cameron firmly. This meant, in a classic Whitehall distinction, that senior members of the Coalition such as Francis Maude and Oliver Letwin would attend Cabinet meetings without enjoying full Cabinet status. 'There was no manual left behind by Churchill,' one senior aide recalled. 'We just had to get on with it.' Llewellyn worked from the file marked 'If We Win', brought over from Conservative Campaign HQ by Cameron's political private secretary, Laurence Mann.

The circumstances of the Government's origins meant that there had been no hoopla of the sort that welcomed Tony Blair when he entered Downing Street in 1997: no 'Britain Just Got Better' T-shirts, no party workers posing as members of the public waving flags to hail the new PM. Just before 8.45 p.m., on the steps of Number Ten, Cameron had said that coalition 'is the right way to provide this country with the strong, the stable, the good and decent government that I think we need so badly. Nick Clegg and I are both political leaders who want to put aside party differences and work hard for the common good and for the national interest.' His Government would stand up for aspiration but always look after 'the elderly, the frail, the poorest in our country'. And he would always, he said, be honest about the limits of what the state could do: 'Real change is when everyone pulls together, comes together, works together, when we all exercise our responsibilities to ourselves, to our families, to our communities and to others.'

Behind him stood his pregnant wife, Samantha, and to his right core members of Team Cameron, including Steve Hilton, soon to assume the deliberately vague title of 'senior adviser'; Coulson; Coulson's deputy, Gabby Bertin; Kate Fall, Cameron's longtime friend and deputy chief of staff; and Liz Sugg, the formidable 'Miss Fixit' of the gang, who would become Number Ten's head of operations. At the fringes of the television screen, the electorate caught its first glimpse of the cohort it had not quite elected to run the country.

The sense of euphoria that sweeps through a party when it returns to office – in the case of the Lib Dems, after decades in the wilderness – was leavened by a sense of surrealism. As one Cameron adviser remembers it: 'There was this incredulity – you know, "How the hell did *this* happen?" ' Hilton, still convinced that the glass of politics was very much half full, was struck by the warmth of the Number Ten staff. Fall sensed that the people who ran the building were ready for a change after the final, grim chapter of King Gordon's reign – projectiles, shouting and fits of fury – but that Sarah Brown would be missed.

By the time Cameron, Osborne and Hague explored the building, it seemed more like the *Mary Celeste*. Only hours before, these offices and halls had still been occupied by Brown, his family and his remaining acolytes, as the outgoing Prime Minister clung to power by his well-chewed fingernails – till even he had to accept that the game was up. Once persuaded that it was time to leave, Brown became the unlikely midwife to the Coalition: it was his insistence in a telephone call to Clegg that he had to go to Buckingham Palace to tender his resignation that forced a decision upon the Lib Dems.

New Labour's thirteen-year tenancy of Downing Street was over, the stage vacated for the clique denounced by Brown as 'public school bullies' and, in more reflective moments, as 'libertarians' – neo-Thatcherites determined, in his view, to dismantle the postwar welfare state while promising 'compassion'; all the more deplorable because they seemed to Brown to be contaminated by the spirit of Regency libertinage. When the alleged use of illegal drugs by Cameron and Osborne became an issue during the Conservative leadership race of 2005, Blair had seen little point in making a prim partisan issue of the controversy. But Brown had been fiercely opposed to the Cameroons' defence that a politician's conduct before he entered public life was private. 'They broke the law,' he muttered to his aides.[4] To the last, he remained convinced that a Cameron Government would stand for private hedonism and public squalor.

The drugs controversy had done nothing to stop Cameron's victory in the run-off five years before against his older rival for the Tory crown, David Davis, or figured significantly in the 2010 general election campaign, despite persistent rumours sweeping the media that this or that juicy story about cocaine-snorting Tories was about to break. In any case, the party's electoral problems proved to have deeper roots than putative scandals about Class A narcotics.

First, the sheer arithmetic scale of the challenge had been eclipsed by the general sense that Labour's time was over. Brown looked exhausted, baffled, even jinxed: the most memorable image of the campaign was the Prime Minister, head in hands, listening to a recording of himself calling a voter in Rochdale a 'bigoted woman'. But if Brown's moment had passed, it did not follow that a Tory triumph was at hand. Osborne, an obsessive fan of Robert Caro's multi-volume life of Lyndon Johnson, often quotes LBJ's first rule of politics, which is that its practitioners must be able to count. In 2010, the numbers were always against him as election co-ordinator. For the Tories to win, a swing of 6.9 per cent between the main parties was required. In the event, the party achieved an average of 5.3 per cent from Labour and gained their highest number of seats in a general election since 1931. But it was not enough: 306 was twenty shy of a majority. The scoreboard did not lie.

Iain Duncan Smith later joked in private that mentioning the election around the new Prime Minister was like mentioning Heather Mills around Sir Paul McCartney: something you tried not to do.[5] But it was a hard subject to avoid – the inevitable backdrop to all the arguments to come, and the root psychological cause of the party's intermittent tendency to self-harm. Cameron's failure to win an outright majority was to become the maypole around which his party danced angrily.

The recriminations began with the first exit polls on 6 May. Some argued that the leader and his circle had been too fixated by abstractions such as the 'post-bureaucratic age' and the 'Big Society', paying insufficient attention to the 'kitchen table Conservatism' that wins elections. Particular scorn was reserved for the blue hardcover Conservative manifesto, entitled 'Invitation to Join the Government of Britain'. The 120-page booklet was handsome and intellectually ambitious, promising a radical redistribution of power from the centre to communities, families and individuals. It deftly knitted together public service reform, social cohesion, localism and active citizenship. But it lacked a sense of crisis, its idiom lofty rather than 'pub-ready'. As striking and imaginative as it undoubtedly was, the manifesto did not speak with sufficient urgency to voters worrying about their jobs, their standard of living, their savings. At a time of economic turbulence and national anxiety, the little blue book just seemed too clever by half.

Much was also made in the post mortem of the tension between Coulson and Hilton. Coulson, a former editor of the *News of the World*, whom Cameron described privately as a 'genius', wanted a crunchy 'retail politics' of practical measures that could be sold to the press and on the doorstep. Hilton did not see why this should exclude a more visionary approach, specifically the 'Big Society' theme that he and the Tory leader regarded as a potential basis for sound government. Osborne stood poised between them, sympathetic to Coulson, but reluctant to trigger a full-blown turf war on the eve of a general election.

Cameron's solution was to put Hilton and Coulson in an office together at Conservative campaign headquarters in Millbank Tower. 'It didn't really work out the way Dave imagined' is the wry verdict of one of their campaign colleagues, now a senior adviser.[6] Raised voices were heard on more than one occasion. 'It was clear that, by the end, Andy and Steve were avoiding each other', according to one veteran of the campaign. 'They were allergic to one another.' Coulson, immaculately tailored, was tidy, even-tempered, used to the disciplines of the newsroom. Hilton, shoeless, unpredictable and fiery, believed in 'creative disruption'. The wheeze of forcing the two men to cohabit doubtless appealed to Cameron's sense of mischief as well as to his unquenchable optimism. In practice, it was an abdication of responsibility and a failure of leadership, albeit relatively minor.

The election had also conspicuously failed to resolve the long-standing argument between 'modernizers' and the Right. Many on the modernizing wing of the party believed that the result would have been better if the so-called 'detoxification' of the Tory brand had been more aggressive, and more effort had been made to present the party as a truly national movement, compassionate and alive to the needs of contemporary Britain.

In Cameron's early years as leader, this campaign had often lent itself to media satire: he posed with huskies on a Norwegian glacier to dramatize his green credentials, paraded his recycled trainers and declared that what young delinquents often needed was 'a lot more love' (translated into the unforgettable headline 'hug a hoodie'). But he and Hilton were untroubled by the mockery. The key was to get the message across that the Conservative Party was undergoing a root-and-branch transformation. Hilton was fond of quoting Gandhi: 'You must be the change you want to see in the world.' Visual shock therapy – the message being: this is a Tory leader unlike any other – was the core of the strategy. The lampooning of Cameron's ostentatious greenery, support for international aid and compassion for troubled teenagers just showed that the message was getting through.

The political risk, as they saw it, was not that the Tory leader might be ridiculed. The danger was that he might be judged fraudulent, and the change dismissed as inauthentic. The Conservatives' private polls showed that the voters had noted and remembered the reports in April 2006 that, as Cameron pedalled to work on his bike, he was followed by a chauffeur-driven car carrying his documents. The defence that no panniers were big enough for the paperwork handled by a party leader made no difference. What mattered was the gap between appearance and reality: the gap which, more than anything else, had eroded the public's trust in politicians.

Yet, that May night in Number Ten, it seemed that the so-called 'Notting Hill Tories' had pulled off a coup without precedent – the formation of a new centrist national government – and one which might have transformative consequences for the political landscape. The young Conservatives around Cameron who admired Barack

Obama's style, charisma and shimmering modernity liked to quote the dictum of his then chief of staff, Rahm Emanuel: 'Never let a crisis go to waste.' The election result was certainly a crisis, but, as far as the Cameroons were concerned, it had been turned to conspicuous advantage. The alliance with Clegg not only added fifty-seven seats to the Government's total, delivering a formal aggregate majority of seventy-six. Potentially, this was also an ideological breakthrough.

For a decade and a half, in opposition and power, New Labour had filled the political sky, while the Tories struggled miserably to achieve a stable post-Thatcherite identity. 'Mods' had fought with traditionalist 'rockers', Europhiles with Eurosceptics, social liberals with social conservatives. Yet the Tory–Lib Dem pact promised a completely new alignment.

In these early, exploratory hours, there were excitable conversations about the medium-term pact turning into something more enduring. Even as the dust of the 2010 election settled, its beneficiaries were already musing about the prospects of a Lib–Con pact in 2015, or a 'coupon election' on the model of 1918 in which the Liberal Lloyd George and Conservative Bonar Law issued letters of endorsement to candidates who agreed to support them.[7] In the first flush of the Coalition's existence such extravagant ideas had a currency that would soon enough seem ludicrous as the two parties got used to the daily abrasions of coexistence.

With fiscally sensible and reform-minded Lib Dems such as Nick Clegg, Danny Alexander and David Laws about to be sitting round the same Cabinet table as Cameron, Osborne and Gove, the centre of political gravity seemed to have moved decisively to the natural terrain of the moderate Tories: economic conservatism, social liberalism, a government at ease with the contemporary world. That impression, as would soon become clear, was only half true: the Coalition was not coterminous with the two parties that had formed it – there were vast, lawless political prairies to the left and right of the Government – and neither tribe was remotely ready to discard its past in the name of an untested shiny future.

But, for now, the Tory centrism represented by Cameron and Osborne deserved its ripple of applause; and, as they and Hague knew better than most, its achievements were hard-won, the yield of a long battle within the party fortress. The process known in Westminster shorthand as Tory modernization was spawned not – as so many media profiles of the new PM claimed – in Notting Hill after the 2005 election defeat, but in a think-tank in Queen Anne's Gate before the 1997 landslide.

There, in the offices of the Social Market Foundation, three young centre-Right policy wonks – Daniel Finkelstein, Rick Nye and Andrew Cooper – began to ask why the Conservatives were failing and what needed to be done to prepare the party for the challenges ahead.[8] What Finkelstein, Nye and Cooper – urged on by David Willetts – quickly realized was that the Conservative Party was perceived by the electorate as indifferent or even hostile to public services. At a deeper level, they grasped that the public had become so suspicious of Conservative motives that the party's association with a policy, however attractive, triggered suspicions in the voters' minds. A painful conclusion followed: that to regain office, the Conservatives would have to change the way they communicated, the way they did business, the language they used, the way they were. This was not a public relations challenge, but an identity crisis: the problem was not Tory policies, but the Tories themselves.

Finkelstein went on to become political adviser to Hague, who, as party leader, was initially an enthusiastic and formidable spokesman for this new approach. In 1997, delivering his first conference speech at the helm, Hague called for a Conservatism that 'believes freedom doesn't stop at the shop counter . . . that listens, that has compassion at its core'. This was not, he insisted, just a question of image, as so many critics of modernization have argued before and since. 'Compassion is not a bolt-on extra to Conservatism,' Hague declared. 'It's at its very core.'

At the same annual gathering, Michael Portillo – recently ousted from the Commons – delivered a memorable speech under the auspices of the Centre for Policy Studies that gave the modernizing cause its foundation text.[9] The distaste the voters had come to feel for the Tories, Portillo argued, 'must be appreciated as a deeply felt distaste, rather than momentary irritation. We cannot dismiss it as mere false perception. Tories were linked to harshness: thought to be uncaring about unemployment, poverty, poor housing, disability and single parenthood; and considered indifferent to the moral arguments over landmines and arms sales. We were thought to favour greed and the unqualified pursuit of the free market, with a "devil take the hindmost" attitude.'

According to Portillo, the party had become associated with arrogance and insensitivity 'using the language of economics and high finance when people's jobs and self-esteem were at stake'. Above all, the Tories were perceived to be at odds with contemporary reality in all its diversity and complexity. 'I believe that it is extremely important for the Conservative Party to deal with the world as it now is': this was the most important sentence in Portillo's 1997 speech.

Thrown by his failure to make electoral ground, and fearful of driving away the Conservative core vote, Hague switched mid-term to a much more abrasive and demotic Toryism that the Blairites found all too easy to parody as 'skinhead Conservatism'. One of the ugliest leadership contests of recent decades followed his crushing general election defeat in 2001: Portillo – back in the Commons and standing as the ultra-modernizer candidate – offered a stark choice to his party: adapt or die. Iain Duncan Smith, mocking Portillo's 'pashmina politics' and dismissing Ken Clarke's Europhilia, emerged the unexpected victor.

IDS, the self-styled 'quiet man', also flirted with some elements of the modernizing agenda, but did not last long as leader. After his abrupt defenestration in 2003, Michael Howard succeeded him by acclamation and – like Hague – promised initial enthusiasm for the modernizers' programme. At the Saatchi Gallery in October 2003, he called for a Conservatism 'broad in appeal and generous in outlook', a party which would 'preach a bit less and listen a bit more', and 'a new kind of politics' distinguished by 'rigorous honesty, measured criticism, realistic alternatives'. But – like Hague – Howard did not (or could not) stick with it. By the 2005 general election, with the Australian political strategist Lynton Crosby at his side, he was blowing the 'dog whistle' on immigration and asylum as the party lumbered towards its third successive heavy defeat. If there is a lesson in this brief history, it is that Tory modernization is an easy cause to embrace, and a very hard one to stay true to.

The mood changed, at least for a while, after the 2005 election. Humbled by Labour's hat-trick, the activists grasped that serious change was called for. At the party's conference in Blackpool, Francis Maude, then chairman, showed them what he called his 'killer slide': polling evidence revealing that public support for a proposal halved when respondents were told it was a Tory policy. In other words, the Conservative brand was so contaminated that it drove voters away from otherwise appealing policies.

Cameron's first two years as leader were a period of systematic change. The so-called 'A list' of candidates was introduced to freshen up the party's parliamentary face. The traditional Conservative emphasis upon Europe, immigration and tax cuts was replaced by new preoccupations: the environment, international development and – above all – the NHS.

After a decade of patience and plotting, Brown finally replaced Blair as PM in June 2007. Cameron and Osborne were sure that if he called a snap election, he would win. They went to the Tory conference in Blackpool fearing, quite rationally, that this might be the last such party gathering they addressed in the top jobs. Labour prepared for just such a rush to the polls, spent prodigious sums on preparing the campaign, and braced itself for battle – until Brown himself pulled the plug at the very last moment, dismayed by his pollsters' findings that a dash to the country was not certain to deliver victory.[10]

Granted a reprieve by Gordon's caution, Cameron faced a more fundamental challenge in the financial crisis, beginning with the credit crunch and the collapse of Northern Rock in September 2007. The closure of Lehman Bros. a year later, on the eve of the 2008 party conference season, brutally dramatized the change in the terms of trade. The Cameroons had initially grazed on the pleasant meadows of 'quality of life', courting ridicule with the idea of a 'happiness index' and public fretting about the cut-price sale of chocolate oranges. Though some of these initiatives – brilliantly satirized in Armando Iannucci's *The Thick of It* as 'tax breaks for aromatherapists' –

survived the journey into government, it was clear that standard of living and economic recovery would be the core issues of the general election and of the Parliament that followed.

Having promised initially to match Labour spending until 2010/11 and to 'share the proceeds of growth' between public expenditure and tax cuts, the Tory leader now decided upon unvarnished candour about the scale of the economic problem. Against the counsel of some of his circle, Cameron began to speak of the 'Age of Austerity' and the necessary pain that this would involve. In his speech to the Conservative Spring Conference in April 2009, he declared that this new era, with all its prospective stringencies, was the necessary consequence of 'the age of irresponsibility' – by which he meant 'the age of Gordon'. In a single address, Cameron used the word 'austerity' eleven times: rarely had an Opposition leader hugged the cactus of future collective hardship so openly.

Osborne was especially clear about the implications for the next Government – and for himself. The kitchen suppers he held at his west London home were his own salon, gatherings at which guests included Robert Zoellick, the president of the World Bank, Jeffrey Sachs, the international development guru, James Murdoch and other senior media figures. At one such dinner in 2009, he said: 'If I'm not the most unpopular Chancellor ever in six months, I'll have failed.'

In all this, the modernizing message became obscured. It was not disavowed so much as crowded out by the argument about economic recovery, the structural deficit (£156bn when the Coalition was formed) and the need to contain public spending. The campaign to change public perceptions of the Tory Party and to reassure voters faded into the background. Traditionalist Conservatives believed that a more robust message on immigration, tax cuts, economic competence and Europe would have cut through and energized the electorate. But in the internal and external audit that followed the general election the analysis which commanded the broadest approval among psephologists and pollsters was that too many voters were still unsure about Conservative motives and values on 6 May 2010 to put their cross by the Tory candidate's name.[11]

This retrospective squabble would continue throughout the life of the Coalition, a battle for the future of Conservatism masquerading as a debate about its past. What is beyond doubt is that the campaign lacked clarity. Cameron himself felt, with a measure of self-reproach, that the party had never settled upon a sufficiently simple message, and that its campaign objectives remained unclear. Part of the Tory pitch to the electorate was honesty about the measures to come: a promise of competence rather than kindness. Yet, at Cameron's insistence, a dash of compassion was also in the mix. As he saw it, there had to be at least a modicum of warmth about the campaign, even if its central message was bleak. On huge posters plastered across a thousand sites in January – before the official campaign was launched – he promised to cut the deficit, not the NHS. But what was the salient point? Was it: 'The Tories have changed and it is safe to vote for us'? Or: 'Only the Tories have the guts to do what is necessary to save the country'? Looking back on the 2010 election, the new PM was sure that sheer confusion about what sort of 'change', precisely, he represented had cost him a great many votes.

As disappointed as Cameron and Osborne were by the result, they were much less surprised than they seemed. The proprieties of a campaign and the necessary fictions have to be observed: in any electoral contest, it is essential that the party leader and his campaign chief exude confidence that they can win until the last vote is counted. But, even as Tory activists pounded the pavements and knocked on doors across the land, Cameron and Osborne were calculating the impossibility of the task.

With only a few weeks to go, they had decided for once to dispense with opinion polls, focus groups and all other generalities, and to go through the full list of the nation's 650 constituencies, from Aberavon to Yorkshire East, estimate the party's prospects in each seat with brutal candour, and thus assess the true state of their overall chances on 6 May. By the time they had completed their laborious tally, the position was clear, unambiguously so: the Conservatives would make great gains in the general election but they would not – could not – win. They had scaled great heights since first assuming control of the party at base-camp. But they would not reach the summit on this assault.

As one of Cameron's closest aides puts it: 'For years, we had said that we had a mountain to climb, to get the number of seats we needed to win. I think we knew rationally that this was true, as something Dave had to say all the time to fight complacency, but emotionally we had never really come to terms with just how great a task we had set ourselves. To win, everything had to go right. I mean, *everything*. And as we got closer to the election, it just became clear that that was too much to ask.'[12]

Thus began an extraordinary and elaborate charade. Cameron and Osborne grasped at once that they would have to begin planning systematically for a hung Parliament and for talks with the Lib Dems. In principle, minority government was possible – but the precedents were scarcely encouraging. Cameron was only seven, and Osborne two, when Harold Wilson formed his minority administration in 1974, but both had served as Cabinet Special Advisers in John Major's Government which lost its Commons majority in December 1996. They had seen for themselves what it was like to live hand to mouth politically, and neither relished the prospect of a second tour of duty.

The Tory Party's instinct, they knew, would be to try minority government rather than to pollute the true faith by dealing with the Lib Dems. But Cameron and Osborne also understood that they stood little chance of enacting their domestic agenda, winning the confidence of the markets, or tackling the structural deficit without command of the Commons. From day one, they would be patching together grubby deals with backbenchers of all parties, buying off nationalists, appeasing Ulstermen, trading votes with their own least biddable backbenchers. Better one big deal than a hundred small ones; better to try for a stable coalition that might last five years than to form a minority government that would probably collapse after a few months.

This much the Tory leader and his closest ally concluded quickly, even as the campaign proper proceeded. Less predictably, they also decided that any coalition had to be based on a system of fixed-term parliaments, in which the date of the general election was decided by law rather than political caprice. This reform – enacted by statute in 2011 – was generally interpreted as a typical example of Lib Dem constitutional tinkering and a concession by Cameron to Clegg. In fact, it was a Tory initiative, based on the Conservatives' assumption that the Conservatives, rather than the Lib Dems, would be the party that slumped in popularity mid-term. 'We have to find a way of stopping Clegg from dumping us,' Osborne told his fellow planners. The stability of a five-year government was what the markets wanted and the Tories needed. For that, it was worth trading the traditional right of the Prime Minister to decide the election date.

In total secrecy, parallel to the daily grid of press conferences, photo ops and media appearances, ran a process of political and psychological preparation for the days and weeks after the election. Having decided to authorize this process, Cameron insisted that its management be delegated to Osborne: if ever there was a case where plausible deniability mattered, this was it. The Tory leader could not afford to be closely associated with these heretical deliberations.

As yet another role was added to his portfolio, Osborne tried to 'war-game' the likely form the talks might take. Two things seemed immediately clear to him. First, that even if Clegg took the bait and entered into constructive negotiations with the Tories, he would break them off at some point to talk to Labour – if only to strengthen his hand. Second, that, if they wanted a coalition, the Tories would have to offer Clegg a referendum on electoral reform at Westminster.

The Shadow Chancellor was right on both counts. But all this lay weeks in the future, on the unexplored, unknown shores of life after the election. For now, it was imperative that the leadership's calculations and Osborne's strategic planning for Lib–Con talks remain clandestine. The merest whiff of their true thinking would smack of defeatism and would certainly undermine party morale and electoral confidence in Cameron personally. In public, the Tories would continue to rail against the horror of a hung Parliament while preparing in private to embrace precisely such an outcome.

Oliver Letwin, the chairman of the Tory policy review, was quietly tasked with a textual assignment to which his first-class mind was perfectly suited: to go through the Lib Dem manifesto line by line and identify potential areas of collaboration, issues where a compromise might be reached – and policies where the two parties diverged irrevocably. The preliminary results were presented to Osborne, Hague and Llewellyn at Osborne's west London home at a private dinner on Sunday, 18 April.

As he worked away, Letwin would occasionally speculate about what parallel investigations might be going on 'on the other side of the fence': meaning among senior Lib Dems. For Nick Clegg, of course, preparing for a hung Parliament was a sensitive but not defeatist task. Since becoming party leader in December 2007, he had mused often about the possibility of power: of Liberals joining the first peacetime coalition since 1931, and taking part in government for the first time since 1945. Clegg disliked the tendency of his party to settle for the status of a protest movement or campaigning think-tank. He believed in politics as the pursuit of power: not power at any price, but power all the same.

In this, he was following a path well trodden by his mentor, Paddy Ashdown, who had engaged in a lengthy *pas de deux* with Tony Blair before and after the 1997 election to steer his party into a governing alliance with New Labour.[13] The first step would be the inclusion of Lib Dem Cabinet ministers in Blair's administration. In due course, the two leaders hoped to move towards 'TFM' – 'The Full Monty' – meaning a merger of the parties and an end to the historic split on the centre-Left that had served the Conservative Party so well. This idealism wilted fast once Blair had secured his first landslide. Why bring Lib Dems into government when Labour had won its own historic victory? Why form a coalition when you had a 179-seat majority? Yet the idea was never entirely ditched. As late as 2007, Brown spoke of a 'Government of All the Talents' that would have space for leading figures from the third party; he was disappointed when Ashdown turned down his offer of a seat in Cabinet and the job of Northern Ireland Secretary.

But Clegg was prepared to go much further. Throughout the 2010 campaign, he insisted that, in the event of a hung Parliament, he had an obligation to talk first to the party that had come closest to victory. 'I tie my hands in the following sense,' he said over the last weekend of April, 'that the party that has more votes and seats, but doesn't get an absolute majority – I support them.'[14] This was a political decision, not the observance of a constitutional duty, for no such duty existed. And – given the state of the polls and the likely outcome of the election – the decision was to go to the Tories first.

This reflected a great deal of thinking and discussion. With more than six months to go to the likely election date, Clegg selected a group to explore the options for bipartisan government, an ad hoc team that included Danny Alexander, his chief of staff; Andrew Stunell, vice-chair of the election campaign; Chris Huhne, the Lib Dem spokesman for Home Affairs; and David Laws, the party's children, schools and families spokesman (and a man considered so Tory-friendly that Osborne had already offered him a place in the Shadow Cabinet).

'Nick wanted to take some early decisions', according to a member of the group. 'We needed to work out our priorities in case we were forced to drop some things.' Clegg said to Alexander: 'We've got to have a hierarchy in place rather than a smorgasbord of policies.'[15] The convergence between the two parties on fiscal policy, civil liberties, greenery and public service reform was as striking as the obvious differences over Europe, tuition fees and constitutional reform. For the Lib Dem leader, the fundamental problem was always going to be persuading his party that any form of deal with the Tories – the old enemy – was not a monstrous betrayal. The more thoroughly prepared his prospective negotiating team was, the better.

Clegg could at least acknowledge his potential role as kingmaker before polling day. Indeed, such speculation enhanced the drama of his position and fed the temporary cult of personality – 'Cleggmania' – that was the unexpected outcome of the leaders' television debates. The Lib Dem leader's occasional display of power-broking ankle was quite deliberate; his apparent reluctance to speculate too deeply about what might happen after the election, artful and carefully choreographed.

The luxury of partial candour was not open to Cameron and Osborne. So keen were they to maintain the pretence that the Tories were heading for outright victory that they over-corrected – occasionally to the puzzlement of the media. Thus, one of the central claims made in the Conservative campaign, almost *ad nauseam*, was that a hung Parliament would be a disaster for the country. When pressed on what he would do if he failed to achieve a Commons majority, Cameron said only that he would behave 'responsibly'. This was a formulaic answer, the stock response of a Prime Minister-in-waiting forced to say something vaguely statesmanlike when asked repeatedly by journalists about a hypothetical result.

In speeches and interviews, Cameron's emphasis was quite clear: that the only remotely safe outcome of the election was a Conservative majority. All other permutations were a sure route to political perdition, policy dither, market anxiety and economic collapse – or so the Tory leader claimed. This line of argument was given toe-curling emphasis in a party political broadcast unveiled by Osborne to the media on Monday, 26 April, and widely dismissed as a dud even before its transmission the following day. Framed as an announcement on behalf of an imaginary 'Hung Parliament Party', and presented by a Clegg lookalike, the broadcast looked forward with mock optimism to a political world in which 'under-the-table deals will be the order of the day, party political wrangling will dominate and policies will be bickered over by secret committees'. If the Hung Parliament Party prevailed, there would be 'no change' to the NHS, schools or criminal justice system, 'a paralysed economy' and 'behind-closed-doors politics – no public allowed'. Fifty-pound notes were shown being flushed down the loo, a supposedly potent symbol of what lay ahead if no party achieved a Commons majority on 6 May.

The Hung Parliament Party even had its own souvenir rosette bearing the image of a hangman's noose. The weakness of the pun was of a piece with the ineffectiveness of the whole stunt, which most journalists dismissed as no more than a panicked Tory response to 'Clegg-mania'. In the days that followed, as the nation's infatuation with the Lib Dem leader began to fade a little, Tory spin doctors briefed more confidently that an outright majority was now in Cameron's grasp.

On the Monday before polling day, the *Daily Telegraph*'s main front-page story reported that 'David Cameron is prepared to rule out any coalition deal with the Liberal Democrats and will try to lead a minority government if the Tories narrowly fail to win an outright majority in the General Election on Thursday. The Conservative leader is increasingly confident of winning an overall majority. Mr Cameron believes the momentum is with his party after his confident performance in last week's final leaders' debate, Gordon Brown's "bigoted woman" gaffe and a series of polls showing a fall in Lib Dem support.'

The speed and vigour with which Cameron made his 'big, open and comprehensive offer' to the Lib Dems on 7 May was hailed as evidence of the Tory leader's quick thinking and political agility. There was truth in this: none of those who witnessed Cameron in action on the morning after the election denied that his resolve was the engine driving events. But the missing element in this portrait is the contingency planning upon which the Tory leader was discreetly drawing.

Indeed, as the election approached, a consensus had grown among Cameron's closest advisers that a Lib–Con deal could be turned to the leadership's advantage at a time of national economic crisis. On election night, Nick Boles, a far more senior figure than his official status as Tory candidate for Grantham and Stamford would suggest, emailed a private memo to Cameron, Osborne, Michael Gove and a few others in the inner circle. After a polite nod to the lingering possibility of an overall majority, Boles confronted reality and argued strongly for a Lib–Con deal: 'It is essential that we make the Lib Dems share equally the blame for the cuts that are to come . . . To secure a coalition agreement, we would need to concede a referendum on electoral reform.' More to the point, Boles argued, this was a chance to show once and for all that the Conservative Party had changed: 'By agreeing to form a coalition and hold a referendum, we would be demonstrating our respect for the will of the people and our openness to a new way of doing politics.' The Boles Memo, protected by password, marked the end of a long, highly confidential process of deliberation and debate at the top of the Conservative

Party. It commanded general assent among those authorized to read it.

Cameron's real achievement had been not to let the Coalition cat out of the bag during the campaign. The only clue before the election – in retrospect, a dead giveaway – was that Shadow Cabinet members tended to say that they were against 'proportional representation' rather than all 'electoral reform at Westminster'. This left Cameron the 'wriggle room' he would need subsequently to offer Clegg a referendum on the Alternative Vote (AV) system in subsequent negotiations. AV requires voters to rank candidates in order of preference: if no candidate is the first preference of a majority of voters, the candidate with the fewest number of first-preference rankings is eliminated and that candidate's votes are redistributed to the remaining candidates. This process is repeated until one candidate secures 50 per cent of the total vote. Arguably, AV is fairer than first-past-the-post. But it is emphatically *not* proportional representation.

Ten days before the election, I appeared on the BBC's *Campaign Show*, interviewing Jeremy Hunt, the Shadow Culture Secretary. Four times, Hunt was asked to rule out electoral reform at Westminster and four times he stuck religiously to the much more specific line that the Tories 'oppose proportional representation'. On the day Cameron entered Number Ten, Hunt apologized to me by text for not 'giving a straight answer . . . now you know why!'

Rarely has politics gripped the public as it did in those five days of inter-party talks: the daily drama at 70 Whitehall as Lib Dem and Tory delegations hammered out the details became the 'Coalition Street' soap opera. Briefly, it looked as if Nick might run off with Gordon after all.[16] But the true plot twist was that Dave had been planning to settle down with Nick all along. And – to the astonishment of several who were in the know – the Tories' biggest secret had held.

The planning and the secrecy mattered because they had helped to tilt the balance. The coalition talks of 7–11 May were notionally even-handed.[17] But – in truth – the playing field was never level. It would be stretching the evidence to claim that Conservatives and Lib

Dems had formally conspired before the election to forge a coalition, or that the outcome was a foregone conclusion. The negotiations in the Cabinet Office were genuinely stressful and came close to collapse more than once. In April 2013, Alan Johnson, the former Home Secretary, revealed that he had been involved in secret talks to take over as caretaker Labour leader and coalition Prime Minister, but was beaten to it by the Tories: 'By the Tuesday morning the Lib Dems came in and it was obvious they'd done the deal.'[18] To an extent that was concealed from public and media alike, much of the spadework had already been done.

What looked like a master-stroke of real-time diplomacy and spontaneous statesmanship was in fact a tribute to the strategic preparations undertaken by Cameron and Clegg before the election: textual, personal and psychological. Both men had fought a public campaign, while bracing themselves inwardly for a much greater challenge. Ground had been made ready. Interests had converged. And a Government had been formed.

It was all so cheerful and decent. On the other side of the Thames, at City Hall, Boris Johnson watched as Cameron defied initial disappointment to seize the prize. In the months to come, the Mayor would conclude that the whole thing was, in truth, a triumph for the English public school system, a credit to its training of young men for office and for the skills of collaboration. Johnson was not the only observer to see the whole thing through this prism – though where Boris saw a social elite justifying its privileges by acting responsibly, others detected a stitch-up by the public school oligarchy. Such schools – Eton (Cameron, Johnson), Westminster (Clegg, Huhne) and St Paul's (Osborne) – were also hothouses of ambition, individualism and elbow-sharpening. The English public schoolboy is groomed for rivalry as much as for teamwork. 'Early laurels weigh like lead' was Cyril Connolly's verdict on his years at Eton. 'It was Competition that turned friends into enemies, that exhausted the scholars in heart-breaking sprints and rendered the athletes disappointed and bitter.'[19] If educational background was truly the glue of the Coalition, it would run into trouble soon enough.

2. Rose Garden: one plan, two guv'nors

Steve Hilton awoke with a start: on this, the first full day of government, he had slept in. Out the night before to celebrate with his friend and fellow Tory adviser, Rohan Silva, he had not got to bed until 5 a.m. And now, on the television screen, he could see Nick Clegg arriving at Number Ten. It was just after 9.30. Through the fog, he recalled that the Prime Minister and his Lib Dem partner-in-government were due to appear in the Downing Street Rose Garden later on – and that he had not yet written Cameron's speech.

For five years, Hilton had been Cameron's intellectual alter ego, the driving force behind the rebranding of the party, famous both for his epic generosity and for his volcanic temper. If early Cameronism had a manual, it was *Good Business*, the book Hilton had co-authored on global co-operation, the benign potential of capitalism and corporate responsibility.[1] It explored methods of 'bringing social values to consumerism and capitalism, not destroying one in favour of the other', and ended with the mock-Marxist rallying cry: 'Capitalists and anti-capitalists of the world, unite! You have nothing to lose but your guilt.'

As with capitalism, so with Toryism. Hilton sought to replace grey skies with blue, and anxiety with optimism: it was his task to make people feel good about voting Conservative. Shaven-headed and casually dressed, he visibly personified the very transformation of the party he was trying to mastermind. This singularity and his unfettered access to Cameron naturally made him the focus of resentment. His ideas struck some of his closest colleagues as uneven and, on occasion, plain silly. Osborne and Coulson believed that his fixation with the 'Big Society' was a distraction from comprehensible policy offerings. Coulson felt that his whole maverick persona was an act, a performance choreographed down to the last shabby T-shirt. But none doubted Hilton's talent or determination.

The question was what role he would now perform in government. Hilton asked for the deliberately opaque title of 'senior adviser' to enable him to roam as he pleased. To the surprise of some of his closest colleagues, he also requested a base away from the Prime Minister's private office, not wanting — initially, at least — to be drawn into the day-to-day detail of government. If he was to carry on being Cameron's visionary, he argued, he needed a measure of detachment to think productively and retain his wild-card energy. But the widespread assumption in Westminster that he would limit himself to image and branding in government was dramatically ill-informed. Hilton had much bigger plans.

Meanwhile, the front-page headlines told a pithy story: the *Daily Telegraph* opted for 'Cameron, PM', *The Times* for 'Embracing Change' and the *Guardian* for 'It's Cameron and Clegg'. Only the *Independent* offered anything remotely spiky: 'David Cameron, leader of brokered Britain'. Hague, already appointed Foreign Secretary, had represented the new Government on the *Today* programme and promised that a basic coalition agreement would be published later in the day (a document not very far removed, it transpired, from Letwin's cut-and-paste draft before polling day).

Osborne was amused to watch inaccurate reports on the rolling news channels that he had been 'confirmed' as Chancellor. Around 10 a.m., he finally prompted Cameron. 'At some point, you do have to appoint me,' he said. 'Well,' replied the PM, with arch formality, 'do you want to be Chancellor?' Osborne then took command of the British economy with a simple 'Yes'. He headed over to the Treasury to be greeted by its Permanent Secretary, Nicholas McPherson, and clapped in by his new staff. Though Osborne had asked not to be welcomed in this way, the officials — remembering the welcome that had been given to Brown — were taking no chances.

Rumours swept Westminster that Michael Gove, the Tory education spokesman, was going to the Home Office, and that David Laws would take the Education brief. But the Home Office had already been earmarked for Theresa May in the provisional plan drawn up on polling day at Hilton's home. As Shadow Home Secretary, Chris Grayling had shown an impressive ability to deliver voter-friendly political messages. But he had fallen foul of the inner circle, apparently comparing Manchester's Moss Side to Baltimore as depicted in the HBO drama *The Wire*, and supporting the right of Christians letting rooms in their own homes to exclude gay couples. Cameron, a former Home Office Special Adviser, simply believed that Grayling was not up to the job. He and Osborne felt that May had displayed sangfroid as Shadow Work and Pensions Secretary. More to the point, they were deeply – and correctly – worried about the prospectively small number of women in the ministerial ranks. With May installed in one of the great offices of state, Sayeeda Warsi as co-chairman of the party, Caroline Spelman at Environment and Cheryl Gillan as Welsh Secretary, the Government would look a little less male-dominated. But the problem of gender imbalance remained: in Opposition, Cameron had promised that at least one third of the jobs in his first Government would be held by women. Of the twenty-nine ministers entitled to attend Cabinet meetings, twenty-five were men.

May's unexpected transfer to her new portfolio also cleared the way for Iain Duncan Smith to become Work and Pensions Secretary. Since the ugly conclusion of his own leadership – sacked by his own MPs – IDS had successfully reinvented himself as a champion of welfare reform, making a much greater impact as the founder of the Centre for Social Justice think-tank than he ever had at the helm of his fractious party. When Cameron stood for leader in 2005, he had told Duncan Smith that he felt that social policy had receded too far during Michael Howard's two years in charge: 'I'd like to get back to this. We've gone down a cul-de-sac.' Liaising closely with Hilton, Duncan Smith allowed Cameron to use the CSJ as a strategic annex, home to the party's Social Justice Policy Group, which he also chaired. It seemed probable to IDS that, if the Tories won the election, he would be retained in some advisory capacity, a backbench sage wheeled out to give moral heft to the new Government's plans for the 'Broken Society'.

Cameron had been weighing up another possibility. Osborne had serious reservations about Duncan Smith's mastery of detail and – as a social liberal – worried that his moral vision might seem too pious and priggish if applied to Government policy. But he recognized that the Tory leader admired IDS's idealism and conviction. During the coalition talks, Cameron made a courtesy call to the former leader to keep him abreast of developments and to seek his counsel. If the party's Right were to be won over to the ostensibly dreadful idea of sharing government with the Lib Dems, it was important to secure IDS's blessing. This was duly delivered – though not unconditionally. 'I'll back you,' said Duncan Smith. 'But you'll need to bring the party with you.' Having done his bit, he headed off to Florence for a break.

On the Tuesday night of the Coalition's formation, he was surprised to be called again by Cameron. This time the new Prime Minister wanted more than moral support. 'Would you think about the Work and Pensions job?' he asked. Duncan Smith was taken aback. 'I don't know,' he answered. 'If you want an answer now, it's "No". But if you let me have a couple of hours, I'll talk to my wife.' Cameron knew Duncan Smith to be an uxorious man, fiercely protective of his wife, Betsy, who was still recovering from a bout of breast cancer the year before. But, an hour later, IDS called Ed Llewellyn and told him: 'If it's still on, I'll do it.'

In government, as in Opposition, Cameron intended to reassure the voters that a Tory Prime Minister could be trusted to cherish the NHS: accordingly, he promised 'no more top-down reorganizations' and appointed Andrew Lansley, his one-time boss at the Conservative research department, to make good that pledge as Health Secretary. The PM's failure to make clear to his old mentor precisely how he wanted to position the Coalition on health was to spawn one of its first true crises. Meanwhile, Cameron assumed that the NHS was indeed in safe hands and despatched Michael Gove to Education with a very different sort of brief.

Cameron was acutely conscious of the political vulnerability intrinsic to educational privilege. The nickname 'Flashman' was dangerous not only because it suggested that he was a bully at heart but because it linked this supposed character trait to his public school background. It was politically essential for him to offer a transformative plan for state education. But, in this instance, political necessity converged with conviction. Cameron had watched the Conservative Education Secretaries of the 1990s – Ken Clarke and John Patten – battle to release schools from local authority control, and applauded Blair's comparable plan to give them academy status. In 2005, he had surprised Michael Howard by asking to become Shadow Education Secretary rather than Shadow Chancellor, choosing this area of policy as the stage on which he made his pitch to be leader. Long before he made it a core theme of his 2012 conference speech, Cameron spoke often of 'spreading privilege' and the duty of the fortunate to improve the prospects of others. After the Crash, he believed that this moral imperative had to become a national mission. Unless Britain's state schools improved dramatically, it would soon falter in the global economic race.

On the Sunday after the election, Gove had told Andrew Marr that he was ready to hand over the Education portfolio to David Laws if it would expedite the formation of a stable Government. In practice, his appointment had never been in doubt. Though the primary task of the Coalition was to deliver economic recovery, both Prime Minister and Chancellor grasped that they had to offer more than austerity. Cameron wanted to be remembered for welfare and educational reform as well as cuts. He was already taking a punt on IDS. He wanted a close ally, who knew the PM's mind, at Education. Gove's legendary politeness was matched by a streak of obstinacy that would be needed if the Government was to take on the vested interests of the education establishment: what the new Education Secretary called 'the Blob'. As he and Cameron were soon to discover, its most jealously guarded lair was the Department for Education itself.

The Lib Dems had five Cabinet seats, and – only half joking – regarded Ken Clarke, the new Justice Secretary, as the sixth. At the age of sixty-nine, Clarke's presence in the new Government was a remarkable achievement of political stamina, his seventh Cabinet post. There was also a symmetry in his appointment: Clarke had been the first senior Tory to call for a coalition, in a *Spectator* interview in 2006. The prescience of his remarks to the magazine's associate editor (and future editor), Fraser Nelson, was remarkable: 'If Brown fights an election that produces a hung parliament, the public will think his duty is to leave No. 10 and accept defeat and people will expect the Conservatives and Liberals to form a working government . . . The Liberals really would look as if they'd ignored the public's message, either refusing to play ball with anybody or helping a defeated Labour party back into office. I'm glad to say the fates could condemn the Conservatives and the Liberals to form a coalition.'[2]

Clarke's contentment was matched by the suspicions of the Tory Right. Even as the infant Government took its first steps, plenty of Conservatives hoped privately that it would fall. The notion that the boundary between centre-Left and centre-Right might be porous was radical indeed. It was also deeply unsettling to those who regarded the Thatcher era as an unfinished revolution to be resumed as soon as possible, and the Coalition as – at best – a necessary evil. Those Tories needed to be represented, too. The senior status accorded to Duncan Smith was some consolation. So too was the appointment of Liam Fox as Defence Secretary and Owen Paterson as Northern Ireland Secretary. This was a bleak hour for the Right – a Tory Prime Minister handing red boxes to Lib Dems – but they were far from beaten.

Some of the changes forced upon Cameron by the reality of coalition were frictionless. Danny Alexander, Clegg's chief of staff, would become Scottish Secretary, a near-sinecure in the era of devolution that enabled him to remain *consigliere* to the Deputy Prime Minister. Lanky, softly spoken and familiar with intermittent adversity as a former spin doctor for the 'Britain in Europe' campaign, Alexander quickly established himself as a pillar of the new bipartisan government – stopping just short of primness in his gentle insistence that everyone stick by the deal and the rules. Although Cameron had taken to calling Hague his 'deputy in all but name', he had never intended to give him the title Deputy Prime Minister in an all-Tory Government.[3] This cleared the way to Clegg's elevation to the office of DPM, with a portfolio that included political and constitutional reform, the chairmanship of the all-important Home Affairs Committee, the right to commission papers from the Cabinet Secretariat, a seat on the new National Security Council, the right to be consulted on the Budget, and 'full and contemporaneous overview of the business of government'. In principle at least, what Cameron saw, Clegg would see too. The Deputy Prime Minister's endorsement was required for all ministerial appointments and the construction of all Cabinet committees. The Lib Dem leader had been granted much more than honorific status. On paper at least, the Coalition would be governed by a duumvirate.[4]

Vince Cable was another matter. The MP for Twickenham wondered whether he should carry on as Deputy Leader of the Lib Dems, 'lobbing things in from the outside' as he put it in private – or immerse himself in the business of the Coalition. But the dilemma was not hard to resolve: aged sixty-seven, he was being presented with the chance to participate in government at the highest levels. How could he justify turning down such an opportunity? Cameron and Osborne toyed with the idea of sending Cable to the Ministry of Justice. But the former economics don and chief economist for Royal Dutch Shell coveted a role in his field. It was hard to envisage him as Osborne's Chief Secretary, the Government's axeman, doing the daily bidding of a Tory boss almost thirty years his junior. That position, in any case, seemed tailor-made for David Laws, a former senior banker who was already on friendly terms with the new Chancellor.

A tussle ensued: Cable told officials that he was surprised at how 'fraught' Osborne became in the negotiations. 'The two of them really clashed', according to one Business Department source. 'It was serious – but they knew they had to reach an agreement.'[5] As irritated as he was, however, the Chancellor recognized that it was important to keep Cable happy: the latter's occasional private boasts that he could bring the Government down at whim were an exaggeration, but they contained a kernel of truth.[6] At an all-important meeting of the Lib Dem parliamentary party during the Coalition talks, Cable said that he 'hate[d] the Tories, I spent my whole life fighting them'; but added that coalition with the old enemy was probably the best available option, and 'I think we could be quite influential.' His endorsement was one of the guy ropes that kept the Cameron–Clegg 'Big Tent' aloft.

The Prime Minister's compromise, accordingly, was to give Cable the Department for Business, Innovation and Skills. He agreed to this – but demanded control of banking reform. To this, Osborne's response was succinct: 'No way.' Again, however, Cable's sensitivities were soothed: this time, with the deputy chairmanship of the Cabinet banking reform committee. Cameron made an early visit to the Business Department to celebrate Cable's arrival and offer his visible endorsement – the symbolism of which was not lost on the new Business Secretary.

For the Cameroon inner circle, this day of patronage and power distribution was tinged with a sense of irrevocable change. All political cohorts are gangs, with a social face as well as an ideological purpose: the architects of New Labour had gone on holiday together and plotted in French and Tuscan villas. But the Cameroons existed as a social set even before they had acquired a clear political purpose. Cameron, Hilton, Kate Fall, Gove, Ed Vaizey (who would shortly be appointed Culture Minister), Nicholas Boles (the leading modernizer and newly elected MP for Grantham and Stamford) and a handful of others had been a gang first, a caucus second. They went on holiday together, were godparents to one another's children and – that greatest of social bonds – shared childcare.

The gang was porous: some lost touch, others were recruited to its social round. Osborne, a few years younger than the core Cameroons, was a natural addition. His wife, the author Frances Osborne, was close to Simone Finn (née Kubes), Gove's girlfriend at Oxford and for several years thereafter. Finn would soon be advising Francis Maude at the Cabinet Office. She was also good friends with Gove's wife, Sarah Vine, the *Times* journalist, who, in turn, was close to Samantha Cameron, helping to look after her children on election night.

Conspicuous by her absence as the business of government began was Rachel Whetstone. Nicknamed 'the Witch' by Cameron in his twenties, Whetstone was one of his closest friends and allies, and had, by common consent, done a formidable job as political secretary to

Michael Howard during his leadership. She was also Hilton's wife. In normal circumstances, Whetstone would have been expected to play a central part in the new Number Ten, perhaps assuming what became known as the 'Leo McGarry' role: a reference to President Bartlet's indispensable chief of staff in *The West Wing*. But her alliance with Cameron was sorely tested in 2004 when it emerged that, prior to her own marriage, she had had an affair with William Astor, Samantha Cameron's stepfather. Cameron and Whetstone achieved a reconciliation of sorts but his wife's feelings were too scalded for the wound to heal entirely. Exiled from political life, Whetstone pursued a highly successful career at Google. There would be times in the years ahead when many in her party would long for her to return and restore grip to the Government.

To those who had watched the New Labour set colonize Whitehall, history seemed to be repeating itself with the arrival of the so-called Notting Hill Tories. But the match was not exact. The Blairite elite had organized itself as an entryist faction, a tightly knit group of politically motivated men and women determined to take over the Labour Party and then the Government. The young Tory gang exuded ambition: Cameron made no secret of his ultimate goal or his belief that a generation had to collaborate if it was to achieve anything. But – crucially – the group would still have existed if he and those around him had failed in their narrowly political objective. There would still have been dinners, tennis, country weekends. The caricature of Cameron as the 'chillaxing' Prime Minister did scant justice to a politician who routinely worked eighteen-hour days.[7] But there was a strand of truth in it: for Cameron and his friends, it was an article of faith that there was more to life than politics.

Not that it seemed like that on the morning of 12 May, as the work began. 'It felt like we had been a group', in the words of one of the PM's closest allies, 'and now everyone was going off in their posh cars to run departments.'[8] In Number Ten, Llewellyn and Fall set about establishing a routine for the PM and his aides. As in their preparations for coalition, so Cameron's team had made clear in advance what they had in mind. Jeremy Heywood, Whitehall's most accomplished shape-shifter, remained Downing Street Permanent

Secretary, a safe bet to succeed Sir Gus O'Donnell as Cabinet Secretary. 'We didn't really have meetings,' Heywood said ruefully of the Brown years. The new boss, in contrast, wanted formal gatherings at 8.30 a.m. and 4 p.m.: himself, Osborne, Heywood, Ed Llewellyn and Kate Fall, Coulson and a few others depending on the order of fare. Hague would usually attend twice a week, and Patrick McLoughlin, the new Government Chief Whip, came to report on the state of the party, the progress of legislation and imminent parliamentary votes. The morning meeting would be news-driven and tactical, the afternoon session (if possible) more strategic in content.

From the start, Clegg held his own meetings with Alexander, attended by his closest advisers, Jonny Oates, Lena Pietsch and John Sharkey, the chair of the Lib Dem election campaign. This meant that the PM and Deputy PM needed to hold a minuted bilateral meeting at least once a week, usually on Monday mornings, to supplement their constant impromptu text exchanges and phone conversations. These face-to-face meetings, also attended by Heywood, Llewellyn, Fall, Jonny Oates and, in due course, Chris Wormald (Clegg's top civil servant) were productive, and often preceded by a lengthy Sunday night phone call between the two party leaders. 'The question at the beginning', according to one Number Ten source, 'was this: did Clegg actually want to run a series of departments or did he want to be a co-pilot? It became clear that what he wanted, at least, was to be a co-pilot.'[9]

The New Labour era had been a binary conflict between two tribes – Blairite and Brownite – in which very few figures straddled the divide. Each faction had its own style, its ideology, its pet policies, its favoured journalists, even its own donors. While the Tories shrank into irrelevance for the best part of a decade, like a gang of bald men squabbling over a comb, the real battle for power was between Tony's Team and Gordon's Gang.

From day one, the story of the Coalition was different, its structures more complex, and its tensions less straightforward. Power under New Labour was radically centralized, an aspiration described by Blair's chief of staff, Jonathan Powell, as 'Napoleonic'.[10] The only struggle that mattered was the turf war between Number Ten and the Treasury: first between Blair and Brown, and then Brown and his Chancellor, Alistair Darling. For civil servants, one of the most unnerving transformations was the ease with which the new Prime Minister and Osborne interacted; the notion of the Chancellor of the Exchequer as part of the same Number Ten team was a radical innovation that would take some getting used to.

Yet that novelty was as nothing compared to the press conference given by Cameron and Clegg in the Downing Street Rose Garden at 2.15 that afternoon. For this moment of bipartisan unity, however glutinous and transient, there was absolutely no precedent. Power is naturally pyramidal: it looks odd without an apex. But here were two party leaders – of similar background, countenance and bearing – apparently sharing power in the national interest.

Unveiling the Coalition's seven-page agreement, Cameron declared that 'we are not just announcing a new Government with new ministers; we are announcing a new politics'. Their Government, he said, would be 'Liberal-Conservative'. Clegg emphasized the need for stability in times of economic uncertainty. 'This is a Government that will last . . . Not because it will be easy . . . This is a Government that will last because we are united by a common purpose.' In the question-and-answer session, Cameron said they had considered the 'confidence and supply' option, wherein the smaller party backed the larger only on finance bills and votes of no confidence, but had found the prospect 'so uninspiring'. Clegg agreed that the Coalition was essentially what the electorate had asked for: not single-party government but stability nonetheless. By this time, the duo seemed as comfortable as a music hall double act. Cameron was asked if he regretted saying that his favourite political joke was 'Nick Clegg'. The Lib Dem leader took his cue and, camping it up, said: 'I'm off . . .' Cameron bit on the bait, wailing: 'Come back!'

However real it was, whatever the future held, the spectacle commanded attention. In their words and body language, the two men betrayed no reluctance, no hint that they were merely settling for this governing arrangement in the absence of anything better. Instead, Cameron and Clegg gave the impression that the Coalition was the ideal outcome for the nation, all they had hoped for personally. They not only looked the part; they seemed to be two steps ahead of every-one else. There could be no more striking way to mark the end of an era overshadowed by the implacable rivalry between two men.

As open to ridicule as the performance was, it dramatized a tough political message with clear resonance: the structural deficit that they had inherited and the grim global economic context provided all the rationale that Cameron and Clegg needed for a grown-up govern-ment of national unity, in which party differences were set aside in the national interest. It looked like pier-end comedy. But it was aimed foursquare at the markets.

The two men had established a quick rapport during and immedi-ately after the coalition talks. Fall, so often Cameron's eyes and ears, believed that the essential affability and optimism they had in com-mon were more important than the shared public school background that transfixed the media. But there was nothing inevitable in their affinity. Not long after he became Lib Dem leader, Clegg and his wife, Miriam, had declined a dinner invitation from the Camerons. Prior to the 2010 negotiations, there was little warmth between them and a measure of public contempt and private indifference on Cam-eron's side. But necessity can be the mother of friendship as well as invention. It helped Cameron – a lot – that he was not Gordon Brown. Clegg had no doubt which of the two main party leaders he would prefer to work with, even if, as Brown had promised, he would be gone as soon as Labour had elected a new leader. In the Cabinet Room before the Rose Garden press conference, Coulson gave his boss and the new Deputy PM a pep talk, but was struck by how comfortable they already seemed in one another's presence. According to one Cameroon: 'Nobody really had to play Cupid.' One would never have guessed that only a fortnight before they had been tearing chunks out of each other in the final television debate at the University of Birmingham. At best, this was indeed a fresh start; at worst, it was a masterclass in political choreography. Osborne was impressed by Clegg's readiness to embrace coalition so unreservedly. 'Their hands really are soaked in the blood,' he later observed.

The Coalition agreement was essentially an inventory of priorities: deficit reduction, a comprehensive spending review, the protection of the NHS, tax cuts for the less affluent, banking reform, an immigration cap, political reform, an overhaul of the welfare system, new financing for higher education, a referendum lock on future EU treaties, civil liberties and the environment. It fell to Letwin, the newly appointed Minister of State in the Cabinet Office, and Alexander, Clegg's representative on Earth, to put flesh on this skeleton and draw up a detailed programme for government.

In July 2005, in a *Sunday Telegraph* article, Letwin had been the first MP to endorse Cameron as a prospective leadership contender – before the then Shadow Education Secretary had even announced his candidacy. Five years on, Cameron wanted his brilliant patron to become the Government's 'mainframe computer': the cerebral cortex of an extremely complex organism that would want to lurch left and right, but had to keep moving forward. Letwin's intellect was his principal claim to the role. But his profound amiability was also important. The 'Letwin giggle' – a high-pitched shriek of delight at the sheer absurdity of most political predicaments – would defuse many moments of tension between the two parties.

Though formally located in the Cabinet Office, Letwin found a temporary base that suited him perfectly for two thirds of the time: a snug in Number Twelve just by the horseshoe that Brown had used as his war room. The lacquered eighteenth-century table was pocked by what looked like the stab marks of a black marker pen – a memento of Gordon's disgust and frustration, Letwin assumed. Unclaimed in the first days of the new Government, the snug was an ideal setting for a rolling conversation with Hilton, James O'Shaughnessy, the PM's policy director, Danny Alexander, Polly Mackenzie, Clegg's head of policy, and a handful of Cabinet Office officials.

The detail was delegated to O'Shaughnessy and Mackenzie, to resolve any conflicts as quickly as possible. The Tory proposal for 'free schools', for instance, had not been fully documented before the election, and the Lib Dems sought reassurances that Gove's enthusiasm for new schools set up by parents, charities and religious groups, independent of town hall control, would not be a recipe for educational anarchy. The remaining areas of tension were addressed at unusual speed, with the core participants turning in long hours.

Letwin was conscious that the Coalition was still in its infancy and might falter if it lost its early momentum. 'A lot of pizza got eaten', according to one of the draftsmen.[11] The document was then handed over to Cameron, Osborne and Clegg for final amendment and published as the thirty-six-page plan *The Coalition: Our Programme for Government*, on 20 May: only a fortnight after election day.[12]

The looming question was: could it be made to work? The greater burden on Letwin – the second objective being pursued around the black-spotted table in the snug – was to set up internal structures that would make the governing partnership function. This procedural deliberation struck some ministers as dull work, but Letwin knew better. All governments depend upon personal chemistry. But a coalition needs formal channels, courts of appeal and early-warning systems. Cameron and Clegg understood that the 'no surprises' rule was essential to any such partnership, however impractical it might prove in the rough and tumble of government and media management.

So, even as the programme for government was being thrashed out, another, distinct process of negotiation was underway. Llewellyn, Maude and Letwin consulted Cameron and Osborne extensively, and had referred their general plans for Cabinet committees to O'Donnell and Heywood before the election. Their secret weapon was Jim Wallace, the Lib Dem peer, former Deputy First Minister of Scotland and its new Advocate General, who had invaluable first-hand experience of managing a two-party Government. The great conundrum – ultimately insoluble – was how to reconcile the differences intrinsic to coalition with the obligations of collective Cabinet responsibility.

When disagreements arose, Letwin hoped that he and Alexander would act as a 'two-person committee of appeal'. If this route failed, the ultimate forum for conflict resolution – in theory, at least – was the Coalition Committee: Cameron, Clegg, five Tory ministers and five Lib Dems, gathering in the Cabinet Room. The general expectation was that this high tribunal would be called into service regularly. In practice, it met only four times in the first two and a half years of the Coalition's existence.

If Blair's style had been Napoleonic and Brown had latterly resembled Macbeth waiting for Birnam Wood to come to Dunsinane, Cameron was minded to restore Cabinet government. The fact of the Coalition turned inclination into necessity. Fresh life was breathed into the Cabinet committee system, sluggish at best under Brown. Lib Dem Cabinet ministers, being fewer in number, found themselves stretched by this revival: Alexander sat on twelve such committees, Cable on seven and Huhne on nine.[13] But it was worth it. The Home Affairs Committee under Clegg and the European Affairs Committee chaired by Hague both became extremely important junctions for the business of government.

Some found the new procedures tiresome. Less could be taken for granted. Ministers could not assume that their colleagues would share their assumptions and intellectual prejudices. This meant that, especially in the first flush of government, everything had to be spelt out. Arguments had to be made from first principles and advanced on the basis of logic. For the more cerebral, such as David Willetts, the Minister of State for Universities and Science, the process was positively invigorating. Richard Reeves, who joined Clegg's team in June as strategy director, was struck by the initially fruitful convergence of talents: the Lib Dems were a party of policy and cerebration, the Tories a party habituated to power and its uses. Clegg, who often referred fondly to the 'kibbutzim' mentality of the Lib Dems, shared Reeves's opinion that his team was learning from partnership with the gnarled old party of power, the most electorally successful political movement in history.

But power, of course, exacts a price.

3. Attention deficit

George Osborne knew he would have to work fast. As the car sped away from Chequers, he hit the phones, making all the necessary arrangements at breakneck speed, hoping he was not too late. In the rough and tumble of forming the Government, it had completely slipped his mind. Indeed, the question had only occurred to him when he was asked by one of the staff at the PM's country residence: 'I suppose you'll be having Dorneywood, sir?' That struck the Chancellor as a good idea: the eighteenth-century house in Buckinghamshire given to the nation by Lord Courtauld-Thomson in 1947, and more recently famous as the venue for John Prescott's croquet matches, would be the perfect retreat in the difficult months and years ahead.

It was obvious to Osborne that he was taking on a formidable task, and one that would, of necessity, make him personally unpopular. Yet it was only months later that he discovered quite how worried Sir Gus O'Donnell, the Cabinet Secretary, and Treasury officials themselves had been in the days preceding his arrival. The deficit bequeathed by Gordon Brown; the larky note left by Liam Byrne for his successor as Chief Secretary ('I'm afraid there is no money'); the flame-torn backdrop of economic crisis in Greece: this was no time for uncertainty, delay or political games. While politicians thrive on the pulse of adrenaline, civil servants crave stability – with due cause, when the global markets are watching. O'Donnell, official midwife to the coalition talks, had delivered a healthy infant (or so he claimed – Cameron would later complain in private that he had hugely exaggerated his contribution). The Government was up and running. Yet, as Osborne took his seat for his first meetings as Chancellor, his civil servants still shuddered at what might have been. To an extent they did not fully confide in him till later, they were simply relieved to have a new boss, speaking for an administration with a sound Commons majority.[1]

Greedy for certainty, they also wanted Osborne's plan to increase capital gains tax to be enacted immediately. There was a case for this: any delay would reduce potential revenues as businesses sold assets quickly to avoid capture by the new rate. But Osborne was firm in his decision that the rise – which required delicate political management on the Tory side – could wait until his emergency Budget on 22 June.

Before that, however, the Chancellor had three immediate steps he intended to take, interconnected measures that would demonstrate to electorate, media and markets that the Coalition was serious about repairing the public finances, that it understood the levels of anger that the banking crisis had spurred, and that, despite its broad ideological composition and shallow foundations, the Coalition was capable of decisive action.

First was the establishment of the Office for Budget Responsibility (OBR) under Sir Alan Budd, a former chief economic adviser to the Treasury. Though not quite as dramatic as Gordon Brown's decision to transfer control of interest rates to the Bank of England in 1997, Osborne's introduction of the OBR reflected the same paradox: that depoliticization is politically popular. It was, as the Chancellor said at the time, 'a rod for my own back': the withdrawal of forecasting and budgetary number-crunching from the political sphere and its wholesale surrender to an independent body. It was well known (and subsequently confirmed in Labour memoirs) that Brown had subjected Alistair Darling to fierce pressure over Treasury growth forecasts.[2] The formation of the OBR would compel the Government of the day to submit its Budget plans and Autumn Statements well in advance for pre-publication scrutiny; 'hugely reducing', as David Laws put it, 'the risk that future Chancellors and Prime Ministers will decide to fiddle the budget figures for their own political purposes'.[3] This, in turn, would keep the figures honest. By draining the politics from the key statistics, the Office would prevent desperate men from doing desperate things. The markets could be certain that the books had not been cooked.

The proposal had been drawn up in Opposition by Rupert

Harrison, Osborne's chief economic adviser. Harrison was an alumnus of the Institute for Fiscal Studies, and, like Osborne, a graduate of Magdalen College, Oxford. Unlike Osborne, he had been tutored by Stewart (now Lord) Wood, who managed to combine for many years the commitments of an Oxford don and the responsibilities of an adviser to Gordon Brown and Ed Miliband. In four years, Harrison, a tall, sleek Etonian, had become as close to Osborne as any of his advisers and discovered a talent for briefing sections of the press on behalf of his master. The near-parity between the two young men invited inevitable comparisons with Brown and Ed Balls. But the parallel had limits: as close as Harrison and Osborne were, and as clearly as the adviser enjoyed plenipotentiary powers when he went roaming across Whitehall or talked to the media, their alliance was not so clearly and furiously *contra mundum* as the Brown–Balls axis. Where Balls had often been public enemy number one in Blair's Number Ten, Harrison and Andy Coulson worked closely together, conscious that the media were foraging furiously for evidence that their respective bosses secretly hated each other. 'The absolute priority was making sure that history did not repeat itself', according to one friend of both men. 'Their genuine fondness of one another was not enough. Dave and George had to be seen, constantly, by colleagues and hacks to be indivisible by a cigarette paper.'

After the OBR was launched, Osborne's second task was to announce £6bn of exemplary in-year public spending cuts. Aside from their intrinsic worth as part of a much greater programme to restore stability to the public finances, the savings were intended to put down a strategic marker. After weeks of political uncertainty, the Chancellor wanted to dramatize the urgency of his plan, and – with Laws at his side – the commitment of the Lib Dems to these painful measures. International Development, Health and Defence were excused from this initial exercise. In an early example of Lib Dem influence, Laws ensured that spending on schools, early years and the education of sixteen- to nineteen-year-olds was also protected.

All other departments (including, of course, the Treasury itself) had to submit their plans to the new Chief Secretary. Not all of his Cabinet colleagues believed that the snap cuts were a good idea:

Huhne, a former economics editor who had also pursued a lucrative career in the City, had grave doubts about the wielding of the axe.[4] 'I soon realized,' Laws recalled, 'that the key for me was to be well briefed to counter the attempts by some Cabinet ministers to defend their budgets. So I needed to know the counter-arguments to those that would be put by the respective Cabinet minister. Treasury civil servants were usually good at anticipating these. What got trickier was if the Cabinet minister was well enough briefed to seek to "counter" my "countering" of his or her points.'[5] Vince Cable and Theresa May proved especially adept at defending their respective departments.

Laws also waged early war on first-class travel by officials, on plants in the Treasury, and on the use of plush Jaguars by ministers – immediately seeking to forgo the privilege of an official car himself. These seemed like obvious efficiencies at a time of austerity. But Whitehall pushed back with surprising vigour. The Chief Secretary was not even able to hand back his chauffeur-driven Jaguar – which cost the taxpayer more than £110,000 p.a. – without a struggle, told by his private office that three months' notice was required. When he asked whether civil servants really needed to take first-class travel, he was told that the lost revenue in ticket sales would in the end be made up by greater state subsidy – 'an ingenious defence', he was forced to acknowledge. Laws was the first, but by no means the last, Coalition minister to experience the collective intransigence of the government machine. It was the first hint of a structural tension between politicians and officials that was to tighten like a garrotte over the next three years, a tension that reflected the most basic question of all: who governs?

The Chief Secretary's team set up a flip chart in his outer office to establish how close he was getting to the £6bn target. According to Laws, the tougher departments were Business, the Home Office, Local Government and Culture, Media and Sport. Theresa May, for instance, did not agree the Home Office settlement until 11 p.m. on Friday, 21 May – perilous brinkmanship, given that the full £6.25bn package of cuts was due to be announced by Osborne and Laws in the Treasury courtyard on the following Monday. For Laws, the rule of thumb throughout was straightforward: 'You just had to remember that we were not in favour of spending any more on whatever was being discussed.'[6]

On 24 May, he and Osborne presented the cuts publicly for the first time. The Chief Secretary went through his inventory with the precision of a well-meaning mortician: the Home Office would lose £367m, Business £836m, Department for Education £670m, Foreign Office £55m, and so on. Compared to the structural deficit of £156bn, these sums were small. But the exercise was intended to be radical in its symbolism if not its fiscal content. Laws captured the spirit of the occasion with his remark that 'public borrowing is only taxation deferred'.

One of New Labour's greatest achievements had been to rebrand public spending as 'investment' and to caricature 'Tory cuts' as a sure road to Dickensian squalor. Now, on a political landscape transformed by the Crash and disfigured by over-borrowing, Osborne and Laws were declaring that era over, warning of much greater austerity to come, and pinning the political prospects of two parties to a new fiscal strategy. True, Alistair Darling (Osborne's Labour predecessor) had already promised to make cuts 'deeper and tougher' than those of the Thatcher years. But Brown remained wedded to the notion that Tories cut and Labour 'invests'. One of the great achievements of the Conservative campaign was to force the idea of the deficit across voters' doorsteps, explain that it was a bad thing, and persuade them that Brown and his gang would never deal with it.

As a signifier of change and of the arrival of a serious new Government, the announcement of £6bn cuts was an unqualified success. But the strategy was also freighted with risk. Osborne, like Cameron, was a fiscal conservative, a child of Black Wednesday and of three successive Labour victories. He was powerfully opposed to unfunded tax cuts, feared their impact upon the markets ('sterling is not the dollar'), and did not share the conviction of those who called for such measures that slashing tax rates yielded instant growth. Long before the election, he had decided that the pain of deficit reduction would be front-loaded at the beginning of the Parliament, accepted that the Government would face a period of extreme unpopularity, but expected that stability would encourage growth and an upswing in the polls. That remained the plan. By the end of the Parliament, Osborne hoped, he would be able to deliver a bonanza Budget and steer the party comfortably towards a second term with its own working majority.

But what if the plan failed, or failed to deliver on time? As dramatic as the Coalition's embrace of austerity undoubtedly was, it risked pleasing nobody. For some on the Tory benches, the Osborne plan was hopelessly timid: the ring-fencing of spending on the NHS and international development made no sense to those who wanted root-and-branch reform of public spending.[7] In private, the Chancellor would express rising irritation with 'people who don't understand how hard it is to cut'. For others across the political spectrum, the problem was not timidity but its precise opposite: the prospect of too much pain, spread across too many years, with too little growth to show for it.

In Government, the fiscal conservative had to be made of stern stuff. In one ear he had the disciples of Reaganomics calling for emergency tax cuts to galvanize the economy; in the other were neo-Keynesians demanding spending 'stimulus' with a similar goal. But Osborne knew, even at this early stage, that his political fortunes would be settled not by economic debate but by practical results. Rarely had the Blairite mantra been so applicable: What counts is what works.

With shocking speed, this auspicious tableau of Coalition unity and purpose was followed by a brutal reminder of political mortality. Only four days after his co-starring appearance alongside the Chancellor, the *Daily Telegraph* revealed that Laws had claimed £40,000 in expenses for renting rooms in properties owned by his partner, James Lundie. It was clear that the Chief Secretary had wished to keep the true nature of their relationship private, and so had maintained the pretence that he was tenant rather than boyfriend. 'I was so determined to keep my sexuality a secret,' he told *The Times*, 'that James and I behaved in every sense as if we were just friends.'

If there was a 'new politics', Laws personified it: fiscally tough, politically pluralist, socially responsible. Could he – and all he apparently stood for – stumble so quickly? Cameron and Clegg were initially drawn to the stopgap measure of an inquiry, referring the matter to John Lyon, the Parliamentary Commissioner for Standards. Laws undertook to repay tens of thousands of pounds he had claimed for rent and other housing costs between 2006 and 2009. But, as Coulson reported to the PM, after talking to Jonny Oates, the media storm showed no sign of receding. Laws himself saw the problem with characteristic clarity. He could explain his actions, but not excuse them.

Why should the taxpayer subsidize his decision to keep his sexuality secret? This would have been a difficult question for any minister to answer. For the man deputed to wield the Treasury axe and get the public finances back into shape, it was impossible. There were painful spending cuts ahead. How could he have begun to explain to a public sector employee paid £40,000 p.a. – the sum he claimed improperly – that she had to lose her job as part of the new fiscal strategy, while he kept his?

Cameron, entertaining at Chequers, battled hard to keep Laws, whom he had quickly grown to admire (and to contrast with Cable, who struck the PM as Eeyorish and potentially wearisome). He took a series of calls on the subject, and conferred with Kate Fall, who was amongst his lunch guests. At about 3 p.m., he spoke to Laws. By then, it was clear that the Chief Secretary was minded to resign, which he did, formally, on Saturday evening. Cameron replied: 'I hope that, in time, you will be able to serve again as I think it is absolutely clear that you have a huge amount to offer our country.'

Laws was fortunate in one respect: his fall was so swift, so sudden, that it was reported with a measure of pathos. Even as Cameron and Clegg brushed off the confetti of the Coalition nuptials, one of their most able ushers was being asked to leave the reception. His place was taken by Danny Alexander, Clegg's right-hand man. It remained an article of faith for the Lib Dem leader that he should have two Cabinet members engaged in the rebuilding of the economy. Alexander might not have Laws's City background, but he compensated in other ways – not least the strong bond he had already forged with Letwin, the Tory with whom he had written the Coalition's digital code.

He knew and got on well with Ed Llewellyn, and had already done business with Osborne in the coalition talks. His elevation was smooth and free of contention.

Having sent an immediate signal about the Government's fiscal plans, Osborne knew he had to be equally clear about its intentions to reform the financial sector. The Chancellor believed that Brown had been mesmerized by the City's potential to subsidize the Labour state, imagining he could exploit the Darwinian forces of capitalism to pay for twenty-first-century social democracy. Osborne saw an economy horribly dependent upon the financial sector, property and state spending. With envious eyes, he looked at California's virtuous triangle of digital entrepreneurship, venture capital and innovative universities.[8] But no amount of pious rhetoric about 'rebalancing the economy' would alter the fact that UK plc required a thriving financial sector, a tax structure that continued to attract high-value earners, and a new regime for the City that was fair but not punitive. In summer 2010, bankers were still global pariahs, vilified for their apparent lack of contrition, the bail-out they had required and the provocative claim that their institutions were 'too big to fail'. No politician could be sanguine about the public anger and anxiety provoked by the Crash. At the same time, Osborne had to acknowledge that, even in 2009, the financial sector accounted for no less than 12.1 per cent of total Government tax receipts and employed over a million workers; a loathed golden goose in poor health is better than none at all.

In his Mansion House speech, Osborne announced his intention to abolish the 'tripartite' system of regulation that divided responsibility for the financial system between three authorities – the Bank of England, the Financial Services Authority and the Treasury – and to consolidate the power of oversight in Threadneedle Street. 'There are real issues of fairness,' the Chancellor told his audience. 'And that is why we will introduce a bank levy and demand further restraint on pay and bonuses.' The structure of the banking sector and its competitiveness would, he continued, be examined by an independent commission under Sir John Vickers, the Warden of All Souls College, Oxford, and a former chief economist at the Bank of England. Osborne had toyed with the idea of a Royal Commission on Banking but decided that such an exercise might be too slow and cumbersome. Vickers, in contrast, was mandated to report to the Cabinet Banking Committee by the end of September 2011: too slow for some, but fast enough to fend off the charge that the Government was soft on the banks.

The initial tranche of cuts and the launch of the Vickers Commission paved the way for the 'emergency Budget' on 22 June. There was some good news: Osborne announced that the state pension would henceforth increase in line with earnings, inflation or 2.5 per cent – whichever was the highest. Corporation tax would fall from 28 per cent to 24 per cent over four years. But taxes would rise: VAT to 20 per cent and capital gains tax to 28 per cent: the first Coalition measure to cause serious disharmony on the Tory backbenches. As promised, a new tax would be levied on banks from January 2011. But the core of the plan was a rolling programme of savings: the rise in the state pension age to sixty-six would be accelerated and public sector pay frozen for two years. Child benefit was frozen for three years and caps on housing benefit were imposed. The NHS and the Department for International Development were ring-fenced, but other budgets faced average cuts of up to a quarter.

The Chancellor's carefully chosen bearing was that of Henry V: 'Presume not that I am the thing I was.' This Budget was intended as a call to action, as well as a shopping list of measures and objectives: it urged the political class and the public alike to grow up, to put away the childish delusions that prevailed in the era of New Labour and to confront the challenges, fiscal and otherwise, that lay ahead.

Osborne's Budget was also ferociously political. It sent the Cabinet a very clear message, which the Chancellor made public on the *Today* programme the following day: 'If over the coming couple of months we can find further savings in the welfare budget, then we can bring that 25 per cent number [for cuts in unprotected departments] down. In the end, that is the trade-off, not just between departments but also between the very large welfare bill and the departmental expenditure bill.' Behind the scenes, the Chancellor was trying to recruit Cabinet muscle to exert pressure on Iain Duncan Smith. It was becoming depressingly clear to him that the Work and Pensions Secretary did not regard welfare cuts as his priority but was engaged (as Osborne saw it) in a quasi-religious programme of mass redemption. 'He resists every cut I propose,' the Chancellor complained to his colleagues. He appealed to them for help. But he also explained that, if IDS wouldn't make savings, they would have to make up the difference from their own budgets. Duncan Smith bitterly resented the way in which he was being singled out by Osborne as the bad guy, the over-spender who had to be brought into line. For the first but not the last time, the sunny official narrative of the Coalition concealed a more brutal reality, in which Treasury muscle was being applied to a Cabinet minister who questioned the writ of the Chancellor.

Another manifestation of the Treasury's tightening grip on the Coalition was the emergence of the so-called 'Quad', the ad hoc group of four (PM, DPM, Chancellor, Chief Secretary) that had met frequently during the Budget's gestation, as the Coalition's primary decision-taking and appellate tribunal. Osborne compared the task to solving a Rubik's Cube where the specific challenge (referring to the respective party colours) was to get 'the yellow bricks to match up with the blue bricks'. Initially, it seemed only natural that he, Cameron, Clegg and Alexander should meet in person as often as possible to hammer out the detail of the statement, not least because it had to reach the OBR well before Budget Day itself. Clegg was particularly concerned about the VAT increase, which he knew his party would see as deeply regressive. 'It's difficult and damaging,' he told Osborne. 'But I can see that it has to be done.' Clegg also noted that Alexander seemed to have gone native almost immediately in the Treasury. 'Danny is like the first special forces guy sent up the river to assassinate Colonel Kurtz in *Apocalypse Now*', according to one Tory observer, 'the one who becomes totally devoted to his original target. Well, Danny was soon wearing warpaint and very much Colonel George's man. No wonder Clegg was baffled.'[9]

The ad hoc meetings quickly became formal and regular. But never that formal. There was no fixed location, and no fixed pattern. It might be a minuted gathering in Number Ten or a kitchen supper in the Downing Street flat. Even the cast list was flexible. When a

specific issue needed to be resolved, it seemed no less sensible to invite
the relevant Secretary of State and often to include Letwin, usually
accompanied by officials from the Cabinet Office and the PM's team.
What had started as a cocktail of good intentions and desperate
necessity – somebody, after all, had to run the country – was becoming
a full-blown experiment. Not 'sofa government', as much as a 'so far
so good' innovation.

That said, it was risky to confuse the new structure of committees
and bipartisan talking shops with the true map of power. In the early
days of the Coalition, Cameron and Clegg consulted one another
almost neurotically, desperate not to violate party sensitivities to
which they were not instinctively attuned. The texting was relentless. Senior ministers were given clunky handsets which had been
modified to make them less vulnerable to interception. To the dismay
of their security minders, most stuck with their own familiar phones,
firing off scores if not hundreds of texts a day to one another. The
tableau vivant of the new Government was undoubtedly the Rose
Garden press conference. The reality was much noisier, more exploratory and back-of-an-envelope. And the only question that truly
mattered was: once his formal obligation to hear Clegg out was dis-
charged, to whom did Cameron actually listen?

Those around the PM answered this question with reference to a
famous line from John le Carré's *Tinker Tailor Soldier Spy*: 'There are
three of them and Alleline' (a reference to the identity of the potential Soviet 'mole' in the intelligence service). To understand the new
Number Ten, you had to grasp an equivalent truth: there were three
of them and Cameron.

Hilton was the first of the trio, the 'senior adviser' with a deliberately
vague brief to chase progress, foster radicalism and combat inertia wherever he found it. The daring with which he had rebranded the party
commanded respect throughout its ranks. Yet, as memories of the election campaign hardened into party folklore, it became orthodox to
blame Hilton for the supposed emphasis upon the 'Big Society' (which
had, in fact, absorbed very little campaigning time). It was also assumed,
wrongly, that his principal preoccupation in office would be image,
tone, branding and strategic message. Hilton's plan was very different.

From the start, he saw himself as a change-maker rather than a campaigner. 'Dave and George are happy to delay things,' he often said, 'but we always have to act as if we only have one term in office.' This was Hilton's prime article of faith. On winning the 1997 election, Tony Blair's chief of staff, Jonathan Powell, said that his main objective was to win again in 2001. Hilton worked on the assumption that Cameron had only five years to accomplish *everything* he hoped to achieve as Prime Minister – not because a Conservative victory in 2015 was out of the question, but because it could not be taken for granted. Hilton believed that the British state required top-to-toe reform: transparency, localism, 'crowd-sourcing' (the quest for information from online communities), the transformative use of digital technology, and the comprehensive application of so-called 'behavioural economics' to the challenges of government.

Advised and encouraged by his close ally Rohan Silva, Hilton was fascinated by the persuasive power of 'social norms', and the work of authors such as Robert Cialdini and Richard Thaler on influence and 'nudging'.[10] It became fashionable in Number Ten policy circles to talk about 'libertarian paternalism': the achievement of progressive goals without heavy-handed state regulation. Hilton and Silva hosted regular seminars in Number Ten for writers and intellectuals whose ideas might stimulate useful policy debate. It was not unusual for a cerebral guest such as Joshua Foer, the American author of a book on memory techniques, to be holding forth to a round table of officials and guests – only for Hilton to wander into the room in his socks to ask whether Foer's researches had any lessons for Michael Gove to implement in the nation's classrooms.[11]

While Hilton gazed upwards at blue skies, the second member of Cameron's trio, Andy Coulson, laboured in the shadow of a cloud that would not budge. The phone-hacking scandal at the *News of the World* had compelled him to resign its editorship in January 2007. But Cameron and Osborne felt that the journalistic and organizational skills Coulson would bring to the Conservative machine outweighed the risk of appointing him. He joined as the party's communications director in July, on a salary of £275,000 – pipping to the post the BBC's Guto Harri, who would go on to become Boris Johnson's spin doctor. The Mayor later formed the private opinion that Harri, in some of his more aggressive briefing, was taking oblique revenge on Downing Street for not getting the job – though Harri appeared to the journalists with whom he dealt every day to be a thoroughly professional communications chief, frequently left to tidy up Boris's mayhem, rather than a rogue operator pursuing a private vendetta.

As with most senior appointments, Osborne was the driving force, and he and Coulson quickly became firm friends. Though scornful of all comparisons between his recruit and Alastair Campbell, the then Shadow Chancellor believed that the party badly needed a street-fighter who could take the battle to Labour and win in a media knife-fight. It was assumed that the former redtop editor had been hired for his tabloid talents. But the real challenge, Cameron and Osborne thought, was to get the Tory message across on television: as much as newspaper coverage and endorsements helped, it was there, and in the hectically expanding digital universe, that they believed the elections of the twenty-first century would be won and lost. Osborne and Coulson shared an entirely practical approach to politics – an approach rooted in Tory conviction but shaped by an unsentimental sense of the possible. It was this that set the George–Andy axis at odds with Hilton, who believed that the Cult of Coulson marked the sacrifice of strategy to tactics. In government, Clegg, who warmed to Osborne and saw him as a fellow metropolitan liberal, was nonetheless astonished by the Chancellor's ruthless pragmatism and scorn for impracticality. Coulson shared with Osborne a desire to root Coalition politics in a language that could be sold on the doorstep and pave the way to an outright Conservative victory in 2015.

Cameron, in contrast, was awestruck by his communications director, whom he privately described in lyrical language. Though the Tory leader liked his original press secretary, George Eustice, and regarded him as competent, he treated Coulson as a redtop shaman, a source of secret knowledge about the world of tabloids, Essex and kitchen-table politics. The phone-hacking story refused to go away, but Cameron was determined not to yield to those who urged him to ditch Coulson.

More than once Coulson said he would have to resign, and he was deeply uncertain about following Cameron into government. He would later describe his decision to do so as the greatest mistake he had ever made. 'None of this would have happened if I hadn't gone with Dave into Number Ten,' he would later say to colleagues. But Cameron was determined not to let his communications chief go – or to ask too many questions. Much of the strength of the Cameroon gang was rooted in its shared history, assumptions and loyalties. But Coulson had the talent of the outsider, and exercised a quietly magnetic influence upon his privileged bosses, bringing Billericay to Bullingdon. The sharp suits, officer's haircut and unflappability marked him out in the team. For his part, Coulson knew the risks and the danger that (even without the baggage of the *News of the World*) politics would consume his entire life if he went with his boss into Downing Street. He had a sense of what was coming when one of his young children – to whom he was devoted – asked him after a crucial meeting between Cameron and the US President: 'Did you get the amount of time you wanted with Obama?' There were so many reasons not to join Dave and George in government. But Coulson was also conscious that he had been offered an astonishing second chance in life, and that he would regret not pursuing the opportunity to its logical conclusion. 'In the end, how can I say no?' he asked allies rhetorically. By the summer of 2009, he had quietly decided to take the plunge. But he did so with a sense that it could all go horribly wrong. 'If I go mad,' he pleaded with one friend, 'please, please, please put me out of my misery with a very large hammer.'

Installed in Number Twelve, Coulson set about drawing a clear line between Special Advisers and civil servants, and integrating the Number Ten and Cabinet Office comms operations. From the beginning, he also intended to collaborate closely with his Lib Dem counterparts – initially Jonny Oates and then Lena Pietsch. After Oates was appointed his deputy, the two men had a frank conversation. 'This could be an unmitigated fucking disaster,' Coulson conceded, 'or we could do something very interesting.' On the day of the Rose Garden appearance, he had made clear to Cameron and Clegg before they went out that 'you've got to show people you can work together'. The Deputy Prime Minister, who had challenged Cameron about Coulson's appointment when the Coalition was formed, came quickly to respect and rely upon the comms chief, calling him frequently and trusting his judgement. When his wife, Miriam González Durántez, found herself at the centre of a media furore about government contracts with her legal firm, DLA Piper, Clegg turned to Coulson for advice. So, from time to time, did Cable and Huhne. Quite at odds with his media image as a tabloid Tory, Coulson was becoming one of the props of the entire Coalition arrangement.

According to one friend of Cameron: 'It was as if Dave believed that the hacking stuff would just peter out, even though there were clearly Labour MPs and non-Murdoch newspapers ensuring that it wouldn't. He had grown dependent upon Andy.' The latter claim is undoubtedly correct. Coulson was one of the indispensable trio – the three men to whom Cameron always listened – and the new Prime Minister was convinced that the delicate balance of the Coalition would be disrupted by his absence.

The third man, of course, was Osborne himself: Chancellor, confidant, chief strategist. To a greater or lesser extent, the fate of every Prime Minister was in the hands of his next-door neighbour in Downing Street. Prosperity did not guarantee electoral victory; nor did hard times ensure defeat. John Major won in 1992, but lost in 1997 (the election of the 'voteless recovery', as Major put it wryly himself). Nonetheless, a Government which owed its existence to a shared economic mission could scarcely expect the voters to show mercy if it failed to restore stability and kickstart recovery.

With the emergency Budget out of the way, the Treasury sent out 'indicative scenarios' to each spending department, launching an 'iterative process' of negotiation that would culminate in October's spending review. Parallel to these talks, a group of top-tier civil servants was seconded from across Whitehall to form a Spending Review Challenge Group, assisted by outside experts, attached to the Cabinet Office and commissioned to find new ways of saving money. As an incentive to ministers in spending departments, Osborne established a 'Star Chamber' to act as a court of appeal: himself, Alexander,

Letwin, Maude, Hague – to be joined by any colleagues who reached a settlement with the Treasury swiftly.

Over the summer, Cameron and Osborne had a series of informal discussions about the spending review, at the heart of which was the NHS and their pledge to ring-fence its budget. The rolling conversation was held in a series of locations – the Cabinet Room, Chequers, the PM's study, though not the Downing Street flat which was undergoing a £64,000 refit (more than half of it paid for by the Camerons themselves). One visitor to Chequers who had been hosted by both Brown and Cameron at the PM's rural retreat noted the contrast: 'Gordon would greet you in a full carriage-built suit then go round the children's table asking them what they were reading. Dave wore jeans and a casual shirt and looked as if he'd lived there all his life.' The Osbornes were no less at home at Dorneywood, the grace-and-favour Georgian mansion in Buckinghamshire: guests at the weekend would find themselves recruited to impromptu shows scripted and directed by the Chancellor's children, complete with costumes and props. On Sunday morning walks in the surrounding woodland, he would take calls from the PM, agreeing the lines-to-take on the stories in the weekend press.

Ironically, in the light of the trouble that health service reform was soon to bring them, the PM and Chancellor agreed that this commitment remained the foundation stone of their governing ethos; the promise that gave this predominantly Tory Coalition 'permission' to be radical elsewhere. In July, Osborne further suggested to Cameron and Clegg that his review should include a substantial settlement for schools. First, this would appeal to Lib Dems and smooth the intra-Coalition politics of the process. Second, it would head off – or at least help to counter – the charge that the early Cameroon infatuation with public services had been purely cosmetic. Third, they believed it was the right thing to do: Cameron and Osborne both regarded Education as the Government's flagship reforming department and Gove as a true Tory radical.

Osborne had a minor tussle with Clarke over the Ministry of Justice spending plan, which he interpreted as no more sinister than an old lion reminding a young lion that he still knew how to play the game. The row with Duncan Smith over welfare was more serious (see Chapter 5). But by far the most difficult department to deal with was the Ministry of Defence. Liam Fox was one of the most able and also most divisive members of the Cabinet. Articulate, fizzing with energy and bristling with ideas, Dr Fox was much more than the blinkered Thatcherite of media caricature. He understood completely the need to modernize the Conservative Party after the 2005 defeat, and fought an impressive leadership campaign in the months that followed – one that earned him the respect of the Cameroons. But he also provoked strong opinions. His portentous manner, syncopated grin and eye-widening tic encouraged the belief he was either mad or a genius. Osborne had mixed emotions about his fellow Atlanticist: he made a point of dining with Fox regularly, but worried that he might go off reservation, behaving erratically or speaking out at precisely the wrong moment. Jokes made by friends about 'how Liam could still become Prime Minister in time for the Olympics' did not strike Osborne as remotely funny.

Fox, for his part, had not forgotten the leadership contest and what he regarded as the shoddy tactics of the Cameron campaign. In order to exclude him from the run-off – the final two candidates chosen by MPs and then put to a vote of the party members – the Cameron team had 'lent' David Davis a handful of MPs; or so Fox believed. Cameron was sure he could beat Davis (which he did, by a comfortable margin) but less sure of his prospects against the Scottish rival with whom he had often played fierce tennis at David Lloyd's chain of courts; or so Fox believed.

As Defence Secretary, his immediate task was to oversee the Strategic Defence and Security Review, a parallel exercise to the spending review which mandated the MoD to graft the Government's fiscal objectives on to its national security strategy. This was no easy task, made harder by the tensions around the Cabinet table. Fox boasted that he did not need to speak to Osborne at all, as he had direct access to the Prime Minister. When the Chancellor was told of this, he simply grimaced.

Sir Jock Stirrup, Chief of the Defence Staff until 29 October, informed Osborne in person that the proposed 10 per cent cut to the

MoD's £37bn annual budget was quite impossible to achieve. Told politely that the savings would have to be found, Stirrup produced a blueprint which – to the Chancellor's amusement – spared the RAF most of the pain (Stirrup having been a pilot and Chief of the Air Staff) but was markedly less merciful towards the Army and Navy. At least Stirrup had a plan: in general, Osborne was appalled by the bureaucracy and complacency of the MoD. 'If people could see how that fucking place is run,' he told one ally, 'they'd be horrified.'

'Horrified' also describes the reaction in Number Ten on 28 September when it became clear that a letter to Cameron from Fox objecting to the cuts had been leaked to the *Daily Telegraph*. According to the Defence Secretary, the Government's position was looking 'less and less defensible'. The cuts, he warned the PM, would have 'grave political consequences for us, destroying much of the reputation and capital you, and we, have built up in recent years'. According to Fox, 'party, media, military and the international reaction will be brutal if we do not recognize the dangers and continue to push for such draconian cuts at a time when we are at war'.

Though Fox insisted that he had not leaked the letter, or arranged for it to be leaked, many around the Cabinet table were unpersuaded by his protestations. The Defence Secretary was at loggerheads with the Treasury over a host of questions. How should Trident be paid for? Could the Navy afford new aircraft carriers? How many soldiers, sailors and airmen faced redundancy?

Such questions were the natural province of the new National Security Council (NSC), formed by Cameron to encourage Government-wide coherence on security and foreign policy. In the words of one Cabinet minister: 'David sees the Iraq War as exactly the way *not* to do things. Find out what they did over Iraq – and do the opposite.' This is only a slight exaggeration. The NSC was meant to be the mature alternative to the 'sofa government' criticized by Lord Butler in his 2004 report on the intelligence failures before the Iraq conflict. The new committee had met on the first full day of the Coalition's existence, bringing together all the key players including the PM, Clegg, Osborne, Hague, May, Fox, Andrew Mitchell (International Development Secretary), Sir Peter Ricketts (National Security Adviser),

Sir John Sawers, the head of MI6, and Jonathan Evans, the director-general of MI5. Its regular meetings were to have a profound effect upon Cameron and his Government's foreign policy. But its initial purpose was to formalize the decision-making process.

Fox's letter, addressed directly to the PM and then (somehow) leaked, was an old-school bid to circumvent the official court of appeal and to embarrass Cameron, on the eve of his party conference, into a compromise. Merely writing the letter was a huge risk. But Fox got away with it – just. On Sunday, 3 October, the PM told the BBC's Andrew Marr: 'I am passionately pro-defence, passionately pro our armed forces. I will not take any risks with Britain's defence.' Fox missed no opportunity to parade his alliance with Cameron. 'In this process, the Prime Minister has been my greatest ally,' he told Sky News the following day. 'The Prime Minister has one duty above all else, which is the defence of the realm, and David Cameron treats that duty with the utmost seriousness.'

The Defence Secretary's gamble paid off. When the Chancellor announced his spending review on 20 October, the MoD was mandated to make cuts of only 7.5 per cent (2.5 per cent less than originally demanded). Thanks to an extra £7bn in savings on welfare and £3.5bn from public sector employee pension contributions, the departmental cuts over four years were reduced to an average 19 per cent rather than 25 per cent as initially proposed. Theresa May faced a 20 per cent reduction in her police budget; Ken Clarke had to manage similar cuts to frontline court, prison and probation staff. Cable's department faced huge cuts, including a 40 per cent reduction in the universities' teaching budget offset by an increase in student tuition fees to a maximum of £9,000 per year. As promised, the English schools budget was protected, and £2.5bn allotted to the 'pupil premium' scheme for less affluent children.

Osborne's strategy was encapsulated in a single sentence: 'It is a hard road, but it leads to a better future.' The internal politics of the review had been scratchy, sometimes positively abrasive. It was the settled opinion of some close to Cameron that Fox was already preparing a carefully choreographed exit: a 'Heseltine moment' when he would march out of Cabinet on a point of Tory principle. But

Osborne was quietly relieved that a Conservative-led administration, having disclosed the most extensive package of cuts in living memory, was not at war with doctors and nurses; not yet, anyway.

As things stood, Osborne's strategy was endorsed by the IMF, OECD and Bank of England and he himself was enjoying a burst of political stardom. The polls suggested that the voters were broadly sympathetic to the Government's main objective: namely, to wipe out the structural deficit in the course of a single Parliament. The question that weighed on Osborne's mind was whether they would stick with it; whether patience played any part in the voters' professed appreciation that this had to be done.

A few days before the review was unveiled, Cameron hosted a party at Number Ten to mark Baroness Thatcher's eighty-fifth birthday – a celebration made poignant by the absence of the guest of honour, who was too ill to attend. The Prime Minister paid tribute to his predecessor and to her radicalism: a spirit of boldness which, somewhat to his surprise, this most pragmatic of politicians now found himself emulating. Lady Thatcher, Cameron said, was much too polite to voice to him the misgivings she must surely have about coalition government with the Lib Dems. But he hoped that she would approve of the consequences of this partnership, if not the form, and soon be able to see for herself 'early signs that the country is getting back on its feet'.

The distinction the PM drew between form and content was instructive. Before the election, the Tories made much of the slogan 'Conservative means to achieve progressive ends' – and that principle had survived the bumpy transition into government. Duncan Smith's welfare reforms were intended to achieve true social justice and to liberate the most deprived.

Osborne's announcement at the Tory conference that higher-rate taxpayers would lose child benefit (see Chapter 5) had been spectacularly controversial: but, in the Chancellor's eyes, it was an indispensable preamble to the spending review, demonstrating as clearly as possible that ministers did not intend to exempt the better-off from their tough measures. It is at least arguable that the whole review would have been impossible – and certainly much harder to present – without the protective endorsement of Clegg and Alexander and the presence of Lib Dem antibodies in the Treasury bloodstream. Cameron often referred to the Deputy Prime Minister as 'the human shield'. For now, the Lib Dem leader was on board. But he fretted about what might lie ahead as the serrated edge of a new fiscal strategy cut into people's lives. He told Osborne that fear of pain was as much a problem as pain itself: 'You've got to understand that you're dealing with a population that feel they or their relatives might fall on hard times. There's a new sense of insecurity, George.'

The stage had been set; a long, demanding process of public diplomacy now stretched ahead. Accepting the need for cuts in principle was one thing; feeling them in practice would be quite another. Though frequently accused of silver-spooned detachment, Osborne often reminded his colleagues that the lives of the neediest and the lowest-paid were finely geared: £10 more or less a week might not look like much on a bar chart, but it could have a transformative effect on those living on benefit or working for the minimum wage. 'It drives me mad when people claim that these savings are easy to find,' he said. 'They really are not.' The plan depended upon public tolerance of austerity; which in turn depended upon the return of growth. The cuts were a necessary but far from sufficient basis for national recovery. 'I don't want to have to come back,' he said as the review went off to the printers; meaning that he did not want to make more cuts in the course of the Parliament. But – as the Chancellor knew better than anyone – the promise was not his to make.

4. 'I wasn't really leading'

In the ante-chamber to Nick Clegg's Commons office hung a print from *The Bystander* given to the Deputy Prime Minister in 2012 by Paddy Ashdown. It was the most famous of Bruce Bairnsfather's First World War cartoons in which 'Old Bill' and another soldier take cover from enemy bombardment in a grim pit. The caption reads: 'Well, if you knows of a better 'ole, go to it.'

For the first six months of the Coalition, Clegg made a conscious effort, as he put it to colleagues, 'to throw myself at Rose Garden politics'.[1] The default position for most Lib Dems was to approach coalition with selective enthusiasm, ensuring that the public was in no doubt when the party disagreed with Tory-inspired policies and that a distinct identity be carved out by Clegg and his ministerial colleagues from the start. The Deputy Prime Minister, strongly encouraged by Richard Reeves, saw things differently. Yes, there would be a time for 'differentiation' – but not yet. In the infancy of the new Government, the Lib Dems had to 'own everything', so to speak. To do otherwise would look gutless and semi-detached, and give a bad name to coalition as a new and untested constitutional structure. The Lib Dems had to risk associating themselves with unpopular policies if they wanted to share credit with the Tories for popular measures. The party could not approach its participation in the alliance as a 'tick-box' exercise, in which Clegg and his colleagues applauded only those policies which were recognizably Lib Dem in inspiration. In public and in private, he was insistent that the party must confound anti-Coalition feeling across the political spectrum by showing that bipartisan government could work.

The Clegg–Reeves plan was to transform a party of protest – a jackdaw with a conscience, aligning itself with the cause of the moment to maximize electoral impact – into a party of government.

Charles Kennedy's eloquent opposition to the Iraq War had helped
to secure the Lib Dems sixty-two seats in the 2005 general election,
its best performance since the 1920s. Under his leadership, these MPs
were the parliamentary wing of a campaigning movement. But
Clegg wanted the party to carry red boxes, not banners.

The problem was that the contents of the boxes were often offensive to a party wedded to a host of pieties, old and new. High on this
sacred list was the principle that higher education should be free, an
engine of social mobility and informed citizenship.[2] That principle
had been practical when 10 per cent of the population went to university. But both the Conservatives and Labour had embraced the
objective of mass participation and ever-widening 'access', driving
the participation figure up to 47 per cent (including further education
colleges) by 2011. Clearly, the traditional model of funding was
incompatible with this dramatic change in social policy.

In 1998, David Blunkett, Education Secretary at the time, enabled
universities to charge tuition fees of £1,000 p.a. But the full toxicity
of the issue only became clear in 2003 when Charles Clarke's proposals permitting annual fees up to £3,000 became proxy terrain for
the Blair–Brown feud. The Commons revolt in January 2004 did not
thwart the reform, but was yet another blow to Tony Blair's waning
authority. Having supplanted Blair in Number Ten, Gordon Brown
was taking no such risks himself. In November 2009, he and Peter
Mandelson – Deputy Prime Minister in all but name – announced a
root-and-branch review of university financing by Lord Browne of
Madingley, the former chief executive of BP.

For the Tories, this posed no immediate threat: the party's 2010 manifesto promised blandly to 'consider carefully the results of Lord
Browne's review into the future of higher education funding'. For
the Lib Dems, on the other hand, the recommendations that Browne
was likely to make – higher fees or a graduate tax – presented a
pre-election quandary. Did the party wish to look serious or sympathetic? Its high electoral ambitions in university towns steered it in
one direction; the desire of the Lib Dem high command to resemble
ministers-in-waiting tugged it in another. Clegg and Vince Cable
urged the party's Federal Policy Committee to embrace fiscal realism

and concentrate on assistance for less affluent students rather than to persist in outright opposition to tuition charges of any sort.

The compromise, if such it really was, still committed the Lib Dems to phasing out, over six years, all tuition fees for students taking their first degrees. Clegg and Danny Alexander insisted that the policy should not be one of the headline pledges in the election campaign. But – disastrously – they still endorsed a statement drafted by the National Union of Students committing parliamentary candidates: 'I pledge to vote against any increase in fees in the next parliament and to pressure the government to introduce a fairer alternative.' Clegg signed up, as – very reluctantly – did Cable, and a total of 400 of the party's parliamentary candidates. Lest there be any doubt, the Lib Dem leader spelt out his position unambiguously: 'Labour and the Conservatives have been trying to keep tuition fees out of this election campaign. Despite the huge financial strain fees already place on Britain's young people, it is clear both Labour and the Conservatives want to lift the cap on fees.' He continued: 'The Liberal Democrats are different. Not only will we oppose any raising of the cap, we will scrap tuition fees for good, including for part-time students . . . Students can make the difference in countless seats in this election. Use your vote to block those unfair tuition fees and get them scrapped once and for all.' The words were strong enough. But the picture was the problem. As the Deputy PM would later reflect to colleagues, the greatest mistake was, in a single photo op, to provide his enemies with such a vivid image of the promise he would go on to break. The detail of the policy was lost in this moment of political theatre as the beaming Clegg knelt to sign the NUS pledge: as it would later seem, treachery with a smile on its face.

On 12 October, Lord Browne published his report, a characteristically elegant analysis at the heart of which was the recommendation that the cap on tuition fees be lifted entirely. Browne also proposed that the earnings limit beyond which graduates would begin to pay back loans rise from £15,000 to £21,000; that there would be no up-front fees; and that part-time students would also be eligible for loans for their tuition costs.

Cable favoured a graduate tax, which he regarded as both

progressive and politically attractive: Gordon Brown had been able
to get away with his 1p across-the-board increase in National Insurance in 2002 because the voters were told that the money would be
earmarked for the NHS. Why not make the same argument to pay
for higher education? David Willetts, the Universities and Science
Minister, worried that such a system would be too centralized at a
time when flexibility was called for. Universities, in Willetts's opinion,
needed to enact a 'supply-side' revolution to make the undergraduate
marketplace more flexible, more open to reform and better able to
meet the variable demand for places.

Osborne had explored a range of options over the summer, including the possibility of a graduate tax, but had concluded that the only
viable system was one that substantially increased the ability of universities and colleges to charge for tuition. The Government response,
delivered on 3 November, endorsed the £21,000 earnings threshold,
but stopped short of abolishing the fees cap entirely, settling on a
limit of £9,000 p.a. As a nod to the Lib Dems, future funding for
further education was secured.

There was some anxiety on the Tory side, especially among those
with longer memories. In 1984, Keith Joseph had proposed that
better-off families should pay a means-tested contribution to tuition
fees – only to be forced into an ignominious climbdown. Cameron
and Osborne knew that the measure would be unpopular with many
Tory voters, too well-paid to apply for bursaries for their student
children, but not affluent enough to have sent them to private school.
'This was their first experience of paying for education, or saddling
their kids with debt', according to one senior Cameroon, 'and they
bloody well hated it. This was as much an issue for Middle Britain
as it was for the Left.' It was to 30 Millbank, the Conservative
Party's headquarters, that 50,000 student demonstrators marched on
10 November. Two hundred protesters broke into the building, a few
dozen of them finding their way to the roof. Police in riot gear
clashed with activists, arresting thirty-five of them, as the smoke
from bonfires curled through the rioting crowd. For the first time in
many years, the chant 'Tory scum!' was heard in London. As they
watched the mayhem on television, Conservative MPs – 148 of them

new to the Commons – were given a first taste of austerity in action, the emotions the Coalition was stirring and the potential response of the aggrieved.

Yet the Lib Dems faced a much more immediate peril than their partners in government. Indeed, the problem that such an outcome would present to Clegg had been anticipated in the Coalition Agreement: 'If the response of the Government to Lord Browne's report [on higher education finance] is one that Liberal Democrats cannot accept, then arrangements will be made to enable Liberal Democrats to abstain in any vote.' One of Clegg's campaign slogans had been: 'No more broken promises'. The Deputy PM faced a crisis of trust.

At regular meetings of the Quad, Osborne noted that Clegg was starting to look tired and to mutter about the workload. For the first time, he seemed seriously harassed and exhausted, as if the full weight of government had suddenly come crashing down on his shoulders. 'What should we do?' he asked his Tory colleagues. Osborne replied: 'I wouldn't sign up to it. I think it's fair – but you're going to have real problems.' But Clegg's question had been rhetorical. 'I respect your candour,' he told the Chancellor, 'but we have to do this.'

In one sense, the Lib Dem leader had no choice, since the proposals were being steered through Parliament by Cable. The Business Secretary himself claimed to be philosophical about the whole business. 'The road to Westminster is covered in the skidmarks of political parties changing direction,' he said. But his public nonchalance did not stop the frenzied search in private for a square-circling solution to this ugly dilemma. In spite of his robust declaration in the Quad meeting, Clegg still wondered desperately whether he might maintain unity among the fifty-seven Lib Dem MPs by directing them to stay on the fence. The uncertainty put Cable in a difficult, parodic position, where he might be expected to commend legislation to the House – and then abstain.

The Business Secretary said that his 'personal instinct' was to vote for the reform, but that 'I'm willing to go along with my colleagues [if they choose to abstain]'.[3] Labour revelled in the muddle. As John Denham, the Shadow Business Secretary, asked: 'When was the last time that a minister – a Secretary of State and a member of the

Cabinet – came to the House to defend a policy that he drew up, on the same day on which he told the BBC that he might not even vote for it?'

In the circumstances, organized abstention was too ridiculous to adopt as official strategy. Clegg had to deploy the whip and hope for the best. In the Commons vote in December, twenty-one Lib Dem MPs rebelled, two of them unpaid ministerial aides who resigned their positions, and a further eight abstained or were absent. Those who voted against included two former party leaders, Charles Kennedy and Sir Menzies Campbell, and the Lib Dem president-elect, Tim Farron. For the Deputy PM, a mere eight months had separated 'Clegg-mania' from the burning of his effigy by protesters. As swiftly as Clegg had become a symbol of hope during the television debates, he no less quickly became a symbol of disappointment during the tuition fees row. It was a brutal disenchantment worthy of the world of celebrity: from collective swoon to the rattle of the tumbril's wheels in less than a year. And it took its toll. According to one of Clegg's colleagues: 'I was more worried about him than at any point. He is a tough guy but all this was happening so fast. He was irritable, too. Snapping, which is unlike him. I assume he wasn't sleeping so well.'

Asked to explain how they saw Clegg at the time, focus groups imagined him as a muzzled dog. As things stood at the end of 2010, the junior party in the Coalition was regarded as silenced and irrelevant, a gang of Tory stooges who acted as a human shield between the electorate and an essentially Conservative Government. The pressure upon the Deputy Prime Minister to produce a reassuringly yellow rabbit from the policy hat was crushing. To this end, he had already insisted to Cameron that the promised referendum on electoral reform at Westminster be held as soon as possible – if not in October 2010, then in May 2011. Behind the scenes, Ed Llewellyn conducted a rolling conversation with Jonny Oates, his Lib Dem opposite number. 'What can we do to help?' was the question. The Deputy PM was no longer kingmaker and had become 'needy Nick'. If that provided Tory Spads (Special Advisers) with a cheap laugh, it was short-lived. Clegg was the bolt that held the whole Coalition structure together. His party was famously inclined to kick out its leaders, which would mean – in all probability – the fall of the Government. It followed that senior Conservatives had to do everything in their power to get Clegg through the ordeal. It did not help that his own feverish refrain during these months was: 'We're stuffed.'

His tribe was restless. The pent-up frustrations of senior Lib Dems were deftly revealed by a *Daily Telegraph* sting operation in December.[4] Undercover reporters posing as constituents visited the routine surgeries of senior Lib Dem MPs and taped conversations, the transcripts of which made embarrassing reading. Michael Moore, the Scottish Secretary, said that he and Liam Fox 'probably couldn't stay in the same situation for very long', and, more significantly, that the breach of his pre-election pledge on student fees was 'the worst crime a politician can commit'. Ed Davey, Business Minister, declared that housing benefit reform was 'deeply unacceptable', while Paul Burstow, the Care Minister, told the paper's reporters that 'I don't want you to trust David Cameron' – not an ideal opening argument to be advanced to voters by one of the Government's lead champions of NHS reform.

Norman Baker, the Transport Minister, sought to equate the participation of the Lib Dems in the Government with the campaign of the great South African MP and anti-apartheid campaigner, Helen Suzman. 'I don't like George Osborne very much,' Baker explained. 'I mean, there are Tories who are all right – Ken Clarke's all right – there are the ones you can do business with. But what you end up doing in the Coalition . . . is we play them off against each other.'

Clegg studied anthropology at Cambridge and is persuaded by the arguments of 'Functionalists' such as Max Gluckman who argue that a measure of conflict is necessary in primitive societies to vent grievance and preserve order: the so-called 'peace in the feud'.[5] In one sense, these conversations showed how disciplined and steady the Coalition was most of the time, and that – for the moment, at least – its senior members were generally willing to submerge their objections in the name of unity. Venting to undercover reporters was scarcely the end of the world.

Naturally, these remarks were annoying for a party leader still struggling to get the Coalition out of the incubator and into the nursery. Yet, in scale, sweep and significance, the reflections of Vince Cable, as related to the *Telegraph*, were of a different order: not simply annoying, but a direct threat to the stability of the Government. 'I have a nuclear option,' the Business Secretary told the newspaper, 'it's like fighting a war. They know I have nuclear weapons, but I don't have any conventional weapons. If they push me too far, then I can walk out and bring the Government down and they know that . . . So it is a question of how you use that intelligently without getting involved in a war that destroys all of us. That is quite a difficult position to be in and I am picking my fights. Some of which you may have seen.'

Having boasted of his ability to bring down the Government, Cable professed himself out of sympathy with both the pace and the quality of reform. 'There is a kind of Maoist revolution happening in a lot of areas like the health service, local government, reform, all this kind of stuff, which is in danger of getting out of control. We are trying to do too many things, actually. Some of them are Lib Dem-inspired, but a lot of it is Tory-inspired. The problem is not that they are Tory-inspired, but that they haven't thought them through. We should be putting a brake on it.'

Cable would later reflect to colleagues that the story 'burst like a bomb' around him.[6] Yet omitted from the first tranche of excerpts were his remarks about Rupert Murdoch, which Robert Peston, the BBC's business editor, posted on his blog on 21 December. The Business Secretary did not mince his words. 'I have declared war on Mr Murdoch and I think we're going to win. I didn't politicize it, because it is a legal question, but he is trying to take over BSkyB . . . I have blocked it. His whole empire is now under attack.'

Murdoch's media conglomerate, News Corp, already owned 39.1 per cent of the satellite television giant BSkyB – chaired by his son James – but was seeking total control of the company. A measure of the bid's potential significance is the breadth of the alliance opposing it, embracing the Telegraph Media Group, Associated Newspapers Ltd, Trinity Mirror, the Guardian Media Group, the BBC and Channel 4.

The *Telegraph*'s decision not to include the remarks about Murdoch on the first day of its revelations looked stranger in retrospect than it did at the time. Conspiracy theorists argued that Telegraph Media Group was somehow trying to suppress Cable's opposition to the bid, which chimed with its own interests. But the plan to hold over the Business Secretary's remarks till the second day of coverage reflected a perfectly plausible news judgement. In December 2010, well before the hacking scandal forced the closure of the *News of the World* and the Leveson Inquiry, the unveiling of Cable's true feelings about the Coalition was simply a bigger story. The question was how Peston, a famously brilliant story-getter, had gained access to the relevant files. An inquiry by a private investigations firm, Kroll International, found that there was strong reason to suspect the involvement of Will Lewis, a former editor-in-chief of the *Telegraph* now working as a senior executive at Murdoch's Wapping HQ. But Kroll was unable to prove its working hypothesis conclusively.[7]

The £7.8bn deal was indeed at the heart of News Corp's global broadcasting strategy, and was approved by the European Commission. In November, however, Cable decided to exercise the quasi-judicial powers granted to him by Section 67 of the 2002 Enterprise Act and refer the takeover to the media regulator, Ofcom, as a potential threat to 'plurality': the number and variety of voices in the media marketplace. 'The independent experts at Ofcom will now investigate and report to me on the media plurality issues that may arise from this proposed acquisition,' he announced.[8]

A chasm separated this sober Whitehall statement and Cable's bellicose boasts and swashbuckling claim to have Murdoch on the ropes. The former was the official language of the economist-as-Cabinet-minister; the latter reflected the strain of irrepressible showmanship Cable also revealed as a contestant in the *Strictly Come Dancing* Christmas special. Cameron could shrug off the private mutterings of Lib Dem ministers about the awfulness of Tories. But he could not ignore – or tolerate – a senior member of his Cabinet telling visitors he imagined to be constituents that he had the power to 'bring the Government down', or boasting of the personal animus driving a ministerial decision about a huge business deal.

The fact that the deal was Murdoch's greatly compounded the political problem, adding the frisson of vendetta to the mix. If the PM sacked Cable, he would be said to be caving in to the media mogul. If, on the other hand, he left him in post, News Corp would object – not unreasonably – that Cameron was allowing his ministers to pursue private crusades under the protective cover of Her Majesty's Government. There was a blizzard of texts and emails – not least from Jeremy Hunt, the Culture Secretary. He texted Osborne: 'Could we chat about Murdoch Sky bid? I am seriously worried we are going to screw this up.' Two minutes later, he emailed Coulson: 'Could we chat about this? I am seriously worried Vince Cable will do real damage to coalition with his comments.'

After a joint press conference with Clegg concluded at 3 p.m., the PM held a rolling series of meetings with the Lib Dem leader and Ed Llewellyn, Heywood and, in due course, Osborne. There was a case for sacking Cable on the spot. The Prime Minister's preference for colleagues who saw the glass as half full was sometimes a symptom of groundless optimism. Even so, Cable, he felt, not only considered the glass half empty but expected it to be knocked over and spilt at any moment. 'Vince is *always* complaining,' he told one ally.[9] The Chancellor found Cable easier to deal with. The Business Secretary had made clear to Osborne from their earliest meetings that 'we could do each other a lot of harm', but that he wanted an entente cordiale: that meant the Chancellor accepting that Cable deserved a serious job and the resources with which to do it. As far as the Business Secretary was concerned, there was much suspicion to overcome. But he and the Chancellor were able to construct a working relationship with the brickwork of confidence-building measures. 'Vince isn't that hard to handle,' Osborne told colleagues. 'You just have to make sure his name is on as many public documents as possible.'

The *Daily Telegraph* story had transformed Cable's public persona, or, more accurately, lifted the veil upon his true character. While none of the claims he made or opinions he voiced were intrinsically surprising – one might expect him to be anti-Murdoch and pleased with the influence he wielded in the Coalition – it was one thing to assume as much; quite another to read it in black and white. Without intending to, he had challenged the authority of the Coalition's most senior figures. It was not a challenge to be ignored, either. Cable might be a 67-year-old economist with a querulous radio manner, but he also had a touch of stardust. Like Ken Clarke and Boris Johnson, he was perceived as a man true to himself, an authentic human being in an age of political clones. In a government of young public schoolboys, his age – the twinkling eye of experience – was an asset.

Cameron and Clegg had no wish to be perceived as hostage to their own Cabinet, presiding nervously over an oligarchy of irreplaceables. If the Coalition was to develop muscle, stamina and authority, it had to amount to more than the people within it. Nobody – except perhaps Cameron and Clegg themselves – should be indispensable. Or so principle dictated.

In practice, however, Cable's claim that he had a 'nuclear option' was hyperbolic rather than utterly absurd: there was a nugget of truth within the braggadocio. He knew full well how important he was to the Coalition's structural integrity. He was one of its moral guarantors, reassuring social democratic Lib Dems that their voice was being heard, and that the party had not sold out entirely. The movement's activists were still reeling from the nasty novelty of the tuition fees row: Lib Dems were used to calling other parties treacherous, mendacious and corrupted by power. To find themselves on the receiving end of the same charge was deeply traumatic, a pitiless crash course in government. If this was what office entailed, was office worth having? The Coalition was still desperately fragile. Cable's departure would not bring it crashing down at once, but might trigger its collapse by stages. When the Business Secretary arrived in Number Ten to see Cameron and Clegg, he was struck by how shaken they seemed. Clearly, he had hit a very raw nerve. The atmosphere was fraught and not improved by Cable's evident lack of genuine contrition. Indeed, he regarded himself as the victim of entrapment rather than the author of the Government's predicament.

In the end, it was a conversation between the PM and Osborne that settled the matter. As angry as they were, they agreed that they still needed Cable. Quoting his political hero, LBJ, the Chancellor said that 'it's better to have Vince inside the tent pissing out'. Cameron agreed. But Cable's remarks about Murdoch meant that he could not conceivably retain oversight of this colossal and colossally contentious bid. Just before 4 p.m., News Corporation issued a statement declaring itself 'shocked and dismayed by reports of Mr Cable's comments. They raise serious questions about fairness and due process.' James Murdoch called Jeremy Hunt to express the same sentiments more bluntly.

The compromise, first suggested by Heywood, was to keep Cable in his post, but to transfer his responsibilities for media and telecoms to the Culture Secretary. Shortly before 5 p.m., the Chancellor texted Hunt: 'I hope you like the solution!' – which was made public forty-five minutes later. The day had been fraught with embarrassment, but meltdown had been avoided. What none of the protagonists could guess was that the public upheavals and private communications of the day – and of many others like it – would soon be scrutinized and picked over in the most searching public inquiry for a generation.

Over Christmas, Cable's home at Twickenham was besieged by reporters. The episode had made him furious but was also, inescapably, traumatic. In particular, he felt that Murdoch's daily redtop, the *Sun*, now had him in its sights. The Tories did their best to be magnanimous. At a Cabinet meeting soon after the debacle, Hague quipped that he was 'disgusted by this right-wing outfit called the *Daily Telegraph*'. This was for Cable's benefit and a typical intervention by Hague to ease tension with wit. But the damage was already done.

For Clegg, the humiliation of his senior colleagues by the *Telegraph* sting not only strained Coalition relations and increased the pressure upon him to repair the damage. It made it all the more imperative that he get back on the front foot, and show his querulous activists that Lib Dem MPs were more than lobby fodder for a Tory-led Government that had fallen short of a majority. For this reason alone, the forthcoming referendum on electoral reform and the AV system was of the highest importance.

The voting system was not Clegg's most passionate preoccupation. He certainly believed strongly in the need for 'political reform' – a vague rubric which covered the number of MPs, constituency boundaries, fixed-term parliaments, Lords reform, party financing and the electoral system used at Westminster. The proximate cause for this enthusiasm (other than Lib Dem principles) was the expenses scandal of 2009. The Coalition Agreement declared that 'Our political system is broken. We urgently need fundamental political reform, including a referendum on electoral reform, much greater co-operation across party lines and change to our political system to make it far more transparent and accountable.'

But the issue that animated Clegg more than any other was social mobility. The ministerial committee exploring the issue came to be seen as a forum where significant decisions were made: Michael Gove, though not formally a member, made a point of turning up to some of its meetings, alongside Willetts and Duncan Smith. The former Labour leadership contender Alan Milburn was appointed as the Government's independent reviewer on social mobility. Schools which educated the poorest children were given the new £430-per-head 'pupil premium', while universities that proposed to charge tuition fees of more than £6,000 p.a. were expected to draw up 'access agreements' – precisely the sort of regulations that Tories traditionally deplored as 'social engineering'.

In April, the Government announced that it was to publish an annual 'report card' on seven key indicators, ranging from infants' body weight and the skills acquired by five-year-olds to GCSE results and adult income. These metrics, Clegg said, would act 'as a series of dials', a dashboard used to monitor the nation's wellbeing and to 'trigger a reaction' when progress faltered. Some Tory Cabinet ministers could hardly conceal their amusement at the Deputy PM's imaginary Heath Robinson machine, monitored by bureaucrats in white coats with clipboards. As Universities Minister, Willetts did his best to support Clegg's well-meaning plan, but struggled to conceal his scepticism that social mobility could be forced by diktat from Whitehall. As he explained to allies: 'My main job has been to keep Vince hosed down during the whole fees story.' Willetts's admirers in the party and media felt that he deserved a more senior post. Those closest to the PM said he was lucky to have a job at all, having supported Davis in 2005. At the time, Willetts had gone to an early meeting of the fledgling Cameron leadership campaign and been put off by the sight of 'all these Etonians'. Most of them were his political friends, including the candidate, and some were close allies: but Willetts could not see – initially at least – how this socially uniform cohort was equipped to save the party. According to one of the PM's oldest friends: 'Dave *never* forgets stuff like that. Even when Nick Boles did a piece in the *Standard* during the contest saying that Davis might not be too bad. That was dicing with death. Nick was lucky not to be exiled from the court.'

Clegg, meanwhile, was unmoved by the playground sniggering and the more serious whispers that he was dragging the Government towards something like 'affirmative action'. Urged on by Reeves, he felt a strong sense of mission – to break up the elites and cartels that still dominated the apex of British society, and to take on the nepotism that ensured that privileged children could expect the best work placements.

This was sensitive terrain for a Coalition dominated by public schoolboys, alumni of the Bullingdon Club and the children of privilege. All the more reason, as far as Clegg was concerned, to confront the question aggressively. He made clear to university vice-chancellors that the rules of the game had changed: how they went about broadening their student intake was up to them, in partnership with the Office for Fair Access; but he expected to see results, particularly in the proportion of state school pupils being admitted to the best universities.

Private school heads complained furiously about a new era of 'differential offers' in which their pupils would have to clear much higher hurdles than rivals from the state sector. Once again, Clegg the 'Old Wet' – a product of Westminster School – was quite content to have triggered such anxieties and to make parents doubt that they could still buy social advantage for their children by paying exorbitant school fees.

Cameron did his best in Cabinet to present Clegg's cradle-to-grave plan as 'Coalition policy'. But there was no concealing the tension between the two parties. In the week that Clegg unveiled his seven indicators, Willetts pointedly declared that he still believed in 'a liberal labour market that doesn't try to achieve social objectives'. The Tories were more at ease with 'supply-side' solutions that removed barriers than with threats to universities. For Duncan Smith, the heart of the matter was the 'broken society' that bred poverty of aspiration. For Gove, it was the culture of expectation and excellence in schools that needed to be addressed. Clegg went further – much further – in his readiness to use the power of Government to compel change. The difference became graphically clear when Cameron admitted that he had recently arranged work experience for a neighbour's son; the PM told the *Daily Telegraph* that he was 'very relaxed' about the disclosure and would continue the practice. Clegg's response during a rally in Norwich was forthright: 'I'm not relaxed about this at all . . . It just can't be right that plum internships are decided by who you know, not what you know.'

If Clegg's highest aspiration was to show that the Lib Dems were a plausible party of government, it was closely rivalled by his ambition to make Britain more socially mobile and less stratified. But, for the movement he led, the great prize (described to the point of cliché as the 'Lib Dem Holy Grail') was electoral reform at Westminster and the strongest argument in favour of coalition was that the party would get a referendum on a change to the voting system as part of the deal.[10] It was an article of faith for Lib Dems that first-past-the-post was wrong in principle, and particularly injurious to them in practice. In the election of February 1974, for instance, the Liberals had secured 19.3 per cent of the vote but only 2.2 per cent of the seats (fourteen). This sense of injustice was, more than any other political imperative, the binding cause of Clegg's party: the redistribution of representative power by a fairer voting system.

In July 2010, the Coalition published two related bills, the first to establish fixed parliamentary terms and the second to overhaul the electoral process itself: the Parliamentary Voting System and Constituencies Bill would reduce the number of MPs from 650 to 600, establish new constituency boundaries, provide for more regular boundary reviews and legislate for a referendum on the Alternative Vote method of election to the House of Commons in May 2011.

This would be the first nationwide referendum since the vote on EEC membership in 1975, and the first ever to be binding upon Parliament. It proposed the greatest prospective change to the parliamentary system since universal suffrage in 1928. The first-past-the-post system invited the voter to choose one candidate, and one candidate only. Under AV, voting became a preferential process, in which the citizen ranked as many of the candidates as he or she wished: first, second, third, and so on. If on the first count, no candidate gained 50 per cent of the vote, the candidate with the fewest first preferences was eliminated and his or her votes were redistributed amongst the remaining candidates.

It was absolutely not what the Lib Dems wanted. Before the election, Clegg had dismissed AV as a 'miserable little compromise'. But it was better than nothing – which is what the party had squeezed out of Labour in thirteen years. Before the 1997 election, Blair had promised a referendum on electoral reform. But when Gordon Brown left Downing Street, Labour had still not acted on its promise. So Clegg's gamble that Cameron would not renege on his pledge during the Coalition talks was essential to their mutual trust. If Nixon could go to China, and de Gaulle extract France from Algeria, then perhaps Cameron could facilitate the end of first-past-the-post. Clegg said that AV was a 'baby step in the right direction' – but knew it was much more.[11] Already, there were *five* electoral systems other than first-past-the-post being used in British elections: to the devolved assemblies, the European Parliament, local authorities and the London mayoralty. Once the crust of conservatism was broken at Westminster – Clegg reasoned – further reform would follow. If a Conservative–Lib Dem Government could introduce AV, what was to stop a Labour–Lib Dem Coalition of the future finishing the job? For once, those Tories who saw every reform as the top of a 'slippery slope' were justified in their anxieties.

The best argument for AV was that the voting system no longer reflected the reality of the nation's party political topography. As the grip of the two main parties loosened, the number of constituencies won with a minority of the vote had risen embarrassingly. In 1951, for example, only thirty-nine MPs out of 625 were elected with less than 50 per cent of the constituency vote. But in 2010, 433 out of 650 seats had been won in this way – with the obvious structural implication that millions of citizens felt that their votes were wasted.[12] By encouraging the voter to express transferable preferences, AV directly addressed this sense of electoral futility by ensuring that no MP could be elected without the support of 50 per cent of his constituency. Clegg's private research in the summer of 2010 suggested that the public was amenable to change.

The proposed new system was clearly in the interests of the Lib Dems, the second choice of so many voters for so many different reasons. In 2010, according to one calculation, the Lib Dems would have won eighty-nine seats under AV instead of fifty-seven.[13] Simulations of previous elections suggested that the impact of the Alternative Vote was unpredictable. In 1945, 1966 and 1997, for instance, Labour might well have won even larger majorities. In 1951 and 1992, narrow victories for the Conservatives under first-past-the-post, AV would probably have delivered hung Parliaments.

That was one of the arguments most frequently deployed by the opponents of the alternative vote. In 1931, Churchill had dismissed this very system as 'the child of folly' which would 'become the parent of fraud'.[14] Electoral reform of this sort would also – its detractors alleged – encourage the politics of the lowest common denominator as candidates sought second and third preferences rather than straightforward endorsement. Blandness, vagueness and evasion would be rewarded rather than conviction, clarity and boldness. The moment of decision would be replaced by an act of ranking – a political act drained of drama and engagement.

In the months that followed, the 'No' campaign tested more than thirty arguments against AV meticulously in private polls. Lynton Crosby, who had masterminded Boris Johnson's mayoral victory in 2008, and Andrew Cooper, strategic director of the Populus polling company, steered the research, with assistance from BBM, a company founded by the former Labour strategists Alan Barnard and John Braggins. Their findings were clear: what the punters most disliked about the proposed new system was its potential cost – £260m, it was claimed – and its complexity. And if AV was such a good system, why was it used only in Australia, Papua New Guinea and Fiji? These three objections (cost, complexity, rarity) would form the basis of the campaign against change.

From the start, Clegg was harried by Tory MPs who saw the referendum and its technicalities as a stick with which to beat the Coalition in general, and the Deputy PM personally. In July 2010, he rejected a motion signed by forty-four of them – including David Davis, Bernard Jenkin, Peter Lilley and John Redwood – to hold the plebiscite on a day other than 5 May, which was already earmarked for elections to the Welsh Assembly, the Scottish Parliament, the Northern Ireland Assembly and some English councils. The notional objection was that these routine party political contests and a referendum on the future of the electoral system should not become entangled. But it was fairly obvious that the point of the ploy was to sabotage the process by any means available.

Even as the Right provoked him, Clegg was certain that he had an understanding with Cameron. Though the Tory leader would notionally oppose AV and make a few appearances in support of the 'No' campaign, these would be token rather than passionate. Clegg would take a symmetrical step back, too. The two party leaders would not let the Coalition collapse over electoral reform.

Initially, the Cameroon inner circle behaved as Clegg had expected, exuding nonchalance about the referendum. Gove, a passionate conservative about most constitutional issues, declared himself 'undecided' on this one. Letwin was said to find the prospect of AV intriguing rather than alarming. Cameron asked his friend and Eurosceptic ally Rodney Leach (Lord Leach of Fairford), the former chairman of Business for Sterling, to assume the same role at the new 'No to AV' campaign. Leach, in turn, appointed Matthew Elliott, co-founder of the TaxPayers' Alliance, as campaign director.

At a stroke, a single act of recruitment changed the nature of the fight, to a much greater degree than Number Ten initially grasped. Elliott was known around Westminster as a restless intellectual terrier, a bespectacled force of nature who would certainly not allow the country to sleepwalk towards a 'Yes' vote. In July, that is precisely what seemed to be on the cards: opinion polls showed about 55 per cent of the electorate supporting change.[15]

The 'Yes' campaign – 'YES! To Fairer Votes' – had plenty of money, thanks to big donations from the Electoral Reform Society (ERS) and the Joseph Rowntree Reform Trust. It could afford to send out plastic dinosaurs as a gimmick to encapsulate the charge that supporters of first-past-the-post were Jurassic in their politics and that AV stood for confident modernity and common sense. Clegg's general election campaign manager, John Sharkey, represented him on the 'Yes' team, which was chaired by Katie Ghose, chief executive of the ERS, and included a number of effective operators, such as the treasurer, Nick Tyrone, and Neal Lawson, of the left-wing pressure group Compass. At its height, the campaign had 110 people on the payroll, twelve regional organizers, a busy phone-bank and full coffers. The odds appeared to be stacked in favour of change.

Elliott grasped immediately that the key variable was the Labour vote. Throughout the summer, the party had been preoccupied by its leadership contest, which ended in a thrilling photo finish between two siblings. In Manchester, on 25 September, Ed Miliband defied the odds and defeated his brother, David, by the tiniest of margins (50.65 per cent compared to David's 49.35 per cent). Most senior Tories, with the notable exception of William Hague, assumed that the Opposition had made a terrible error, choosing the more left-wing of the two Milibands, indebted to the trade unions whose votes had pushed him over the finishing line – just.[16] Cameron was now facing his third Labour leader across the Despatch Box, an unlikely veteran at the age of forty-three.

Miliband himself stuck by the pro-AV position taken in Labour's 2010 election manifesto: to campaign in favour of a system that ensured 'every MP is supported by the majority of their constituents'. But Elliott knew that many in the party's ranks preferred the status quo, and that there were plenty of furious David Miliband supporters who might relish the opportunity for a rematch against the impostor Ed. He hired Joan Ryan, former Labour MP for Enfield North, as deputy director, and Jane Kennedy, former Minister of

State for Farming and the Environment, as national organizer. Kennedy spoke at 200 meetings of Labour activists around the country. Ryan was to head the sub-campaign, 'Labour NO to AV', established to rebut the charge made by Chris Huhne and others that the main organization was a Tory front, and to bring on board politicians like John Prescott who disliked politically ecumenical groups.

Elliott also deployed the formidable talents of Bruce (Lord) Grocott, former aide to Tony Blair and Chief Whip in the Lords, to construct a Labour network opposed to AV. If the Labour vote could be split, the 'No' camp might prevail. But the pressure had to be relentless. By polling day, 130 Labour MPs had declared themselves strongly opposed to the alternative vote. It was no accident that David Blunkett presented NO to AV's last television broadcast. The message was: this is about saving a tried-and-tested system, not an opportunity to bash the Tories without consequence.

In November, Elliott met Kate Fall and Stephen Gilbert, Cameron's political secretary, to brief them on his progress. Quietly spoken, rarely seen in public and one of relatively few women in the inner circle, Fall was extremely important to Cameron's daily life and one of the people whose counsel he trusted. She was almost invariably at his side, briefing him and steering him away from errors of judgement. When her marriage to the property developer Ralph Ward-Jackson ended in late 2010, her colleagues were impressed by her dignity and ability to keep going. She was also wrongly assumed to be the model for (or even the author of) Tamzin Lightwater, the *Spectator*'s diarist sending suspiciously well-informed despatches from Conservative HQ.[17]

As Elliott made his pitch, Fall and Gilbert were impressed – but also taken aback. Fall quickly realized that Elliott's unexpected success in building a cross-party 'No' campaign could have serious strategic implications that had nothing to do with electoral reform. 'What will this mean for the Coalition?' she asked at the meeting – rhetorically, but prophetically. If the AV referendum was lost, 'needy Nick' would be in even deeper trouble, with all that this implied.

As the 'No' campaign started to look serious, the opposing team began to show the strain. 'We weren't engaging in the intellectual argument', according to one veteran of the 'Yes' campaign. 'Who would be the figurehead? We kept Nick [Clegg] away from it and that was a mistake. People knew perfectly well that this was his idea. The problem was that nobody owned it.' The same source recalls meetings with far too many campaign groups chipping in and far too little focus: 'It illustrated why anarcho-syndicalism didn't work.'

Thus far, Cameron had gone to great lengths not to wreck Clegg's great reform. Fall kept him in the loop about Elliott's progress – but he could hardly tell the 'No' team to stop doing its job. Instead, obstacles were discreetly placed in its path. The 'No' campaign was not even granted space for a stall at the Conservative conference in Birmingham; donors were being told to give money to the party rather than to the campaign. Cabinet ministers did not wear 'NO to AV' stickers – although Osborne wore his on the inside of his jacket lapel, flashing it with a grin to those he thought would enjoy this (very minor) act of insubordination.

So starved of funds was the 'No' cause that Elliott toyed with the idea of declining the status of lead campaign or 'designated organization'. Under the Political Parties, Elections and Referendums Act (2000), the Electoral Commission may name one campaign to represent each outcome of the referendum: each such organization receives a grant from the Commission of up to £600,000, has its spending capped at £5m, and is given a free campaign mailshot to every household in the referendum area, free broadcasts and free use of public venues. Elliott considered sticking with the lesser status of 'permitted participant', simply to deny the 'Yes' campaign all these publicly funded goodies. According to his clear understanding of the referendum rules, the contest had to be fought on a level legal playing field: if the 'No' campaign waived the right to be the 'designated organization', the 'Yes' campaign could not be unilaterally granted a bonanza of public assistance.

Elliott need not have worried. The PM was uncomfortable with this ploy to undermine the 'Yes' campaign, which he knew would be seen by Clegg as a 'dirty trick'. The 'No' campaign's finances were transformed by the donation of £400,000 by Peter Cruddas, the founder of the CMC spread betting firm, who also became co-treasurer of the campaign. Meanwhile, the parliamentary party had had its fill of Cameron's disengagement from the issue. At a meeting with back-benchers in January, Sayeeda Warsi, the Tory chairman, was asked pointedly by Jenkin whether the campaign was being given adequate resources. In Number Ten, the Prime Minister himself was con-fronted by the executive of the 1922 Committee and told face to face that the party was drifting towards disaster. Tories in the Upper House began to voice similar frustration. The barely coded message sent to him by the 1922 executive and picked up by the whips from their allotted backbenchers was that defeat in the referendum would seal his reputation as a loser and persuade every Tory MP in the House and every candidate in the country that his lack of grip had made it harder for them to win in 2015. His relationship with the par-liamentary party was already rocky: in the five years of his leadership, the grievances had stockpiled, over his robust handling of the expenses scandal, resentment of the ruling clique, and a ham-fisted bid shortly after the election to weaken the 1922 Committee. Defeat in the referendum would make a scratchy mood positively poison-ous. The fractious Tory tribe would become openly seditious.

Here, once again, the multi-dimensional geometry of the Coali-tion asserted itself. Cameron wanted to help out Clegg, badly damaged as he was by the tuition fees debacle. But the PM could not afford to provoke the collective wrath of his own MPs – not so early in the Parliament, not with so many battles ahead, and not (to be blunt about it) simply to cheer up the Lib Dems. He had tried to prop up his deputy, but he could not risk a full-scale Tory uprising. 'So Nick was suddenly left swinging in the wind', according to one ally. 'No warning – nothing.'

From February, Cameron did precisely what Clegg had under-stood he would not – namely, lead from the front. He and Osborne started to canvass editors and pundits. In a speech at the Royal United Services Institute, the Prime Minister warned that AV would result in a 'Parliament of second choices', in which 'someone who's not really wanted by anyone [wins] an election because they were the least unliked'. Aligning himself clearly with the 'NO to AV' script, he argued: 'If you vote for a mainstream candidate who is top of the ballot in the first round, your other preferences will never be counted. But if you vote for a fringe party who gets knocked out, your other preferences will be counted. In other words, you get another bite of the cherry.'

In March, at the Conservative spring forum in Cardiff, the 'No' campaign was at the heart of the message from the platform – a dramatic contrast to its total exclusion from the October conference. 'On May 5th,' Lady Warsi said to the assembled party, 'I want you to defend the seats we hold. Of course, we've got to take the seats we can. But above all on May 5th, we need to win the one election which will affect every single general election to come.' On the Sunday of the conference, Ken Clarke joined the assault on AV, praising the historic wisdom of the decisions taken by the British people under first-past-the-post. Cameron asked his audience to imagine themselves at the 2012 Olympics: 'We're all watching the 100 metres. Usain Bolt powers home over the line. But then he gets to the podium, it's the guy who came third who gets the gold. We wouldn't put up with this in the Olympics. We shouldn't put up with it in our democracy.'

In the space of five months, the 'No' campaign had been promoted from an embarrassing necessity to the party's principal battlefront. But it was not until 18 April, when Cameron shared a platform with John Reid, the former Labour Home Secretary, under the 'NO to AV' banner, that Elliott believed that victory was in sight. Cameron's close identification with the 'No' campaign would steer Tory voters on 5 May; while Reid's presence at his side made clear the serious cross-party character of the endeavour. It was an embarrassment to the 'Yes' campaign that Miliband would not share a platform with Clegg, whom he regarded as a liability. The team pushed the Labour leader's office to be flexible, but his mind was made up.

Though the business of government continued, the tensions within the Coalition were now severe and overt. In March, Chris Huhne was infuriated by Warsi's claim that AV would help the BNP and declared that 'this is another example of the increasingly Goebbels-like campaign from the anti-AV people, for whom no lie is too idiotic given the truth is so unpalatable to them'.[18] Officially, Downing Street claimed to be relaxed about such crossfire, shrugging it off as an inevitable feature of a fiercely contested referendum. Privately, the Cameroons wondered if the governing partnership could take the strain, and how easy a female Muslim who had been compared to a Nazi by a Cabinet colleague would find it to resume business as usual after the vote. Warsi was indeed shaken by the exchange though (at this stage) confident of the PM's support. Clegg was torn between anger at the content of the campaign literature and anger at Huhne for his shameless show-boating. 'Chris was getting ready to slip into the leader's chair if and when Nick fell, that much was clear', according to one supporter of the Deputy PM.

The Lib Dems' growing conviction that they had been deceived by the Tories came to a head at a Cabinet meeting two days before the referendum, when Huhne (again) confronted Cameron with anti-AV leaflets that attacked Clegg personally. Huhne then challenged the Prime Minister to justify the campaign literature and to sack any Tory official involved in their production or distribution. Osborne intervened, telling Huhne: 'This is the Cabinet, not some kind of sub-Jeremy Paxman interview.' Clegg's silence was eloquent. It was his habitual role in Cabinet – and outside – to seek common ground when senior Lib Dems clashed with the Tories. But in this instance he wanted Cameron and Osborne to savour the embarrassment he was feeling. Osborne increasingly thought that Huhne was a joke, and was no more impressed by his occasional attempts at camaraderie – 'You and me, George, we're operators' – than by his antics in Cabinet. He also thought that Clegg had too thin a skin, and had yet to come to terms with the price a governing politician pays for exercising power. Cameron was more concerned that Clegg was close to the limit and what that might mean for the Coalition.

In fact, it had been the Labour members of the 'No' team who had insisted on using Clegg's image in such leaflets. To energize the Labour vote, they argued, it had to be spelt out that the referendum was an opportunity to punish Clegg and the Lib Dems for letting the Tories in. But such nuances were lost in this heated, intensely awkward Cabinet exchange. The incident was leaked almost immediately after the Cabinet meeting. If Huhne's intention had been to redefine the 'No' campaign in voters' minds as underhand and untrustworthy, he had left it much too late. A ComRes poll published by the *Independent* on the same day showed the 'No' campaign ahead by 66 per cent to 35 per cent among those who were certain to vote.

On 5 May, the following question was put to the electorate: 'At present, the UK uses the "first past the post" system to elect MPs to the House of Commons. Should the "alternative vote" system be used instead?' The second nationwide referendum in British history resulted in a crushing defeat for AV: by 67.9 per cent to 32.1 per cent. More than nineteen million citizens had voted, a turnout of 42 per cent. The 'Yes' campaign had spent £3.4m, compared to the 'No' team's £2.6m. Clegg's unpopularity had played its part in the outcome. But the deciding factor was Miliband's conspicuous inability to unite Labour behind the proposal – or, perhaps more accurately, his reluctance, so early in his party leadership, to expend political capital on a cause that most voters regarded as marginal.

When Tyrone went to visit one of the 'Yes' campaign's offices to wind up the accounts, he found the team playing *Battlestar Galactica*, decked out in science fiction outfits. Elliott, for his part, noted the bathos with which the world moved on almost instantly. In 1975, on the question of Britain's relationship with Europe, there was a sense that history had been made by the *vox populi*; not so on this occasion. But that was precisely the point, the message of the referendum. It was an instruction to the Coalition to stop tinkering and to get on with the business of fixing the country. Yes, the public was indifferent to the reform. But it had made its indifference very clear. In this respect, the timing was cruel: only six days before the vote, the country had been treated to the royal pageant of Prince William's wedding to Kate Middleton, the subliminal message of which was more striking than any political broadcast. No institution better embodied the British preference for evolutionary adaptation rather than constitutional upheaval than the monarchy. Amid all the bunting and Middletoniana, the closing arguments of the reformers stood little chance of a fair hearing.

In a useful analysis of the campaign, Tim Montgomerie, founder of the Conservative Home website, remarked that Cameron had shown that he had 'fight in him. He proved he can still be a winner . . .

In an alliance with Britain's centre right newspapers he gave a taste of the campaign that could see him win a second term.'[19] The implicit question posed by Montgomerie and others was whether the PM could preserve and nurture this campaigning alliance.

Clegg was stunned rather than surprised. 'I wish I could say this is a photo finish but it isn't and the result is very clear. I'm a passionate supporter of electoral reform but we've got to accept this. If, in a democracy, you ask someone a question and get an overwhelming answer, you just have to move on.' It was, he conceded, a 'bitter blow'. In the closing weeks of the campaign, he had railed against the nastiness of the 'right-wing elite, a right-wing clique who want to keep things the way they are'.[20] The scales, at any rate, had fallen from Clegg's eyes. His relationship with Cameron had survived, for the simple reason that it had to. But where Clegg had previously seen his governing partner as a reasonable, moderate man with broadly similar instincts to his own, he now regarded him as the acceptable face of a truly appalling party. 'Can you control your people?' was what he now asked Cameron time and again. It was a question that was to have momentous consequences when posed the following year in the very different context of Lords reform.

From the humiliation of tuition fees to the humiliation of the referendum: the period from October 2010 to May 2011 had carved a terrible arc through Clegg's fortunes, a remorseless series of political adversities. Public trust in the Lib Dems had plummeted over the party's broken promise on fees. And what had he got in return? Power, yes, but power to what end? The referendum had (it was assumed) settled the question of electoral reform for a generation and wrecked the dream of centre-Left realignment. Labour MPs watched the Lib Dem collapse in 2010 and 2011 and wondered if there would be much of a third party left after the Coalition with which to 'realign'. Recalling these months, Clegg would admit to colleagues: 'I wasn't really leading.'[21]

The collateral damage to the Coalition was immense. Clegg urged Cameron to see it from his point of view: 'Consider what it's like. There can't be many leaders who can survive that kind of shock.' The Tories had not planned to fight the referendum so hard, so personally, so pitilessly. But – having decided to do so – they let Clegg and his fellow reformers have it with both barrels.

In the words of one senior Downing Street official: 'Nick realized what we're like, what Tories are capable of.'[22] The age of innocence was over, never to return. As another Cameron ally put it: 'The Rose Garden had been well and truly napalmed.'

5. Political benefits: the fraught politics of welfare

'I thought we were a team!' Iain Duncan Smith exclaimed. 'If we are going to do this . . . you know, we have to work as a team!' David Cameron listened as the Work and Pensions Secretary let off steam about George Osborne's alleged perfidy and realized this was one of those occasions where he would have to intervene. 'Yes,' he promised. 'Yes, I'll talk to him.' His first party conference as Prime Minister, and already – this.

As a former leader of the party, Duncan Smith disliked such moments intensely. During his brief chieftaincy, Cameron and Osborne had been the up-and-coming duo who prepared him for his bouts with Tony Blair at PMQs. Now they themselves were the ruling duumvirate of the party: one was his boss, the other his troublesome senior partner in the enactment of welfare reform. In the words of one familiar with IDS's sensitivities: 'Imagine waking up one morning to find out that Ant and Dec are running the country.' Duncan Smith had agreed to take the Work and Pensions job because he believed (correctly) that it was a once-in-a-lifetime opportunity to translate at least some of his social vision into reality and to take on the culture of welfare dependency. But he had not fully grasped the extent to which Osborne would loom over everything he did and tried to do. Nor did he have an inkling of the ferocious turf war that would soon rage between the two of them.

The Tories' first conference in power for fourteen years should have been an occasion to savour, but was never fated to be a victory lap. For a start, there had been no victory – other than the negotiating triumph of the Coalition itself, about which Tory activists had decidedly mixed feelings. Second, the new Government was already unveiling measures to deal with the deficit that would have jarred badly with a celebratory, ticker-tape event. What did matter was that Cameron's team should exude competence, reliability and a spirit of collaboration.

It mattered, too, that party and public alike should believe that the Coalition was united on welfare reform. On the day he became Tory leader in December 2005, Cameron had declared the need for 'social action to ensure social justice, and a stronger society. I want to set free the voluntary sector and social enterprises to deal with the linked problems that blight so many of our communities, of drug abuse, family breakdown, poor public space, chaotic home environments, high crime. We can deal with these issues, we can mend our broken society.'[1] This was an ambition to which Cameron had repeatedly returned as Leader of the Opposition, and welfare reform was at its heart. At the Centre for Social Justice, Duncan Smith's policy group had produced two substantial reports, *Breakdown Britain* and *Break-through Britain*, while the *Sun* had run a series of stories under the rubric 'Broken Britain' that paved the way for the newspaper's even-tual endorsement of Cameron. When Boris Johnson described the claim that 'we have a broken society' as 'piffle' in his *Daily Telegraph* column, the Tory leader was infuriated.[2] Though he headed a Gov-ernment whose primary task was economic, Cameron saw himself first and foremost as a social reformer.

So it was a poor start to the 2010 Tory conference when Duncan Smith was completely caught off guard by Osborne's announcement that higher-rate taxpayers would now lose child benefit. Suddenly faced by a bank of cameras, the Work and Pensions Secretary impro-vised as much as he could, while his media adviser, Susie Squire, did her best not to be knocked over by the scrum of reporters. Child benefit cut? For the middle classes? What was happening? IDS replied: 'I'm going to find out.'

In his conference speech, the Chancellor went out of his way to praise Duncan Smith, who, he said, had 'done more than anyone in our Parliament to expose the deep unfairness that traps millions of our citizens in dependency, and makes millions of others pay for it'. He and the Work and Pensions Secretary were 'working together on the biggest reform of the welfare system since that great liberal

William Beveridge'. There would be a cap on benefits per household. But 'the public must know that the burden is being fairly shared'.

As Osborne put it: 'a system that taxes working people at high rates only to give it back in child benefit is very difficult to justify at a time like this. And it's very difficult to justify taxing people on low incomes to pay for the child benefit of those earning so much more than them.' He repeated the slogan he had used the year before: 'We are all in this together.'

That was not how it seemed to Duncan Smith at all. He felt excluded and driven to the margins. He believed he had been made to look fool-ish, bounced into a radical decision on a deeply sensitive issue, and that what seemed bold on Monday might look reckless on Tuesday. Cuts to the £12bn child benefit bill had certainly been discussed as part of a much broader debate on the future of welfare. He had discussed the options with Osborne's chief economic adviser, Rupert Harrison, before the summer recess. But – as far as IDS was concerned – the moment had not arrived for a definitive announcement.

Part of the problem was that child benefit was not administered by the DWP but by the Treasury. Technically, Osborne was not treading on his colleague's toes at all – which only aggravated the latter's anger. In the first weeks of the Coalition. Duncan Smith had made a bid to take control of this particular benefit but had been seen off by Osborne, who knew a land-grab when he saw one. Indeed, by conference, the Work and Pensions Secretary felt that the Treasury was essentially treating his own department as an annex. He warned Osborne of this 'power trip' and chafed at the constant reminders, explicit and impli-cit, that child benefit was part of his empire. 'You say you control child benefit, George,' he said. 'But we're a Government.'

The Chancellor was certainly taking a risk in his conference speech, though a calculated one. The universal children's allowance was one of the main pillars of the benevolent state proposed by Bev-eridge in his report of 1942. It had long been regarded as sacrosanct: central to the 'progressive universalism' whereby the needy got most but everybody got something. As Nicholas Timmins writes in his masterly history of the welfare state, Margaret Thatcher always understood that it 'had never been a mere safety net for the poor'.

Amongst many other things, 'it paid for the child benefit which middle-class mothers might use to buy a better bottle of wine, but which they none the less used'.[3] The means-testing of child benefit would have disagreeable consequences for 1.2 million higher-income families. But its symbolic impact would be much greater. Or so, at least, Osborne's internal critics claimed. What the Chancellor presented as an example of Coalition 'fairness', they interpreted as an intolerable assault upon Tory principles – doubly offensive, since it supposedly penalized those who worked hard and did well, and (it was claimed) undermined support for the family.

The backlash in Birmingham was something to behold: an eruption of fury from which, it sometimes seemed, Osborne's relationship with the right-of-centre press and some sections of the party might never truly recover. Some of the anomalies presented by the proposal were indeed absurd: it was clearly ridiculous that a single wage-earner on £44,000 would lose the benefit, while the hypothetical dual-earners next door with a joint salary of £80,000 would be unaffected. But it was not really the anomalies that caused offence. It was the prospect of a Conservative-led Government failing to exempt its traditional supporters from the toughest measures. Could it possibly be that when Cameron and Osborne said 'we are all in this together' they actually *meant* it?

Tories who had for years, and in some cases decades, argued for cuts and railed against handouts had suddenly discovered the social democrat within. The withdrawal of child benefit from those who earned £44,000 p.a. or more was presented as an atrocity, a betrayal or both. This was the first sighting of what I termed at the time 'fiscal Nimbyism': the desire to see the deficit wiped out – as long as you or the people you profess to represent are not affected.[4]

For Duncan Smith, the episode had a more specific significance. Politically bold as it was, Osborne's announcement struck him as personally evasive. He considered the Chancellor to be the polar opposite of Ken Clarke, with whom he felt he could have a good-natured confrontation without imperilling their working relationship. In contrast, he felt that Osborne liked to make a decision and act upon it without lengthy consultation.

The Chancellor regarded the Coalition as one long consultation – the matching of 'yellow bricks and blue bricks' – and was certainly not afflicted by a deep sense of penitence after the conference spat. More than any of his colleagues, he expected the Government in general to become unpopular with uncommon speed and to be vilified himself no less quickly. He was right on both counts. The corollary was impatience with those ministers who – as he saw it – complained and moaned about everything. According to his own private audit, Duncan Smith had resisted more or less every Treasury initiative. 'He opposes every cut,' Osborne complained to one friend. Nor was he confident that IDS had the IQ. 'You see Iain giving presentations,' he confided in allies, 'and realize he's just not clever enough.' Cameron was much less scathing. He recognized Duncan Smith's limitations but regarded him and Owen Paterson as his ambassadors to the Tory Right; he felt a special connection with him, as with Hague, both former leaders of the party; and – to a much greater extent than Osborne – he shared Duncan Smith's inclination to see welfare reform as a moral task.

From the start, the tensions between the Chancellor and IDS were palpable. Not surprisingly, Osborne wanted to bring the £192bn welfare budget under control. No deficit reduction programme that did not include substantial benefits savings would be taken seriously. Duncan Smith, on the other hand, hoped to transform the social landscape, attacking welfare dependency at root. Though there was an intersection of objective – eventually, welfare reform reduces the burden upon the taxpayer – their priorities were radically different. The Chancellor sought rapid fiscal action. Duncan Smith wanted to redefine 'social justice' in Tory terms. Osborne believed that workers should not subsidize shirkers. Duncan Smith did not want to attack those on benefit as scroungers but to usher them virtuously towards the world of work.

At the heart of the IDS plan was the 'Universal Credit': a scheme that would, in theory, harness the power of technology and force simplicity upon the hopelessly complex jungle of credits, benefits and allowances. Starting in October 2013, a single benefit would take the place of the income-based parts of the Jobseeker's Allowance and the Employment and Support Allowance; Income Support; Child Tax Credits; Working Tax Credits; and Housing Benefit. A colossal computer system was developed in consultation with HM Revenue and Customs to provide up-to-date information on individuals' earnings: the so-called RTI (real-time information) system, which relied upon bosses and banks making the correct use of a hashtag to identify each employee. In scale and aspiration, it was the biggest prospective change to the payroll system since PAYE was introduced in 1944.

The meetings at the Treasury were persistently testy. Osborne was not convinced that the system was practical or cost-effective. Worse, he believed that the urgency of cuts to the welfare budget was being eclipsed by the construction of Duncan Smith's magical mystery machine. 'We've got to get the costs of this down,' he told the Work and Pensions Secretary, 'and the costs of welfare *have* to come down, Iain.' As far as the Chancellor was concerned, Duncan Smith was more concerned with moral crusades than the imperatives of the fiscal crisis. 'Look,' IDS would say when a cut was mooted, 'this is going to be very difficult for these people.' Osborne wondered whether Duncan Smith had the political nerve to do what had to be done – and whether the Universal Credit was more than an expensive distraction from the difficult work in hand.

Hilton, too, was deeply worried about the plan – not because of its ambition, which he instinctively admired, but because it was a centralizing solution to a problem that, in his view, required ultra-local, tailored solutions as well as the national system of incentives and disincentives that constituted the welfare state. 'Iain's answer to it all is a bloody big computer,' Hilton told one ally.

Duncan Smith believed that Osborne had been captured by the Treasury and its institutional arrogance. 'I can see his whole sense of government changing,' he told colleagues. 'He's not a gambler at all.' In August, the feud spilt into the public domain as the *Mail on Sunday* reported that Duncan Smith had told the Chancellor: 'I am not prepared to tolerate the appalling way you treat my department. Your officials must show more respect to my staff. They do not deserve to be treated in such an arrogant and rude way.'[5] Osborne reportedly replied: 'If you come up with proposals that work, they will be treated with respect.'

In fact, by the time the story appeared, the Prime Minister had already been forced to intervene. Returning from a controversial trip to India, Cameron found IDS and Osborne 'at no speakers' in August, as one of the frustrated negotiators put it. The PM could hardly believe that his most senior lieutenant and a former party leader were simply not talking to one another – but wearily agreed to mediate. 'George is under stress,' Cameron told Duncan Smith. 'I'll sort it out.'

The Work and Pensions Secretary was not alone in his frustrations. One of the great shocks that awaits any new minister outside its precincts is quite how powerful the Treasury is. It is certainly true that Gordon Brown's long reign as Chancellor, frequently at war with Number Ten, had strengthened its institutional grip upon Whitehall. But that grip long predated Brown's war with Blair. Though Osborne considered himself a potential successor to Cameron, he saw the office of Chancellor as much more than a stepping-stone to the top job. In this, and in many other respects, he was influenced by Nigel Lawson, who had been a mentor to the young Shadow Chancellor, and continued to advise him in office. 'For George, Nigel is Yoda,' says one friend of Osborne. In his memoirs, Lawson declared that 'just as a company cannot be successful without a strong finance director, so the economy cannot be run successfully without a powerful Treasury'.[6]

Clegg, in particular, had not anticipated what it might feel like to be on the receiving end of this elemental power. As a Sheffield MP, he could never quite forgive the Treasury for its withdrawal, in June 2010, of an £80m government loan to the heavy-engineering firm Sheffield Forgemasters (although it did secure an investment of £36m from the Regional Growth Fund in October 2011). To compound the ignominy, it fell to Clegg's former chief of staff, Danny Alexander, now Chief Secretary to the Treasury, to make the announcement – thus rubbing the Lib Dems' noses in the austerity which they themselves were making possible by propping up the Tories.

The focus of Clegg's ire became Harrison, who exuded confidence, gave people the impression that he considered himself the smartest guy in the room and rarely deferred to anyone. The Deputy PM felt patronized and let his irritation show. On several occasions, Clegg found himself snarling at the Chancellor's closest adviser – consoling himself with the thought that, in a coalition, this was better than snarling at the Chancellor himself. The relationship between Clegg and Osborne required elasticity and goodwill so that the two did not fall out – a breach that would put the Coalition in mortal danger. Even so, there were days of high tension. One such moment arose when Clegg announced his intention to deliver a speech on tax policy in January 2012 – calling for the personal allowance to be raised to £10,000 more quickly and the introduction of a 'mansion tax' of 1 per cent per annum on properties worth more than £2m ('the mansion tax is right, it makes sense and I will continue to make the case for it. I'm going to stick to my guns'). Clegg told Osborne: 'I know you don't like this.' The Chancellor replied tersely: 'I don't.' Clegg absorbed this. 'I know,' he said to the Chancellor. 'But I have to do it.'

Osborne understood such necessities – Clegg tickling the belly of his party and its supporters – as intrinsic to the Coalition, and was not strongly opposed to the idea of the mansion tax, believing, like the Lib Dem leader, that wealth was under-taxed compared to income. Where Duncan Smith was concerned, the disagreement was more irritating. His respect for his colleague's reinvention of himself as a social reformer had been eclipsed by a sense that IDS was just not up to the job, technically, intellectually or temperamentally. For now, he struck a deal with him. If Duncan Smith could find £18bn in savings, the Treasury would take £16bn and the DWP could keep the remaining £2 billion for its welfare reform programme. It was this compact that Osborne announced in his first spending review on 20 October 2010 – only sixteen days after his announcement on child benefit.

Not surprisingly, the Coalition's tough rhetoric on welfare was popular, a snug fit with the twitching anxieties and instinctive parsimony of bleak economic times. The capping of benefits claimable by working-age people at £26,000 per household struck a particular chord. The redtop press obliged with grotesque instances of benefit abuse and – to Duncan Smith's dismay – the popular debate was framed not as a mission to help and to rescue, but as a punitive exercise to stop the 'skivers' from leeching off the 'strivers'.

In slogan form, welfare cuts met with strong approval. But the reality was more nuanced, troubling and abrasive when the slogan was disaggregated into millions of realities. Some ministers were quicker to grasp this than others. Chris Grayling, Minister of State at DWP, rapidly became the target of those campaigning against the reforms, caricatured as a cruel ideologue striking fear into the hearts of the most vulnerable members of society.

Nicknamed 'the Terminator' when Shadow Home Secretary, Grayling was indeed a man of the Right. But he was keenly aware of the risks implicit in welfare reform, and particularly the transitional problems triggered by replacing one benefit culture with another. As far as he and his colleagues were concerned, the end was wholly desirable. But the means were riddled with difficulty and – in some cases – bound to inspire the deepest anxiety. 'I am worried that this will drive some people to suicide,' Grayling was heard to say.

Reform of disability benefit had always been an extremely sensitive matter, and the Coalition's plans were no exception. The new Personal Independence Payment replaced the old Disability Living Allowance, a reform that was driven, at least in part, by the need to save money. But the migration of all disabled or severely ill claimants on Incapacity Benefit and Income Support to the Employment and Support Allowance (launched by Labour in 2008) was not a consequence of Treasury pressure. It reflected the belief that, where possible, those able to work should do so, and that welfare dependency was as potentially isolating as disability itself.

The aim was to get all claimants to take the Work Capability Assessment (WCA) by 2014. These tests were deeply contentious and had already spread panic on websites frequented by disabled people. Grayling sought specific reassurances that the assessments, and the prospects of the assessments, would not make those taking them so wretched that they took their own lives. Under the system he had inherited from the previous Government, claimants were summoned to assessment by a computer-generated DWP letter. As part of the reform, they were telephoned. That was something. But it did not eliminate the fear of the disabled that a faceless bureaucracy was conspiring to remove their only means of financial support.

According to an ICM survey of more than 1,000 GPs published in October 2012, 6 per cent of doctors had encountered a patient who had attempted or committed suicide as a result of 'undergoing, or fear of undergoing' the Government's fitness to work test.[8] Professor Malcolm Harrington, the independent reviewer of the assessment system, resigned in 2012 after declaring that it needed to be 'more fair and humane'.[9] Atos, the private contractor paid £112m a year to carry out the tests, fast acquired the reputation of a bureaucratic bulldozer, crushing the most vulnerable under its tracks. In August 2012, demonstrators in wheelchairs and other activists protested outside the multinational's London headquarters and scuffled with police after occupying the lobby of the DWP.

While GPs questioned the value of a tick-box system when judging the nuances of human affliction, especially mental illness, MPs produced alarming anecdotal evidence of constituents whose lives had been wrecked by the insensitivity of the WCA. By the summer of 2012, the involvement of Atos in the sponsorship of the London Olympics and Paralympics had become intensely controversial. A report by the Commons Public Accounts Committee blamed the department for letting loose the lumbering force that had caused 'misery and hardship' to thousands of people. In 38 per cent of appeals, the department's decisions were being overturned. 'This poor decision-making is damaging public confidence and generating a lot of criticism of the department's contractor for medical assessments, Atos Healthcare – but most of the problems lie firmly within the DWP,' said the committee's chair, Margaret Hodge. 'The department is too often just accepting what Atos tells it. It seems reluctant to challenge the contractor.'[10]

The Atos furore was only one case study of welfare reform in action and the powerful emotions it understandably released. It encapsulated the risks of contracting out sensitive tasks to private companies and – as Hodge complained – credulity within the

Government. Another such case was the furore generated by the Work Experience Scheme in 2012. This particular programme targeted 16–24-year-olds who had been unemployed for three to nine months and gave them a work placement lasting two to eight weeks. The scheme was voluntary; and for the first week the participant could walk out if he or she considered the placement a waste of time. Thereafter, he or she faced penalties (up to two weeks' docked benefits) for bad behaviour, failure to turn up, or rudeness to staff or customers. But even these sanctions were discretionary. The idea was not to drive the young into 'forced labour' but to give them a basic sense of what work involved: teamwork, correct clothing, punctuality.

Quite separate from this was the £5bn Work Programme, launched in June 2011, which Duncan Smith considered his contribution to the 'Big Society'. In general, it was compulsory after nine months' unemployment for young people and after a year for those aged twenty-five and over. In March 2013, the DWP reported that 'more than 200,000 people have already got into a job thanks to the Work Programme'. At its heart was a financial incentive structure that rewarded voluntary and private sector contractors for finding employment or training positions for jobseekers. In February 2012, one of the principal eighteen contractors selected by the Government, A4e, was pummelled by allegations of fraud and poor practice – with such ferocity that its chair, Emma Harrison, resigned both from her company role and from her position as the Prime Minister's 'family champion'.

This was a moment of maximum danger for Cameroon statecraft. The Work Programme was intended to be a ladder of hope for the jobless from despair and worklessness to dignity and autonomy. But it was also a trial run for payment-by-results or PBR – the system whereby public sector tasks were contracted out to independent bodies which were then remunerated according to performance. This was the practical application of Cameron's mantra, 'rolling forward the frontiers of society', a means of harnessing the experience of business and charities to carry out tasks that had previously been the preserve of the state.

The A4e scandal was a dire precedent: Harrison had paid herself an £8.6m dividend in 2011, though unable to secure long-term positions for more than 3.5 per cent of the jobseekers under the company's supervision. The 'Right to Work' campaign, an offshoot of the Trotskyite Socialist Workers Party, scented an opportunity to strike a blow against 'state capitalism' generally and the Coalition's 'workfare' blueprint specifically. But instead of targeting the Work Programme, the group stepped up its attack on the much smaller Work Experience Scheme, adopting a deft strategy of 'brand contamination'. Fearful of 'reputational damage', Argos, Burger King, Matalan, Waterstones, TK Maxx, Maplin and others terminated or suspended their participation.

Mobilizing on Twitter and other social media, Right to Work frightened the big retail companies sufficiently for them to seek a meeting with Grayling. The minister insisted that the summit was no more than a 'courtesy' meeting but he also knew that concessions would have to be made if the scheme was to survive and prosper. Accordingly, he announced that participants could now leave their placements *after* a week without losing benefits. Sanctions would be applicable only in cases of gross misconduct. 'The dropping of sanctions for the work-experience scam is one battle won,' said Mark Dunk of Right to Work, 'but the wider fight goes on.'[11]

Of this, Grayling had no doubt – although promotion was to move him to another battlefield (see Chapter 15). What had become abundantly clear in the Coalition's first two years was that welfare reform was very easy to talk about and very hard to do. It was more straightforward to secure popular support for cuts in general than for a particular cut. Even before its tougher measures had been implemented, the Government's benefit reforms had provoked strong opposition – an unpredictable mix of sincere and deeply felt anxiety on the one hand, and manipulative, ideologically driven street-fighting on the other.

Osborne pushed Duncan Smith hard on welfare savings – and would push him harder still in due course. For the time being, he could do so with political impunity. But he and Cameron knew that public support for austerity measures could never be taken for granted. As the cuts took their toll, heart-rending case studies would flicker on our screens. The voters would tolerate tough measures – perhaps even applaud them – if they were a sign of competence. But no Government could afford to be seen as both heartless and incompetent.

According to the polls, welfare reform was still a vote-winner for the Conservatives and a problem for Labour, which had not shed its image, reported in focus groups, as the party of the lazy man on the sofa. Yet at the heart of it all, as ever, was the ticking clock of public impatience: would success in the Coalition's central mission of national recovery come in time?

As months turned into years, reliable tabloid anger at 'scroungers' was bound to compete with the growing suspicion that the gilded governing class, immune to adversity and insulated from real life, was squeezing the neediest – including hundreds of thousands of working families – but failing to deliver growth, prosperity and renewal. At some point, without a strong economic recovery, the first sentiment would be overtaken by the second. The only question was when.

6. 'So big, you can see it from space'

It was the first time the Chancellor had truly lost his temper since taking office – and he was seething. 'Nobody told me this was coming,' he said, pointing to the document on the table. '*Nobody.*' His colleagues, used to his equable manner, squirmed at the genuine anger that was evident in his tone.

The fifty-page text that had provoked his wrath was the health service White Paper, finally published on 12 July 2010 under the heading 'Equity and Excellence: Liberating the NHS'.[1] The culmination of many years of work and analysis by Andrew Lansley, the Health Secretary, it proposed a dramatic overhaul of the system, a transformation of the way in which the service was run, and was certain to be contentious. How, exactly, had the Chancellor of the Exchequer not been informed of a plan to put £80bn of public money into the hands of general practitioners? And what about the Tory election campaign, masterminded by Osborne, which had a reassuring message about health at its very heart?

Lansley, for his part, was surprised that Osborne was surprised. Surely it was clear from the Tory manifesto that big change was on its way, and in the first half of the Parliament? It is true that Number Ten and the Treasury had been alerted to the White Paper's approaching publication. A Whitehall circular on the day of the Queen's Speech had further declared that 'subject to legislation' strategic health authorities would be abolished. That said, the Health Secretary was, by temperament, a problem-solver rather than a collaborator, and liked to be left alone until he was ready to present his proposals. In Cabinet, he had scarcely gone out of his way to prepare his colleagues for the sheer scale of what was coming, and how quickly. 'He's like a mad professor in the shed', according to one adviser at the time. 'We never quite know what he's doing in there.' Osborne's eye was firmly on the ball of cuts, not NHS reform. His outburst was a combination of anger at Lansley, and self-reproach that he had not spotted the runaway train heading towards the Coalition.

The Chancellor was a fan of *Crimson Tide*, a 1995 Tony Scott thriller set in a submarine, in which two naval officers fight over the interpretation of orders received to launch nuclear missiles. The commanding officer, played by Gene Hackman, wants to proceed with the order received – to fire off the warheads. The executive officer, played by Denzel Washington, urges caution, since a second order has been sent, but not fully received. It may, he argues, be a retraction of the first. Mayhem, naturally, ensues. Osborne, after many screenings, liked to joke that he agreed with Hackman's position and his insistence on sticking to the rule book.

The Chancellor – who had always loved late-night DVD sessions followed by analysis – was not serious about *Crimson Tide*. But he did believe in sticking to procedure, especially in Coalition. The advice that he, Cameron and Clegg had been given by political friends in countries where coalitions are routine was always the same: no surprises. A bipartisan Government would only survive if its senior members knew what was coming and what difficulties to expect. If a Conservative Health Secretary could not keep a Conservative Chancellor properly informed – which meant more than the occasional memo – what hope was there for the broader alliances upon which the Coalition depended?

The NHS White Paper and Michael Gove's radical blueprint for schools were the heart of the Government's plans for public service reform. The Cameroons' belief that education and healthcare could be dramatically improved by decentralization, transparency, accountability, diversity of provision and choice was something they had in common with the so-called 'Orange Book' Lib Dems – named after a 2004 collection of essays entitled *The Orange Book: Reclaiming Liberalism*. The volume had been co-edited by David Laws, and the contributors included Clegg, Cable, Huhne, Ed Davey and Steve Webb (who had since become Pensions Minister, working well alongside Duncan Smith). This convergence of priority was a powerful bond, especially in the early days of the Coalition. Both Cameron and Clegg acknowledged that Blair had understood the importance of reform – witness academy schools, free of town hall control, and semi-independent foundation hospitals. But it was no less clear that Brown had never believed in decentralization and had watered down or thwarted many of his great rival's plans. Labour was also disproportionately the home of public sector workers, the 'producer interest' in this case, and, with Blair gone and his supporters scattered to the winds, the party was liable to revert to type, representing them more aggressively than the demands of patients and parents.

What lingered was the feeling that Conservatives did not really care about what Blair had called 'schools'n'hospitals' – as if it were one word – since, in popular perception, they all sent their children to private schools and paid for private healthcare. In Opposition, the party had done little to help itself. When Peter Lilley made a speech in 1999 declaring that Conservatives must make peace with the public services, it was his own side that howled him down. But Lilley was absolutely right. At the heart of what Cameron, Osborne, Gove, Hilton and others had tried to do since 2005 was the recognition that the Conservative Party would not win – would not deserve to win – until it was seen to regard state schooling and the NHS as more than necessary safety nets for those who could not afford to take the private route. The fact that so many of the most prominent Cameroons had been to famous public schools only made the task more pressing.

The political strategy devised to deal with this was straightforward. On education, Cameron ruled out a return to grammar schools, to the fury of many Tories.[2] His purpose was to distance his party from anything that smacked of social segregation and from what David Willetts called 'bring-backery' – the reactionary impulse to turn the clock back and revive lapsed or abolished practices. Having fought that symbolic battle, which contributed to a rocky summer in 2007, Cameron proposed to finish what Blair had started and make schools freestanding civic institutions rather than bleak local branches of a national bureaucracy. His appointment to the Education portfolio of Gove, one of his closest and most able lieutenants, was intended to signal the seriousness of his commitment.

On health, the overwhelming priority was reassurance. It was no accident that Thatcher had felt driven in 1983 to pledge that the NHS was 'safe in our hands'; or that Nigel Lawson had, no less famously, written that the 'National Health Service is the closest thing the English have to a religion'. Like all parishioners, they had their complaints about the way the church was run, the leaks in the roof, the inadequacy of the vicar's pastoral care or preaching. But that did not make a jot of difference to the strength of their belief. The NHS had come to enshrine powerful group instincts and ancestral solidarities. No Tory leader who ignored this stood a chance of becoming Prime Minister.

Cameron grasped all of this. He understood that the NHS played a particular role in the psyche of the nation as a symbolic guarantor of fundamental decencies that any prospective reformer had to respect. One of his first measures at the helm of the party had been to ditch the 'patient's passport' proposal, a system that would have partially subsidized those who went private. He ring-fenced the NHS budget and even had the chutzpah to launch a campaign against 'Labour's NHS cuts'. As he told his party conference in 2006: 'Tony Blair explained his priorities in three words: education, education, education. I can do it in three letters: NHS.' As the father of a severely handicapped son, Ivan, Cameron knew what he was talking about. 'When your family relies on the NHS all of the time – day after day, night after night – you know how precious it is.' This was no exaggeration. The Camerons' daily routine was interspliced with local NHS services; they had spent many nights sleeping in hospitals. What the Conservative leader said about the health service, he meant.

As a campaigning politician, his specific task was to reassure the voters that he would not desecrate the service they treasured. But what, precisely, did that mean? Did it imply steady management, incremental change but nothing dramatic? Or did it mean something completely different? A root-and-branch overhaul of the NHS to preserve it and make it capable of withstanding the transformed pressures of the twenty-first century? This question was never fully or collectively addressed – an omission for which the Coalition was to pay dearly.

If Cameron's approach to the NHS was led by the heart, Lansley was governed by the head. He had been Shadow Secretary of State for Health since June 2004 and held on to the portfolio in government. As a former head of the Tory research department, he had employed or knew well most of the principal Conservative figures at Number Ten, including, crucially, Cameron himself and Hilton, the latter supporting radical changes to the NHS. The implementation unit headed by Nick Boles, tasked with preparing the party for office, found that Lansley made few demands on its time compared with other Shadow Secretaries of State.[3] But this did not set alarm bells ringing. The Prime Minister was predisposed to trust his old boss, especially when it came to the technicalities of health reform.

The fatal divergence was captured in a single phrase. In a piece for the *Yorkshire Post* in May 2008, Cameron promised that 'we will stop the top-down reorganizations and pointless structural upheavals that have done so much damage in the NHS'.[4] In a speech to the Royal College of Nursing the following year, he pledged that 'there will be no more of those pointless re-organizations that aim for change but instead bring chaos'.[5] Lansley made no such commitment because this was precisely what he was planning. Rashly, he seemed not to believe that such articles and speeches would be binding once the reforms were underway. There was a logic-chopping side to his character, too, which enabled him to argue that Cameron was only ruling out 'pointless reorganizations' – not reorganizations per se. In any case, the pledge did not appear in the Conservative manifesto, which set a clear enough trajectory: 'We have a reform plan to make the changes the NHS needs. We will decentralize power, so that patients have a real choice. We will make doctors and nurses accountable to patients, not to endless layers of bureaucracy and management.'[6]

It is mysterious that the two men failed to see the imminent collision only if one forgets the rollercoaster reality of political life, especially in the punishing day-to-day routine of an election campaign that lasted years rather than months, against the backdrop of global financial crisis. Unless a contradiction of this sort is causing immediate difficulty, its resolution is often postponed. Cameron, who was present at all the important policy sessions, and Lansley, who knew what his boss's political strategy was, should have addressed the obvious tension. But they never got round to it – with the consequence that the Conservative Party went into the 2010 election offering absolute reassurance on the NHS while plotting one of the most dramatic reforms in its sixty-two-year history. Cameron was simultaneously promising absolute stability and total disruption.

The inevitable collision was the consequence of the Coalition *Programme for Government*. As far as Lansley was concerned, the document had been drawn up much too quickly, by much too small a group of people, with too little regard for the parties' existing proposals. Neither Tory nor Lib Dem manifesto promised to 'stop the top-down reorganizations of the NHS that have got in the way of patient care'. Yet there it was on page 24 of the new text that was meant to be the founding document of the bipartisan Government. In a single paragraph, Lansley had been shackled, his ambitions to reform strangled at birth.

Or so it seemed. Undeterred, the Health Secretary and his Lib Dem Minister of State, Paul Burstow, decided that the Coalition Programme was no basis on which to proceed and got to work with senior officials to draw up the document that became the White Paper. The civil servants, at least, had been taking careful note of Lansley's detailed proposals before the election, and had prepared policy documents based on their understanding of his intentions. Sir Hugh Taylor, Permanent Secretary at the Department of Health, was closely involved before his retirement at the end of July. The Coalition Programme proposed the inclusion of 'directly elected individuals' on the board of the nation's 152 Primary Care Trusts (PCTs), the bodies which commissioned health services. As appealing as this might have sounded, Lansley wanted such decisions to be clinically led.

The White Paper proposed the outright abolition of PCTs and Strategic Health Authorities and their replacement by commissioning consortiums of GPs themselves. The regime of targets introduced by New Labour would be ditched in favour of much greater transparency so that patients and professionals could judge services by results. Lansley also wanted to encourage competition amongst providers, delivering the greater value for money that was needed if the NHS was going to match growing demand – even with a ring-fenced budget of more than £103bn. Wherever possible, patients would be given a choice of 'any willing provider'. More than ever, payment would be decided by results. The Lib Dems contributed the idea of Health and Wellbeing Boards to bring together commissioning groups and local councils in strategic forums. Patients would also have a champion in the consumer organization Healthwatch. The existing independent foundation trust watchdog, Monitor, would acquire new powers as an 'economic regulator' to promote effective provision, competition, fair prices and continuity of service. As one scholarly study of the reform concludes wryly: 'The only way to reconcile the White Paper with the [Coalition *Programme for Government*] was to argue that the restructuring was bottom-up rather than top-down.'[7] Obviously, it was no such thing.

The revolutionary principle at the heart of the reform was the transfer of commissioning powers to family doctors. A voluntary system of GP fundholding had been introduced in 1991 with some success. This time, however, the change would be nationwide and not optional. Indeed, Sir David Nicholson, the chief executive of the health service, said that the reform was so big 'you can see it from space'. The *Daily Telegraph* called it 'the biggest revolution in the NHS for 60 years'.

For that and many other reasons – not least weariness with 'top-down reorganizations', of which there had been about twenty over the years – most health professionals and NHS employees were sceptical from the start. The Royal College of GPs welcomed the prospective enhancement of its members' powers – but had doubts about the sheer scale of the upheaval. Even before the White Paper's publication, Unison, the public sector union, said the plan would be a bonanza for private managerial consultants, performing administrative work for which GPs did not have the time or, in many cases, the skills. Osborne, in particular, was conscious of the stern warning in Lawson's memoirs. Remembering that the NHS had acquired the mystique of a religion, politicians should never underestimate the power of its priesthood: 'For a bunch of laymen, who called themselves the Government, to presume to tell the priesthood that they must change their ways in any respect whatever was clearly intolerable. And faced with a dispute between their priests and Ministers, the public would have no hesitation in taking the part of the priesthood.'[8]

The battle for hearts and minds in such struggles involved persuading the voters that those objecting were protecting vested interests. The print unions and the miners were one thing. But the public did not regard the Royal Colleges as trade unions; and grateful patients did not see doctors and nurses as 'interest groups' but as the magicians who had delivered their babies, treated their illnesses and cared for their elderly relatives. Lansley insisted that his entire purpose was to save the service and to make it capable of withstanding demographic and galloping technological demands that would have astonished Nye Bevan. The service already needed to find £20bn in efficiency savings before 2015. Whoever was in power would have had to squeeze more value for money from the system. But his argument struggled to compete with the growing outcry from the professional bodies and unions and the corrosive claim that the plan's emphasis upon competition would mean 'privatization by the back door'.

In fact, many NHS services were already provided, free at point of delivery, by private companies. But that did not make the slightest difference to the increasingly emotional struggle. In Cabinet, Ken Clarke, Health Secretary under Margaret Thatcher, tried to cheer his colleagues up, guffawing that 'this is nothing compared to the trouble we had with my reforms'. Osborne, still annoyed at the way in which he had been blind-sided, told Lansley that, whatever ingenious structure he came up with, the public would make a very straightforward judgement: 'In my view, the only thing that matters is that waiting times don't slip and get longer.'

The Coalition Committee, the Government's court of appeal, with all the Government's senior figures present had discussed the gathering storm of protest in July, but agreed only that the Prime Minister would sort it out with Lansley – who was absent. Questioned by colleagues subsequently, the Health Secretary found it hard to conceal his exasperation at their confusion. Which bit did they not understand? He was irritated that his *grand projet* had been debated in his absence, but confident that his former employees at the research department would see things his way in the end. 'They all used to work for me, anyway,' he said – which was indeed true of Cameron, Osborne and Hilton.

Though Oliver Letwin had been notionally involved with the plan from the start, Cameron now asked him as all-purpose trouble-shooter to scrutinize the plan line by line before its publication as the Health and Social Care Bill. Letwin, working closely as ever with Danny Alexander, identified a range of questions which needed to be answered before the legislative process could begin and posed them in a series of meetings at his own office in the Cabinet Office, Richmond House (the department's main building) and Number Ten. Lansley and Burstow were subjected to a protracted interrogation. Did the proposals make sufficient provision to deal with institutional failure? If a hospital or clinic did not respond to better management, would it be taken over or closed? Was there a sufficient number of doctors willing to take on the commissioning responsibility and the management of a budget? And – most important of all – would it work? Would the new system squeeze inefficiency out of the NHS and reduce waiting lists?

What struck Letwin as he and Lansley met the various interest groups affected by the reforms was that their anger was mounting. The Health Secretary believed that the British Medical Association had understood and broadly endorsed his plans for GPs' compulsory involvement in commissioning before the election. 'I've got them on board,' he boasted to officials. But Dr Laurence Buckman, the chairman of the BMA's GP committee, later told a different story – yet again one of messages misunderstood and crossed wires. 'I can say that I was listened to, but wasn't heard.'[9] But now, in any case, the initially mixed response given to the White Paper was hardening into a wall of outright hostility. The ministers had expected the public sector unions to oppose the Tory-led plan on principle, but the surging antagonism of the Royal Colleges was a puzzle. 'I can't quite fathom what it is that they object to *quite so much*,' Letwin was heard to say.

The bill was published in January 2011, all 550 pages, 300 clauses and 24 schedules of it – three times as long as the founding 1946 Act. Its sheer scale strengthened Lansley's determination and Cameron's growing recognition that it was too big to fail; and the conviction of its opponents that the threat was every bit as comprehensive as they had feared. Meanwhile, the growing confidence of medical professionals and unions that they could kill the bill reflected two big changes in the political landscape.

The election of Ed Miliband as Labour leader in September relieved most Tories, who regarded his older brother, David, as a greater threat. But the collective sigh of relief that coursed through the Coalition was premature. Miliband was a more agile and cunning opponent than had seemed likely during the leadership contest.

In the NHS reforms, he identified an immediate opportunity to present the Government not only as heartless, but as insensitive to national tradition. In a speech to the Royal Society of Arts, he hailed the health service as a 'great British institution and one we need to preserve and renew for the next generation'. At Labour's Welsh conference in February, he portrayed the Conservatives as a party that had forgotten how to conserve: 'Look around Britain and we see the biggest assault that we have seen in a generation on our common life.' The Government had been forced into an embarrassing U-turn over its proposals to sell off the forests ('We got this one wrong,' the Environment Secretary, Caroline Spelman, admitted to MPs on 17 February). But the original plan, Miliband said, was characteristic of a Government prepared to 'carelessly destroy the institutions that people value. We all know the institution Britain values perhaps more than any other and where the stakes are the highest: the National Health Service.'

The Labour leader grasped that change could be alarming as well as energizing, particularly when its pulverizing power seemed to threaten treasured institutions, social forms and communal habits. Downing Street policy wonks were fond of quoting the Swedish psychologist Claes F. Janssen and his 'Four Rooms of Change' theory: the four rooms being Contentment, Denial, Confusion and Renewal. At best, the NHS reform programme was stuck in the Confusion Room.

In this context, Miliband had found his own (temporary) guru, who had been churning debate on the Left under the banner of 'Blue Labour': Maurice Glasman, who had been recently ennobled as Lord Glasman of Stoke Newington and Stamford Hill, and, unusually for a socialist academic, believed profoundly in the value of institutions and traditions. Though its influence upon Miliband's thinking was exaggerated, 'Blue Labour' undoubtedly helped him develop a language in which to express his championship of the health service and to present Lansley's plan as an act of desecration.

The second political shift that greatly compounded the problem of the NHS plan was the plight of the Liberal Democrat Party. Clegg had taken a political beating for breaking his promise on tuition fees – and then another over the referendum on electoral reform at Westminster. When his party gathered for its Spring Conference in Sheffield on 11 March, it was furious and spoiling for a fight over health. Baroness (Shirley) Williams, still a hugely respected figure in her party, had read the bill – and not liked it one bit. 'Why we should dismember this remarkably successful public service for an untried and disruptive reorganization amazes me,' she said.[10] Burstow put forward a motion that was supportive of the plan. The assembled activists made clear that they were almost unanimously against Lansley's bill. Confronted with certain defeat, Clegg was forced to accept two amendments to the motion, supported by Williams and the former MP Dr Evan Harris. The Deputy Prime Minister lacked the necessary political capital to risk a confrontation with his membership, and could only promise to take the message back to Cameron.

Never had a Lib Dem Spring Conference been so influential or monitored by the media so carefully. Watching nervously, Lansley was taken aback by the strength of feeling in the party with which the Tories were supposedly in coalition. He and his fellow Conservatives were used to the 'Orange Book' Lib Dems with whom they sat in Cabinet. But Clegg and co. were not typical of the party they led, which had shifted to the Left during the Blair era. A great many of its members were active in politics precisely because they mistrusted Conservatives, and the Health and Social Care Bill confirmed the worst suspicions they had harboured when Clegg led them into the pact. Collectively at least, the Lib Dems were behaving like an Opposition party again. Lansley was now squarely on the defensive. 'We've already made changes,' the Health Secretary told the BBC. 'We are not sitting there thinking we must know the answers and nothing can change. If we can clarify and amend in order to reassure people, then we will do so.'

Reflecting on the painful passage of the Health and Social Care Bill, Clegg later said: 'If I'd known it was going to be as badly handled as it was, and it was going to become such trench warfare, we wouldn't have started on it, of course not.'[11] But before the Spring Conference he had been happy to take credit for it. 'I agree it's an ambitious programme of reform,' he told Andrew Marr in January, 'but over time I think it'll leave patients with a feeling that they are at the centre of it. They're not constantly at the beck and call [of] a system over which they've got very little control.' Asked in the same interview whether the impending 'huge change to the NHS' had been in the Lib Dem manifesto, Clegg replied: 'Actually, funnily enough, it was.' In the second reading division of the bill on 31 January, not a single Lib Dem MP had voted against (and only one, Andrew George, had abstained). It was only at the Spring Conference that the junior governing party discovered its principled objections, forced to do so by grassroots rebellion.

Lansley turned to Alan Milburn, the former Labour Health Secretary, for advice and asked him if he would be interested in chairing the new commissioning board. As Milburn told one journalist: 'I said to him "do you think I have the letters M.U.G. tattooed on my forehead? Why would I use my political capital to rescue you from the mess you have made of yours?"'[12]

His political antennae had not deserted him. As the furore over the bill started to contaminate everything the Government was doing, the question was now being asked: was it worth it? Why jeopardize everything the Coalition had fought to achieve in less than a year and make Miliband's life easy, in order to salvage a reform so complex it made the Schleswig-Holstein question seem simple? It was not even clear that the bill would make it through the House of Lords, where Lib Dem peers and many of the 200 cross-benchers were already preparing to raise objections. There was much medical expertise in the Upper House, as well as deep political cunning.

At this point, Clegg was urged by many senior Lib Dems, including Richard Reeves and Tim Farron, the party's new president, to withdraw his support altogether from the faltering plan. He was frustrated by Lansley and Burstow and by their inclination to answer political questions with answers about the technicalities of health policy. It sounded like an alien language. 'They speak NHS Nanu Nanu,' he complained (in a reference to the late-seventies TV show *Mork & Mindy* that dated him).

The Prime Minister was as vulnerable as he had ever been to the whim of his governing partner. The 2015 election, he believed, would be dominated by the success or failure of the Coalition's economic programme. But he had always thought that the NHS would be high on the list of electoral priorities. Had the Conservatives held to their promise to treasure and nourish the NHS? It was what Letwin called a 'high-octane issue'.

Cameron, Osborne and Hague made it their practice to meet discreetly from time to time, for candid discussions about the Coalition's progress – gatherings which some regarded as the true heart of the Government, its most powerful caucus, more important even than the Quad. At these sessions, the Foreign Secretary was sometimes called upon to play the role of elder statesman and to confront his younger colleagues with unpalatable truths. At one meeting in the spring of 2011, he told Cameron and Osborne that the Coalition had simply taken on too much and that the overhaul of the NHS, whatever its intrinsic merits, was probably one reform too many. But it was not open to them to ditch Lansley's plan, as Miliband demanded, whatever their most private wishes might be. The squeeze on public spending meant that, even with its ring-fenced budget, the health service had to be reformed and to deliver better value for money. To that end, some GPs and health authorities had already started to make transitional arrangements in readiness for the Lansley revolution. Primary Care Trusts were being wound up. The Prime Minister could hardly tell them all to restore the status quo.

'So,' Cameron asked Clegg, 'are you going to kill it?' Clegg told him that this was not his plan – but that Cameron had to understand how high a political price he was paying for his complicity. Lib Dems were tearing up their membership cards in disgust at what they saw as wholesale destruction of the world's greatest healthcare system. Some senior Tories still believed that Clegg had allowed the Spring Conference debacle to unfold so that his own party would not take the blame for the health reforms as they had for tuition fees. But the Deputy PM accepted that Cameron could not turn back, and that, if the Lib Dems pulled the plug, the ultimate consequences might be very ugly indeed.

On 31 March, Cameron, Clegg and Lansley met at Number Ten in Cameron's office before a larger meeting to discuss the bill. Cameron was behind his desk, Lansley perched on the settee, Clegg sitting edgily off to the side. The Health Secretary quickly realized that this was not going to be a conversation but an issuing of instructions. 'Look,' the Prime Minister said, 'we've got a problem here and we've got to reset.' Lansley disliked the word 'reset' and particularly disliked what it meant in this context – which was Downing Street seizing control of his life's work. The following week the Government launched a 'Listening Exercise' that would last two months, 'to pause, listen, reflect and improve', and the formation of the NHS Future Forum, chaired by Dr Steve Field, to marshal opinion on the bill and its implications. What became known as the 'Pause' was without apparent precedent and announced without enthusiasm. Though presented as an example of the Coalition's democratic credentials – its readiness to heed public anxiety and take advice – everyone involved knew it was a colossal humiliation and an amateurish last resort.

At this relatively early stage in the life of the Parliament, the only new resource ministers had to throw into the unpromising mix was time. There would, indeed, be amendments. But the real purpose of the 'Pause' was to cauterize the wound, get the two governing parties past the local elections on 5 May – and hope that tempers had cooled when business resumed. Lansley was kept under close watch by Number Ten and Cabinet colleagues to ensure that he did not resign in fury. As angry as he was, the Health Secretary did not seriously consider flouncing out – but Cameron and Clegg were not to know that. The

PM had treated his former patron as Prince Hal does Falstaff – not quite 'I know thee not, old man', but close enough to leave Lansley looking like the loneliest man in Whitehall.

Even with the 'Listening Exercise' up and running, Letwin was still concerned that the bill would not succeed in Parliament: the sort of disaster that damages Governments irreparably. A new and unexpected complication arose in Steve Hilton's enthusiasm to *add in* material. The near-universal assumption was that the 'Pause' would culminate in at least some dilution of Lansley's original plan. But, with his genius for the counter-intuitive, Hilton wanted to make the bill more *radical*, more supportive of competition in the NHS and particularly among GPs so that patients had much greater choice when it came to signing up with a family doctor. He wanted stronger language on the entry of new providers to the system. Everything he proposed was consistent with the spirit of the existing reforms. But it was additional material. It fell to Letwin, the Cabinet minister most ideologically close to Hilton, to rein him in. This made for some of the more surreal conversations of an already surreal situation. According to one involved in the negotiations: 'Oliver had to moderate Steve's demands, and explain to him that, you know, now was not really the time to be flexing our muscles *more*.'

The Lib Dems were badly mauled in the local elections, losing 748 seats (unlike the Tories, who gained eighty-six). Cameron understood the need for Clegg to differentiate himself by any means available. But Conservative backbenchers were furious with the Lib Dem leader and his party for what they regarded as the self-inflicted wound of the health furore. It became commonplace for Tory MPs to speak of the '[Lib Dem] tail wagging the dog', as resentment grew at the concessions made to keep the NHS bill alive. One of the many bequests of the Lansley plan was the cementing of this feeling that the Lib Dems were getting more than their proportionate due; matched only by the Lib Dems' growing suspicion that the Tories were exploiting their support and giving too little in return. Yes, the Lib Dems were in office at last. But what was the Coalition doing that was distinctively in the Liberal tradition?

As Clegg told Lansley: 'I don't disagree with the policy. I've just

somehow got to get it through Shirley and David Owen.'[13] The concessions were indeed considerable, and had to be. The original, tight
timeline was dramatically relaxed so that a revolutionary change
became much more evolutionary in character. The new clinically led
commissioning organizations would begin their work in a gradual
fashion rather than a public sector equivalent of the financial services'
'Big Bang' in 1986. The 'assumed liberty' of these groups was changed
to 'earned autonomy': only when they had proved their readiness to
the commissioning board could they get going. The words 'any willing provider' were changed to 'any qualified provider'.

Even after the changes, Milburn called the legislation 'the biggest
car crash in NHS history', and one that had set back the cause of
market-based reform by a generation.[14] The bill cleared the Commons but the Lords still had plenty to say – as did the BMA, which
called again for the bill to be dumped. Andy Burnham, a former Secretary of State for Health, returned to his old beat to shadow Lansley
in October, and stepped up the attack with considerable success,
meeting the various organizations opposed to the plan and advising
them. In January, the Royal College of GPs released an online survey
which suggested that 98 per cent of its members wanted the bill to be
put out of its misery. The *Health Service Journal*, *British Medical Journal*
and *Nursing Times* published a joint editorial declaring the legislation
an 'unholy mess'.

There had been times when Lansley had not felt supported by
Number Ten and the 'Centre'. In the summer of 2011, his Special
Adviser, Jenny Parsons, had attended a meeting in Downing Street
with Jeremy Heywood, Jonny Oates and other officials. She had
warned them that speed was now of the essence: 'We have to move
hard before the recess otherwise everything is going to get unravelled.' Her concern was that Labour would do exactly what Burnham
then did in the autumn – which was to meet and co-ordinate the
forces ranged against her boss. Her fears were dismissed. Oates told
her: 'Don't worry about the stakeholders.' On 7 February, a *Times*
column by the influential commentator Rachel Sylvester quoted a
'Downing Street source' saying that 'Andrew Lansley should be taken
out and shot.' The Health Secretary's allies believed the source must

be one of: Andrew Cooper, the Number Ten director of strategy, Patrick Rock, Cameron's political adviser, or Craig Oliver, the director of communications. Needless to say, nobody was putting his or her hand up. But the episode was a measure of the poison now flowing through the Coalition's IV drip. Cameron, who hated conflict, did his best to remain on friendly terms with Lansley. But those around him briefed that the Health Secretary's resignation 'would be accepted' or expressed tepid confidence: 'If Andrew decides to stay, we'll stand by him.' This was the PM at his most passive-aggressive – officially supportive of a colleague, while his advisers polished a dagger in the background.

An unexpected blow – of a sort which no previous Government had faced – was the call on 10 February by Conservative Home, the political website, for the bill to be dropped. The post, by the site's founder, Tim Montgomerie, began: 'The NHS was long the Conservative Party's Achilles heel. David Cameron's greatest political achievement as Leader of the Opposition was to neutralise health as an issue. The greatest mistake of his time as Prime Minister has been to put it back at the centre of political debate.' This was, indeed, the crux of the matter. Cameron's sin had primarily been one of omission – failing to keep an eye on Lansley and to master the detail of what his own party was proposing. That failure, which was Osborne's too, had forced the issue back to the fore. It was a colossal failure, an inexcusable lapse in political vigilance.

The bill, Montgomerie continued, was 'neither transformational nor necessary' but jeopardized everything else the Government was doing. In conclusion, the blogger urged the Prime Minister to kill it off 'before it's too late'. He also let slip that three Cabinet ministers had spoken to ConHome, expressing varying measures of despair. 'One was insistent the bill must be dropped. Another said Andrew Lansley must be replaced. Another likened the NHS reforms to the poll tax.'

A former Conservative speech-writer and chief of staff to Iain Duncan Smith, Montgomerie was now much more powerful than he had ever been in a formal political role. During the 2005 leadership contest, a series of right-of-centre blogs had emerged backing one of the candidates – or none of them – and exploited the new speed and availability of broadband to provide the Tory grassroots with a series of bulletin boards. Some were serious, others scabrous: what they had in common was energy and, in a few cases, success. Affable, assiduous and highly intelligent, Montgomerie had been fast to spot the political potential of so-called 'Web 2.0': social media, real-time interactivity, digital networks and virtual communities. Though ConHome was founded before the 2005 election, its rise corresponded with Cameron's as watchdog, intermittent supporter and market square for Conservatives. It was not the only force in the right-of-centre blogosphere: Paul Staines's fearless Guido Fawkes and the *Spectator*'s Coffee House blog were both required reading around Westminster.[15] But ConHome had a specific role, the product of Montgomerie's political background, media knowledge and ability to attract the eyeballs of Tory activists to his site. Much more than any formal body, it represented the views of Conservative members – and potential members – and, as such, was a force in the party. Montgomerie enjoyed the access of a newspaper editor and the influence of a Cabinet minister. His scepticism about certain aspects of the Cameroon modernization programme and the social liberalism of those he called 'Soho modernizers' could not be ignored. His call for Lansley's bill to be ditched was an appreciable political blow. By 9.45 a.m., the party chairman, Sayeeda Warsi, had posted a response.

The desperate stalemate, unexpectedly, was broken in the Lords. Disaster in the Upper House – a quite conceivable outcome – was largely averted by the genial manner and impressive workrate of Earl Howe, a junior Health Minister who knew the Upper House as well as he knew the Lansley reforms. Acting as go-between, he was able to negotiate final amendments: the Secretary of State would retain responsibility for the NHS and remain accountable to Parliament. But progress, however slow, was being made. The small nudge made all the difference. Both sides had fought to a standstill and recognized that it was time to draw stumps. About 2,000 amendments had been made to the bill. A final bid by Burnham to thwart its passage failed and, on 27 March, after fifty days of debate in Parliament, the Health and Social Care Bill was given royal assent.

Even as they heaved a collective sigh of relief, ministers asked themselves: how did that happen? Since the Act only came into force in April 2013, the success or failure of its content cannot yet be judged. Lansley may yet be proved right by the improvements his vilified reforms deliver. But the form the plan took – the political confusion in which it was wrapped from the start – was an unforced error of epic proportions. Though the Coalition had eventually united behind it, it never attracted more than a handful of true believers in the upper echelons of Government: Lansley, Letwin, Hilton (up to a point). When Osborne professed ignorance of the White Paper, he and others should have insisted that the process be stalled until the precise implications of the proposals had been established and the politics debated. The time for the 'Pause' was June 2010, not April 2011. The case for killing it off was always powerful. But nobody volunteered to switch the machine off. The Government, after all, was acquiring a reputation for U-turns. Could it survive a legislative reversal of this scale?

The bill was frequently described as Cameron's poll tax: a monumental policy mistake that might yet do for him. But a closer parallel was the price Blair had paid domestically for Iraq, and what Alastair Campbell called this 'huge stuff about trust'. The voters were always going to feel misled by a plan of this sort after the campaign that Cameron had led from his first day in the party leader's office. In all this lay the danger that his core identity would become blurred. Was he a radical reformer or a guardian of what the voters cherished? Did he care most about price or value? Was he presenting himself to them as a transformative Prime Minister in a hurry, or as the personification of reassurance in a time of doubt and global insecurity? Cameron argued that he was both a conservative and a radical, preserving that which was good and repairing whatever was broken. The NHS bill had angered voters precisely because he was now turning upside down the very institution he had pledged most passionately to preserve. All that the controversy had vaguely in its favour was its timing. On the Statute Books before the Coalition reached its second birthday, the Health and Social Care Act would at least not overshadow the second half of the Parliament – unless it unravelled.

The timing of the bill, of course, was no accident. Cameron and his team had been much influenced by Blair's conclusion that he had squandered too much time and left reform until too late in the life-cycle of his premiership. If there was radical work to be done, the Tories concluded, then let it be done quickly. But a Government needs priorities, too. Fiscal reform, education, tuition fees, a transformation of the welfare state, localism, a changing relationship with Europe, a referendum on AV – and a root-and-branch restructuring of the NHS. Hague was right: Cameron was trying to do too much.

Lansley cannot be blamed for wanting his long-planned reforms to be at the front of the queue. He also insisted that the plan be enshrined in legislation so it could not be torn up instantly by another Secretary of State. Like Hilton, he believed that a Government should behave as if it only has one term and assume that its opponents will try to undo its work as soon as they win power. The Act was devised to resist future ministerial fiat. What Lansley never came close to devising was a story – or a 'narrative' – with which he could make sense of his legislative bulldozer. Where healthcare is concerned, voters care only that it is effective, quick and free. Everything else they hear is white noise – or, much worse, makes them fear that the services they depend upon are being undermined. Gove presented his reforms as a continuation of New Labour's stalled programme rather than a fresh start with all the risk that entailed. Lansley could easily have done the same, promising to finish what Milburn had started; overseeing evolutionary change rather than an unwanted NHS revolution. Ironically, Milburn regarded the bill as a missed opportunity. All the amendments, he told Hilton, had limited the competitive aspect of the reforms: 'You have sent a message from the centre that competition has been watered down.' Hilton agreed: he thought enhanced competition between providers was much more important than the establishment of the new commissioning groups, an aspect of the plan which he would have been willing to ditch.

Osborne blamed himself for failing to see the disaster coming and 'not stopping it'. The absence of a well-resourced policy unit in Number Ten meant that the early-warning system at the centre of the Government malfunctioned. Reflecting on the whole debacle,

Cameron lamented the lack of 'pitch-rolling' before the White Paper. He and his colleagues had certainly prepared the public for Osborne's deficit reduction programme. But they had not done the same for Lansley's plan and paid a grievous price for it.

Lansley himself paid more dearly, losing the only job he had really wanted in government. Cameron and Llewellyn had agreed with him that he could not go into the 2015 general election as Secretary of State for Health – by which point he would have held the same party portfolio for almost eleven years. But he had expected to be moved in 2014 or the autumn of 2013 at the earliest, not transferred in September 2012 to the position of Leader of the House – a role he had scarcely coveted. His real ambition was to see his reforms implemented and to be vindicated by posterity. His successor, Jeremy Hunt, let it be known that the best and kindest thing he could do when asked about Lansley's policies was not to talk about them. In that ignominious postscript lies a lesson for all politicians: that few good ideas for reform go unpunished.

7. Civil action: the Gove revolution

'It doesn't feel like it now, but you will be a better minister for having gone through that.' Michael Gove had not expected to hear such a verdict on his first real mishap in government – least of all delivered by David Davis, Cameron's final-round rival for the leadership in 2005 and no admirer of 'Dave's gang'. It was, after all, Derek Conway, Davis's chief enforcer, who had first identified the 'Notting Hill Set' in 2004 – and not in a friendly fashion, either.

Before running into Davis, Gove had apologized to the Commons for errors in a list about school building programmes that the Government now proposed to scrap. 'DD', a Commons veteran who had written a book on Parliament, might have been expected to gloat, however subtly, over Gove's discomfiture. But it was clear to the Education Secretary that his remark was sincere.

In 2008, Davis had, quite unexpectedly, resigned as MP for Haltemprice and Howden – forcing a by-election as a mini-referendum on Labour's plan to allow detention of terror suspects without charge for up to forty-two days. He was handsomely re-elected with 72 per cent of the vote. But the episode had marked a decisive break between Davis, who had been Shadow Home Secretary until standing down from his seat, and the Cameroons. His impulsive behaviour had cost him one of the great offices of state (for he was still on track to be Home Secretary) and, as far as Cameron was concerned, exiled him for good. This was a mistake. Davis may have been in error – and was foolish to act unilaterally – but his 'moment of madness' (if such it was) was an act of principle rather than a personal scandal, or a breach of parliamentary standards. It would have served Cameron well in the difficulties ahead if he had found a way of bringing this talented politician back into the tent.

Gove pondered Davis's observation that his ritual humiliation in

the Commons would ultimately serve him well. Clementine Churchill famously suggested to her husband that his general election defeat
in 1945 was 'a blessing in disguise'. To which Churchill replied: 'If so,
it is well disguised.' But – on reflection – Gove realized that Davis
was right. His parliamentary ordeal had been a salutary warning of
what was to come, what was at stake – and the extent and source of
the opposition he faced.

On 5 July 2010, Gove had cancelled the £55bn Building Schools
for the Future (BSF) scheme, complaining that 'throughout its life it
has been characterised by massive overspends, tragic delays, botched
construction projects and needless bureaucracy'.[1] It was an aggressive
intervention, a warning not only that the fiscal incontinence of the
New Labour era was at an end, but that Gove's legendary civility
should not be mistaken for diffidence. 'There are some councils
which entered the process six years ago which have only just started
building new schools,' he said. 'Another project starting this year is
three years behind schedule. By contrast, Hong Kong International
Airport, which was built on a barren rock in the South China Sea and
can process 50 million passenger movements every year, took just six
years to build – from start to finish.' At a stroke, rebuilding projects
at 715 schools had been cancelled.

Rick Nye, the former director of the Conservative research
department, now strategy director at the polling company Populus,
had once mocked Labour's inclination, when faced with public
service under-performance, 'to throw carpet tiles at the problem'.
Though Gove scarcely objected in October to Osborne's above-
inflation settlement for schools each year till 2015, he also wanted to
send an early signal about his own priorities. Reform was more
important than faddish architecture. Shortage of money was not an
excuse for shoddy standards. The adept targeting of resources – such
as the Lib Dem 'pupil premium' – had a part to play. But the spending carnival of the Labour years was emphatically over. Symbolic of
this was the scrapping of the Education Maintenance Allowance
(EMA) for sixteen- to nineteen-year-olds in England and its replacement by a much more tightly targeted £180m bursary system.

Unfortunately for Gove, and for the credibility of his argument, there were at least twenty-five errors in the BSF list he disclosed. To make matters worse, he failed to ensure that the list was widely available to MPs during the debate, which meant that they were scrambling in an undignified fashion to discover whether schools in their respective constituencies were affected. The Labour MP Tom Watson advised Gove to apologize: 'You should volunteer. If you do, we'll be gentle with it.' Wise counsel, perhaps – although, in the event, it did not stop Watson shouting at Gove that he was a 'miserable pipsqueak' (a remark he was in turn ordered to withdraw by the Speaker, John Bercow).

By his own admission, Gove had missed the 'EQ point' – the 'emotional intelligence' – required in handling such an announcement. However strong the rational case or fiscal imperative for ditching BSF, the individual MPs whose constituency schools were affected were always going to feel a sense of outrage. Worse, if understandably, he had assumed that the information reaching his desk for use in a parliamentary statement had been subjected to due diligence. It was clearly unsafe to make such assumptions. Was it possible that he had been sabotaged?

Gove was quickly learning that, at the Department for Education (as he had re-named the Department for Children, Schools and Families), a radical Conservative Secretary of State could take nothing for granted. If this made him seem paranoid, that was a price worth paying. And just because the minister was paranoid didn't mean they weren't out to get him. Gove's fear that the department had its fair share of pro-Labour 'sleepers' was exacerbated when Julie McCandless, a diary secretary who had worked for Ed Balls for many years, announced after a few months of the new regime that she wanted to leave – only to pop up as Balls's office manager and diary secretary at the Commons. That was at least public and honest. But Gove worried that, after thirteen years of Labour, his department was full of 'moles'. Too often, he would be given dud information to announce (the number of playing fields closed by the Government, for instance). The Secretary of State was ultimately responsible for any data he released and suffered politically every time inaccurate statistics were published by his department. But Gove was not a slipshod politician. At the very least, he concluded, there were officials at the department's HQ, Sanctuary Buildings in Great Smith Street, who were more than content to see him embarrassed.

To compensate, he had strong ministerial support from Nick Gibb, a longstanding believer in education reform, and – initially at least – the Lib Dem Sarah Teather. As in many other departments where Tories and Lib Dems were getting to know one another, Gove and the diminutive Teather seemed at first to make a formidable duo. According to one observer: 'It was like watching a Scottish Enlightenment philosopher make friends with a Weeble.'

Clearly, the department would need to be overhauled if Gove was to get anywhere – though the Civil Service does not allow for 'nights of the long knives'. In October 2011, the departure of Sir David Bell, the Permanent Secretary since 2006, and three other senior officials prompted claims of a purge. Officially, this suggestion was dismissed as sensationalist nonsense. Off the record, politicians and mandarins alike spoke of growing tensions and frustrations.

The real problem was cultural rather than personal. Conservative ministers had always referred to the 'education establishment' of mutually supportive teacher unions, local authority officials, academic specialists on education and teacher-training institutions. This establishment, Tory and Blairite reformers argued, resisted any change of any sort that threatened Tony Crosland's comprehensive revolution, the grip of the town halls on local schools, national pay-bargaining and the homogeneity of the system. Since Kenneth Baker's Education Reform Act of 1988 introduced the National Curriculum, this 'establishment' had lost many battles. When Blair spoke of the 'forces of conservatism' and public sector 'wreckers', he included those who refused to accept the need for radical educational reform.

But Gove believed that what confronted him was less akin to an arthritic establishment than a self-regenerating monster from a fifties monster movie: a 'Blob'. The term had been adopted by William Bennett, President Reagan's Education Secretary, to describe the bloated bureaucracy that stifled reform of American schools, and now it became part of the Cameroon lexicon.[2] It is hard for a coalition, always

seeking unity, smoothing over differences, urging emollience, to identify an 'enemy within'. Just as a committee that sets about designing a
horse ends up with a camel, so a Quad trying to find a common foe
would end up remitting the problem to a sub-committee, probably
headed by Oliver Letwin. The 'Blob' was the closest the Coalition
ever came to naming such an enemy.

It is hard to exaggerate Gove's importance to Cameron's plans. To
win an election – which he had not done yet – the Tory leader had to
convince the electorate that he stood for more than austerity and (as
Labour would have it) tax cuts for the rich. As he told the *Sunday
Telegraph* in January 2013, he would have liked to push harder on
immigration reform but this was 'just an issue where there is quite a
profound disagreement between the Liberal Democrats and Conservatives'.[3] The two principal areas in which he wanted to claim
radical success by the 2015 general election were welfare reform and
education.

The fate of the benefits revolution would be settled by the performance of Iain Duncan Smith's Universal Credit, the extent to
which Labour remained associated with welfare dependency, and the
electorate's trust (or lack of it) in the Government's motives. Education, on the other hand, required dynamism at the top to deliver
change fast, intellectual conviction to power the changes, and the
political guile required to deal with sabotage in its many forms.

Gove had succeeded David Willetts as Shadow Secretary of State
for Children, Schools and Families with a brief to put the grammar
schools row firmly behind the party, but to argue for radical reform
of a quite different sort. There was to be no fatal divergence between
political rhetoric and policy detail of the sort that caused so many
problems for Andrew Lansley. After the 2005 election, Cameron had
asked to be appointed Shadow Secretary of State for Education and
Skills rather than, as might be expected, Shadow Chancellor. He and
Gove were as one in their belief that a structural revolution was
required in the nation's secondary education, and that a centrally
directed return to grammar schools and selection at eleven was the
opposite of the radical decentralization that the sclerotic system
really needed.

Cameron was often amused by his colleague's enthusiasm – 'You occasionally have to restrain him' – but preferred that to the alternative. In the new Conservative constellation, Gove stood out not only because of his talent, but because he was not from a privileged English background. Born in Edinburgh in August 1967, and named Graham, he was adopted four months later by a couple in Aberdeen, where his adoptive father ran a fish-processing business. Renamed Michael Gove, he attended a state primary school and then won a scholarship to Robert Gordon's School in Aberdeen. At Oxford, he read English and was President of the Union (Hilary Term, 1988), two years after Boris Johnson (Trinity Term, 1986). Returning to a Union debate years later, Gove was surprised to be offered a lift back to London by Mick Jagger 'in the boot'.

Initially, Gove's wit and eloquence led him to a career in journalism and broadcasting. As a trainee reporter at the *Press and Journal* in Aberdeen, he had joined a strike for several months, earning him the semi-ironic nickname of 'Red Mike'. In 1992, the year in which Cameron was alongside Norman Lamont on Black Wednesday, Gove was alongside David Baddiel and Tracey MacLeod on the Channel 4 satirical show *A Stab in the Dark*. He worked on the BBC's *On the Record* and the *Today* programme, where, as an increasingly confident Conservative, he feared himself out of place.

At *The Times*, however, he felt at home almost immediately, his gifts quickly recognized by the editor, Peter Stothard, and, in due course, Rupert Murdoch. As comment editor, news editor and columnist, he was clearly being groomed for an editorship at News International – unless another newspaper group poached him first. But his thoughts were already tending towards the political arena, as a participant rather than an observer. Assumed at first to be a man of the Right, he was indeed a passionate Unionist and champion of Israel's right to defend itself, and alive to the global nature of the Islamist threat.[4] But he was also one of the first Tories – outside Parliament until he became MP for Surrey Heath in 2005 – to recognize fully the need for the party to change, 'detoxify' itself, and shed its image as a cross between an ideological sect and a rich man's club. In 2002, the informal leader of the modernizers, Francis Maude, established a new think-tank in Westminster, Policy Exchange: Gove was chairman and his former flatmate, Nick Boles, its director.

Biography and background were central to his distinctive political significance. To adapt Blair's familiar line about why he had joined Labour, Gove had not been born into the Conservative Party; he had chosen it. For cradle Tories, Conservatism was like membership of the Church of England or a passport; it came with the birth certificate. But Gove had thought about it. He understood what it was like to be a voter, weighing up his options.

Like Hilton, he was a scholarship boy who had risen via university to the commanding heights of his profession. He was socially amphibious, not remotely chippy among the trustafarians of west London, but proud of his Aberdonian origins. There were no toe-curling attempts to make him mimic what spin doctors imagine to be the authentic voice of the proletarian milieu: the telltale guttural Mockney into which Blair and even Osborne sometimes lapsed. It was his insights, as well as his political brain and determination, that made Gove so essential to Cameron.

Almost 60 per cent of those entitled to attend Cameron's Cabinet meetings had been privately educated, soaring above the national average of 6.5 per cent. Gove was among them. But, for his family, a place at a top independent school had been a mark of aspiration rather than the default position of an elite. He was also that near-oxymoron – a Scottish Conservative – who understood what it was like to be going against the grain. His objective was profoundly radical: to ensure that the 'supply-side' improvement in the state sector was so dramatic that successor Cabinets would no longer be dominated by former pupils of fee-paying schools. As a father of young children, he could also see what was happening beneath the veneer of twenty-first-century egalitarian culture. There was now an appreciable risk of social cantonization, whereby a 'superclass', composed of the 6.5 per cent of children who went to the world's most competitive private schools and to the tiny number of comparable state schools, effectively seceded from everyone else. As politicians talked piously of social mobility and equal opportunity, the 'superclass' was sewing up every profession, every institution, every source of power. It was

Gove's mission to break that cartel – not by social engineering, or quotas, or affirmative action, but by radical education reform.

In so doing, he was challenging the world that had produced many of the Coalition's most senior figures. Though better camouflaged than ever before, there was still a caste system that defined the privileged Englishman: such an individual grew up surrounded by Tories, took for granted the fact that he would have homes in the country and in London (in the 'Royal Borough of Kensington and Chelsea', of course), and inhabited a social milieu in which everybody knew everybody. It was the world described in Allan Hollinghurst's *The Line of Beauty* and, with savage brilliance, in Edward St Aubyn's Patrick Melrose novels.[5] Those who knew both men said it was impossible to understand the relationship between Cameron and Boris Johnson without reference to their respective positions at Eton. Boris was the older boy and a 'Colleger' (a scholar) rather than (like Cameron) a regular fee-paying 'Oppidan' – a vintage example of what Freud described as the 'narcissism of small differences'.[6] Though officially indifferent to class – 'It's not where you've come from that counts, it's where you're going' – Cameron and Osborne fretted often about the politics of privilege and its capacity to rear up and bite them unexpectedly. The pictures of the two men in their Bullingdon Club regalia – Osborne's more recent than Cameron's – followed them around in documentaries and profiles like criminal mug shots follow Hollywood stars. As austerity bit and the economic recovery stalled, the photographs did their brutal semiotic work. How could anybody willing to wear such gaudy tailcoats claim, with a straight face, that 'we are all in this together'? All in what, exactly?

Like the comprehensive-educated Hague, Gove was sometimes a much-needed ambassador from outside the west London Tory demi-monde. Like Hilton, he enjoyed dual citizenship, firmly rooted in his past but happily assimilated to the world that the late Frank Johnson, former editor of *The Spectator* and *Telegraph* sketch writer, had christened 'the Hill'. He had stepped out for several years with Simone Kubes (later Finn), who became a Special Adviser to Francis Maude, was a longtime friend of Kate Fall and had known Frances Howell long before George Osborne met and proposed to her. Gove's wife, Sarah Vine, whom he had met at *The Times*, was independently close to Kubes/Finn and to Sam Cameron. Three degrees of separation were rarely necessary, let alone six.

Vine's friendship with Sam led many in Number Ten to suppose that she would soon be running her office. Cameron's wife had official assistance from Isabel Spearman, who had previously worked for the world-beating designer Anya Hindmarch. Gabby Bertin, number two in the communications team, was also deeply loyal to Sam. But the pressures on a Prime Minister's spouse – especially one with a career of her own, at Smythson's, trying to raise a young family in the Downing Street flat – were ever more intense.[7] Cameron's aides would chase Sam trying to integrate the two spouses' diaries. According to one adviser: 'When we raised the matter with Dave – delicately, I have to say – he rolled his eyes as if to say: "You know what she's like." End of discussion.' But Sam was popular in Number Ten and regarded as well-mannered and decent. According to one Cabinet minister: 'Living in the public eye, even living above the shop, it's harder than people imagine. She is very supportive of Dave. But the pressure is amazing. You know, the truth is that the Camerons don't much like Larry [the Downing Street cat]. But they have to go along with it.' The Prime Minister was certainly adamant that Freya, Osborne's bold and itinerant tabby, was not coming into his flat, 'tearing up the bloody furniture'.

Having Vine on-site would make life easier, many in Number Ten thought. It was not to be, but the same Cabinet minister said that Gove and his wife performed a function in the Coalition as a couple that was completely distinct from their individual roles as a Cabinet minister and a newspaper columnist. 'Michael and Sarah are the couple the Camerons can hang out with and talk shop or not talk shop with. They help out with the kids, they are great company.' Another Cameron ally puts it thus: 'Michael is like a cross between Jeeves and Che Guevara. He has got a brain the size of a planet and can help Dave in most situations. But he's also a true believer. As much as Steve.'

The Education Secretary was most certainly in the Cameroon milieu, but not of it. Like Hilton, he was an outsider. The PM's senior adviser brought to the table the energy, enterprise and anti-authoritarianism of the Cold War refugee. As an adopted child, Gove understood that biology was not destiny, and that a child's future could be transformed by opportunity: the embrace of a loving home or a first-rate school. He saw secondary school education not as conveyor belt preparation for the path predetermined for you by class – an ancient university and a job in the City, or a life of worklessness – but the phase of an individual's life in which his or her political and social self acquired its muscle and sinew, and the consequent ability to make meaningful choices in life. School should not be a place for homogenization but a disruptive force – where expectations were confounded, ambitions realized and human energy released.

More, perhaps, than any of his postwar predecessors, Gove was also an unashamed humanist, who believed that the teaching of a core of knowledge, history and literature was an essential part of citizenship. In June 2012, he called for pupils to learn poetry by heart from the age of five. In the same spirit, he stoked controversy by sending a 400th-anniversary copy of the King James Bible to every school – in a scheme funded by philanthropists – not as an act of religious piety, but because, in his opinion, its language was the foundation stone of modern English. It was Gove's contention that a diverse society such as contemporary Britain needed, more than ever, to identify and commemorate a common cultural heritage.

To those who shared the Education Secretary's perspectives, this was merely common sense. To those who were opposed to his programme of reforms, it was laughably at odds with the reality of an inner-city comprehensive, proof that Gove's priority was not the rescue of disadvantaged children from Ignorance (one of Beveridge's 'Five Giants'). For the most assiduous campaigners against his blueprint, such as Melissa Benn, author of *School Wars*, and the journalist and blogger Fiona Millar, its true purpose was to dismantle the comprehensive system and the spirit of equality it embodied.[8] Just as the opponents of Lansley's reforms saw ill-defined 'privatization' lurking in every line of his bill, so Gove's antagonists believed that he was 'centralizing' the schools system by reducing the role of town halls, reviving academic selection by the back door and nurturing social segregation. The ferocity of the conflict was undisguised: it was the closest Britain was likely to come to the 'culture wars' that have so scarred American politics in recent decades.

Gove's office in Sanctuary Buildings was his command and control centre. A poster of Obama with the word 'Hope' caught the visitor's eye as did the slogan 'Cut through the red tape' and a picture of Martin Luther King. When it came to content, the Secretary of State did not mind being regarded as prescriptive. He wanted to administer shock therapy and knew that the Blob would hiss, fizz and exhale smoke as he did so. It was considered bad manners to talk about 'grade inflation' in exam results, or the debasement of the currency after years of political pressure. Like citizens of the Weimar Republic pushing barrows full of cash to buy bread, Year 12 and 13 pupils (sixth formers) were now compelled to take an ever-greater number of A levels to distinguish themselves. Gove believed that the problem had to be confronted. In her public correspondence with him, Glenys Stacey, the chief executive of Ofqual, the qualifications watchdog, declared that grade inflation was 'virtually impossible to justify and . . . has done more than anything to undermine confidence in the value of those qualifications'.

When, in 2012, the proportion of A or A* marks awarded to A level candidates fell for the first time since 1991, ministers were quietly encouraged that the 'gold standard' of the education system might yet be liberated from political targets and manipulation, its prestige gradually restored so that it served not ministers, but the teenagers who sat the papers, and the universities and employers who depended upon the qualification's resilience as hard currency. The small dip was not statistically significant. But its cultural meaning was potentially immense – the first stirrings, perhaps, of a shift from a system that had enabled ministers to make absurdly hyperbolic claims about soaring standards to one that simply measured excellence.

In June 2012, the *Daily Mail*'s Tim Shipman reported that Gove was planning 'to axe GCSEs and return to an O-level style exam' – a scoop that energized the Tory Party as much as it horrified Lib Dems.[9] The Education Secretary's stock within and outside his party shot up, and his leadership credentials began to be examined seriously. Cameron kept a cautious distance from Gove's swashbuckling moment – conscious that today's swashbuckling moment is tomorrow's reckless folly. But he had known about the plan to abolish the GCSE for some weeks and offered broad support. Clegg's position was quite different. As far as he was concerned, this was simply the beginnings of a Tory 'differentiation' strategy – the mirror image of his own – and not to be taken seriously as Coalition policy. The Deputy PM was adamant that the GCSE would not be abolished on his watch. Gove was no less adamant that the changeover would begin in 2014 or 2015 at the latest.

On this occasion, however, the Education Secretary had overreached himself, and knew it. His plan for an English Baccalaureate Certificate overseen by a single examination board, whatever its merits, was never going to be implemented by a Coalition Government. The Commons Education Select Committee sucked its teeth and ruled that the reforms would be 'too much, too fast'. In February 2013, Gove conceded to the Commons that this had been 'a bridge too far' – and, by implication, he did not want to risk everything by fighting his own personal Battle of Arnhem. He made no attempt to conceal the setback: 'When the arguments overwhelm me and I recognize that I am wrong, I think it best to retreat. We only make progress in this life when we know when to cut our losses.'

Instead, he settled for a toughening up of the GCSE and a reformed National Curriculum – fact-based, exam-tested – that reflected his aggressive faith in the power of education. Without this kind of core knowledge, he said, 'students from poorer homes will continue to perform less well in the exercise of every basic skill that one needs to be employed in the modern world'. This was Gove's credo, his version of Gray's *Elegy* – the poet's famed lament for talent never permitted to blossom – and his riposte to those who said he was a social segregationist: 'The accumulation of cultural capital – the acquisition of knowledge – is the key to social mobility.'[10] He described Jonathan Rose's pioneering book, *The Intellectual Life of the British Working Classes*, as his 'Bible'.[11]

Form, in any case, was more important than content. It had taken Blair a few years to grasp that higher standards followed from better

structures, rather than vice versa. The essence of secondary education reform was to transform the very nature of schools: from high
street branches of a town hall and national education bureaucracy
into genuinely local civic institutions, in which teachers, parents and
pupils alike would feel a strong sense of collaborative investment.
The Treasury would fund them, Ofsted would inspect them, and
they would be legally required to teach a 'broad and balanced
curriculum'. But within those minimal parameters, the twenty-first-
century school would become a genuine example of Burke's 'little
platoons' and a concrete example of the 'Big Society'.

The Tories had been here before. In the early nineties, John Patten
had fought a bold campaign to enable schools to opt out of town hall
control and become 'grant-maintained', keeping a totalizer on his
desk of those which did so. But, under the legislation Patten inherited, schools had only been able to opt out after a parental ballot – a
natural opportunity for the Blob to frighten parents and spread mis-
information. Hilton, in particular, was an admirer of what Patten
had tried to achieve. But this time, the tactics would have to be different. In Opposition, he urged Gove to 'make the case for why the
system needs change urgently. You know, and I know, but we need a
broader constituency.'

While in health reform the policy and politics had diverged disastrously, schools policy was always destined to be radical under the
Tories. So it mattered that Gove prepare the ground – that he get
stuck into what Cameron called 'pitch-rolling' – explaining that
what he proposed was intended to empower parents against town
hall bureaucrats, enable good schools to grow, and encourage new
schools to replace bad ones. To parents worried about their children's
basic literacy and numeracy this was an opportunity to change the
odds.

The purest manifestation of the new educational ethos was the
right granted to voluntary groups, teachers, parents, charities and
businesses to set up their own schools. Central government would
assess applications (so no state-funded Jerry Falwell Academies or
Aleister Crowley Colleges), provide funding and stand well back,
intervening only in emergencies. The most obvious model was the

US 'charter school', of which there were approximately 6,000, most of them over-subscribed. Gove decided, however, to make his explicit template the Swedish system, since the importing of a policy from social democratic Scandinavia would almost certainly provoke less controversy than the emulation of American practice. A charitable body, the New Schools Network, was established to help groups set up their own schools. No less influential in spreading the word was the journalist and author Toby Young, one-time *enfant terrible* of the *Modern Review*, now the driving force behind the West London Free School. His despatches from the front line of educational reform were an entertaining inspiration to other parents.[12]

Once again, Gove found that he was grazing the limits imposed by the fact of coalition. The Education Secretary wanted to allow free schools to be run at a profit, knowing that the involvement of business had been vital in Sweden. For the Lib Dems, however, this was a step too far, the commercialization of a core public service. At different moments, it seemed that Clegg, Richard Reeves and Danny Alexander might be open to it. But they could never quite be coaxed to make the leap, unleashing market forces in the secondary education system. Jeb Bush, the former Governor of Florida, counselled Gove not to allow the issue to become all-consuming. 'I've got nothing against profit,' Bush said. 'But I just think it's a distraction from all the other things you're trying to do.'

The first twenty-four free schools opened in September 2011, followed by an additional fifty-five a year later. In March 2013, Cameron and Gove announced that 102 more had been approved. The progress was encouraging – but both men knew this was the work of a generation, especially without the incentive of profit to accelerate the process. Free schools might be the absolute encapsulation of their education model – new institutions literally rising from the ground – but the existing 'academy' system established under Labour was also a foundation worth broadening and building upon.

Though he had sent a copy of the King James Bible to every English state school, Gove's own political gospel was Blair's memoir, *A Journey*, which struck him as the *cri-de-coeur* of a frustrated reformer. New Labour had been right, he believed, to introduce academies, self-governing institutions free of town hall control and the constraints of the National Curriculum, often with a subject specialism. He frequently praised Lord (Andrew) Adonis, former head of Blair's policy unit and schools minister, who, more than anyone, had made a reality of this idea.[13] David Willetts, when Shadow Education Secretary, had also paid homage by declaring: 'I am more authentically Andrew Adonis than Andrew Adonis is.'

Willetts's quip captured the essence of Gove's strategy with academy schools – which was to present himself as an evolutionary reformer, completing Blair's unfinished work, rather than the Tory radical that he actually was. 'In matters of ideology, I'm a Blairite,' he said in June 2012. 'I believe that what's right is what works.' To those who said he was encouraging a two-tiered schools system, he replied that he was doing no such thing. In fact, the whole purpose of liberalizing schools, as far as he was concerned, was to give communities the chance to escape the centralized segregation of the status quo, a multi-tiered system about which they could do nothing. Academies were intended to be heterogeneous rather than uniform, each attracting a different form of sponsorship, whether by an individual, a business or a charity. There were 203 academies in May 2010 when the Coalition was born. By April 2013, 2,886 were open in England.

As far as Gove was concerned, this was the single most important metric. What had started as a Blairite wheeze, never fully accepted by the Brownites, had become a movement, and one that would survive a change of governing party. Just as Lansley hoped to entrench in law a new structure for commissioning healthcare that could withstand and survive future ministerial caprice, Gove wanted academies and free schools to spread like antibodies so that the nation's immune system might resist the Blob. It was obvious that the next Labour Prime Minister, given the Opposition party's post-Blair funding arrangements, would be deeply indebted to the public sector unions. It was vital, therefore, to ensure that the shift by schools to embrace independence had its own clear momentum by the mid-point in the 2010–15 Parliament. Though it attracted less coverage than the rows about curriculum content – historical facts, poetry, languages – this was the battle which, in Gove's eyes, had to be won at more or less any cost.

The Education Secretary was a famously polite man, a quality that served him well in the Coalition. In a bipartisan Government, trust between colleagues is even more important than usual. The radicalism of Gove's measures was clear to those who were looking. Despite his gifts as an orator and his debating talent – his capacity to crush an opponent in argument – he knew that parents wanted to be reassured and inspired rather than intellectually awestruck. If the Tories were to stand a chance at the 2015 election, they had to be trusted as custodians of public services.

This left a lot of work to be done by his Special Advisers, Henry de Zoete and Dominic Cummings. The reputation of spin doctors during the New Labour era had encouraged Cameron to promise a limit on the number of 'Spads' in government – as pledged in the Coalition Agreement. Yet, by July 2012, his Government was employing more of them (eighty-one) than Gordon Brown at the time of his departure. As the case of Adam Werritty would show (see Chapter 9), senior ministers needed political appointees to liaise with officials, chase progress, brief the media, write political speeches, massage their egos or – much more valuable – tell them the truth.

Whitehall had always resisted the continental *cabinet* system, in which ministers were free to appoint a team of senior advisers, financed by party as well as taxpayer. This meant that the role of Special Advisers was opaque, covering everything from glorified valet to chief of staff (sometimes in the same overworked individual). In September 2010, Christopher Myers had resigned from his position as a Spad to William Hague, after 'untrue and malicious' allegations circulated about their relationship. Hague, appalled and outraged, felt compelled to issue a personal statement to protect his wife, Ffion, revealing that the couple had struggled with infertility for many years and that she had suffered 'multiple miscarriages'. Hague continued: 'We have never made this information public because of the distress it would cause to our families and would not do so now were it not for the untrue rumours circulating which repeatedly call our marriage into question. We wish everyone to know that we are very happily married.'[14] Other than causing the Hagues immense pain, the episode showed only how vaguely defined the Special Adviser's function was. Myers was a 25-year-old who had acted as Hague's constituency aide and driver: a bright, affable minder. In contrast, Hague's chief of staff, Arminka Helic, was one of the most impressive foreign policy experts in the Government. His other adviser, Denzil Davidson, an expert on the European Union, was also a cerebral force.

Gove depended upon his Special Advisers and was proud of it, thanking their 'much-maligned tribe' as he accepted a prize at the *Spectator* Parliamentarian of the Year awards in 2012.[15] For media relations, he deployed de Zoete, a sharp Etonian, alumnus of Portland PR and member of the de Zoete banking family. In theory at least, Cummings was kept in a deep vault in the department, working on strategy and policy. His powerful intellect had secured him a First in Ancient and Modern History, and made him a formidable campaigner against British membership of the euro and EU federalism. Like Hilton, he was mild-mannered by temperament – except when he wasn't. His volcanic outbursts had astonished Duncan Smith in 2002 when he had been, briefly, the party's director of strategy. 'You would go and see Iain at HQ in Smith Square', according to one observer, 'and there Dom would be in the leader's office – not even thirty, I'd guess – with his shirt unbuttoned, down to the bottom two buttons, shouting the odds. Iain would be completely silent. He was like a long-suffering courtier dealing with a furious princeling.'

Andy Coulson had used his power of veto to keep Cummings out of Gove's departmental team but, once Coulson had gone, he resumed his place at the Education Secretary's side. In theory, he was not supposed to get involved in the media operation. But, not for the first time, he became the story. He and James Frayne, the department's former director of communications, were named in an internal grievance report involving a DfE staff member who had served twenty-seven years – a case that would have been referred to an employment tribunal if not for a reported private settlement of £25,000.[16] The complaint described a 'macho culture of intimidation, favouritism and "laddism"'. But Cummings was also resented as one of the architects of Gove's plan to slim down the department progressively until it was no more than a managerial hub. In November 2012, plans were announced to cut its workforce by about 25 per cent by 2015 – the first phase, it was rumoured, of a blueprint to reduce the size of the department by 90 per cent. In this, Gove and Cummings were at one with Letwin and Hilton, for whom the 'post-bureaucratic age' was not just a slogan, but a signpost to a future in which Whitehall would be unrecognizably leaner and more cost-effective.

Small wonder that Gove was so popular with Osborne. Not only did the Chancellor admire what his colleague was doing to raise educational standards. He was impressed by the vigour with which he approached departmental cuts – not as an evil necessity but the right thing to do in the twenty-first century. It was axiomatic to Gove that the gentleman in Whitehall did not know best, and that the less intervention the centre was forced to make, the better. Until schools taught the basics reliably, there would be a role for the National Curriculum. Under Charlie Taylor – a highly successful head teacher who was also a friend of Cameron – the new Teaching Agency would get a grip on teacher training and regulation. But the objective was to replace central direction with neighbourhood initiative, to end the era of educational Gosplan once and for all and let schools develop their own character and strengths, competing for pupils and sponsorship.

None of this would happen if the Blob had anything to do with it, and it was clear enough that the battle would be brutal, bloody and prolonged. In late 2011, the Information Commissioner, Christopher Graham, ruled that Gove's team should not use private email accounts or texts from personal phones to conduct official business: the implication was that senior advisers were using unofficial routes to brief journalists and otherwise communicate without risk of subsequent scrutiny. Graham's point was that this ruse – if such it was – would not work, as all such messages, whether from departmental email accounts and mobile phones or otherwise were covered by Freedom of Information legislation.

Gove's supporters were not to be so easily tamed and corralled.

Sacked from his job as Children's Minister in the September 2012 reshuffle, Tim Loughton made a personal attack on Gove and his management of the department that provoked a savage response. According to Loughton: 'Most officials have never met the Secretary of State other than when he'll troop out a few chosen people for the New Year party, Mr Grace-like, tell us "You've all done very well" then disappear. That's no way to run an important department. It is terribly anachronistic, terribly bureaucratic, terribly formal.'[17] On 17 January 2013, the *Spectator*'s political editor, James Forsyth, reported on the magazine's Coffee House blog the view of 'one senior Department for Education source' that 'Loughton was a lazy incompetent narcissist obsessed only with self-promotion.' As part of his defence, Loughton told the magazine that, far from being lazy, 'I was always the first one in and the last one out.' He proceeded to table a series of parliamentary questions about staff complaints, clearly designed to force Cummings into the open and out of the department. Appearing before the Education Select Committee on 23 January, Gove was asked by the Labour MP Ian Mearns: 'Are there elements working within the department that are out of control, Secretary of State?' Gove answered: 'No.'

That was not the view of Toby Helm, the political editor of the *Observer*, who suspected himself to be the target of 'some kind of "black ops" campaign', fought in the Twitterverse by the anonymous @toryeducation.[18] Helm's 'new stalker', as he described the tweeter, accused him of being 'like [Alastair] Campbell . . . an activist not a professional hack' and a 'Labour stooge'. Helm continued: 'This Twitter feed is always up to the minute on policy announcements, highly informed, and is very unlikely to be the work of some outside obsessive. It is swift with robust, politically charged comment and rebuttals, fiercely pro-Gove but at the same time often deeply personal.' De Zoete denied all knowledge, while Cummings said: 'I am not toryeducation.' Gove requested any evidence the newspaper had to prove its insinuation.

Behind the scenes, he had asked all the suspects whether they had anything to do with @toryeducation and been reassured to his satisfaction. He was heard to compare the Twitter feed to the ever-controversial midfielder Joey Barton: 'You think: "Oh no, what's he done now."' Whoever was writing the tweets was a passionate defender of the Education Secretary – but might damage the very reputation he or she sought to protect by going too far.

Courtesy and intellect get you a long way: Gove had always commanded loyalty, amongst his friends but also in politics. As Osborne sustained wounds on the economic front, the Education Secretary began to be sized up by the party as a potential contender himself. Could Gove be Thatcher to the Chancellor's Keith Joseph – the junior partner who ended up in the top job? The parallel was scarcely exact. Osborne had never been called a 'mad monk' and his political resilience far outstripped Joseph's. But it was true that Gove had a broad range, as he showed by his many interventions in Cabinet and his presence at the National Security Council when Islamic extremism was concerned. He was a deeply serious man but witty, affable and alive to the ironies of life – not least those of which he was the victim. His profound sense of mission posed the question: why not go further, all the way to Number Ten?

To this, he answered that he had watched Cameron and that he was not up to the job. He did not want to make further demands of his family – his children being his first blood relations, and all the more miraculous for that. Unlike some senior politicians, he both loved and liked his wife and wanted to see more of her. And he was not so foolish as to think, as others did, that his friend George was out of the running. But what if the call came? What if the moment of decision arrived, and the clamour to take a stand was louder than he expected? If his colleagues implored him to be a candidate, would he really send them away? To that question, not even the wise owl of Sanctuary Buildings knew the answer.

8. 'A huge event in the life of the nation'

'You've got to come back,' Ed Llewellyn told his boss. 'You've got to come back now.' It was Monday, 8 August 2011, and the Prime Minister was still on holiday in Tuscany – even as riots tore through the cities of England, shops were looted and flames filled the urban skyline. Gangs taunted the police and stocked up on plasma screen TVs and trainers. The social order, it seemed, was on the brink of collapse – all of it televised and tweeted.

Cameron and Llewellyn shared a distaste for over-reaction and theatricality. Their initial instinct had been that the disturbances were localized outbursts of criminal activity and deserved to be treated as such, rather than dignified as a national emergency. But by Monday the contagion was still spreading, the police were struggling to maintain order – and, as Cameron himself admitted, 'the captain was not on the deck'.

Just as Cameron never actually used the words 'hug a hoodie', Jim Callaghan did not say 'Crisis? What crisis?' in January 1979 – but, in both cases, it was the pithy headlines that stuck. On the Sunday morning, as the people of Tottenham sifted through the wreckage of the rioting the night before, Cameron was photographed wearing a polo shirt, tanned and smiling, in a café in Montevarchi, with his arm round a waitress he had forgotten to tip on a previous visit. The juxtaposition of this image with the pictures from Tottenham was political tinder, and invited the snap judgement that the PM was out of touch, as well as out of the country. Crisis, what crisis?

A special RAF flight was arranged to get Cameron back to his desk by Tuesday morning. Nick Clegg had returned from his holiday in Spain on the Monday. But Theresa May, the Home Secretary, and Boris Johnson, the Mayor of London, were still out of the country. May flew back overnight from Switzerland to join the PM at his first meetings with the Metropolitan Police and for a full gathering of the Civil Contingencies Committee, Cobra. Facing angry calls for his return, Boris also broke off a Winnebago holiday in the Canadian Rockies, racing back to the airport to catch a transatlantic flight. 'It was tough,' he later reflected. 'And then people felt angry because they'd seen their shops, their property, attacked and, sod it, the sodding Mayor had been somewhere else.'[1]

The collective absence of the governing elite for the first three nights of the riots was a perilous low point for the Coalition. For once, the charge that Cameron spent too much time 'chillaxing' – grotesquely unfair, given his normal working hours – rang dangerously true. Precisely when leadership was most needed it was visibly absent. Inevitably, the vacuum was filled by fear, rumour-mongering and a sense that the anarchy was now viral, and perhaps unstoppable. It was also far from clear what sort of disturbances these were, and whether any social or political message lurked within the frenzied looting and destruction.[2]

In the stuffy upper floors of Number Ten – airless and quite unlike the grand reception rooms – normal routine was being replaced by coffee-fuelled round-the-clock attention to the rolling news channels, blogs and Twitter. As the PM was quickly informed, the notional trigger was the death of Mark Duggan, a black 29-year-old, in a police shooting in Tottenham on Thursday, 4 August. Duggan's relatives and other local residents were furious about the manner in which his bereaved family had been treated by the police, and by their refusal to divulge details about the fatal incident. Two days later, 120 demonstrators converged on Tottenham Police Station, arriving at 5.30 p.m. and demanding answers. By 8.30 p.m., the protest had escalated, as the police station came under attack and a squad car was set alight. Officers were pelted with eggs, bottles and bricks, and faced a mob armed with baseball bats and crowbars. A double-decker bus and nearby shops were set ablaze. Police on horseback were called to the scene, and a helicopter loomed over the conflagration. The Acting Commissioner of the Met, Tim Godwin, was reported to be monitoring the situation closely, as well he might: the worst of the disorder had been contained by 11.30 p.m. but looting continued throughout the night, as thieves filled up their car boots and trolleys with stolen goods from stores such as Argos, JD Sports and Boots. May stayed in close touch, asking for up-to-date intelligence, watching and waiting as thousands of young men across the capital witnessed the scenes on television and decided that, the next night, it would be their turn.

On Sunday evening, what had started as a pretext – Duggan's death – became an irrelevance. The riots spread across London to Enfield, Edmonton and Brixton, a wave of destruction and looting that pitted armies of hoodies against far too few police officers. Watching in Downing Street, the PM's advisers realized that the Met was in trouble – and so were they. In less than twenty-four hours, a confrontation over the death of a young father had become a battle for control of the capital's streets, in which the rioters seemed always to be one step ahead of the authorities. The world watched London in flames and wondered whether the city was, after all, capable of mounting the Olympics in a year's time. Johnson, the man who was slated to be master of ceremonies at the Games, was thousands of miles away in a Winnebago. 'He is not going to come back and allow these criminals to set the agenda,' declared Kit Malthouse, Deputy Mayor for Policing. Downing Street briefed reporters mischievously about the Mayor's absence – though the PM's aides were increasingly concerned about their own boss's political truancy.[3]

As a cohort, the politicians looked as if they had been caught on the hop – one of the worst fates that can befall a practitioner of their trade. Though police officers reported that the sky was sometimes dark with bricks and other projectiles, the rioters' most valuable weapon was the BlackBerry smartphone and, specifically, BlackBerry Messenger (BBM), a service that was not only free, but secure. Developed for business users who sought confidentiality, the BBM network was private to recipients, encrypted and almost impossible to monitor. The call-to-arms on Sunday – resent thousands of times – seems to have been one particular message: 'Everyone in edmonton enfield woodgreen everywhere in north link up at enfield town station 4 o'clock sharp!!!! . . . Fuck da feds [police], bring your ballys [balaclavas] and your bags trollys, cars vans, hammers the lot!!'[4]

As Sir Denis O'Connor, Her Majesty's Chief Inspector of Constabulary, later told MPs, the use of social media was a 'game changer' for which the police were simply 'not geared'. Assistant Chief Constable Sharon Rowe of the West Midlands Police expanded in her evidence to the Commons Home Affairs Select Committee: 'I do think there is a challenge for policing nationally . . . on how we . . . evaluate that information to turn it into intelligence. We are into a totally new game now and a new world of fast dynamics where we have to put a policing operation in very quick time in place. We have that challenge of being able to evaluate what is true and what is rumour.'[5]

That challenge was at the heart of the emergency facing the police on Monday, 8 August, as the violence spread to Hackney and Croydon, where the 140-year-old Reeves furniture store was burnt to the ground. There was now disorder in Huddersfield, Reading, Bristol, Leeds, Leicester, Milton Keynes, Birmingham and elsewhere. The rioters kept coming because they believed they could get away with it. There was absolutely no reason to assume that the rioting would peter out.

On Tuesday, the Prime Minister chaired the first full Cobra meeting of the crisis. As businesslike as the discussion remained – Cameron's trademark – the air was thick with tension. In the grey, featureless setting of Cabinet Office Briefing Room A (which gave Cobra its misleadingly exciting name), the PM looked a little too tanned for comfort. There was real concern about the failure of the police thus far to control the situation and barely controlled friction between the politicians and Sir Hugh Orde, president of the Association of Chief Police Officers. In the words of one present: 'Orde clearly felt that we had a cheek coming back from our holidays and telling him how the response had been inadequate.' In theory, the police had operational control, but, in practice, felt that they were receiving mixed messages from absent politicians. Was this a threat to public order that needed to be contained? Or an outbreak of criminality that had to be stopped? In the words of one Cabinet member present at the Tuesday Cobra meeting: 'The police were bloody angry, it was obvious. Their line was: "You told us to do one thing, now you're telling us to do another."' On Saturday and Sunday, 3,000 uniformed officers had been on duty in London. On Monday that number had been doubled – but the violence and looting had continued. It was decided that no fewer than 16,000 police officers would be present on the streets of the capital on Tuesday night, adopting a tougher arrests policy and intervening sooner to disperse crowds.

This was effective – in London at least. But the disorder escalated elsewhere on Tuesday night, in Birmingham, Nottingham, Gloucester and Salford. On Wednesday, 10 August, there were disturbances in Manchester city centre, while, in Birmingham, three men were killed on Dudley Road in Winson Green. Tariq Jahan, the father of one of the three dead, made an impromptu statement from his doorstep that captured the mood of a nation weary of the violence and frightened of where it might lead: 'I lost my son. Blacks, Asians, whites – we all live in the same community. Why do we have to kill one another? Why are we doing this? Step forward if you want to lose your sons. Otherwise, calm down and go home – please.' Cameron was moved by this intervention, which he felt justified his gut feeling – not shared by all his colleagues – that the riots would bring out the best as well as the worst in people.

If Mark Duggan's death was the tragedy that had triggered the riots, Jahan's moving plea was the bookend that marked their ending. Though the Home Office and the police remained on high alert, and Cobra continued to meet, the disturbances were over, fading away as suddenly as they had arisen. Five people had been killed, 299 police officers injured, about 2,500 shops and businesses looted, and £300m of insurance costs rung up. Courts sat through the night in London, Manchester and the West Midlands to expedite justice and dramatize the restoration of order. Cameron and Johnson, bonded in adversity and shaken by the criticism that they had both waited too long to come back, had a convivial dinner in which they seemed as close as they had ever been.

As the danger of anarchy receded, an angry political inquest began. Social media, exploited by rioters to co-ordinate their actions, were now used to mobilize clean-up operations and 'broom brigades'. Heckled in Clapham on Tuesday, Boris knew he had ground to make up and was soon out on the streets with a green broom – or at least holding one aloft. Cameron's aides urged him to do the same, but he declined. 'No,' he told them. 'It's not prime ministerial.' In Opposition, he had been a willing mannequin, happy to go along with the visual stunts required to achieve a political objective – whether that meant hugging a husky or wearing recycled trainers. But Cameron believed that dignity was essential to the office he held and not something to be frittered away in moments of panic.

There were weightier matters to consider, in any case. Relations with the police remained fraught. On *Newsnight*, Orde said that 'the fact that politicians chose to come back is an irrelevance in terms of the tactics that were by then developing'.[6] The Acting Met Commissioner appeared to back him against the politicians who had been absent for the first three nights of violence. 'I think after any event like this, people will always make comments who weren't there,' said Godwin. Number Ten let it be known that this was 'stepping over the line', while continuing to declare total confidence in the police in all official statements. 'Godwin was playing a very dangerous game', according to one Home Office source, 'because we could have made a lot more of the police fuck-ups. The politicians were taking most of the big hits for being absent. The Met should have recognized that – and shut up.'

The riots had also prompted inevitable questions about police funding – stoked, to Cameron's fury, by Boris in a *Today* programme interview. 'If you ask me whether I think there is a case for cutting police budgets in the light of these events,' declared the Mayor, 'then my answer to that would be "No".' So much for convivial dinners. Cameron insisted that the cuts were necessary and reasonable, and that the priority should be to release more officers from bureaucratic tasks.

'I have looked at this, and looked at it again, and looked at it again,' he told the *Sunday Telegraph*, 'and frankly what we're asking the police to do [is] to find on average 6 per cent cash cuts over the next four years. Now, there isn't an organisation in the country that hasn't had to find those sorts of efficiencies. I sat down with my Chief Constable, who comes to my constituency surgery, who took me through her budget line by line by line, and she showed me where she was going to find the savings, how they are going to cooperate with other forces, how they are going to do better on procurement, how they are going to get people out from behind their desks, how they are going to cut paperwork, and how they are going to do that without reducing visible policing. I absolutely believe it can be done and it's no good just immediately saying: "Well, it's been a difficult week, so let's tear up police budgets and let's give up on that part of dealing with the deficit." '[7]

For May, this was a test with potentially far-reaching implications. Those who saw her in the moments after her appointment as Home Secretary in May 2010 said she was 'almost speechless with shock'. Having done her bit in a range of senior Opposition roles, culminating in the Work and Pensions brief since January 2009, she had earned a Cabinet post. But she had not remotely expected to be appointed to one of the great offices of state – only the fourth woman (after Margaret Thatcher, Margaret Beckett and Jacqui Smith) to achieve this distinction. She was also keenly aware that the Home Office was a graveyard of political ambition, even though the management of prisons and probation had been hived off to the Ministry of Justice in 2007. As Home Secretary, she was still responsible for policing, immigration, border control, counter-terrorism and national security. The work was grinding and detailed, and generally attracted attention only when things went wrong. Less than a month after her appointment, she was confronted with the high-profile tragedy of the Cumbria shootings, when a lone gunman, Derrick Bird, killed twelve people and injured eleven, before turning the weapon on himself.

May was almost as famous in Whitehall for her caution and indecision as she was in the media for her kitten heels – a preoccupation that said more about media sexism than it did about her. She could drive her officials mad with her vacillations – notably over control orders, the restrictive arrangements for terror suspects, and whether or not to abolish them.[8] 'Theresa May – but, then again, she may not' ran the joke. Her response was to let the mockers mock and to get on with the job. She was famously discreet, which accounted for

some of the media's frustration, and rarely relaxed even with colleagues she had known for years. Again, this singled her out in a
testosterone-charged alliance of men. 'You have to ask why it was
always Dave, George and William and never Theresa', according to
one insider. 'She held one of the great offices of state, she was a former party chairman, she knew the ropes. But it would never have
occurred to them to include her. It was a boys' club, always was.' Her
handling of crises was never awe-inspiring, but she was always
sure-footed – a reliable media performer who could be trusted on
Newsnight or the *Today* programme. She presided over falling crime
and immigration. She had also embarked upon the most ambitious
reforms of the police in a generation, taking on vested interests that
had seen off many of her predecessors.

In this sense, the tensions across the table of Cobra meetings during the riots were highly intensified variants of existing emotions.
Orde's anger at what the PM and May were saying about police tactics during the first days of the disorder matched the loathing he
already felt for the Government's plans for elected police commissioners. As the man leading ACPO, he foresaw grave local tensions
with chief constables. May also faced huge opposition from the
Police Federation over her proposed overhaul of police pay and conditions – reforms designed to meet the immediate requirements of
deficit reduction but also to minimize the number of officers stuck
behind a desk rather than visibly maintaining order on the streets.
Pay accounted for 80 per cent of the £9bn spent on policing per
annum: given the fiscal context, its structure had to be addressed. But
the Home Secretary also wanted to liberate officers from the tyranny
of paperwork. In addition, she had plans to fast-track graduate
recruits to inspector level within three years. In Number Ten, Hilton
cheered on anything that upset the old police establishment.

As a symbol of dynamic change, Cameron had wanted to appoint
the legendary Bill Bratton – former police commissioner in New
York and Boston, and ex-chief of the Los Angeles Police Department –
to take over the Met after Sir Paul Stephenson's resignation in July.[9]
The Home Secretary resisted, insisting that the new Commissioner
had to be British-born, and tipping the scales back from audacity to

the cautious option (in the end, the job was given in September to Bernard Hogan-Howe, the former Chief Constable of Merseyside). As a compromise, Bratton was taken on as an adviser on policing and gangs. Once again, Orde was furious: 'I am not sure I want to learn about gangs from an area of America that has 400 of them.'[10]

The riots and their aftermath were May's most public test to date as Home Secretary. But there was a deeper, barely articulated question lurking within the scrutiny. As it became clear that economic recovery was going to take longer than the Coalition had inevitably hoped and suggested, the Tory Party began, as it always does, to consider its options. Before she revealed robust instincts on crime and law and order at the Home Office, May had been resented by many Tories for daring to say in 2002 that 'some people' called them 'the nasty party' (not, please note, that she herself did so). But as Home Secretary she had shown herself to be more than an over-promoted modernizer with elegant footwear. Without fanfare, Conservative MPs and activists started to assess her potential as a prospective successor to Cameron: 'the British Angela Merkel' became the shorthand. John Major had padded noiselessly to the very top of the Tory Party and into Number Ten, slipping between Douglas Hurd and Michael Heseltine. There were plenty of possible contenders already: George Osborne, Boris Johnson, Michael Gove, Jeremy Hunt. What was to stop May testing the waters?

At the 2011 party conference in Manchester, she played to the Tory gallery with relish, claiming in her speech that, thanks to the European Convention on Human Rights, an illegal immigrant had escaped deportation because he had a pet cat. But it was the way she told the story – 'I am not making this up' – that told a political tale. To the delight of her true blue audience, the former ultra-modernizer was now talking like Richard Littlejohn or Jeremy Clarkson. Ken Clarke, the Justice Secretary, helped her considerably, keeping the story going by complaining that her claim was 'laughable' and 'childlike'. He also resisted her Cabinet campaign to impose mandatory jail sentences on juvenile offenders convicted of knife crime. May and Clarke had what one minister described as a 'curt exchange' after their conference clash. But, as far as the party and popular press were concerned, she was a comfortable winner.

In the days following the riots, her performance at the Despatch Box and on television was assured enough. But was it possible to imagine her chairing Cobra meetings as Prime Minister? The seed had been sown. The more immediate question was how the present occupant of Number Ten would handle the political fall-out of the disturbances. Having recalled the Commons for an emergency debate on Thursday, 11 August – a week after Duggan's shooting – Cameron answered questions from 160 MPs in a marathon 165-minute performance. His objective was threefold: to characterize the riots as primarily an outbreak of criminality; to praise the police to the skies, but make clear that their tactical response had been wrong; and to shut down the row over police funding. 'It is simply preposterous,' he told the House, 'for anyone to suggest that people looting in Tottenham at the weekend, still less three days later in Salford, were in any way doing so because of the death of Mark Duggan. Young people stealing flat-screen televisions and burning shops – that was not about politics or protest, it was about theft.' The officers in the front line had shown remarkable courage, the PM continued, but 'what became increasingly clear earlier this week was that there were simply far too few police deployed on to our streets, and the tactics that they were using were not working . . . Initially, the police treated the situation too much as a public order issue, rather than essentially one of crime.' And to those who claimed that the riots made cuts unthinkable, he replied that 'the problem was not about police budgets in four years' time, but about the availability of the police right now'.

Politically speaking, and through a combination of luck and judgement, Cameron had escaped the flames – just. As it was, more than 60 per cent of voters believed that ministers had 'failed to return to their desks quickly enough'.[11] If he had stayed in Tuscany a day longer, or if the disorder had continued over a second weekend, his premiership would have been plunged into a serious political crisis. 'Who governs?' Heath had asked in the first election of 1974 – to which the voters' answer had been: 'Not you, mate.' Cameron had been spared such a fate. His Government had lost control, its senior members scattered around the world as London burned. But he had returned just in time, asserted himself through Cobra and the Commons, and insisted, as politely as he could, that it was the police rather than the politicians who had been caught napping.

Even so, the riots nagged at him, offending not only his fundamental view of human nature, but also his ambitions to stitch together the tears in British society. Since 2008, if not before, it had been clear that the principal challenge facing any Government he headed would be the state of the economy: he and Osborne knew that their fate would be settled by their success or failure as economic repairmen. But Cameron was, by inclination, a social reformer rather than a fiscal technician. What animated him was not the control of public expenditure – much as he understood its importance – but the matrix of education, welfare and social cohesion policies that, he believed, could strengthen the social fabric and bequeath to the next generation a country a little more at ease with itself.

To an extent that has not been fully appreciated, this aspect of Cameron's political character was deeply influenced by his first experience of fatherhood. Throughout his life, Ivan Cameron suffered from cerebral palsy and severe epilepsy, and died aged six in 2009, a terrible tragedy from which no parent could ever fully recover. His death subjected Cameron and his wife to pain that could scarcely be imagined. Quite naturally, he considered leaving politics altogether after the loss of his eldest child. Close friends worried that he was not giving himself time to 'process' his grief – to which Cameron's answer, in private and public, was that such grief can never be fully 'processed'. It is a constant presence. Yet, in his all-too-brief life, Ivan also undoubtedly transformed his father, planting in him a deeply felt belief that those in power had a duty to help the weakest members of society as well as to foster aspiration and self-reliance. It was impossible to grasp what he meant by 'progressive Conservatism' without reference to this deeply personal and private narrative. The poster-size photograph of Ivan that hung in the Downing Street flat was symbolic not only of enduring parental love but of a moral commitment.

As Cameron often had cause to declare in the days after the riots, he is an incorrigible optimist: a disciple of David Hume rather than Thomas Hobbes.[12] His Conservatism was neither the paternalism of the old Tory 'Wet', nor the rugged individualism of the Thatcher years. It was not just personal responsibility that he called for but – more ambitiously – 'social responsibility': the sense of duty and community that would (for instance) inspire a group of parents to set up a free school, state-funded but free of town hall management, or enable a volunteer group to take over a local amenity they treasured, or encourage charities to help provide drug rehabilitation and probation services. The challenge was to persuade pundits and sceptical voters that this was more than a fraudulent way of wrapping public spending cuts in moral language, a conjuror's distraction technique to enable him to shrink the state. Who were all these people who had the time to be as socially useful as Cameron hoped? Was this anything more than public services on the cheap?

His first and most pressing task on returning from Tuscany was to restore order, shore up public confidence and denounce the criminality that had raged through the streets. Yet the context of that criminality perplexed, intrigued and dismayed him. Subsequent studies have suggested that the riots were a strange brew of crude acquisitiveness, opportunistic looting, copycat behaviour, and a pitiful attempt by the hopeless and the marginal to claim some sort of power. Of the retail sites looted in the disturbances, the highest proportion were electrical stores, closely followed by clothes shops.[13] Foot Locker, JD Sports, PC World, Currys and mobile phone shops were all targeted – systematically, in many cases, by thieves seeking to sell on desirable stolen goods. One sixteen-year-old girl from Wandsworth told the *Guardian*/LSE study of the riots: 'It was literally a festival with no food, no dancing, no music, but a free shopping trip for everyone.' According to a nineteen-year-old from Tottenham: 'We could have changed the whole everything, the whole government, man, but people wanted Nikes and crap on their feet.' The biggest spur to the rioters was watching others defy the police with apparent impunity. These were the first viral disturbances to afflict English cities.[14] But there was also a perverse, misguided sense among some of the rioters that they had empowered themselves, that 'we had [the police] under control. We had them under manner for once. They never had us under manners. We had them on lock . . . They was the criminals today.'[15] According to one north Londoner in his mid-twenties: 'When no one cares about you you're going to eventually make them care, you're going to cause a disturbance.'[16] Gangs had been heavily involved in the riots. But they had also, in many areas, declared a truce and set aside deadly postcode rivalries for the duration of the uprising. What, beyond acquisitiveness, had driven them to suspend their grievances and 'beef' with one another?

Cameron had cut his teeth as a Special Adviser to Michael Howard at the Home Office. He had no patience with those who sought to excuse crime as a necessary consequence of economic deprivation or of political disenfranchisement. But he did not believe the argument ended there. This was, he said, 'a huge event in the life of the nation'. On the Tuesday of the riots, Cameron spoke to David Lammy, MP for Tottenham, to express his sadness at what had happened in his constituency and to reassure him about policing in the days ahead. 'I suspect we're going to be hearing a lot more about the broken society in the next few days,' said Lammy. 'I suspect you may be right,' the Prime Minister replied.[17]

In this response, Lammy showed that he understood Cameron well. His preoccupation with the 'broken society' might strike Boris as 'piffle' but the PM was as sure as he had ever been that Britain needed a social revolution in 2011 as much as it had required economic transformation in 1979. He asked Duncan Smith and May to investigate gang culture and violence with help from American police chiefs. But he was not among those who believed that gangs were the core problem. If anything, their intimidating strength in certain areas was a symptom of much deeper problems connected to the rudiments of human behaviour and interaction.

The heart of the matter, he told the *Sunday Telegraph*, was the identity of young men and the need for role models. 'You can see in boys that they yearn – I see it in my son [Elwen, aged five at the time], he yearns for time with his Dad alone, he wants to go for walks. It is extraordinary, this sense that you should do things together, and talk about things, and explain things, and it is brilliant. But, God, it's testing – no one tells you how to do it. I think we all rely on our friends to tell us "You need to do this differently", and we watch our friends and how they parent, and we listen a bit to our Mums and Dads. If you haven't got that network, where do you get it from?'

To that rhetorical question he had no ready answer – nor to the related problem of scale that had been revealed in the riots. 'The complicated bit is why are there so many, why is there this sizeable minority of people who are prepared to do this?' It was essential to Cameron's beliefs that the world was a better place if you trusted people and shared responsibility. But what could you do for those who sneered when told that 'we are all in this together'?

In a speech in his Witney constituency on Monday the 15th, he offered a situation report on his conclusions. As Lammy had predicted, he declared that 'the broken society is back at the top of my agenda'. While acknowledging that the Government could not 'legislate to change behaviour', he insisted that it could not be 'a bystander' either. The rules it set, the manner in which they were enforced, the services it provided and the signals government sent 'about the kinds of behaviour that are encouraged and rewarded': these were powerful forces. 'From here on,' he said, 'I want a family test applied to all domestic policy. If it hurts families, if it undermines commitment, if it tramples over the values that keep people together, or stops families from being together, then we shouldn't do it.'

Many Tories hoped that this was, at last, a cue for Cameron to make good his promise to recognize marriage in the tax system. This was one of the few areas of policy where he and his Chancellor disagreed. Belief in marriage as the cornerstone of a stable society was part of Cameron's 'irreducible core'. His case for a tax break worth – say – £20 a week to a married couple was never that a financial 'incentive' of this sort was going to drive millions of young people to the nearest registry office or church. The idea was to change the message that individuals were sent as they stumbled through the dense thickets of the welfare system, already encountering symbols and prompts freighted with meaning.

In Cameron's opinion, the signal the state sent was at best neutral, and at worst actively hostile to marriage. In his 1988 Budget, Nigel Lawson had introduced the Married Couple's Allowance, which was then steadily eroded and restricted by Norman Lamont and Ken Clarke before its abolition by Gordon Brown in 1999. Perversely, the new credit structure had entrenched a 'couple's penalty' – the price a couple pays for staying together. According to figures compiled by Duncan Smith's department, a family earning £35,000 a year would gain £186 a week if the parents split up. Cameron did not imagine that any single policy could stop the onward march of divorce. But he was intrigued by the lessons of the 'Nudge' school of behavioural economics, and the claims of 'libertarian paternalism' that government could do as much through encouragement as it could through the compulsory force of legislation and regulation. In 2010, Cameron had set up a Behavioural Insight Team at the Cabinet Office, headed by David Halpern and advised by Richard Thaler, an economist from the University of Chicago, who had co-authored *Nudge*, the founding text of this school of policy-making. Rohan Silva, as ever Cameron's conduit to the intellectual and technological cutting edge, also ensured that Robert Cialdini, the celebrated author of *Influence*, was invited to one of his seminars for officials and media commentators at Number Ten. The 'Nudge' strategy was not a comprehensive approach to government – 'how do you nudge Osama bin Laden?' became the in-house joke – but it offered an appealingly fresh way of looking at the state.

In this context, Cameron felt that couples could be 'nudged' gently towards marriage – an institution that was currently invisible and irrelevant to the tax credit and benefit system Brown had bequeathed to the Coalition. When still in government, Ed Balls had accused the Tory leader of wanting 'to socially engineer family life', but this was to overstate the case dramatically. Cameron reasoned that the welfare system was already a maze of prods, nudges and winks. It was already, inescapably, a moral system, bristling with moral messages and moral signals – about work, the homes in which we lived, the children we raised, the incapacities we suffered. Brown's system favoured work and lone parenthood. Cameron, who had been a Cabinet Special Adviser during John Major's 'Back to Basics' disaster in 1993, knew the risks of treading on this terrain and had no plans to play the preacher. What he wanted was nothing more than to give marriage a voice in the ethical cacophony.[18]

Osborne, a metropolitan liberal in such matters, simply did not agree. He did not think it was the state's role to offer preferential treatment to married couples – however limited and symbolic – through the tax and benefit system. Nor was it certain that such a measure would be approved by the Commons. The Con–Lib programme for government promised that Lib Dems could 'abstain on budget resolutions to introduce transferable tax allowances for married couples without prejudice to the coalition agreement'. The promise to recognize marriage in the tax system had figured in Cameron's very first speech as a leadership candidate in 2005, and helped to persuade many traditionalist Tories that the young modernizer was still a Conservative to his fingertips and a friend of the most basic social institution. To such MPs, the riots and the ensuing debate on family breakdown seemed the ideal circumstances in which to make a reality of the six-year-old promise. But they were to be disappointed.

Instead, the PM unveiled the £448m 'Troubled Families Initiative' in December, presenting the scheme as a coherent policy response to the flames and rage of the summer. 'While the Government's immediate duty is to deal with the budget deficit,' Cameron said, 'my mission in politics – the thing I am really passionate about – is fixing the responsibility deficit.' There were, he continued, 120,000 families that had cost the taxpayer £9bn in the preceding year – or £75,000 per household. His Government would set its face against the 'compassionate cruelty' that trapped such families in welfare dependency, subjected them to 'endless state schemes and interventions' and judged success 'by how much is spent on the consequences of failure'.

From now on, he said, each such household would have 'a single port of call and a single face to know' – a named 'family worker' – rather than multiple state agencies contradicting one another and entangling themselves and others in bureaucracy. In the jargon, the help offered to these families was too 'silo-based', and that had to stop.

The driving force behind the initiative was Hilton. Usually a passionate decentralizer, Cameron's senior adviser argued that, in this case, central control was essential. He persuaded the PM to appoint Louise Casey to head the new Troubled Families Unit, in spite of her New Labour pedigree (she had already led Blair's Respect Task Force and, since March 2010, held the post of Commissioner for Victims and Witnesses). Eric Pickles, as Secretary of State for Communities and Local Government, would take the lead in Cabinet, but Hilton's plan was for the unit to have the status of a semi-independent agency and to assume direct supervision of the 120,000 families. 'Their names and addresses should be written on the walls,' he said, speaking metaphorically – but only just. He agreed with Casey that there should be three very simple measurements of success. First, those in the family who could work should be employed or on their way to employment. Second, children should be attending school and truancy scorched out of the family's habits. Third, no member of the family should be in trouble with the law for six months – or another agreed milestone.

To Hilton's fury, these three tests were sent out to Whitehall – and returned, in dramatically expanded form, as eighty-seven measurements. On this matter, he prevailed, eventually. But he was unable to persuade his colleagues that local authorities had to be excluded from the management of these families if anything was to change. Heywood was adamant that town halls retain a role, in partnership with Casey's unit. Hilton feared that the people who had already failed these families would still be responsible for them, albeit in a new configuration. The compromise was that Heywood's solution should be tested and, if it was found wanting, ditched in favour of direct control by the unit. But Hilton knew a Whitehall stitch-up when he saw one.

What Cameron announced was the mixed scheme: 40 per cent of the cost of promising new schemes would be centrally funded if town halls could find the remaining 60 per cent. Never before had a family intervention policy been so localized – or risky. What if town halls 'cherry-picked' the more biddable families to work with, so that they could claim success – leaving the truly hardcore cases to their own devices? Would a few 'spot-checks' be enough to ensure town halls were playing fair? But the most important question could only be answered in Westminster and Whitehall. In the first instance at least, the initiative would last only until 2015, and was founded on optimistic assumptions about the pace of change. According to its own guidelines: 'you should be able to claim your results-based payments around 12 months after the intervention has started'.[19] In most cases, a year would barely be long enough to lay the foundations of change in a family's behaviour. What the initiative needed more even than resources was political stamina: the determination to keep going when the cameras moved on and the pundits lost interest in the mutilated social landscape revealed by the riots.

It was hard to disagree with the intentions of Cameron's project. But even in Number Ten, his advisers wondered how long it would command his attention, competing as it was with grim economic news, the Leveson Inquiry into the hacking scandal, the demands of Afghanistan and the stabilization of Libya, the European Union, pressure from Clegg to press ahead with House of Lords reform, and the increasingly restless mood of the Tory parliamentary party. Without the PM's hand firmly on the tiller, the initiative would become just another gravy train for shrewd town hall officials.

Clegg wanted in on the act, too. On 31 August, he announced the appointment of a 'Riots Communities and Victims Panel', under the chairmanship of Darra Singh, the chief executive of Jobcentre Plus. This was emphatically not a full public inquiry but a straightforward investigation that would report to all three party leaders and satisfy political honour without committing the Government to anything much. Singh was joined by Simon Marcus, the founder of the Boxing Academy in London, Baroness Sherlock, former chief executive of the National Council for One Parent Families, and Heather Rabbatts, a Jamaican-born British lawyer and former chief executive of the London Borough of Lambeth.

The panel delivered its interim report, *5 Days in August*, in November and then its final findings, *After the Riots*, in March 2012. Singh's panel heard representatives of the main public services describe a group of about 500,000 'forgotten families' which 'bump along the bottom' of society – four times as many as Cameron had identified.[20] Though the report was written in the language of the sociology seminar, the idea at the heart of its recommendations was surprisingly old-fashioned: namely, 'character'. This, the report concluded, was an amalgam of 'self-discipline, application, the ability to defer gratification and resilience in recovering from setbacks'.[21] Primary and secondary schools, it recommended, should 'undertake regular assessments of pupils' strength of character' and be required 'to develop and publish their policies on building character'.[22] Amongst its many recommendations, the final report proposed a series of unbreachable 'red lines': notably, that every child should be able to read and write to 'an age-appropriate standard' by the time he or she left school (and schools that failed should face penalties); that no offender should return to the community from prison without 'wraparound support'; and that every child should have 'the skills and character attributes to prepare them for work' when he or she left education.[23]

There was little in this document with which Cameron could disagree and much which meshed completely with his professed desire to repair the 'broken society' and to nurture 'social responsibility'. But this was always going to be a marathon rather than a sprint, in a political culture that increasingly valued speed over endurance and (for all the claims to the contrary) rewarded what Blair had called 'eye-catching initiatives' more generously than the long haul. Lammy complained that only eleven out of sixty-three proposals made by the panel were being implemented a year after the final report's publication.[24] On the social front, as in the economic battle, Cameron counselled patience. Though his Government had never agreed to adopt all the report's recommendations, he remained committed, he said, to the social policies that he hoped would be his true legacy. The question was whether Cameron would last long enough to test that commitment.

9. Gamble in the desert: the war against Gaddafi

David Cameron, dressed in casual black shirt and jeans, strode across the lawn of Dorneywood, enjoying the early-evening sun, and greeted the guests gathering for his host's party. It was Saturday, 18 June 2011, and George Osborne had invited friends to celebrate his fortieth birthday at the Chancellor's grace-and-favour home in Buckinghamshire (a few weeks late, in fact: he had begun his fifth decade on 23 May). The Prime Minister had just spoken by phone to Nicolas Sarkozy about progress in Libya, and was amused by the French President's gung-ho demands – which he duly mimicked: 'Zere must be more of ze raids! More raids!'

Osborne's wife, Frances, teased him that the party was an opportunity to marry himself – a celebration of his all-round wonderfulness – a joke the Chancellor had the good sense to repeat in his after-dinner speech. A cake with an image of his face in the icing was brought out and the host, Cameron and Hague chatted quietly for a moment amid the blue balloons as the revelry continued. The next-door squash court had been converted into a disco for the evening. Pictures were taken of the assembled veterans of Hague's leadership years – Osborne, Daniel Finkelstein (by then a senior executive at *The Times*), Baroness (Tina) Stowell and the Foreign Secretary himself. A coalition governing in times of austerity enjoys few moments of celebration, its grip on power always provisional and uncertain. But more than one guest remarked that the Conservative Party was at last permitting itself to believe that it had escaped thirteen years of Opposition – albeit by an unconventional route.

Cameron, too, was evolving as Prime Minister. When he first contemplated a run at the leadership in 2005, one of his priorities had been to restore the focus of politics to domestic matters and away from the global adventures of 'you neo-cons'. In this, he differed markedly from two of his closest lieutenants, Osborne and Gove, both of whom were strong believers in interventionist foreign policy. Indeed, Gove had written a book on fundamentalist terror that became required reading for policy makers on both sides of the Atlantic and was seen in the hands of John McCain, the Republican presidential nominee in 2008.[1] Had the Tory leader been told then that one of the principal acts of his first years in Number Ten would be to lead an Anglo-French campaign in Libya, he would have laughed out loud.

Though persuaded to vote for the Iraq War by party loyalty and Blair's passionate parliamentary rhetoric, he had harboured grave doubts about its wisdom. Nor did he sign up to the so-called 'Chicago doctrine' of liberal intervention as defined by Blair in 1999 in response to the Balkan tragedy. On the fifth anniversary of 9/11, Cameron had delivered a speech that had caused considerable offence in the US, distinguishing 'neo-Conservatism' from his own fledgling brand of 'liberal Conservatism'. According to Cameron: 'We will serve neither our own, nor America's, nor the world's interests if we are seen as America's unconditional associate in every endeavour.' Democracy, he continued, 'cannot quickly be imposed from outside', just as 'liberty grows from the ground – it cannot be dropped from the air by an unmanned drone'. The principle of multilateralism, so badly mauled by Iraq, must be mended. It was time for 'humility and patience'. The Bush White House had clashed with Michael Howard. Republican strategists wondered whether his protégé was cut from the same cloth.

By the time Cameron entered Number Ten, Barack Obama was President and – he made directly clear to the new Prime Minister – more interested in 'ending wars than starting them'. He liked to quote the warning of the sixth President, John Quincy Adams, that America should not go 'abroad in search of monsters to destroy'. Cameron had no quarrel with that principle. He had established the National Security Council to bring week-by-week coherence to foreign and security policy; and launched the Strategic Defence and Security Review to align Britain's defence capability with contemporary threats and (more painfully) with the fiscal realities inherited by the Coalition. Visitors to Number Ten in those first days were left in absolutely no doubt that his remorseless priorities would be economic recovery, public service reform and social cohesion: no more wars, in other words.

As for the conflict in Afghanistan, Cameron believed that the original intervention in 2001 had been just and necessary; but that, nine years on, there were severe practical limits to what could still be achieved. In principle, he backed the surge strategy drawn up by General Stanley McChrystal, commander of the International Security Assistance Force in Afghanistan. But he suffered no delusions about what was achievable, given the resources and political capital that the international community was now willing to expend. Like Obama, he wanted to leave Afghanistan in a state of comparative stability, making progress in the development of civil society and the maintenance of law and order. Like William Hague, he believed there were elements of the Taliban who could be recruited to this cause, if only because they themselves wanted a secure stake in postwar Afghanistan. But he dismissed as ludicrous the idea that Britain should stay as a nation-building garrison power for the decades it would take to construct a fully functioning democracy. If that had ever been a realistic objective, it had long ceased to be so.[2]

Though he landed in hot water for using a medieval allusion, Liam Fox spoke for the Government when he told *The Times*: 'What we want is a stable enough Afghanistan, able to look after its own security so we can leave without the fear of it imploding . . . But let's be clear – it's not going to be perfect . . . We are not in Afghanistan for the sake of the education policy in a broken 13th-century country. We are there so the people of Britain and our global interests are not threatened.'[3]

Cameron's aides angrily denied any suggestion of defeatism. When it came to the Afghan campaign, they pointed out, the weather was made in Washington – and the weather forecast was absolutely unambiguous. The US Vice-President, Joe Biden, who had always been sceptical about the surge in Afghanistan, spelt it out: 'We're going to be totally out of there, come hell or high water, by 2014.' For Cameron, the question was not whether to withdraw, or even what the deadline for departure should be, but how to achieve a dignified and secure exit – bearing in mind that military withdrawal is always perilous.

Immersed in a huge fiscal project, busy with welfare and education reform, distracted by the debacle of the NHS plan, drawn ever deeper into the hacking scandal, and struggling always to please both his own backbenchers and his Coalition partners, the last thing Cameron needed in 2011 was a military engagement. Yet this is not only what he got, but what he actively sought when he realized the potential human cost of inaction in Libya.

The backdrop to the conflict was the Arab Spring, the astonishing wave of insurgency, civil resistance and democratization that began on 18 December 2010, in Tunisia, after the self-immolation of a street vendor, Mohamed Bouazizi, in protest at harassment by police and municipal officials. In less than two years, the governments of four countries fell, unrest spread throughout the region and the geopolitical landscape was transformed from Mauritania in the west to Oman in the east. Hague quickly drew the radical conclusion that this wave of change was of greater historical significance than 9/11.[4]

The Gaddafi regime was awkwardly poised as the sands of an entire region shifted and shuddered. In March 2004, Blair had met the dictator at a dune summit symbolic of Libya's conditional return to the family of nations. Over fish couscous, the Colonel and the New Labour Prime Minister sealed a deal that secured for Britain a strategic and commercial foothold in the Arab world, ended Gaddafi's WMD programme, and played a part in the disclosure of the illicit Pakistani trade with the Middle East in nuclear technology. Blair hoped that this would be no more than a transitional arrangement – as proved to be the case. But in 2004 it was the only deal on the table.[5]

The Arab Spring had transformed the terms of trade in Libya, as elsewhere. Saif Gaddafi, the dictator's son, called Hague and made a bizarre request for help. The Foreign Secretary's advice was brusque: 'Start being democratic.' There were scattered protests against the regime in mid-January, mostly in the east, but it was not until the following month that the uprising began in earnest. On 15 February, the arrest of Fethi Tarbel, a lawyer and human rights activist, triggered a riot in Benghazi, in which 600 protesters clashed with the police. The disturbances spread quickly to Quba, Zintan, Derna and al Bayda, and were met with bloody reprisal and the deployment of water cannon. Gaddafi was clearly willing to do anything to cling to power: in Benghazi he released inmates from prison, gave them weapons and recruited them as mercenaries to fight the rebels. There was some early evidence of scattered side-switching by police and of fighter pilots defecting to Malta. But hospitals were fast running out of supplies and vulnerable to attack by loyalist militias. On 20 February, the protest spread to Tripoli and Saif Gaddafi appeared on state television to blame the unrest on the intervention of 'foreign agents'. In fact, it was the regime that was now importing mercenaries from Chad, Mali, Niger, Zimbabwe and Liberia, paying them up to $2,000 a day. Saif's peroration might have been delivered by his father: 'We will fight to the last man and woman and bullet. We will not lose Libya. We will not let Al Jazeera, Al Arabiya and [the] BBC trick us.'

The Coalition's initial response to the crisis was inglorious. Hague publicized a baseless rumour that Gaddafi was on his way to Venezuela. It became a private joke among officials to get the Foreign Secretary to say 'Benghazi' as often as possible – the long second syllable bequeathed by his northern accent ('Bengh*aaaaaz*i') causing stifled giggles on more than one occasion. Cameron was on tour with arms manufacturers, while Clegg, on the Swiss piste, 'forgot' he was meant to be Acting Prime Minister. At this point, only the French President, Nicolas Sarkozy, had the measure of the threat, calling on 23 February for a no-fly zone to 'prevent the use of that country's warplanes against [its] population'.[6] Such an intervention would prevent Gaddafi from importing mercenaries by air and attacking his own people from the skies, and would enable allied jets to take out his defences and military infrastructure. Elsewhere, heads of government were afflicted by a sort of global aphasia that had been intermittently apparent since the Iraq War: an inability to speak meaningfully about such emergencies. The silence was punctuated only by banalities.

Within a week, hundreds were reported to be dead – perhaps more than a thousand – and, as the riots continued in Tripoli, Cameron declared that the violence was 'appalling and unacceptable'. In addition to his regular updates from Hague, he was reading intelligence briefings, talking to Llewellyn and watching the saga unfold on television. On 22 February, in a speech that lasted an hour and a quarter, Gaddafi promised to 'fight until the last drop of blood is spilt' and to 'cleanse Libya house by house'. The despot blamed hallucinogens, Islamists and foreign powers for the collapse of order. Clearly, the Colonel's grip on reality – long tenuous – had loosened decisively, and it was no longer safe to assume that he would respond rationally to diplomacy or face-saving solutions. Llewellyn regarded this speech as a turning-point and told his boss so.

Major General Abdul Fatah Younis, Interior Minister and often regarded as the ruler's de facto deputy, had had enough. 'I told Gaddafi, we have too many unemployed youth,' he told Al Arabiya. 'I want that dirty person who shot my cousin to face justice. I am not a two-faced man. I worked with Gaddafi for forty-two years, I was shocked at his speech today.' Sufficiently shocked, indeed, to sign up as commander-in-chief of the rebel forces. Meanwhile, Mustafa Abdul Jalil, the former Justice Minister, claimed that the Colonel had personally masterminded the 1988 Lockerbie atrocity in which 270 people were killed. The 42-year-old regime of the 'mad dog' seemed to be unravelling by the hour. But that perception was premature. In Number Ten, Cameron and Llewellyn were examining the options in ever greater detail – military intervention being one of them.

At this point, Hague's priority was the safety of the 3,500 British nationals who had yet to leave Libya, and the despatch of chartered planes to bring them home. According to one Cabinet minister who was wired into Downing Street's thinking: 'William was getting a kicking in the media for not moving into gear fast enough. There was a tremor of alarm in Number Ten – I'll put it no more strongly than that – that he was dragging his heels a bit.' The frigate HMS *Cumberland* was sent to international waters nearby so it could quickly assist with the evacuation if necessary. For now, Cameron confined himself to stronger language. In remarks disclosed on 24 February, he said: 'These actions, yes, they must have consequences – consequences in the UN Security Council, consequences for those responsible for them and we should, as Barack Obama said, look at the full range of options in doing that.'[7] Behind the scenes, Cameron was increasingly convinced that at least the threat of a no-fly zone would be needed – and probably its imposition. On the same day, anti-regime militias seized control of the north-western coastal city of Misrata.

Now the rebels had shown themselves capable of seizing territory. In the National Security Council, Cameron put to the meeting the pivotal question: 'Is it in our national interest or not to get involved?' As far as the PM was concerned, the question answered itself. If Gaddafi crushed the opposition and Libya became a pariah state once more it would be a grievous source of instability on Europe's door-step – a refugee crisis waiting to happen. The country was already responsible for 2 per cent of global oil production, with much greater potential in its reserves. Libya was central to Britain's strategic and commercial interests in the region. What message would it send to the world if the mad Colonel was now left to crush the rebels and embark upon bloody reprisals?

After early successes in the oil port of Ra's Lanuf on 4 March and in Bin Jawad the next day, the rebels had faced a ten-day loyalist counter-offensive. Bin Jawad was back in the hands of pro-Gaddafi forces by the morning of Monday, 7 March. As battle raged in Zawiya and the dictator's jets pounded Ra's Lanuf, Cameron told his Cabinet at a special regional meeting in Derby that a no-fly zone was now absolutely essential, and that all diplomatic and political forces must be deployed to achieve international agreement.

Strategic calculation aside, the PM had no wish to be a bystander as a massacre unfolded in North Africa. His critique of Blair's liberal interventionism and American neo-conservatism did not, he explained, mean that he proposed to 'pull up the drawbridge'. He had often quoted Gladstone's Midlothian maxim that 'the foreign policy of England should always be inspired by a love of freedom'. A liberal conservative foreign policy, he insisted, was neither isolationist nor drained of all ethical content.

When it came to foreign affairs, he was much influenced by his chief of staff, Ed Llewellyn, who had a detailed knowledge of the world's chanceries and supranational institutions. Llewellyn had worked alongside Paddy Ashdown when he was High Representative for Bosnia and Herzegovina (2002–6) and brought to the table a folkloric memory of the Srebrenica atrocity in 1995 when 6,000 Muslims had been massacred by Serbs in the 'Marathon of Death'.[8] Cameron did not share Blair's ambition to 'reorder this world around us'. But he could not, in all conscience, stand aside as the horrors of Srebrenica and Rwanda were replayed in North Africa.

His decision to support Sarkozy in calling for a no-fly zone and to deploy what leverage he had with Obama in favour of engagement was a serious risk. In lighter moments, the PM had always enjoyed characterizing the foreign policy positions of his senior ministers. Osborne and Gove were the 'neo-cons' – especially the Education Secretary, who, Cameron joked, 'is only allowed to talk about foreign policy occasionally in case he gets too excited'. Letwin, though fiercely proud of his Jewish ancestry, was often sceptical about Israel's actions. Clegg was known by the PM and his aides as the 'Rt Hon. Member for Palestine'. Hague and Fox were Atlanticists to the core, but had greater sympathy with the Realpolitik of, say, Henry Kissinger than with the nation-building ambitions of the truly Jeffersonian neo-cons who had steered US policy towards the invasion of Iraq.

Ken Clarke had defied the party whip to vote against the attack on Saddam Hussein in 2003, and he had little interest in foreign policy adventures – the offices of Foreign Secretary and Defence Secretary being two of the very few senior Cabinet posts he had not held in his illustrious career. With the knowing chuckle of a minister who has seen it all – including the tribal cartography – he said that Libya would be better off partitioned. Even as RAF Typhoons and Tornadoes were flying into Libyan airspace, the Justice Secretary still insisted that he was 'not totally convinced anyone knows where we are going now'.[9]

As Cameron would later find in the furore over gay marriage, the Tory Party and its supporters in the press had little patience with enterprises that, in their view, distracted him from the central object-ive of economic recovery. He could be no more certain of the conflict's potential duration, scope and human cost than the Desert Rats had been in 1940. Gove and Osborne backed him from the start, while the Defence Secretary and Hague took longer to be persuaded.

Fox was a friend of his US opposite number, Robert Gates – 'they talked all the time', according to one senior British official – and shared the concerns of the Pentagon: they were more worried about Yemen and Iran than Libya, and concerned that a protracted war with Gaddafi – if so it became – would drive the West's already over-stretched defence capability to breaking point. What if the Iranians took advantage of American and British absorption in the Maghreb to accelerate their nuclear enrichment? Fox regarded Europe as woe-fully under-prepared for conflict without US assistance in a broad range of areas – air-to-air refuelling, for instance, and ISTAR (Intel-ligence, Surveillance, Target Acquisition and Reconnaissance). The two defence secretaries were also sceptical that there was a fireproof plan in place for the post-Gaddafi aftermath. 'What outcome do we really want?' Fox repeatedly asked at NSC meetings.

Like most Prime Ministers, Cameron enjoyed dealing with the military and intelligence agencies – 'the professionals' as Blair had called them, a term sometimes borrowed by his self-styled Tory heir. But in this case the PM's team were sure that Sir John Sawers, chief of the Secret Intelligence Service ('C'), and General Sir David Richards, who had become Chief of Defence Staff in 2010, were opposed to the whole scheme. 'In the end, spooks and soldiers will do what their political masters tell them', according to one ally of Cameron, 'but they obviously thought: "Here we go again, another Prime Minister with a hare-brained war he wants to fight."'

In Cabinet, Gove was the most passionate supporter of action and, at the Cabinet's first thorough discussion of the crisis on 1 March, had made an intervention that, in a leak to *The Times*, was described as 'messianic' in its intensity.[10] Fox muttered that this was 'all very well for those who won't have to write the letters of condolence'.

Hague was on the back foot, expressing regret for intelligence failings in the Foreign Office. On Monday, 7 March, he came under further pressure in the Commons over a botched attempt to infiltrate a group of SIS officers and SAS members by helicopter – a diplomatic mission which ended with the British team under house arrest in Libya for four days. Sir Christopher Meyer, the former British ambassador to Washington, described the episode as a 'stonking, copper-bottomed fiasco'. The rebels themselves were mystified. 'It's just people coming from the sky and saying: we want to negotiate,' said Iman Bugaighis, a spokesman for the rebel council. 'They said they want to see the new government. But it was really weird because there are other ways to negotiate than landing by helicopter in a field without telling us you're coming.'[11]

'You are seeing the slow eclipse of William,' claimed one senior colleague at the time, 'and the emergence of George as the real Deputy Prime Minister.' This Tory underestimated Hague's resilience (and Osborne's loyalty to him). As the Chancellor's mentor, and a former party leader quite familiar with the peaks and troughs of politics, he felt much less threatened than some colleagues assumed. Nonetheless, it was clear that, for the time being, the Osborne–Gove axis was in the ascendant. Pressed on the matter, the Foreign Secretary maintained his zen-like calm. When the *Sunday Telegraph* asked him whether there were any neo-cons in the Cabinet, he replied: 'Well, there might be one or two.'[12] It was obvious whom he meant.

Clegg was hardly a neo-con, and felt uncomfortable when subjected to the full force of Gove's conviction. But his role in the crisis has been glossed over in most accounts, as if his support for Cameron reflected only the reluctant acquiescence of a Coalition partner anxious to preserve unity rather than agreement on the substance. In fact, the Deputy Prime Minister was as robust as Cameron and Osborne. 'He is, at heart, a liberal interventionist', according to one senior source, 'and he is good at the big picture stuff, too.' As others became lost in the quagmire of detail on Libya, Clegg would chip in at meetings: 'We *must* be doing this. It is the right thing to be doing.'

In the end, Cameron's decision to act was a lonely one, the action of a gambler rather than a risk-averse manager. What he now needed was utterly dependable counsel from people who would not panic if the campaign got sticky. In addition to Llewellyn, he had an experienced National Security Adviser in Sir Peter Ricketts, former Permanent Secretary at the Foreign Office and ex-chairman of the Joint Intelligence Committee. To run a central team on Libya and act as a point-man for the many departments and agencies involved, he appointed Hugh Powell – an official he regarded highly and trusted implicitly, who had been director of the Strategic Defence and Security Review and inherited the intellectual confidence of his father, Charles (now Lord Powell of Bayswater), Margaret Thatcher's closest adviser in Downing Street.

On 28 February, Cameron took the plunge and called publicly for a no-fly zone – only to be slapped down three days later by Gates, who witheringly scorned the proposal as 'loose talk'. Although the US Defense Secretary had not named the British Prime Minister, he did not have to. The message – offhand and dismissive – was loud and clear. The campaign did not need American leadership, but it did require American involvement. Cameron saw that, amongst everything else, the Libyan crisis was an opportunity to demonstrate to the US that such a campaign was possible: that Washington's support need not entail Washington assuming full responsibility, and that 'the Atlantic alliance' was not just a diplomatic way of describing US servicemen putting their lives at risk to solve all the world's security problems. Hillary Clinton, the US Secretary of State, was edging closer to Cameron's position – as was her husband, who still regretted his failure to act over the genocide in Rwanda. Obama remained positively sphinx-like, veering from the apparently robust to the confusingly reticent. On 23 February, he said that 'the suffering and bloodshed is outrageous, and it is unacceptable' and that he had ordered US forces 'to prepare the full range of options that we have to respond to this crisis'. Yet on 11 March he presented his continued indecision as somehow virtuous, a sign of considered statesmanship, and pledged only a 'wide range of actions' against the Libyan dictator.

Cameron found the President congenial company, admiring his poise, confidence and the apparent ease with which he took to the leadership of the free world. His own preference for smooth surfaces and civility meshed well with the measured political heartbeat of

'No Drama Obama'. But he grew increasingly exasperated, as the months passed, by the Commander-in-Chief's reluctance to get his hands dirty in the global workshop. 'I can't really get him to focus on problems like Iran and the Middle East,' he told one ally. 'He won't commit. It's unbelievably frustrating.' The President regarded war not only as a horror but as a personal affront, precisely because it marked the failure of the things at which he believed himself to excel: conciliation, diplomacy, the healing power of debate and rhetoric. The Obama story depended to a considerable extent upon the claim that he would end the wars he inherited from Bush, and reposition America by 'forging a new relationship with the world based on mutual interest and mutual respect'. To the extent that he wanted to spend political capital on the world stage it was in the Pacific region, where he believed America's destiny lay in the twenty-first century. On Libya, Cameron knew that the absolute maximum he could expect was a time-limited commitment to give strictly defined support to the Anglo-French initiative. With this President, in these circumstances, even that was a lot to ask.

Relentless British diplomacy helped to turn the tide in Washington as it had when Blair persuaded Bill Clinton to follow his lead in Kosovo. Cameron spoke to Obama, sometimes daily as the moment of decision drew near. He found the President scarcely more precise on the phone than he was in public, but hoped that the message was getting through. Hague spoke often to Clinton and Llewellyn to Elizabeth Sherwood-Randall, senior director for European affairs on the US National Security Council. Was the world's mightiest power really content to be trumped in the defence of liberty by the supposed 'cheese-eating surrender monkeys' of the Élysée? In essence, the answer to that mischievous question was: yes. But three women helped steer Obama away from paralysis and towards the minimal level of US commitment which Cameron sought: Hillary Clinton; Susan Rice, America's UN ambassador; and Samantha Power, director of the Office of Multilateral Affairs and Human Rights and author of *A Problem from Hell: America and the Age of Genocide*. Rice had worked for Bill Clinton's National Security Council at the time of the Rwandan atrocities in 1994 and was famously reported to have said: 'If we use the word "genocide" and are seen as doing nothing, what will be the effect on the November [congressional] election?' In an article written by Power for *The Atlantic* in 2001, Rice said: 'I swore to myself that if I ever faced such a crisis again, I would come down on the side of dramatic action, going down in flames if that was required.'[13] Now that moment had come.

Obama's counter-terrorism chief, John O. Brennan, and his National Security Advisor, Thomas E. Donilon, were no more enthusiastic than Gates. The Secretary of State herself remained sceptical about committing US troops to a third conflict well into March. Welcome as it was that Arab powers were ready to join the fight, she now realized that Gaddafi might not fall without Western intervention, and that there was a clear and present danger of unconscionable slaughter in Benghazi. Admiral Mike Mullen, chairman of the US Joint Chiefs of Staff, drew up a military plan that was signed off by the President after an hour-and-a-half-long meeting at the White House on Thursday, 17 March. There would be no boots on the ground, and the campaign would be strictly time-limited: 'days not weeks', Obama said.[14] The White House was soon briefing that America's commitment was 'time-limited and scope-limited'. The President's aides insisted that what might have looked like uncertainty was simply his usual deliberative method: careful assessment and analysis followed by a clear decision. Cameron was not so sure about that. He wondered whether Obama would ever have reached a verdict on Libya without a firm nudge in the right direction from the impressive Clinton–Rice–Power trio.

From the first Cabinet conversation about the Libyan campaign, the Prime Minister also made clear that the lessons of Iraq had to be taken on board. Andrew Mitchell, the International Development Secretary, assembled a Stabilization Response Team under Ben Mellor, a senior official in his department, to liaise with the National Transitional Council (which had been formed on 27 February and declared itself Libya's sole representative on 5 March) and to offer the fledgling administration whatever help it needed in restoring basic amenities and civilian governance. Long before the strongholds of Sirte and Tripoli had fallen, reconstruction was being discussed systematically. The most scandalous failure of the Iraq invasion had been the Pentagon's refusal to heed Colin Powell's warning about post-invasion instability and his plan for the restoration of civil order after Saddam's fall. Cameron was determined that the error would not be repeated.

Mindful of the controversy that still chased Blair's decision to take on Saddam, he also wanted to establish beyond reasonable doubt the legality of what he proposed. The punctilious Attorney General, Dominic Grieve, was involved at every stage and took the Prime Minister at his word – even vetoing a plan to drop 200 million new Libyan banknotes, worth £1bn, into the country to assist the rebels. It was patiently pointed out to the incredulous Cameron that the proposal would be a technical breach of a UN freeze on all Libyan assets.[15] 'What's the downside to doing it?' asked the PM. 'Can I be sent to jail?' Grieve answered calmly: 'Well, yes. You can.'

Even formal legality was not enough. Cameron wanted widely expressed international backing for the campaign – again, to forestall later arguments about its legitimacy, and, as one Cameroon put it, 'to get as many dabs as possible on the weapon'. At a special meeting in Cairo on 12 March, the Arab League formally backed the Cameron–Sarkozy proposal – compensation for the European Union's much more cautious statement, which promised only to 'examine all necessary options' to protect civilians, and for the lukewarm language adopted by the G8 in Paris on 15 March. The Arab League's endorsement was hugely important, as was the specific promise by the Emirates that they would pull their weight against Gaddafi.

The spotlight now moved to the United Nations, where Britain's ambassador, Sir Mark Lyall Grant, set about collecting enough votes for a Security Council resolution authorizing a no-fly zone.[16] In principle, Libya was the first real test of the 'Responsibility to Protect' (or R2P) doctrine in international law, codified by the UN World Summit in 2005, which mandated the 'collective use of force' by other nations where necessary, in order to prevent genocide and the slaughter of non-combatants. Theoretically, this represented a fundamental challenge to the idea of national territorial sovereignty rooted in the 1648 Treaty of Westphalia.

International jurisprudence was one thing; geopolitical reality quite another. 'The expectation in London was that the negotiations would fail', according to one close to the talks. 'We really didn't think it could be done.' Such a resolution requires nine affirmative votes but can be vetoed by any of the Security Council's five permanent members (America, Britain, France, Russia and China). Cameron and his colleagues hit the phones, the Foreign Secretary coming into his own as a calm but relentless persuader. Hague was a believer in bilateral relationships, rather than supranational institutions or blocs, as the most reliable foundation for multilateralism, and it was on that basis that he proceeded, drawing on the many personal alliances he had built since becoming Shadow Foreign Secretary in December 2005. At the Commons Foreign Affairs Select Committee, Bob Ainsworth, the former Defence Secretary, had tried to needle Hague about the 'percentage chance' of securing an agreement at the UN.[17] He was determined to prove the Labour MP wrong.

As the motion was tabled on Monday, 14 March, it seemed all too likely that Russia would throw it out. Vladimir Putin, the Russian Prime Minister, considered the resolution to be 'deficient and flawed; it allows everything and is reminiscent of a medieval call for a crusade'. But the Arab League's endorsement of the proposal made it less attractive for Putin to stand in its way. Russia agreed to abstain rather than oppose the plan; China, Germany, India and Brazil followed suit. On Thursday, 17 March, the UN Security Council passed Resolution 1973 with ten votes in favour and five abstentions – though only after Ambassador Rice had rushed from the chamber to find the South African representative. The text demanded 'the immediate establishment of a ceasefire and a complete end to violence and all attacks against, and abuses of, civilians', explicitly called for a no-fly zone and authorized member states 'to take all necessary measures . . . to protect civilians and civilian populated areas under threat of attack in the Libyan Arab Jamahiriya [Libya], including Benghazi, while excluding a foreign occupation force of any form on any part of Libyan territory'.

With a UN resolution of this clarity in his back pocket, Cameron knew that the support of the Commons would follow. But – again – it was essential that it be secured. On Monday, 21 March, Cameron reassured MPs repeatedly that this would not be 'another Iraq', that there was no prospect of an invasion, that there would be no 'occupying force'. Gaddafi's position might look untenable, but 'Libyans must determine their own future' – the alliance's task was simply to enforce the resolution. The Lower House supported the UN-backed intervention by 557 to thirteen. Only one Conservative MP, John Baron (Basildon and Billericay), voted against.

They had cut it fine. The UN had authorized intervention at the very eleventh hour, even as Gaddafi's forces closed in on Benghazi, on the north-east coast of Libya, his tanks rolling towards the city as supporting aircraft criss-crossed in the skies ahead. The loyalist counter-offensive had shaken the rebels to the core and snatched the initiative from the NTC. What had looked initially like a swift regime change threatened to become a civil war. 'It was absolutely clear', according to one Cabinet minister, 'that there was going to be a bloodbath if nobody stepped in.'

Gaddafi's representatives had repeatedly promised a ceasefire as the Security Council deliberated. But at first light on Saturday, 19 March, the battle of Benghazi began as his artillery unleashed its havoc on Libya's second city. Rocket launchers did their work along the southern side. Approaching from the west, past Garyounis University, T-72 tanks rolled towards the rebel strongholds, making bloody progress in their exchanges with rag-tag units armed only with Kalashnikovs, old howitzers, grenades, rocks and bricks. By 10.30 a.m., it seemed as though the loyalist forces were going to prevail and Gaddafi keep his terrible promise to exact vengeance.

Unexpectedly, the rebels bought themselves precious time by blasting at the Colonel's tanks from an old armoured vehicle that had been taken from a military store until the loyalist column started to beat a retreat. It was a brief reprieve. A rebel MiG-23BN crashed in the outskirts of the city, apparently shot down in error by friendly fire – a desperate image of amateurism in the face of veteran military dictatorship. But help was finally at hand.

In Paris, Sarkozy had gathered twenty-two senior figures – including Cameron; Hillary Clinton; the UN Secretary General, Ban Ki-Moon;

the Arab League Secretary General, Amr Moussa; and the French Prime Minister, François Fillon – for a meeting in the Élysée presidential palace. With unashamed theatricality, Sarko declared that France had 'decided to assume its role, its role before history', and that French planes were already airborne and about to strike. On one level, he had taken an outrageous liberty, indulging his love of showmanship at the end of a fantastically delicate diplomatic process. But it was difficult to deny Sarkozy his moment of triumph: he had been the first to venture out on a dangerous branch and had not lost his nerve. At that stage, Cameron and the other allies were less interested in who had fired the first shots of the allied campaign than in how effective the initial raids had been, and how Gaddafi would respond. Later, Cameron would recount Sarko's theatrical coup to his aides with a shrug as if to say: 'That's show business.'

As the French President had announced, sorties had indeed begun, Rafale fighter jets launching their first strikes at around 6.45 p.m., bombarding vehicles and tanks on the outskirts of Benghazi and on the main road into the city. It was only a few hours before a hundred British and American missiles were raining down on Gaddafi's communications infrastructure and airfields in the north. Air attacks resumed at 4 a.m. the following day, destroying at least seven tanks and two armoured personnel carriers.

A pattern of attack and counter-attack now asserted itself. Heavy fighting continued, not least in Misrata and Ajdabiya. Amid the skirmishes and full-scale battles, the rebels struggled to unite as a coherent force. On 23 March, an interim government was formed under Mahmoud Jibril, a Western-educated former protégé of Saif Gaddafi who proved essential in the early negotiations with Sarkozy, Clinton, Hague and others. But the NTC had a long way to travel before it could claim to control the country.

In London, Fox continued to fret about the trajectory of the campaign. Even those who found him a difficult colleague admired his application. So it was no surprise that, having taken personal control of the tactical dimension of the campaign, he set aside his concerns and focused upon it totally – even insisting on secure communications when he was on holiday in Spain so that he could assess its progress in real time. The question that worried him was: what next? Regime change was not in the UN mandate; Resolution 1973 explicitly forbade 'a foreign occupation force of any form' – no 'boots on the ground', in other words. As the weeks turned into months, and Gaddafi remained at large, the Defence Secretary was increasingly concerned about mission creep. How long, Fox wondered, before the option of sending in euphemistically titled 'military advisers' – as John F. Kennedy did in Vietnam in 1961 – started to be discussed seriously?

A book highly regarded by British defence strategists was *The Utility of Force* by General Sir Rupert Smith, which argued that we had moved from an age of 'industrial war' to an age of combat 'amongst the people'.[18] The Libyan campaign had been triggered by the urgent need to prevent slaughter in Benghazi. Its continued legitimacy – at home, as well as in Libya – depended upon the best targeting in the history of warfare, so that Cameron and his Coalition colleagues would be able to claim that civilian casualties had been kept to an absolute minimum.

The accuracy of the targeting was indeed extraordinary. Fox told colleagues delightedly of the successful use of precision weapons – notably Storm Shadow and Brimstone missiles. He was especially proud of a strike on a building in Tripoli where a snipers' nest had been destroyed without significant damage to the floors below. The first Gulf War had bequeathed an ugly fame to the euphemism 'collateral damage'. Fox dared to propose that, in such a conflict, no such loss of life was excusable.

In fact, this apparent triumph was the cause of serious tension behind the scenes. When a target was identified, a full and formal Collateral Damage Estimation (CDE) was conducted. As a guide to military decision-making, a computer-based Collateral Damage Model (CDM) was deployed to estimate the likely effect of different weapons on particular structures in given locations – rural, semi-rural, urban, and so on. In the Iraq War, any US estimate higher than thirty had to go to President Bush or Donald Rumsfeld, the Defense Secretary, to be signed off personally. The CDE system was the polar opposite of old-fashioned 'carpet bombing': the estimate had to be as small as possible, proportional to the military value of the target. As macabre as this calculation was, defence planners regarded it as an essential tool for military decision-makers operating under great pressure, often with very little time to authorize or veto a strike.

In the case of the Libyan conflict, Cameron's team discovered to their collective fury that Fox had unilaterally, without consultation, set the CDE at zero. Legally, the Defence Secretary was within his rights and believed himself to be pursuing an honourable and humanitarian course. Politically, it was an astonishing decision to have taken without informing the Prime Minister – ruling out, at a stroke, all targets where there was even a slight risk of civilian casualties. Cameron was furious that the Defence Secretary had not raised the issue. 'This is fucking *ridiculous*,' he exclaimed when informed of Fox's ethical freelancing. The Defence Secretary later told the *Guardian*: 'I was absolutely adamant that our collateral damage was set at zero. That was a bit controversial with some of our allies, but I argued we would need to exorcise the ghost of Iraq post-Gaddafi, and we could do that if we showed we had a higher regard for the lives of civilians, and had a different perception of the value of life, than the regime that was being replaced.'[19] Other senior figures drew a very different conclusion, arguing that the moral straitjacket in which Fox had tied up the planners often made it impossible to attack military targets and was, in the words of one member of the NSC, 'one of the reasons the war took so bloody long'.

America's involvement in the campaign was known by the code-name Operation Odyssey Dawn. On 31 March, Nato assumed sole command of the international effort under Operation Unified Protector: a disappointment for Sarkozy, who wanted an Anglo-French command to direct the operation next. At the same time, General Sir David Richards was urging Cameron to think hard about the acceptable duration of the campaign. 'We have done what we can militarily,' he would say. 'It is time now to act politically.' Though it had always been clear that Richards had reservations about the entire enterprise, Cameron and Osborne were impressed by his intellect and candour. 'We should have brought him in to replace [Sir Jock Stirrup] as soon as we arrived,' one senior minister observed. Thanks to cuts in the defence budget, he was also the last CDS to live in an apartment in Kensington Palace.

Though Cameron wanted a decisive ending to the military operation, he took Richards's point about political reality. Quietly, he kept his options open. There were signs that the Colonel might accept some form of internal exile – as long as he were allowed an adequate protection force to ensure his security. Not surprisingly, this was dismissed as impractical and certain to be completely unacceptable to the Libyan NTC. Secretly, therefore, Cabinet Office officials and MI6 officers prepared an exit strategy for Gaddafi in case it was necessary to strike a deal to end the conflict. Idi Amin had spent his last years in Saudi Arabia. But, for Gaddafi, Equatorial Guinea was chosen as a prospective retirement home: oil-rich but awesomely corrupt – one in five children died before they reached the age of five and 70 per cent of the population lived in deep poverty – this tiny republic did not recognize the jurisdiction of the International Criminal Court, which issued a warrant for Gaddafi's arrest on 27 June. Although the UK had no bilateral links with Equatorial Guinea and contributed only small amounts of aid to it through multilateral programmes, Andrew Mitchell, as Development Secretary, was able to assist the officials tasked with these delicate contingency plans, helping them make the necessary contacts in the capital, Malabo, and elsewhere.

Although the military campaign now bore the 'Nato' brand, much of the heavy lifting was carried out by the so-called 'Four Amigos': the UK, France, Qatar and the United Arab Emirates. Meanwhile, a strategic penny had dropped. Richards advised the Prime Minister – and the alliance as a whole – to shift the military focus from the east of Libya – Benghazi and Ajdabiya – to the west, a moment widely identified as the turning-point in the campaign. Sawers, the MI6 chief, was also fast to identify this fundamental error in the operation's first phase, and to suggest a transfer of resources and military focus to the west. According to one defence source: 'It was a case of everyone, the Prime Minister included, realizing: "Fuck, they're useless – fat colonels and amateurish students who didn't do peace-keeping."'

The question was what to do with this strategic insight. A top secret plan was drawn up, to be co-ordinated by a special ops cell in Paris at the offices of the French operational headquarters (CPCO). Allied special forces and intelligence officers would be sent into areas such as Misrata and Zintan – twelve teams of four to six, plus support infrastructure – to assist with rebel activity, tactical advice and targeting intelligence. The director of UK special forces, Major General Jacko Page, handled the London end of the operation – although, as one Cameron aide comments, 'Jacko took his time.' The Ministry of Defence, represented by Fox and Richards, and MI6 were unpersuaded. 'It won't work,' said one senior opponent. 'This is not decisive.' It was Cameron, Osborne and Clegg who recognized the potential, as well as the hazards, and authorized the operation. 'It was always the political leadership who were willing to take the risks,' said one Whitehall source. 'It was the senior officials who were fantastically risk-averse.'

The journey from UN Resolution 1973 on 17 March, to the storming of Gaddafi's Bab al-Aziziya compound in Tripoli on 23 August, to the death of the fallen dictator, as he tried to flee Sirte, on 20 October, was far from linear. The death of the rebels' army chief, Abdul Fatah Younis, on 28 July – at the hands of the men he had notionally commanded – was a measure of the disunity and mistrust which bedevilled the interim government. It frequently seemed that the conflict was doomed to degenerate into bloody stalemate. In London, even the more hawkish ministers and officials accepted that a negotiated settlement might be inevitable. Only in August did Cameron and his closest security advisers become privately convinced that victory was on the cards. Three factors had tilted the balance: the sheer martial determination of the Misrati and Zintani militias; the emerging connections between the towns, forming the basis of an urban governing network; and the unpublicized actions of special forces.

Long before its conclusion, Cameron was reaping a diplomatic dividend from his conduct in the Libyan conflict. In July 2003, Blair had told Congress that it remained America's responsibility to fight for freedom around the world, 'because destiny put you in this place in history, in this moment in time, and the task is yours to do'. America was tired of hearing about its destiny. Cameron had grasped that, and requested only that Obama make a limited commitment to the Libyan campaign. Operation Odyssey Dawn was indeed headed by General Carter Ham, head of US Africa Command. But, fourteen days after the original Security Council resolution, operational control had been transferred to Nato. Cameron, Sarkozy and Obama continued to hold regular three-way video-conferences: when it came to military might, America was still in a class of its own. Hague had forged a good relationship with Clinton, and spoke to her regularly – sometimes daily. But the Libyan conflict had shown America that it was no longer expected to be the ubiquitous global policeman, taking the lead every time a humanitarian disaster had to be averted or a tyrant overthrown.

In May, Obama paid a state visit to the United Kingdom, dramatizing the growing warmth between the two leaders and the enduring bond between their respective nations. 'Ours is not just a special relationship,' he and Cameron wrote in a joint *Times* article, 'it is an essential relationship – for us and for the world.'[20] They served burgers to military veterans and servicemen at a barbecue (Obama gave the PM a barbecue grill, which he often mentioned to guests at Chequers). The President addressed both Houses of Parliament in Westminster Hall, declaring his hope 'to reaffirm one of the oldest, one of the strongest alliances the world has ever known' and his belief that 'the United States and United Kingdom stand squarely on the side of those who long to be free. And now, we must show that we will back up those words with deeds.' Of Libya, he said that 'we will not relent until the people . . . are protected and the shadow of tyranny is lifted'. The President had moved a long way since early March, and for that Cameron was at least partly responsible.

Only days after the death of Osama bin Laden, Obama was surfing high in the opinion polls. The Prime Minister did not expect his visible affinity with the leader of the free world to translate into a transfusion of popularity: politics, he knew, did not work like that. But Cameron also understood that a British Prime Minister could not achieve much on the world stage unless he enjoyed at least cordial relations with the President of the United States. Blair, he believed, had turned this principle into a fetish. But the principle remained sound. It was essential for any occupant of Number Ten to be taken seriously by the White House. And Cameron was already making plans involving Britain's relationship with Europe that might have transformative implications for its perceived position in the world (see Chapter 13). It was more important than ever that he be taken seriously as an international statesman, rather than seen by other heads of government as a struggling party leader in hock to his ideologically fixated backbenchers. In that context, Obama's blessing – his status as the First Friend – was worth having.

After the fall of Gaddafi, Fox was heard to say: 'We were lucky.' But he himself was not. In October, his friendship with a 34-year-old fellow Scot called Adam Werritty became the subject of daily media coverage. Werritty was one of Fox's closest friends, a longtime business associate and the former chief executive of the Atlantic Bridge, an Atlanticist research and campaigning body set up by Fox in 1997 with Margaret Thatcher as its president. He had also been best man at Fox's wedding to Esme Baird in 2005. But what attracted attention was Werritty's adhesive proximity to the Defence Secretary, even when he was on Crown business. Though he had not been security-cleared by the MoD, he was present at forty of Fox's seventy official recorded engagements, visited him twenty-two times in sixteen months, and was present on eighteen of his trips abroad. Salacious insinuations of Edwardian homoeroticism (strongly denied by friends of Fox) helped keep the story alive. But its essence was the question of operational security and the ease with which Werritty had apparently swanned into the inner sanctum of the MoD. The intensity of the two men's friendship would have been entirely their own business had it not become so entangled with Fox's work. The scandal made the Defence Secretary seem like a modern-day Bob Boothby: a liability and a law unto himself. The impression was scarcely fair: even Fox's detractors acknowledged that he was ferociously patriotic and dedicated to his work. But his judgement had unquestionably faltered.

Pressed in the Commons on Werritty's access to sensitive material, the Defence Secretary insisted that 'at no point did he attend departmental meetings, at no point did he have access to classified documents, and at no point was national security at risk'.[21] But Werritty had allowed quite the opposite impression to arise, handing out business cards, embossed with the House of Commons logo, that described him as 'advisor to the Rt Hon. Dr Fox MP'. It emerged that Ursula Brennan, Permanent Secretary at the MoD, had spoken to Fox in August about the cards. It was also reported that Sir Jock Stirrup, the former CDS, had warned the Defence Secretary about Werritty's omnipresence – a conversation Fox could not recall.

Brennan was tasked with investigating Fox's links with his friend, prior to a full report by Sir Gus O'Donnell, the Cabinet Secretary. Each day, the saga acquired a new twist. Werritty was alleged to be a Mossad asset, unwitting or otherwise. He was said to be plotting regime change in Tehran. He had links to the radical Right in the US. What had started life as an investigation into lax security was becoming a comic opera. Struggling under the weight of speculation, intrigue and sheer absurdity, Fox resigned on 14 October. Philip Hammond moved from Transport to take the post of Defence Secretary, while Justine Greening was brought in from her ministerial position at the Treasury to replace Hammond.

The Tory Right, still represented in the Cabinet by Iain Duncan Smith and Owen Paterson, felt that they had lost their most robust champion in the Coalition oligarchy. But the true lessons of the Werritty affair were structural. Access to Cabinet ministers is the most precious currency in Whitehall, but – time and again – it had been debauched. The Coalition Agreement promised that 'we will regulate lobbying through introducing a statutory register of lobbyists and ensuring greater transparency' – but such regulation had scarcely been a priority for a Government confronted by economic crisis. Why had Werritty behaved as he did? Because he could. In Number Ten and the Cabinet Office, the scandal had been a wake-up call. 'There is Before Werritty,' one official said, 'and After Werritty. That can never happen again, and we'll have to let ministers have more official, vetted Special Advisers if that's what it takes.'

About no senior colleague did Cameron and Osborne feel such ambivalence. By the time Fox left they could not wait to see the back of him, appalled at the sheer recklessness of the Werritty connection. 'Dave did his best to be sympathetic when Liam was resigning', according to one source. 'But it was getting pretty terse all round.' Fox was disowned by Downing Street in the immediate aftermath of his resignation, though privately Cameron and Osborne expected him to return to the Government before the 2015 election. He would never be part of Dave's gang, and never wanted to be. Some of the Cameroons regarded him as odd, edgy or even plain weird, inclined to bring unease to the table. But the Prime Minister and Chancellor respected his talent and the political belligerence they had faced first-hand in the 2005 leadership contest. He would be back.

Fox's resignation was a sour postscript to a remarkable period in the life of the Coalition, in which the two governing parties had shown that they could collaborate on foreign policy as well as fiscal strategy. Cameron had also confounded the notion that he was a bloodless pragmatist, averse to risk and unpredictability. 'He is actually a gambler,' said one who was close to him during the conflict. 'It goes back to the side of him that loves playing bridge, and all that.' Of course, Cameron wanted to stick to the rules and avoid the controversies of Iraq. But – to an extent that has never been properly appreciated – he was prepared to go into battle even without UN approval. At the special Cabinet in Derby on 7 March, he had told his colleagues that a no-fly zone would not require a specific UN Security Council resolution. Though the idea was not discussed formally at the National Security Council or in Cabinet, his closest advisers even considered the possibility of going it alone, without American support. 'Not desirable, but possible,' said one Cabinet minister at the time. It is doubtful that a successful no-fly zone could have been imposed in time to save Benghazi without US assistance. But the fact that Cameron's inner circle was even contemplating such a prospect is a measure of the Prime Minister's readiness to risk all on the fate of a single North African city.

For those who had long acquaintance with him, Cameron's experience in the Libyan conflict was pivotal. It was, in the words of one friend, 'the moment when Dave said to himself – "Wait a moment – I have the levers of power."' Like Thatcher, he grasped that a Prime

Minister had to dominate the detail (as he had failed to do in the case of NHS reform), to have the courage to insist, and to be counter-cultural within the Government, questioning received wisdom and stale orthodoxy. Cameron was 'visibly energized', according to an NSC attendee, by the process. 'It was tense, but he was physically different – as if he had really found his form and his role', in the words of one source.

The National Security Council – or, more accurately, its Libya committee, NSCL – met sixty-eight times during the conflict. At the end of the operation, Osborne rewarded each member with a commemorative set of dinar coins. But the greatest reward was the satisfaction that a horrific slaughter had been averted by allied intervention. When Hague visited Benghazi in June, he was touched by the sight of people rushing up to him in the street, shouting: 'Mr William! Mr William!' Cameron knew there would be no political dividend from the fall of Gaddafi, and had expected none. The days of the khaki election were long past. But that was not why he had thrown the dice. As one Cabinet minister put it: 'Whenever things get bad, and the press is saying what a rubbish government we are, I remind myself that there are people alive in Benghazi tonight because we decided to take a risk.'

10. The ballad of Steve and Jeremy

'You fucking lied!' Thus did the Prime Minister's senior adviser address the Head of the Home Civil Service. The words hung in the air, crackling with unanswerable belligerence. Steve Hilton's colleagues were used to his temper – but this outburst of incandescent rage was of a different order. He was now addressing Sir Bob Kerslake, who (Hilton believed) had seriously misrepresented what he, the PM's right-hand man, had previously said on the sensitive matter of Civil Service cuts and the size of Whitehall departments. The bearded Kerslake could barely believe his ears.

It was the afternoon of 8 May 2012, in Francis Maude's office at the Cabinet Office overlooking Horse Guards. Maude himself intervened: 'You can't talk like that, Steve.' The minister and his colleagues waited uncomfortably for the next move. Hilton, red-faced and inconsolable, was standing up now. At least one of those present wondered if he might try to hit the astonished Kerslake. Instead, Hilton marched out, swearing ('fuck it!') as he slammed the door behind him.

What none of the astonished participants in the meeting knew was that, as real as Hilton's fury was, the form it had taken was a private joke. He had been much amused by a passage in Walter Isaacson's biography of Steve Jobs. During the development of the iPod, Jobs had been determined that the new device should only be available to those who used Apple computers. For obvious commercial reasons, his team also wanted PC users to be able to own iPods. After one such meeting, Jobs yelled: 'Screw it. I'm sick of listening to you assholes. Go do whatever the hell you want.' It was this incident that Hilton had in mind – and mimicked – as he berated Kerslake.[1]

By this point, Hilton was behaving recklessly and theatrically, having revealed in March his intention to take a 'sabbatical' from

Number Ten. Officially, he was leaving for family reasons: his wife, Rachel Whetstone, was now based at Google's global headquarters in Mountain View in California, and, with two young sons, the couple had to make some difficult decisions about their medium-term future. These questions were real enough. But the sharpest incentive to leave was Hilton's growing sense of isolation in Number Ten and sadness that what he had assumed was a shared philosophy of government was no such thing.

By the time he left Downing Street, he felt an ideological kinship only with Oliver Letwin, Gove and Rohan Silva. Osborne, he knew, was positively hostile to his drive for decentralization – and openly so. Ed Llewellyn, he believed, had gone completely native, siding with the mandarins, always anxious about upsetting Heywood or Kerslake. More than once Llewellyn took him aside after the latest round of mutterings and urged Hilton to cool it. 'Look, Steve,' he would say, 'you've got to watch it.' There was a background of complaints, he continued, and 'we don't want that sort of reputation'.

In such situations, Hilton knew he was always likely to lose. As intermittently mesmerized by him as Cameron undoubtedly was – 'Steve is the Dave Whisperer', according to one friend of both men – he knew that the Prime Minister would always back Llewellyn in matters of protocol and practice. Cabinet ministers had learned not to broach the subject. On one occasion, Eric Pickles suggested that Number Ten needed new staff who were more overtly political. Cameron interpreted the remark as an attack on his chief of staff. 'No, no,' the PM said, 'Ed has served the party for so many years. And he's loyal.' Pickles tried again, being as jovial as he could. 'Prime Minister, I love you like a brother, but –' To his astonishment, Cameron exploded: 'Eric, I'm not listening to any more of this!'[2]

Hilton's detractors claimed that he was never a team player and that he was too easily distracted by stunts. Why, colleagues wondered, was he so keen to get the pop singer Prince to come to Number Ten? What could possibly be achieved by an awkward encounter between the Prime Minister and a diminutive rock legend long past his peak? It was assumed that he and Osborne felt a residual fondness for Hilton – they were co-creators of the Cameron Project –

but were also exasperated by his impatience, his wilful eccentricity and his refusal to accept the pace and parameters of government. There were times when he reminded Osborne of Michael Heseltine and his love of the *grand projet* – but without Heseltine's political magic.

Hilton's capacity for fury – the flipside of a mostly gentle and generous temperament – had often been an issue, too. During the election campaign, he and Coulson had clashed over his offhand treatment of staff in meetings. 'You're pissing me off, and you're pissing them off,' the communications chief was heard saying. In late 2012, Andrew Mitchell lost his Cabinet post over an alleged altercation with the police in Downing Street. In this respect, as in others, Hilton was the trailblazer, often having rows at security checks around Westminster over his bike or inability to find his pass. A passionate streak of anti-authoritarianism coursed through him – and on one occasion nearly landed him in the cells.

After Cameron's conference speech in October 2008, Hilton scrambled into the vehicle that would take him to Birmingham New Street station, where the Tory leader's train was about to depart. At the barrier, he could not find his ticket and was furious when the station staff refused to let him through. He became abusive and police officers were quickly called to the scene. Attempts to calm him down had the opposite effect. He swore under his breath – at which point he was arrested. Kate Fall was calling desperately from the train, wanting to know where the rest of the Tory leader's entourage had got to.

By now, Hilton was in plastic cuffs, with his head up against a wall. He was led to an upstairs office, where the red mist subsided sufficiently for him to realize the scale of his predicament. In the event, profuse apologies did the trick, and Hilton was not locked up – escaping with an £80 penalty notice for disorder under Section 5 of the Public Order Act. Escapes do not come much narrower: only a few hours before, Cameron had used his speech to berate our society's shoddy treatment of the police and its 'culture of incivility'. Much of that speech had been drafted by Hilton himself.

So it was no surprise to any of his Number Ten colleagues when

Heywood referred to his combative nature in evidence to MPs in January 2013. 'The way Steve operates is to challenge,' he told the Commons Public Administration Select Committee. 'Steve is a very challenging person.' In Hilton's absence – now that he was teaching at Stanford University – an orthodoxy had hardened in Whitehall that he had been essentially unsuited to government: a talented campaigner and brand manager but not a reformer. But that was a lazy caricature of a complex personality whose exit said as much about the system he had tried to change and the Prime Minister for whom he worked as it did about him.[3]

As a former protégé of Maurice Saatchi, Hilton had 'made his bones' looking for messages and ads that could keep the Tory Party in power; his professional background was a gravitational force that drew him naturally towards political imagery, communications and sloganeering. This led many to suppose that his preoccupations were essentially cosmetic and his convictions pliable. In fact, the opposite was true. Hilton, the son of Hungarian refugees, believed passionately in personal liberty and social responsibility and deplored the extent to which the words 'society' and 'state' had become interchangeable. The 'Big Society' may not have swayed many hearts and minds in the 2010 election, but it reflected a coherent philosophy, and one that welded Cameron's patrician Toryism to Hilton's profound belief that individuals, families, neighbourhoods, businesses and charities were the true building blocks of a civic order.[4] The twentieth century had belonged to the state – benignly in the introduction of universal healthcare, free education and (at first) the postwar welfare revolution; pathologically so in the abominations of Nazism and the Soviet system. In Hilton's eyes, the twenty-first should be the 'post-bureaucratic age' in which power was radically decentralized and devolved so that decisions really were made at the lowest conceivable level. The engine of change, he believed, would be the digital revolution, which would empower citizens with data to an extent that was previously unthinkable.

In this crusade, his principal ally was Rohan Silva, senior policy adviser to the PM and former fast-stream analyst at the Treasury, who had initially been talent-spotted while still in his mid-twenties by Osborne and recruited to the Tory cause. Young, clever and cultured – he was a trustee of the Whitechapel Gallery and Battersea Arts Centre – Silva had been an intern in the office of the Labour MP Nigel Griffiths. But the writings of Isaiah Berlin and Karl Popper had made him sceptical about left-wing statism. His belief in the liberating power of digital technology and openness matched and sometimes surpassed Hilton's: a passion expressed in his championship of 'Tech City', the digital hub at Old Street in east London.

In the first days of the Coalition, Hilton and Silva had urged Cameron to send out a series of papers to Whitehall immediately, demanding transparency. They were struck – though not surprised – by the force with which O'Donnell resisted the requests, insisting that only demonstrably accurate information be released. Since one of the principal objectives of the initiative was to subject raw government statistics to outside scrutiny – to check their accuracy *externally* – this was an aggressive counter-punch by the Cabinet Secretary. It was clear from the very beginning that Whitehall knew exactly what was coming and was ready to fight.

Hilton had masterminded the rebranding of Toryism in Cameron's early years as leader, and cemented his own reputation as an ingenious, nimble and idiosyncratic political guru. Before the election, he was often regarded with suspicion by the Conservative Right as a dangerous iconoclast who had no reverence for the party's rituals, institutions and folklore. It was widely believed that he voted Green in 2001, appalled by Hague's flirtation with 'skinhead conservatism' and abject failure to modernize his flailing party.

At this point, Hilton was seen by Tory traditionalists as a tieless heretic who had more in common with his New Labour friends than with the party for which he had once worked: he was close to Ben Wegg-Prosser, Mandelson's former chief aide; Tim Allan, who had been Blair's press adviser; and Tom Baldwin, the *Times* journalist who would go on to become Ed Miliband's communications director. As Cameron swathed the party in greenery, hugged huskies, and changed the Tory logo from a torch to a scribbled drawing of a tree, Hilton became the lightning conductor for the wrath of the Right and for senior Tories who felt disenfranchised by the modernization project. Paid more than £250,000 p.a. for his work, he was blamed (correctly) for the Tory leader's fixation with change and his pursuit of the unexpected to transform public perceptions of the party.

In December 2006, for instance, the *Daily Telegraph* reported the disquiet as follows: 'Shadow cabinet ministers have privately expressed misgivings about the advice given by Mr Hilton, whom they regard as highly intelligent and motivated but misguided. The tension is most palpable with Francis Maude, the party chairman, who is frustrated by the sway Mr Hilton holds over Mr Cameron. There was also a dispute with Dr Liam Fox, the defence spokesman and former leadership challenger, who was astonished that Mr Hilton had used a focus group to test whether the party should support the case for replacing the Trident nuclear deterrent. Mr Hilton is one of the few advisers permitted to interrupt and contradict Mr Cameron at meetings with shadow ministers. One source said: "Steve just interrupts Cameron and says: 'Shut up Dave, you don't know what you are talking about.' Cameron takes it from him because he trusts him so much."'[5]

Hilton's licence to speak directly to Cameron survived the transition to office. But his role and position in the Conservative constellation changed dramatically. As the Prime Minister's senior adviser, he wanted to move beyond rebranding to a much more substantial role, enforcing Cameron's will (or at least what he assumed to be Cameron's will) and driving change across Whitehall. His premise, as he repeatedly told Cameron and Osborne, was simple: 'We may only be here for five years, so let's behave as if that's all the time we've got.'

In Hilton's mind, this meant more than the stable government provided by the Coalition and the fiscal responsibility demanded by Osborne. He wanted Cameron to use power aggressively and impatiently, to identify himself unambiguously as a transformative Prime Minister and to set his senior adviser loose in Whitehall. He told the Cameroon circle that each generational cohort was granted one shot, one turn at the wheel, and that this was theirs. 'Dave and George just want to get re-elected,' he complained to colleagues. 'They say about stuff – "Oh, this is for the second term." But what if there is no second term? What if this is it?'[6]

In collaboration with a core group of colleagues, including Letwin and Maude – the reported grievances of 2006 now a distant memory – Hilton had drafted plans for structural reform in every department. These were amended by James O'Shaugnessy and Polly Mackenzie, working with a group of officials to ensure that the proposed changes and timetables were consistent with the Coalition Programme. But, even in edited form, the plans survived as calls to action and templates for change, embodying the new Government's commitment to public service reform as well as to deficit reduction.

Letwin agreed with Hilton that speed was of the essence. In Eric Pickles, the Communities and Local Government Secretary, they found a shrewd and robust ally, prepared to take on town halls and the well-entrenched apparat of local government. 'We are in the workshop of the Big Society,' Pickles told one ally, 'while all the posh lot are off doing the Latin.'[7]

Some true believers in localism such as Ferdinand Mount, former head of the Downing Street policy unit and a practised social analyst, were sceptical. 'Until local councils themselves raise the bulk of their revenue,' he wrote, 'all talk of localism can only be a charming *tableau vivant*.'[8] Fiscal decentralization of this sort was a remote prospect indeed while Osborne was at the Treasury. But – *pace* Mount – the direction of travel was clear enough. The Localism Act of 2011 established a framework for decentralization: local authorities were granted a new 'general power of competence', which meant they were free to do as they pleased except when the law specifically prevented them from doing so – a reversal of the historic assumption that councils could act only when legally bidden to do so. But they were also required to be more transparent and open to scrutiny. Major cities were encouraged to seek the leadership of directly elected mayors. But community groups were also empowered to take over pubs, libraries and shops put up for sale, and to exercise the 'right to challenge' the local authority's delivery of a particular service with a view to providing it themselves. In Number Ten, it was said that Pickles was 'too big to fail'. But the joke at the expense of his girth was made in a spirit of respect as well as mischief.

In parallel, Maude took charge of the Open Public Services White Paper, the aim of which was to find fresh ways of performing core public functions, such as tax collection, probation services and administrative services. The Prime Minister's opening words, published in July 2011, suggested an uncompromising spirit at work: 'The contents of this white paper will be felt in every state school, hospital and prison, by every doctor, teacher, parent, patient and citizen. I'm not going to make the mistakes of my predecessors blocking reform, wasting opportunities and wasting time.' In a speech in July 2011, Maude spoke in similar vein: openness, he argued, was more than a courtesy to the taxpayer. It had 'the power to absolutely transform the way government and society work for the better', saving lives, driving growth and transforming social relationships.

Clegg and Alexander liked the principles of localism and transparency well enough, but were sometimes alarmed by the combative language that Hilton and his colleagues used. Letwin, in particular, was conscious of the need to phrase the white paper in a way that did not unnecessarily jangle the nerves of the average Lib Dem activist. 'It sounds less radical than it is,' he said to a fellow Tory who was concerned that the teeth of the reforms were being quietly removed one by one to save the Coalition.

Cohabitation with the Lib Dems was often aggravating to Hilton. But his considered view was that the Government's work was imperilled by three much deeper and intimately entangled forces: judicial review (which he could do little about); red tape and bureaucracy; and the interventions of the European Union. As Cameron's brand manager in Opposition, he had urged him to embrace 'quality of life' issues and to make the Conservative Party genuinely 'family-friendly' by supporting maternity and paternity leave. An important component of the Tory 'detoxification' strategy was to persuade voters that the party was not in the pocket of big business, or the political wing of the CBI and IOD, and would stand up for the employee seeking reasonable 'work–life balance'.

In office, Hilton had become persuaded that high levels of flexibility in the workplace, however desirable, could not be expected of employers struggling to survive ghastly economic circumstances. Economic growth was a higher priority than the right to change a newborn's nappies. Indeed, Hilton's view was that radical supply-side reform was needed to help companies – especially small- and medium-sized firms – to escape the tangle of labour regulations. To this end, Cameron was persuaded to commission a report on employment law from Adrian Beecroft, the venture capitalist and Tory donor.

From the start, his inquiry caused trouble. Notionally, it was established by the Business Department as part of its 'Red Tape Challenge' and the responsible minister was Ed Davey, reporting to his fellow Lib Dem, Vince Cable. But this was a matter of formality rather than political substance. When Davey went to the Cabinet Office to listen to Beecroft with Letwin and others, he was dismayed by the apparent deference shown towards the financier by Silva. As the conversation turned to the controversial matter of 'no-fault dismissal' – the right of employers to sack arbitrarily – Davey wanted to know if there was a factual basis for the claim that such a reform would encourage growth. 'So where is your evidence?' Beecroft was lofty in his dismissal: 'There is no need for evidence.'

Before his promotion to the Cabinet, Davey regarded the fending off of left-field schemes from Number Ten – which is to say from Hilton and Silva – as one of his core ministerial duties: the proposed deregulation of inflammable sofas and nighties being an example that stuck in his mind. But the Beecroft process was different. This was not just another '*Thick of It* idea', as eccentric, irrelevant or unworkable proposals to emerge from Downing Street became known around Whitehall (in homage to Malcolm Tucker's furious line: 'let's set up a department to count the moon'). The inquiry was a matter about which Hilton felt passionately, and in which he had invested the plenipotentiary powers of the Prime Minister.

In October, Beecroft delivered his report – a slender sixteen-page document that made up for its brevity with ambition. Instead of befuddling his readers with tables and graphs, the author offered a series of straightforward proposals to liberalize the labour market. The rules on unfair dismissal would be rewritten; it would become much easier to sack 'under-productive' staff; businesses would find it less difficult to opt out of compulsory pension contributions, parental leave allowance and pay audits. Firms with fewer than ten staff would be given special dispensation from a range of employment regulations.

The official report was disclosed in May 2012 after a late draft was leaked by the *Daily Telegraph*. Missing from the final document was Beecroft's admission in the draft that his plan would enable an employer to sack a worker simply because he did not like him or her: 'While this is sad, I believe it is a price worth paying for all the benefits that would result from the change.' This bleak candour was expunged from the official report. But it showed that Beecroft, at least, was absolutely honest about what he was proposing.

Hilton and Silva believed that the proposals would create jobs and that this, more than an inventory of 'social rights', was what the unemployed really cared about – especially the young, desperate to experience the dignity of labour in some form or other. Cable and Clegg, in polar contrast, saw Beecroft as an intolerable provocation and a shoddy exercise in ideological polemic dressed up as an officially sanctioned investigation. The Business Secretary wrote in the *Sun* that he was 'opposed to ideological zealots who want firms to fire at will'. Parts of the report, Cable said, were 'bonkers'. Clegg claimed that the proposed deregulation would create 'industrial scale insecurity amongst millions of workers'.

In an interview with the *Daily Telegraph*, Beecroft himself replied that Cable's opposition was 'ideological, not economic', and dismissed him as a 'Socialist who found a home in the Lib Dems . . . I think people find it very odd that he's in charge of business and yet appears to do very little to support business.'[9] The internal opposition to his report was grist to the mill of those who believed that the Coalition was structurally averse to radicalism, and that aggressive supply-side measures to stimulate growth would never be taken as long as the Tories were governing in partnership with the Lib Dems.

Yet Beecroft identified the much more intriguing question and one that had been nagging away at Hilton during 2011. 'I am constantly struck,' the venture capitalist said, 'by how un-robust the

Prime Minister and the Chancellor are when it comes to pushing back.' Why, during the negotiations over the report's final form, had Cameron not let it be known that he backed his senior adviser to the hilt? Instead, Heywood had been empowered to negotiate a compromise – the implication being that the PM wanted a settlement rather than a particular answer. Osborne, for his part, regarded the report as fundamentally un-serious: an inventory of assertions rather than a forensic inquiry. In his conference speech in 2012, he nonetheless thanked Beecroft 'for the work he has done' and offered a new voluntary three-way deal to small and medium-sized companies. Employees would trade their rights of unfair dismissal and redundancy for a stake in the business, while the Government would charge no capital gains tax on any profit made from those shares. 'Owners, workers and the taxman, all in it together': Hilton's dream had been reduced to the Chancellor's one-off soundbite.

Whatever its merits, the Beecroft inquiry always lacked the political support it needed at the apex of the Government. Though its supporters continued to speak wistfully of its total or partial resurrection, and the unions still referred to the report as a bogeyman lurking in the dark, it was dead before its publication.

On the EU, Hilton had been arguing since before the 2010 election that the Conservative Party should be systematically preparing Britain for exit. According to one senior Cameroon: 'When Steve said this, the reaction was: "That's mad."' But the strategy guru was thinking years ahead. 'You can't leave every EU summit and say it's a triumph for Britain,' he warned Cameron. 'We need to be building a picture of constant defeat.'

This at least had logic on its side – if escape from the EU was your clear objective, it made little sense for British politicians and officials to emerge from Brussels declaring that 'Europe is going the UK's way.' The whole point, Hilton argued, was that it was manifestly failing to do so. As so often, however, he was charging ahead of a pack that embraced a much broader range of opinion about Britain's future in the EU.[10]

In September 2007, Cameron had written an article for the *Sun*, offering the voters 'this cast-iron guarantee: If I become PM a

Conservative government will hold a referendum on any EU treaty that emerges from these negotiations'. The intergovernmental talks to which he was referring spawned the Lisbon Treaty, an agreement which reheated much of the failed EU Constitutional Treaty. When it became clear in November 2009 that Lisbon was going to be ratified by all twenty-seven member states, Cameron announced that, since the treaty was now part of European law, his referendum promise was henceforth null and void. What the Tory leader hoped would be seen as a mature recognition of reality was almost universally scorned as a screeching U-turn. Lord Mandelson, the Business Secretary, told Sky News that Cameron was being dishonest: 'It looks as if that cast-iron guarantee has become very rusty indeed.' In years to come, Cameron came to regret bitterly not adding a phrase or a sentence to the original *Sun* piece, if only to make clear that his guarantee would expire if Gordon Brown and his EU counterparts all ratified Lisbon.

William Hague, then Shadow Foreign Secretary, had long promised enigmatically that, if Lisbon did indeed become part of EU law, a Tory government would not 'let matters rest there'. The plan (fully discussed in Chapter 13) was always to introduce a referendum lock on future transfers of sovereignty to Brussels; to announce an audit of the impact of EU law on British sovereignty; to renegotiate the terms of the UK's membership; and then to hold a referendum after the 2015 election. 'We've got to be clear with this,' Hilton said to his colleagues. 'If we're heading for a referendum in the second term, we have to have changed the terms of the debate.' By then, he explained, the case for exit had to be absolutely manifest. The public had to believe that the EU was holding Britain back in what Cameron came to describe as the 'global race'. As Prime Minister, he would have to emerge from every EU negotiation looking despondent and frustrated: or so Hilton's strategy demanded. This was a lot to ask of any Prime Minister, let alone a politician as addicted to calm deliberation and as temperamentally optimistic as Cameron.

Hilton, of course, was positively persuaded of the case for exit. The PM was far from ready to commit himself to this objective, or to concede its desirability: he believed it was still possible to rebalance the relationship between Whitehall and Brussels, and to salvage Britain's membership.

Cameron was open-minded. Hilton, in contrast, believed that the mandarinate was determined to keep the UK in the EU at almost any cost. In an exquisite dramatization of the problem, he clashed with Heywood over the true enforceability of EU law. Why should the Prime Minister obey European regulations on temporary workers, he asked the civil servant. 'Because,' Heywood replied, 'he could end up in prison.'[11] Though it was hard for Hilton to top this, he thought the argument unworthy of a senior civil servant whose intellect he admired. It also confirmed his worst suspicions that Whitehall would link arms with Brussels if Britain made a serious bid to exit the European Union.

The question was: what sort of Whitehall? Hilton spoke of a spectacular reduction in head-count, perhaps of up to 90 per cent, and the housing of the Civil Service in a single building, like Somerset House. 'You could never quite work out how much of this was said for effect and how much was meant literally', according to one friend. As Hilton spoke of revolution, his ministerial colleagues proceeded with reform. Maude, in particular, believed that his Civil Service Reform Plan, published in June 2012, was a radical blueprint that would make the service 'smaller, flatter, faster, more focused on outcome not process'.[12]

The number of civil servants would fall from 500,000 to 380,000, there would be fewer management layers and the digital provision of services would become the default position in government. It required all permanent secretaries in 'delivery' departments – principal public services such as education and health – to have had more than two years' experience in a commercial or operational role. The plan also proposed a tougher appraisal system to identify the top 25 per cent and the bottom 10 per cent.

Maude – one of Cameron's best ministers, who preferred discreet effectiveness to flashy theatricals – was not seeking combat for combat's sake. But he had his run-ins with the mandarinate. He and his colleagues resisted the pressure from Whitehall to install Dame Helen Ghosh, Permanent Secretary, as Head of the Civil Service – an appointment that Maude believed would have been a disaster. Not all such selection processes ended happily. Maude came to regard the choice of Sir David Normington as First Civil Service Commissioner (Whitehall's independent regulator) in December 2010 as his own worst decision, a form of self-sabotage. Civil service reform would always be a bumpy ride, especially in times of austerity and under a Coalition Government where power was more widely dispersed. But Maude, aided by his sharp Special Adviser, Simone Finn, wanted there to be no doubt about his intentions. In a speech in October, he spelt out with quiet menace the need for officials to do as their political masters instructed. 'Once a Minister has made up his or her mind and given a decision the constitutional role of the Civil Service is explicitly clear: it is to implement that decision.'

By then, Hilton had left, on extended 'sabbatical'. It had taken him many months and much reflection to inch towards a conclusion that was personally painful as well as professionally dismal. As a practitioner of the rites of statesmanship, Cameron had exceeded even his closest friends' expectations. The list of set-piece occasions on which the PM had judged the tone with calm accuracy was impressive – notably, his apology in June 2010 for the 'unjustified and unjustifiable' Bloody Sunday killings. After Hilton's exit, there was the PM's dignified response to the findings of the Hillsborough Independent Panel in September 2012; his statement on the Algerian crisis in January 2013; and the bowing of his head in memory of the Amritsar massacre the following month. On such occasions, even the most truculent Tories conceded that their leader was a politician of immense ability and presence.

Yet, by the end of 2011, Hilton had come to regard Cameron as a reactive rather than a transformative Prime Minister. Though he continued to press him to shift up a gear, he had realized, with something close to despair, that his words, though politely received, were not getting through, and that there was little point in carrying on. In the Downing Street flat, he had a framed copy of a cover image from *The Economist* in August 2010, depicting Cameron as a mohawked punk under the headline: 'Radical Britain: The West's most daring government'. This is precisely what Hilton had hoped for: his friend as agent provocateur and guerrilla-statesman, turning the system upside down. But – he had reluctantly concluded – the magazine cover was a triumph of hope over reality. Cameron, his senior adviser had realized, was not a political punk, shaking a fist at the Establishment, but one of its instinctive guardians, looking down from the battlements of the ancient English fortress. By Hilton's standards, he was an evolutionary reformer: a Whig, not a radical.

The personal bond between the two men remained strong. On occasion, moreover, Cameron was every bit as combative as Hilton had hoped. In March 2011, he used his speech to the Conservative Spring Conference in Cardiff to attack the 'enemies of enterprise' – including, most provocatively, 'the bureaucrats in government departments who concoct those ridiculous rules and regulations that make life impossible, particularly for small firms'. Whitehall's most senior mandarins were furious to be thus characterized. Here was an opportunity for the PM to stand firm. But when O'Donnell asked Heywood to 'calm things down', he was reassured by the Downing Street Permanent Secretary that Number Ten understood the grievance and accepted that the matter had not been handled adroitly.[13]

The fact that Heywood felt able to say this to O'Donnell, with no fear of contradiction, is an eloquent measure of a power shift within Number Ten away from Hilton and towards the genial mandarin. Jeremy, not Steve, was the PM's vicar on Earth – or at least seen as such. Indeed, it was heavily rumoured – though never substantiated – that Heywood had even had a hand in the *writing* of the speech: running with the hares and hunting with the hounds, so to speak. There was nothing unexpected about any of this, no overt sense that the politicians were being manipulated any more than was usual. Heywood was not by any means unpleasant to work with, or grand in his demeanour. Initially, he and Hilton looked set to be firm friends: privately, Heywood claimed to agree with much of what he stood for and urged him to persist.

Hilton's allies later wondered whether this was all part of a grand set-up – encouraging him to be ever more radical to enable the civil servant to slide into his place at court. Heywood always laughed off such suggestions, as if to say 'Machiavellian, moi?' Peter Mandelson had enjoyed being portrayed as the Prince of Darkness, pulling the strings behind the scenes. Heywood's response was quite different. He shrugged off his media image as a gross misrepresentation of an honest official doing his job.

Certainly, he was easy to get on with. His cheerful countenance and gift for friendship made him an unlikely villain. 'Jeremy looks like a bank manager doing his best to help a student with his over-draft', according to one insider. 'He doesn't do the alpha male thing of dominating the room. But he is always in the room.' Silva, in par-ticular, saw no tension whatsoever between his own loyalty to Hilton and collaboration with Heywood: he found the civil servant sup-portive on issues great and small. So when Silva wanted to exert pressure on the Business Department and David Willetts over online access to academic journals – notoriously expensive to access digitally – it was Heywood who put his shoulder to the wheel in the name of greater openness.

What unnerved some in Number Ten was simply the speed and apparent ease with which the civil servant accrued greater and greater authority and influence. In the colourful image of one senior Tory source: 'Jeremy is like Batman. Gotham City *needs* Batman – and Jer-emy fills that space.'[14] Power seemed to gravitate towards him like iron filings to a magnet. He had been Principal Private Secretary to Norman Lamont on 'Black Wednesday' – working alongside a young Special Adviser called Cameron. He had served as PPS to Tony Blair in Number Ten, and Downing Street Permanent Secretary to Gor-don Brown and Cameron, before becoming Cabinet Secretary in January 2012. In the words of Nick Pearce, the former head of the Number Ten policy unit: 'If we had a written constitution in this country, it would have to say something like: "Notwithstanding the fact that Jeremy Heywood will always be at the centre of power, we are free and equal citizens." '[15]

Inevitably and intrinsically, the circumstances of coalition were an opportunity for a civil servant of Heywood's intellect and guile. Describing his role to the Commons Public Administration Select Committee in May 2012, he was diplomatic. 'I would not use the word "referee",' he said. 'I am a civil servant; I don't arbitrate between elected politicians. They have to come to agreements themselves. Obviously, the Deputy Prime Minister, the Prime Minister and other Ministers ask the civil servants occasionally to help them try and find areas of common ground, to filter through issues and pinpoint the issues that really do need to be resolved at a political level, so I do get involved a lot in issues that divide them.' A referee, in other words.

What also amazed ministers was how ubiquitous Heywood seemed to be. As Osborne confirmed in his evidence to the Leveson Inquiry, it was Heywood who suggested that responsibility for the BSkyB bid and media plurality be transferred from Vince Cable to Jeremy Hunt.[16] It was said that he was behind the NHS 'Pause', the twisting of arms necessary to ensure that Fred Goodwin, the disgraced boss of the Royal Bank of Scotland, lost his knighthood, and, in 2013, the decision not to sack Sir David Nicholson, the chief executive of the NHS, immediately over the Mid Staffs hospital scandal. Apocryphal or not, such stories embellished Heywood's reputation as chief courtier and choreographer of the Coalition. Kerslake, who often travelled into work with him at 7.30 from south-west London, was increasingly seen as no more than Heywood's sidekick, Sancho Panza to the bespectacled knight. The Head of the Home Civil Service also became well known for other reasons. 'It's unpleasant to say this', in the words of one Cabinet minister, 'but Bob Kerslake really does have awful BO. I mean, *really* smelly.' Whitehall is a cruel place, indeed.

Hilton had wanted a 70 per cent head-count reduction written into Civil Service legislation. Heywood told the Commons Public Administration Committee that such targets were not 'remotely' the policy of the Government. There could be no clearer indication of who had prevailed. It was not a contest of personalities, or of briefing, or even of political will. It was a battle for the ear of Cameron.

This was what aggrieved Hilton most. He had truly believed in 2010 that he was at the heart of a collective enterprise to revolutionize the structure, ethos and performance of the British state. He had been pleasantly surprised to discover that there were people in other parties who harboured similar ambitions – notably, Richard Reeves, Clegg's strategy adviser. He and Hilton prepared Cameron and Clegg for a presentation at Chequers to the first political Cabinet of the whole Coalition. They offered two themes: a 'horizon shift' that would compel the new Government to forge policy for the long term rather than for tomorrow's headlines or the next minute's tweet. The second idea was the 'power shift' that Hilton believed in so deeply: decentralization to individuals, neighbourhoods and local institutions on a scale never previously countenanced. But even as he watched the Prime Minister and his Lib Dem deputy address their colleagues, Hilton feared that the ambition would not last, that the warm words would freeze in the permafrost of day-to-day politics. The 'Big Bang' of measures he envisaged – all concentrated in the first two years of the Parliament – did not stand a chance.

Initially, he ascribed the loss of momentum to the weakened position of the Lib Dems. The tuition fees debacle and defeat in the AV referendum had scarred Clegg and forced him to differentiate his party from the Tories – claiming sufficient victories in what became known in Number Ten as the 'Moroccan souk' of tit-for-tat policy transactions.

On closer examination, however, Hilton reached a diagnosis that was much less palatable. The Cameron Government was doing good and important things: deficit reduction, education reform, localizing measures, steps towards a more effective Civil Service. But – Hilton concluded – its *idée-force* was the maintenance of power, rather than its radical redistribution.

According to this analysis, the ascendancy of Heywood was a symptom rather than a cause. Cameron and Llewellyn had, in Hilton's eyes, found themselves at home amongst the mandarinate. Why lead a revolution, when you like the status quo? As he saw it, they had too readily accepted the argument that the Number Ten policy unit should be primarily staffed by civil servants rather than political advisers. Accordingly, in March 2011, Paul Kirby was appointed head of policy development, in charge of around a dozen officials, working alongside Kris Murrin, head of implementation. Both Kirby and Murrin – of course – reported to Heywood.

The Downing Street Permanent Secretary was well aware of the suspicion that he was empire-building, transforming a unit that ought to have been an engine of Cameroon reform into another Whitehall fiefdom. As so often, however, he was simply doing his political masters' bidding. When the new Government arrived in May 2010, Heywood felt that, in practice, Letwin *was* the policy unit. When the spending review began to exercise the Coalition, however, Osborne told him: 'I think you need more capacity.'

It was clear to Heywood that Clegg would not accept unvarnished Tory advice from a beefed-up brains trust staffed exclusively with Conservative appointees. Nor could he really justify the creation of two policy units, arguing cacophonously at the taxpayers' expense over whether to privatize the M25. The only conceivable solution – at least in Heywood's eyes – was a team of technocrats working to the Coalition script rather than a specific party line.

Hilton saw matters very differently. Yes, he had never been persuaded that the Tory policy director, James O'Shaughnessy, had the energy or the breadth of interest to do the job in Downing Street. O'Shaughnessy, for his part, felt that he was being driven out by stealth – obstructed, excluded, not always invited to key meetings – and that he had more than proved his stamina and resourcefulness in the early weeks of the Coalition (not to mention in Opposition). O'Shaughnessy finally left the post of director of policy to the PM in October 2011.

But what Hilton wanted instead was not a team of technocrats. He himself craved a new role as chairman of policy, with Silva running the policy unit under his guidance. Up to a point, Cameron was happy to indulge the pair's undoubted creativity. The PM, for instance, was delighted by Silva's creation of an iPad app with which, in theory, he could govern the country. Developed at a cost of £20,000, the 'management dashboard' was intended to give the PM real-time data on government performance, opinion polls, inflation, the markets, even Twitter trends. Easily dismissed as a stunt, the app was – at least in aspiration – a sophisticated attempt to import to Number Ten the 'sabermetric' system of analysis made famous by the Michael Lewis book and film, *Moneyball*, in which baseball players were selected by the Oakland As with reference to hard empirical data rather than the scouts' visceral decisions.[17]

Apps were fine. But what the PM and Llewellyn would not accept was any configuration that had Steve and his sidekick in senior managerial positions. It grated with Hilton that he had to fight hard to secure a small team of four people when what he wanted was a hefty platoon of like-minded reformers and intellectuals to launch a permanent revolution that would turn Whitehall upside down.

This, of course, was precisely the problem. Cameron and Llewellyn thought of the Government as ambitious, reformist and committed to more than austerity. But permanent revolution – Tory Trotskyism – was something neither of them was temperamentally suited to. They liked smooth surfaces and courteous negotiation rather than the deliberate disruption that Hilton quite candidly favoured. Cameron joked that Steve had become a 'raving right-winger'. But the gulf between the two friends was not ideological. In the end, it had more to do with temperament, social background and the connection between the two. The sadness for Hilton was that the experience of government revealed to him a social isolation in the Cameroon gang he had not before suspected. As he saw it, Cameron, Osborne, Llewellyn and Fall had shown themselves to be creatures of the Establishment. He wanted to rock the boat. And they didn't.

Pre-announced in March 2012, Hilton's departure was far from neat. Cameron and others in Number Ten felt that his protracted exit was self-indulgent and provocative in form, designed to test their collective restraint. His call as he left Number Ten for £25bn extra welfare cuts did not amuse Danny Alexander, who remarked that 'most people would bring in a cake on their last day'. There was a measure of relief, even amongst those who enjoyed Hilton's flamboyant presence. 'He was no good at playing with the team', in the words of one colleague. The Number Ten machine adjusted to the loss. With Hilton gone, Craig Oliver and Andrew Cooper got to work on the message they hoped would carry Cameron into the next election: the challenge of the 'global race' and the promise that the Tory Party would be 'on your side'. As the PM saw it, there was a masculine and a feminine component to this strategy. The warning that Britain must be lean and nimble to survive in the coming planetary contest was for the left side of the brain: the rational and competitive. The pledge to be 'on your side' appealed to the right side: the emotional and nurturing aspects of the human psyche.

Yet in politics, as in life, friendship is complex, contradictory, non-linear. The bond between Cameron and Hilton was much too strong and fraternal to perish for political reasons. As disappointed as Hilton was, he was angrier with himself for misjudging the limits of Cameron's ambition as a reformer. Heywood's great skill, he acknowledged, was in understanding his political masters and giving them what they wanted.

If Hilton returned to politics full-time, it would be as a practitioner – possibly as the mayor of a city. He held discussions with Boris Johnson before the Mayor's re-election in 2012, in which Hilton made it clear that he was interested in a substantial role such as Deputy Mayor with responsibility for business and enterprise. In the end, he decided not to make the leap. According to one ally of Johnson: 'It would have been too big a jump and so many people would have seen it as disloyal to Cameron. Steve admires them both. But this would have looked like dumping Dave and signing up with Boris.'

Instead, Hilton headed to California to be with his family, and to teach at Stanford University. He flew back to help Cameron with his conference speech in October 2012; and he retained an almost umbilical connection with the Prime Minister. Gove and Silva, for instance, wanted Michael Lynas, a member of the Number Ten policy unit, to become chief executive of the National Citizen Service, a £200m voluntary scheme that gives sixteen- and seventeen-year-olds the chance to undertake community work. The NCS was close to Cameron's heart and one of the projects he hoped would be part of his legacy. Lynas was well-suited to the job, but faced a number of internal obstacles. In the end, Gove and Silva contacted Hilton to fix from California what could not be fixed in Whitehall. With Maude also recruited to the cause, Lynas was set fair for a senior role at the Service.

The departure of Hilton left a hole so distinctively shaped that it could not be filled (although he himself had suggested for consideration either George Bridges, the seasoned Tory strategist, or Malcolm Gooderham, former chief of staff to Portillo). Though the circumstances of his exit were complex, what it signalled to the Conservative family – from grandest Cabinet minister to lone blogger – was that the radical had been driven out and the mandarins had moved in. Heywood reportedly complained to a meeting of bankers about the lack of unity among Cabinet ministers on economic strategy – as if the pesky politicians were making his life unnecessarily difficult.[18] Duncan Smith told his advisers that 'not a day goes by without me missing Steve'. One well-known right-wing backbencher went much further: 'The day Steve left was the day things really started to go wrong.' That was an extreme version of a sentiment widely felt: that the Prime Minister, in losing Hilton, had surrendered a source of governing energy he could ill afford to spare. Yes, Steve could still call his old friend Dave at any time, and be sure of a hearing. But, in the day-to-day life of Number Ten, the Age of Hilton was already over and the Age of Heywood well-established. That said more about Cameron than it did about either talented man.

11. The Boris Situation

'I'm hoovering up all the credit! All this credit!' As the London Olympics drew to a close, Boris Johnson was heard joyously claiming his own political dividend in boisterous conversation with a fellow Olympic Board member. There was always an edge of irony and self-mockery to the Mayor's outbursts. But it was hard to deny that the London Games, a triumph of sport and spectacle seen by billions, had also been the most extraordinary leadership campaign launch in history.[1]

Ken Livingstone had been the Mayor when the capital secured the Games at a meeting of the International Olympic Committee in July 2005 (the day before the 7/7 bombings). But it was his Tory nemesis who got to welcome the world's athletes to London for the first time since 1948. In a single fortnight, the Boris 'brand' had gone global.

As Johnson later recalled, 'a sort of euphoria took hold of the population . . . it struck me as a sort of benign mental contagion, a bit like the sentimental affliction that hit us after the death of Diana, Princess of Wales, except that this time it was positive'.[2] So gloomy had the prophecies of disaster been – infrastructural, meteorological, athletic – that the sensational reality of the Games was all the more gripping than it might have been if the nation had been confidently expecting a triumph. The two politicians who had done more than anyone else for almost a decade to make the Games a triumph were Lord Coe and Dame Tessa Jowell (who had persuaded Blair to take a chance on the bid in the first place). Along with Sir Keith Mills, Deputy Chair of the Games organizing committee (LOCOG), Paul Deighton, chief executive officer, and Hugh Robertson, the Tory Sports Minister, they had collaborated with conscious reference to Truman's maxim: 'It is amazing what you can accomplish if you do not care who gets the credit.' Indeed, they had assumed that whoever won the 2012 mayoral election would, indeed, 'hoover up' the credit. Livingstone had given Boris a run for his money, losing by only 3 per cent (in contrast to the double-digit lead Johnson had commanded in some opinion polls during the campaign). But Londoners gave the Tory incumbent a second term – a result that burnished his credentials as a winner and persuaded the national leadership that his Australian political guru, Lynton Crosby, should co-ordinate the 2015 general election campaign. To the victor, meanwhile, went the spoils: Boris was now, *ex officio*, master of ceremonies at the greatest show on Earth. As he said in Michael Cockerell's 2013 documentary about him: 'It was a jammy old trick to pull.'

And what ceremonies. Danny Boyle's extravaganza to mark the opening of the Games set the tone for the Olympic fortnight and the Paralympics a few weeks later. Taking 'Jerusalem' as its central theme, the ceremony spoke in an idiom of dream and myth, the language of fear and of hope that mediates troubled times. The country was being tested, and there was worse ahead. Boyle's production seemed to pose the necessary question: what was Britain made of?

A squall of ideological outrage followed the show, but missed the point spectacularly. The NHS, Beveridge Report and immigration were indeed celebrated. But so too were the achievements of the Armed Forces, the great hymns, the Union. The thematic power of the ceremony flowed not from political history but the unrelenting spirit of innovation and invention. Boyle took as his text the words of Caliban: 'Be not afeard; the isle is full of noises.' He presented Britain as a revolutionary nation, whose revolution was not ideological, but scientific, creative and intellectual, its greatest creations the fruits of the mind, whether the songs of the Beatles or the World Wide Web. Beijing had celebrated its Games with a colossal display of regimented uniformity. London greeted the world with a show that was magical rather than bureaucratic, meandering, and polychromatic to the point of psychedelia. It was worthy, indeed, of what the city's biographer, Peter Ackroyd, has called 'Infinite London'.[3] It helped to cauterize the wounds of the riots the year before, and to hint at the eventual return of national confidence and prosperity. This was not the work of a second-rate nation.

Such moments fizz with politics, even though political life is officially suspended. Cameron hoped the Games would be a punctuation mark, a breathing space to alleviate his difficulties. In practice, this unforgettable summer was more like a poetic report on the state of the nation, expressed in sport, spectacle and celebration. There was no dividend for the Coalition. But Cameron was quietly pleased that his instincts about the public's basic optimism remained sound. At the time, I wrote that true Britishness straddles the boundary that separates irony from determination.[4] It was entirely apt that we had satirized our own Games pre-emptively in the brilliant BBC comedy series *Twenty-Twelve* – Hugh Bonneville's mantra, 'So that's all good', capturing perfectly the constant battle between hope and experience. But, as is so often the case, life trumped art. The ceremony's most daring moment involved the Queen herself in a skit with Daniel Craig as James Bond, the visual gag being that Her Majesty, rather than 007, had parachuted from a helicopter into the stadium.

In the Diamond Jubilee celebrations the month before, the 86-year-old sovereign had stood before the world as a living symbol of lifelong service, institutional continuity and personal dignity. The parachute stunt was breathtakingly camp, monarchy as music hall. It was also a moment of unprotected audacity. But it worked perfectly, as gracious an expression of British self-deprecation as one could possibly imagine. The message beamed around the world could not have been clearer. Being good at sport is important, but being a good sport is what really counts.

Cameron had been consulted by Buckingham Palace about the Queen's involvement in the Bond stunt and, as it turned out, given the correct advice. During the Games, he chaired regular meetings of Cobra, the Civil Contingencies Committee, to ensure that UK plc was looking its best every day. He predicted that the Olympics would boost the economy by more than £13bn over the following four years – a prophecy that was always going to be difficult to verify or disprove. He and other Cabinet ministers schmoozed business leaders relentlessly, keeping a tally of deals done and investments secured. But this was always going to be the Mayor's party. Clegg warned him that this would happen and, knowing there was nothing to be done about it, urged the PM to smile his way through the fortnight. Boris, too, admitted in private that he knew the situation was sometimes 'embarrassing for Dave', but could not quite see what he could do to prevent that.

In the Cockerell documentary, the Mayor was shown watching footage of himself addressing an adoring crowd in Hyde Park, chanting his name. He admitted to the film-maker that this sonic boom of flattery was 'very, very bad for the ego. But you do understand why Roman emperors put on great games and great spectacles. I mean, suddenly you think – wow!' According to one senior organizer of the Games: 'It felt like it was Boris's show, and it was awkward for Cameron sometimes. There was one occasion when Boris was talking to William and Kate at the back of the box and the PM was just sitting there. He was notionally the senior guy but there was no doubt who the host was.' As the Coalition faltered in the mire of the 'omnishambles', the supposedly shambolic Mayor was having the time of his life. George Osborne was booed by the 80,000-strong crowd as he awarded medals at the Paralympic Games, his rictus the best he could muster in the circumstances. On another visit to the Olympic Park in Stratford, as the Chancellor sat down to eat some food, he was asked by one of the young 'Games Makers': 'So, George – is that your austerity dinner?'

The Mayor, meanwhile, could do no wrong – or so it seemed. In an attempt to woo spectators to one of the big-screen 'Live Sites', he tried out a zipwire in Victoria Park – and got stuck, thirty feet above the ground:

> The harness was starting to chafe, especially in the groin area.
>
> 'Has anyone got a ladder?' I asked.
>
> No one had a ladder. At length I spotted my Special Branch personal protection officer, a nice chap called Carl. He had been seconded from his normal job of guarding Tony Blair, and was supposed – I reasoned – to rescue me from embarrassing predicaments.
>
> 'Carl,' I said, 'is there anything you can do?'
>
> Slowly, he reached into his breast pocket, took out his mobile phone, aimed carefully, and took a picture of my dangling form . . .[5]

The episode, of course, merely added lustre to the Boris legend. As Cameron acknowledged: 'If any other politician anywhere in the world was stuck on a zipwire it would be a disaster. For Boris, it's an absolute triumph.'[6] The political alchemy involved was indeed unique. As the passage above illustrates – with its apparently casual mention of Blair's Special Branch minder – the Mayor's trick was to be simultaneously at ease with the trappings of power and nonchalantly unimpressed by them. He had always wanted his rivals to underestimate him, and emphasized his apparent weaknesses. In speeches and interviews, he would frequently use the classical rhetorical device of *captatio benevolentiae*, declaring himself unworthy of praise and saying it should be directed at others. Almost invariably, those who sought to mock him found that he had got there first. It was not until 2012 that some of the most senior Tories realized how deadly serious was his ambition.

Quentin Crisp's definition of charisma – the ability to influence without logic – certainly applied in Boris's case. But there was more to his method than likeability and showmanship. His path to the imperial purple would be to play the part of tribune, the representative of the people. Though he sounded more like a character from Wodehouse than any Cabinet minister – his rich baritone seemingly a benign echo from the past – he distanced himself from what he privately called 'Dave's patrician politics', which he likened, pejoratively, to Harold Macmillan's.

The voters admired what they believed to be his 'authenticity': he made no attempt to disguise his privileged upbringing and spoke often of his good fortune. He was a passionate believer in cycling and often to be seen on his 'pushbike' careering down Farringdon Street towards Blackfriars. Cycling had worked well for Cameron, too – until it was discovered that the Tory leader's bike was followed by a car carrying all his papers.

Boris seemed, at least, to be comfortable in his skin, and less of a phoney than most politicians. When John Lydon, aka Johnny Rotten of the Sex Pistols, was asked by the *NME* about the mayoral contest, he declared Livingstone to be 'a living nightmare of repression. He'll find the way of killing the fun in anything – he's misery personified.' But then the man who had sung about 'Anarchy in the UK' offered this unexpected endorsement to another spikey-haired showman: 'Who would you like to have dinner with? It would be Boris . . . Boris would fit happily in any of my surroundings.'

The Conservative Party's relationship with its leaders, actual and prospective, is often hysterical, veering from hero worship to disgusted disappointment. Boris's Olympic moment coincided with a low point in Cameron's relationship with his querulous tribe. Twenty years had now passed since the party had won an election outright, seven of them with Cameron as leader. Why was he bothering with schemes apparently designed to upset Conservatives, such as Lords reform and same-sex marriage? Where was the economic recovery? Where was the opinion poll lead over Miliband? Where was the moment of reckoning with Europe? Why was Salieri running the country when Mozart was available?

The relationship between Cameron and Johnson was the most obsessively followed of the Coalition – even though the Mayor was not part of it, and enjoyed the political advantage of not having to run everything important at City Hall past Brian Paddick, the Lib Dem candidate in the 2012 mayoral election, as Cameron did with Clegg. The two Tory titans intrigued and baffled one another, a fascination that became a media parlour game: two Etonians, both Bullingdon boys, both Oxford graduates, both Tories, both products of the political-media class.[7] As already discussed in Chapter 7, the distinctions between the two on paper seemed marginal – Freud's 'narcissism of small differences'. Yet they were conspicuously unlike one another.

There were times when Cameron found Johnson erratic and selfish. There were moments, too, when Boris could not conceal his irritation that Dave the Plodder had reached the top of the greasy pole first. In October 2011, Jeremy Paxman interviewed the Mayor at the Tory Party conference and teased him about his relationship with the PM:

> Paxman: You mention 'Dave' . . . Isn't it true that you've always felt yourself slightly intellectually inferior?
> Johnson: [looking puzzled] Inferior?

Paxman: Inferior.

Johnson: No . . .

Paxman: No.

Johnson: To who?

Paxman: To David Cameron, your leader . . .

Johnson: No, well, that's a new one. No, I haven't. But, on the other hand, I can see where this is leading . . .

Paxman, visibly enjoying himself, persisted.

Paxman: This goes back to the days, of course, when he got a First [at Oxford] and you didn't.

Johnson: Ah, yes.

Paxman: Does that still rankle a bit?

Johnson: Well, it would, if it wasn't that his First was in PPE . . .

No intellectual slouch himself, Paxman appeared to have genuinely astonished the Mayor with the suggestion that Cameron might be cleverer – and manoeuvred him into a classicist's expression of fruity disdain for 'Modern Greats', as the Honour School of Philosophy, Politics and Economics was originally known. PPE at Oxford had become the British equivalent of the French École nationale d'administration. Cameron was the third Prime Minister, after Wilson and Heath, to have graduated in this Oxonian combination of subjects. So too, amongst many other senior politicians, had Hague, Hilton, Danny Alexander, David Willetts, Chris Huhne, Jeremy Hunt, both Milibands, Ed Balls and Michael Heseltine (Boris's predecessor as MP for Henley). But Johnson was a true believer in the saving power of *Literae Humaniores*, the impregnable wisdom of Homeric epic, and the effortless brilliance of Balliol College.

He had been one of the first MPs to support Cameron, not expecting him to win. The pacemaker in a race – the runner who sets off quickly and then drops out – is not meant to triumph. Boris had assumed after the 2005 general election that he still had time to establish his generational claim to the leadership. It was a deeply unpleasant shock to watch a fellow Etonian – a *younger* Etonian – cruise past him to the top job. They had known each other long enough for resentments to fester. In particular, Boris suspected that Cameron had encouraged Michael Howard to send him to Liverpool in 2004 to apologize in person for an article in *The Spectator*. In its weekly editorial, the magazine had claimed the city was wallowing in its 'victim status' after the death of Ken Bigley, an engineer from Liverpool hideously executed by hostage-takers in Iraq. Boris was also dismayed by the way he was treated by Cameron in the reshuffle of July 2007 – remaining higher education spokesman but demoted, in practice, as Willetts assumed the role of Shadow Secretary of State for Innovation, Universities and Skills. This was the rut from which Boris sought to escape when he ran for Mayor. Had Cameron given him a decent Shadow Cabinet role in 2007 he would almost certainly not have risked all on London.

On Cameron's side, there was what one aide calls the 'weekly mind-fuck' of Boris's *Daily Telegraph* column. In August 2008, for instance, the recently elected Mayor, in celebrating the success of Britain's athletes in the Beijing Olympics, managed to scorn one of Cameron's most deeply felt beliefs: 'If you believe the politicians, we have a broken society, in which the courage and morals of young people have been sapped by welfarism and political correctness. And if you look at what is happening at the Beijing Olympics, you can see what piffle that is.'[8] The Cameroons scoured the weekly despatch from City Hall for messages blunt and nuanced, aware that a prose stylist as accomplished as Johnson could wreck a day – or longer – with a single well-crafted phrase. It did not help the Tory leader's ambitions as a social reformer that the most popular Conservative in the country considered his analysis to be 'piffle'.

Once Cameron was installed in Number Ten, these interventions mattered less – and more. They mattered less because the Prime Minister has the power to do, whereas the Leader of the Opposition only has the power to speak, and is always in danger of being defined by the media. But it mattered more now what Boris said, precisely because his party was sharing power and he was a national figure as well as a civic leader – a hugely influential Tory standing conveniently outside the smoke-filled souk of the Coalition. In September 2010, he described the new immigration cap as 'a bit of a shambles'.[9]

He called for an end to the 50p tax band even as Cameron and Osborne conducted their delicate negotiations with Clegg on how and when to abolish it (see Chapter 12). He insisted that politicians stand up for bankers. He demanded a new airport.

He and his champions were busy outside the pages of the *Telegraph*, too. At the 2009 Tory conference, he insisted that there be a referendum on the EU Lisbon Treaty – the last thing Cameron wanted to dwell upon at the last such gathering before the general election. As the exit polls showed that the Tories had failed to win a majority, his sister, Rachel – a well-known author, editor and columnist herself – tweeted: 'It's all gone tits up. Call for Boris.' In October of that year, the Mayor said that he would not countenance 'Kosovo-style social cleansing' in the capital as a consequence of the Government's proposed housing benefit cap. 'On my watch,' he insisted, 'you are not going to see thousands of families evicted from the place where they have been living and have put down roots.' To that provocation, Number Ten replied with chilly fury. 'The Prime Minister doesn't agree with what Boris Johnson has said, or indeed the way he said it,' a spokesman announced.

Some of this was not only legitimate but necessary. Boris was not a Minister of the Crown, subject to collective responsibility, or an MP, managed by a party whip. He was bound by the basic standards of Tory discipline – but that was it. As Mayor of London, his prior responsibility was to the citizens of that global megalopolis – which was why he was so outspoken on the subject of aviation and so opposed to tax rates that deterred mobile high earners from coming to London or staying there. The capital city's relationship with immigration was unique; its Mayor was bound to resist a cap that would snarl up its age-old dependency upon newcomers. In Guto Harri he had a clever and active comms director, a former chief political correspondent at the BBC, who wanted to cement Boris's image as a statesman as well as a celebrity.

In the truest sense, Cameron had asked for it. The 'Big Society' he championed meant the devolution of power – or it meant nothing. The New Labour state was unitary, uniform, controlled and homogeneous. The Big Society was meant to be untidy, disaggregated and cacophonous. To be more than just another political slogan, it had to involve mayors being truculent, and police commissioners arguing with the Home Office, and neighbourhood groups campaigning against Whitehall decisions. No figure more clearly incarnated the sheer bloody-minded, restless awkwardness of the Big Society than Boris.

Cameron and Osborne understood this and saw a measure of disagreement between City Hall and Whitehall as healthy. Not so the Mayor's Eurosceptic sabotage of the 2009 conference or his claim, days before the same event in 2012, that the Government's 'intended timetable [on aviation capacity] sets a course for economic catastrophe'. Such interventions were interpreted as hostile and provoked a sharp response – by telephone call, email or – most often – text. As Boris told friends: 'Dave was pretty bloody direct.' According to one aide: 'Boris would end up apologizing. I went into his office once and Boris was sending him a message: "Mate, sorry, I messed up." And then the reply from Dave: "Don't worry, I'll sort it out."' Osborne sent him a text complaining: 'Your support for the bankers is hurting us on the doorstep.' Yet, as the election drew closer, the national campaign wanted more and more from him. Boris thought that the 2010 campaign was disastrous – much too vague – and would shout at the screen: 'They're not giving people a *reason* to vote Tory!'

Just as the Coalition was, in practice, without precedent, so too was Boris's political position. His stardom was one of the signals that the postwar unitary state was breaking up. Neither a minister nor a parliamentarian, he nonetheless wielded great power and influence as Mayor of a global city, a master of the media and the only true political celebrity in the country. By the time Cameron was ready to unveil his strategy for the EU he needed Boris's approval.

On 30 September, the Mayor and his family arrived at Chequers for lunch. The gathering, says one who was there, was like 'a scene from a gangster film where there's food and kids running around and normal family life but the two dons are actually doing business and agreeing who's going to get whacked'. There was high confidence on both sides that they could agree on the EU. If Boris could soft-pedal his demands for a referendum for a month or two, his patience would be rewarded by Cameron's speech. At one point, his wife Marina teased him: 'I don't think your position makes any sense at all!' The biggest disappointment of the day for Johnson was that Cameron said the tennis court was not fit for play. The irrepressibly competitive Mayor knew that the PM had given him an easy time when they had faced one another in Trafalgar Square in September 2011: Johnson, after all, had an election coming up in May 2012. But he wanted to show Dave that he could beat him fair and square, and was frustrated to be denied the chance. 'Something about his racquet, a likely story,' the Mayor muttered.

The great Conservative division of the Coalition years was not Cameron versus Johnson. For a start, there was no real prospect of Boris trying to supplant his fellow Old Etonian, as much as some Tories wanted him to. By choice, he was not an MP, and despite the suggestion made by his father, Stanley, in the Cockerell film that the party 'change the rules', could not become leader until he returned to the Commons. By standing for a second term, he had taken a rational decision to be London's Mayor during the Olympics rather than to wait for a parliamentary by-election and then a reshuffle. And – in all honesty – how many of the Cabinet jobs he was likely to be given in the short term could compete with the once-in-a-lifetime thrill of standing astride the capital city during the Games?

Those who knew the Mayor best said that, ruthlessly ambitious as he undoubtedly was, he also felt constrained by a classical sense of loyalty to Cameron that verged on sentimentality. Though Heseltine was one of his mentors, he did not see Cameron as his predecessor MP for Henley had seen Thatcher. He would not be one of the assassins wielding the dagger in Pompey's portico. 'I have a dirty secret,' he confessed to one friend in the privacy of his City Hall office, 'which is that I'm actually very fond of Dave and one of his greatest admirers.' Cameron, too, wanted Boris rather than Ken to be Mayor.

Johnson's battle was with everyone else. On the night of his second victory over Livingstone, he spoke to Cameron. 'This is my last election, Dave,' he said. 'I want to go and earn some money.' Cameron could not conceal his disbelief. 'That's bollocks,' he said. Indeed it was. Johnson's formula when asked about his prime ministerial

ambitions had been to issue a non-denial denial. 'My chances of
becoming Prime Minister,' he told an audience at the Hay Festival in
June 2012, 'are only slightly better than being decapitated by a fris-
bee, blinded by a champagne cork, locked in a fridge or being
reincarnated as an olive.' It was psychologically revealing that he
always spoke about probability rather than volition. By the middle of
2012, he was beginning to tiptoe towards candour about his ambitions. In the same month, he told *New York* magazine: 'We have to
have a new airport. One of the only reasons I want to assume supreme
power in England is to make sure that happens.' Pause. 'For God's
sake, don't quote me saying that.'[10] In the Cockerell programme,
broadcast in March 2013, he finally admitted that 'if the ball came
loose from the back of the scrum' he'd quite like to be Prime Minister. He was saying it more and more. 'The thing that makes me want
to drive a T54 into Number Ten is aviation,' he told one friend in
early 2013. Increasingly, it was not just ambition. In his own eyes, he
had a mission to make Britain unbeatably attractive to business, and
to install the infrastructure and tax regime to make that possible. Like
Cameron promising to 'spread privilege', he had long declared the
enemy to be 'inequality of ambition'.[11] Unlike Cameron, he was ill at
ease with the idea of the 'broken society' and preferred the persona
of national cheerleader – part Tigger, part Churchill – to the image
of smooth statesmanship cultivated by the incumbent.

With candour came a new form of scrutiny. In a BBC interview
pegged to the documentary, Johnson was subjected to a brutal grilling by the broadcaster Eddie Mair. None of the issues raised by Mair
was new: the fabricated quotations that had led to his sacking as a
Times trainee in 1988; a phone call with his distraught friend Darius
Guppy, in which he appeared to promise information about a reporter
so he could be beaten up; and the lies he had told to conceal his affair
with fellow journalist Petronella Wyatt. What was startling about the
interview was its ferocity. 'You're a nasty piece of work, aren't you?'
Mair asked him. Johnson resembled an English sheepdog who had
gambolled up expecting a pat only to be smacked squarely across the
chops. Afterwards, Johnson conceded that Mair had done 'a splendid
job'. But the interview was like a whisper of harsh words from the

future, filtered back into the studio through some tear in the space-time continuum. Mair's questions were a pitiless reminder to the Mayor of what lay ahead if he ever stood for the leadership. To get anywhere near the top job, he needed to be able to handle such cross-examination. There were plenty of backbenchers who hoped he would try: a YouGov poll in the same month suggested that, with Johnson at the helm, the Tories might win forty to fifty more seats than they would under the present leadership.

The Conservative oligarchy – the tier of Tories beneath Cameron, many of whom rarely impinged upon the public consciousness – took a very different view. To the outsider, politics looked like a series of energized interventions and counter-interventions: from the start of the *Today* programme at 6 a.m. to the end of *Newsnight* at 11.30 p.m. and the first reviews of the next day's newspapers. It was a cascade of tweets, soundbites across the Despatch Box, the spats on *Question Time*, the snippets of speeches, shots of Cameron in shirt-sleeves hosting a 'PM Direct' session, talking heads on College Green, Nick Robinson standing in Downing Street explaining it all. And all that was important enough. But it was not the end of the matter.

Just off-screen, beyond Twitter's 140-character limit, away from the cameras and the oratory and the interviews, there was another form of politics, much of it never expressed explicitly. The late Philip Gould used to insist that a strategy did not really exist until it was written down. But 90 per cent of politics, far from being written down, is barely articulated: it exists in the pauses, the silences, the body language, the apparently casual aside. It exists in the lethal remark that only reveals its deadliness in retrospect. It is the briefing that looks parenthetical but is actually the whole point of the conversation. It is the politics that made John Major, rather than Heseltine, Prime Minister in 1990. It did for Brown in 1994, when Blair succeeded John Smith.

It was also the principal hurdle facing Boris Johnson. I was not the only journalist to be struck by the withering briefing against the Mayor by Tory oligarchs at the 2012 conference in Birmingham: middle-ranking Cabinet ministers, precisely those one would expect to feel threatened by Johnson's ascendancy and resentful of the way in which he was mobbed around the conference halls. They chipped away at the cult of Boris, questioning his capacity to head a team rather than nurture his own brand, his command of detail (although Whitehall officials who have seen him in meetings say he knows how to master a brief), and his priorities. They underestimated the power of celebrity (and a track record as a winner) in contemporary culture. The Obama phenomenon had shown that, with star quality, an apprenticeship need not be long (Obama had been Senator for less than four years when he was elected President). But the oligarchic forces of resistance could make life difficult for him.

Unlike some of his admirers, Boris did not underestimate his prospective rivals – especially Osborne. He might have beaten the Chancellor in a game of squash at Dorneywood, and trump him easily in popularity polls. But the Mayor knew toughness when he saw it. The only danger when thousands of people chanted your name in Hyde Park was that it went to your head. But it took steel to keep smiling while 80,000 people booed you. Unlike Boris, he had a well-established team of representatives in Parliament: Claire Perry, Matt Hancock, Greg Hands, Sajid Javid. The Mayor knew that Osborne considered him to be a remarkable celebrity and a unique politician but far too much of a maverick to lead the party, let alone a Government. He was linked to Cameron by memories of school and university. No such threads bound Osborne and Johnson.

By the end of 2012, Boris had become convinced that Michael Gove was being pushed by 'Dave and George' as a potential 'Stop Boris' candidate. And here New Labour did provide a precedent, for the Blair camp had groomed a series of potential successors to stand, when the time came, as the 'Stop Gordon' contender: David Blunkett, Alan Milburn, John Reid, David Miliband. All of them had been flattened by Brown's tartan juggernaut. Boris did not yet have the destructive firepower nor the inclination to do to Gove – or anyone else – what Brown had done to his prospective Blairite rivals. Gove, as we have seen, was well protected by two of the sharpest and most effective Special Advisers in Whitehall. Well-known for his oratorical gifts and talent as an after-dinner speaker, the Education Secretary liked to joke that his gravestone would bear the inscription:

'They couldn't get Boris.' But as one friend of the Education Secretary put it: 'I think if George said to Michael, "You have to stand against Boris because you have the best chance of winning, and I will back you", then Michael would find it difficult to resist the call.'

That, of course, was speculative. Beyond speculation, however, was the fact that Boris had given the Tory Party an itch it had to scratch. In politics, legitimacy depends not only upon the observation of the rules but – much more vaguely – upon the public's sense that it hasn't been hoodwinked or cheated. Because of its curious origins, the Coalition struggled every day to prove its legitimacy, not only arithmetically but in the mandate of a unifying national mission. One of the many reasons that Hague had struggled as Tory leader was that Michael Portillo, the front-runner before the election, had lost his seat and was therefore ineligible to stand. By the end of the Olympics, the Mayor's popularity had reached such a level that whoever succeeded Cameron as leader had to be Boris – or someone who had beaten Boris fair and square. All other outcomes were a recipe for trouble.

Though he talked of standing for a third term as Mayor, that sounded evasive. What Quentin Tarantino would have called 'the Boris Situation' required a collaborative solution. For the Mayor to seek a Commons seat in a by-election would look like skulduggery and a preparation for treachery. But Cameron had frequently and publicly said that he hoped Boris would carry on in public life after he left City Hall. To do that – at least at national level – he needed a seat. If he stood in the 2015 general election, with Cameron's encouragement and blessing, he would be breaking his promise not to play both roles. But he had broken promises before and been forgiven. And on this occasion he would have a reasonable, public-spirited defence – namely his wish to serve the Conservative Party and the country after eight years serving London. There was a recent precedent in Ken Livingstone, who had served as Mayor and MP for Brent East for just over a year before the 2001 general election.

Towards such a solution – or something similar – both sides edged. But it seemed unlikely that the rollercoaster ride of Johnson's career could ever submit to such a logical, calm and routine trajectory. How much more probable that it would take an unexpected turn, in some unpredictable direction. In such a saga, there were bound to be plot twists.

In the meantime, other, younger, Tories were staking their claim to define the party's future. In April 2013, Cameron appointed a 41-year-old MP, one of the promising 2010 intake, to head up his policy unit as a Cabinet Office minister, and to add political weight to the Number Ten operation. The MP in question was a friend and Bullingdon contemporary of Osborne, who had taken a First at Oxford and seemed to be headed for an editorship before he left journalism for politics. All who knew him agreed he had all the necessary talents to get to the very top. He had watched and learned, too. What better preparation for power, after all, than to be the Mayor's very own younger brother – Jo Johnson? In some households, rivalry, like charity, begins at home.

12. Omnishambles

For George Osborne, it was one of the most significant moments of the Parliament: perhaps, strategically speaking, the most symbolic. Hours after he had delivered the 2011 Autumn Statement, his Lib Dem Chief Secretary, Danny Alexander, was being grilled by Jeremy Paxman about its implications for the economy – and for his own party:

> Paxman: So you are going into the next election promising further billions of pounds of cuts in spending? That's what you're going to say in your manifesto at the next election?
> Alexander: I'm afraid so, yes.

The Chief Secretary could have kept Paxman at bay with a stock politician's answer about the folly of writing manifestos in advance. He could have alluded, politely, to the Coalition's limited lifespan and the inability to speculate on party policy beyond 2015. But Alexander did not resort to the usual stalling devices. To his interviewer's visible surprise, he accepted the principled logic of his own position. Having signed up to the austerity programme in 2010, the Lib Dems were not going to turn their backs on it at the next election. 'This is important,' the Chancellor was overheard to say after the interview. 'It really shows that the political commitment to deficit reduction is intact.'

The Coalition had taken a battering in the previous twelve months, as Nick Clegg reeled from the tuition fees row and the ignominy of the AV referendum. Now might be just the time to put some clear yellow water between himself and Cameron. But on the central mission that had brought the two parties together – deficit reduction – he and the Prime Minister, and Alexander and Osborne, remained as one. Hard as it was to envisage the Coalition lasting beyond the next election, the Chief Secretary, in a single sentence, had ensured that it might; or, at the very least, that there was not yet an impediment to it doing so embedded in the Chancellor's fiscal strategy.

This mattered enormously to Prime Minister and Chancellor alike. In January, Alan Johnson – always an odd choice as Shadow Chancellor – had resigned from Labour's front bench for personal reasons, and Miliband had handed the portfolio to Ed Balls. Nobody doubted Balls's intellectual qualification for the job, or his political abilities. But the appointment also limited Miliband's freedom of manoeuvre. The Tories believed that Labour could not win, or translate its potential support into votes, unless it took clear, unambiguous steps to distance itself from the party's past public-spending sprees. The speech that David Miliband would have given if he had won the leadership – leaked to the *Guardian* in June 2011 – addressed this problem head-on. 'George Osborne says we are in denial about the deficit. Because he wants us to be. So let's not be. It is a test.' Miliband Sr's victory-speech-that-never-was would have continued: 'However much [the Tories] are hated we will not benefit until we are trusted. Trusted on the economy as we were in the 1990s. Trusted because we show in word and deed that the alternative to mean government is lean government.'

Balls had no intention of distancing himself from past expenditure or signalling any form of contrition for Labour's fiscal strategy. He would admit that the Blair and Brown governments had not regulated the City strictly enough. But – as he put it in a *GQ* interview: 'The simplistic idea that if I stand up and say, "Yes, you're right, we spent loads and loads of money badly and we are really responsible, but the fact that I am willing to admit that now means you should trust me for the future" – people would laugh at me. So it's wrong and it's not true, and it's also a foolish thing to say.'[1] One of Cameron's private laws of the Universe was that 'if something has to happen in politics it does, sooner or later'. Pursuing his own logic, he argued that Miliband would have to get rid of Balls well before the election. But – for once – he hoped he was wrong. His own plan for a Commons majority depended considerably on Miliband and Balls failing to reassure the electorate that Labour in 2015 was substantially different from Labour in 2010. 'Same old Labour' tested well with focus groups.

One of Osborne's prime objectives in setting spending totals beyond the next election was to force Labour to respond; to show that the two Eds had learned nothing and would try to solve a borrowing crisis by borrowing more. Cameron had been known to complain to Clegg about this aspect of the Chancellor's political style: 'Sometimes George gets a bit too clever about trying to create dividing lines.' But not on this occasion. It mattered more than ever that Labour be forced to come clean about its spending and borrowing plans because the parameters for 2015 had changed.

Originally, in kitchen strategy meetings before the 2010 election, Osborne had set out a road map for his party's first term. As far as possible, the painful measures would be front-loaded. Economic stability would follow the announcement of these measures. Growth would follow stability. Finally, the 'proceeds of growth' – a phrase much used in the early days of Cameron's leadership – would be distributed in an electorally friendly fashion, so that, by 2014, the country was feeling sufficiently prosperous to reward the Conservatives with a working single-party majority.

By the summer of 2011, those pre-election supper meetings seemed a very distant memory. It was becoming clear that the Coalition was not going to fulfil Osborne's commitment to eliminate the structural deficit – the part of the deficit unaffected by growth – by 2014–15. Much of his year had been dominated by the Eurozone debt crisis and its implications for the UK economy. Indeed, senior ministers, Treasury officials and the Bank of England undertook contingency planning for the collapse of the euro: an outcome that was not yet probable but no longer inconceivable, and one that might test the very social fabric. Osborne knew full well that Labour and some economists would pin the blame on his own fiscal conservatism for the absence of growth. They were already doing so. But the Eurozone crisis, intermittently leading news bulletins, at least put his own setback in some sort of geopolitical perspective. It had thrown a great Greek spanner in the engine of global recovery.

Delivered on 29 November 2011, the Autumn Statement was, first and foremost, an inventory of bleak figures and forecasts by the Office for Budget Responsibility (now headed by Robert Chote, the former director of the Institute for Fiscal Studies). The Government would have to borrow £111bn more than it had expected only nine months before; the existing pay freezes for public sector workers would be followed by a 1 per cent cap on future increases; 710,000 public sector worker jobs would have to go by 2016/17; the rise in the state pension age to sixty-seven would be brought forward by eight years, to 2026; real household income was likely to fall by 2.3 per cent that year, the highest annual drop since the Second World War. It was a grim, autumnal inventory.

The political leap, however, was the Chancellor's decision to announce new spending totals for two years beyond the plan set out in the spending review of October 2010: total managed expenditure would fall by 0.9 per cent a year in 2015/16 and 2016/17, which is to say, beyond the election. 'It was a defining moment', according to one senior source, 'vote Tory for more cuts! The risk was huge.' But not, the same source says, as huge as it seemed. First, Osborne and Alexander had no real option, without tearing up their fiscal strategy entirely: there had to be more cuts. Second, the Chancellor's shocking candour put immediate pressure upon Miliband and Balls to decide whether they would match Coalition spending plans or not. That is always a difficult decision for an Opposition. But Miliband had no wish to answer it little more than a year after becoming leader.

Working in the engine room of the Treasury with Alexander, Osborne had come to believe more and more in the need for a new age of realism. The dominant culture of Western politics was still steroidal and hyperbolic – Obama's 'Yes We Can!' continued to resonate as the outstanding recent example of that culture's electoral potential. The President's campaigning slogan was the purest (and perhaps final) expression of the baby boomers' expectation that you could have it all, that nothing was unaffordable, that this new credit card, or second home, or fourth holiday, was within your grasp. Property was worth having as collateral for yet more credit. But – as the Eurozone countries were now being painfully reminded – the global debt party was over.

The only question was how quickly it was politically possible to clean up the mess – the complaint from some on Osborne's own side being that his measures were too modest and slow. By the Left, he was accused of dismantling the state and paralysing the economy; by the Right he was caricatured as Alistair Darling with a blue rosette, only marginally tougher than the last Labour Chancellor.

Osborne would never satisfy those who saw politics as a branch of economics. True radicalism, he understood, had to go with the grain of humanity. Revolutions in advanced democracies are rarely fast. Like Bismarck, he believed that politics was the art of the possible and that it was not trimming, or woolly compromise, or betrayal, to embrace this reality. He liked to remind those who demanded that he be more 'Thatcherite' that spending had risen in real terms under the Iron Lady and that when she tried to force through a reform – the poll tax – that offended the distinctly British sense of social justice, she was finished. Like his mentor, Nigel Lawson, he had little interest in ideology when it strayed beyond the limits of the politically feasible.

His Autumn Statement stayed within those boundaries, but hinted at tougher measures to come, especially in its paragraphs on the public sector. The end of national pay-bargaining, for instance, was now within sight. Pay represented 30 per cent of all public spending, so the localization of wage rates was a potentially huge structural change.

These measures were announced on the eve of the biggest strike in three decades, as more than thirty unions took action in protest at the cuts to public sector pensions. Around two million strikers ensured that most schools were closed, refuse was not collected, hospitals and town halls struggled to function, and transport services were thrown into disarray. The Civil Contingencies Committee, with Osborne and Michael Gove among those present, held a series of meetings to discuss the detail of the response. As we have seen, each time such an emergency arose – as it had in the riots, as it did again in May 2012, when a fuel strike was threatened – the same basic question was posed: who governs? Who is in charge round here? In such circumstances, the Coalition's task was invariably to exude competence. It had to be ready to trade tactical unpopularity for strategic respect.

The Autumn Statement of 2011 reframed the central political contest. At a stroke, a one-term fiscal strategy became a two-term fiscal strategy: a realignment of policy that required a corresponding realignment of the Conservative campaign for 2015. The principal argument would not be a bid for gratitude – 'Look how well you've done out of us' – but a plea for patience – 'Let us finish the job'. In due course, Bill Clinton would provide a template for such a campaign in his speech to the Democratic Convention nominating Obama for a second term. 'No president – not me, not any of my predecessors – no one could have fully repaired all the damage that he found in just four years,' Clinton said. 'But he has laid the foundations for a new, modern, successful economy of shared prosperity. And if you will renew the president's contract you will feel it.'

That – or a version of it – was going to be Cameron's pitch in 2015, and the PM started to quote the speech as a text for the campaign. What mattered was the idea of a trajectory, a direction of travel, and the risks of deviating from it. As long ago as the Tory conference of 2009, Cameron had warned that 'it will be a steep climb. But the view from the summit will be worth it.' Six years on, he was going to have to renew that pledge to an increasingly impatient nation. The forbidding question was how to persuade the voters that progress had been made and the path up which they were all trudging was still the right one.

Having steered the Autumn Statement through the political shoals, Osborne began to plan the 2012 Budget and a series of crunchy decisions. Though he was unimpressed by claims that the Coalition lacked a 'growth strategy', he sympathized with prospective investors in the UK, entrepreneurs and mobile high earners who told him that the 50p rate of income tax was a serious disincentive to them. The Revenue reported that it had raised only £1bn – a disappointingly small compensation for its deterrence effect.[2] In practice, the top rate was no more than a symbolic levy, dramatizing the 'fairness' of the measures made necessary by fiscal crisis. It was a crude and ineffective instrument, penal taxation masquerading as social democracy. But it was hard for politicians – especially those from privileged backgrounds – to quarrel with the principle that those who earned more than £150,000 a year should pay tax at a higher rate. Why would a Government insisting that it would not 'balance the books on the backs of the poor' be reducing the burden on those who earned more than 5.5 times the average wage? Why, when it was cutting public spending across the board, demanding co-payment from students, cutting benefits and public sector pensions, and squeezing savings from the NHS, should this Government, before its second birthday, be giving help to the rich? For the political-media class living in London, £150,000 p.a. might seem no more than a desirable salary, but to the overwhelming majority of the forty-six million registered to vote in the UK the sum was almost unimaginably huge.

Osborne picked his battles within the Government very carefully, but, in this case, he believed the cost of caution would be too high. The Chancellor understood the need for reform of the financial sector, which was why he had established the Vickers Commission. He continued to raise the bank levy. Later in the year, he backed a parliamentary inquiry – though not, as Labour did, a judicial investigation – into the Libor scandal that had driven Bob Diamond from the chief executive's post at Barclays.[3] But on the 50p rate the Chancellor had reached a clear conclusion in favour of abolition.

And not just abolition. 'I want the 50p rate to go back to 40p,' Osborne said. Cameron, who was profoundly anxious about the whole idea, turned to Clegg: 'What do you think?' Clegg did not mince words: 'I think it's unbelievably difficult.' The PM agreed. Poll after poll showed that his party was widely perceived not to care about the vulnerable and the struggling.[4] That suspicion would be deeply compounded by the abolition of the 50p rate; he would, he feared, be marching into the elephant trap left for him by Brown's Government in the 2009 Budget.

As a Lib Dem, Clegg did not have to worry as deeply as Cameron did about the electorate's perception of his motive. Defeated on electoral reform, his priority was to secure a decent policy victory that was recognizably of Lib Dem origin. He and Cable sensed that

Osborne had some sympathy for the argument that income was taxed too heavily and wealth too little. The Lib Dem manifesto had called for a 'mansion tax' of 1 per cent for properties worth £2m, 'paid on the value of the property above that level'. The problems implicit in such a measure were manifold – not least the fate of elderly home-owners living on modest incomes whose properties had shot up in value over a long period of occupancy (a relatively common phenomenon in newly desirable parts of London). What would such a person do when presented with an unexpected bill from the Revenue of £10,000? These and other anomalies would have to be addressed. There was a more general fear that such a tax would necessitate property revaluation and higher council taxes. But the Chancellor was open to discussion.

Clegg saw the scope for a grand deal: despite his serious reservations, he would endorse the outright abolition of the 50p tax rate, so that the top rate would be 40 per cent for those earning more than £42,475 (where the limit stood in 2011–12). In return, Osborne would agree to a mansion tax – a shift in the structure of taxation for which the Lib Dems could noisily claim responsibility. The Chancellor was tempted. 'What is really the problem with this?' he mused aloud. But Cameron was appalled by the whole idea and ran his prime ministerial blue pencil through it, vigorously and definitively. The political impact upon London and the South-East of such a tax would, he argued, be terrible for the Tories: 'How are we going to get Boris re-elected?' he asked. And that wasn't all. 'Our donors will never put up with it,' the PM declared. 'At least he's honest,' Clegg mused to aides after the grand bargain had been stopped in its tracks.

Though the mansion tax was dead in the water, Cameron was coming round to Osborne's position on the top rate of tax. The Chancellor piled on the anecdotal evidence and argued – persuasively – that every Budget and every Autumn Statement would be overshadowed by this issue until they resolved it. 'If not now, when?' was a potent question. Clegg pressed Cameron for a quid pro quo. 'You're pushing me way beyond my comfort zone,' he told the PM. 'You are cutting the upper rate at a time of austerity.' But he could see that the Chancellor had won the argument in principle.

In practice, two variables remained: how far to reduce the top rate of tax, and what to give the Lib Dems in return? A tense meeting in the Prime Minister's flat followed to resolve these questions. Much as he wanted to abolish the 50p rate altogether, Osborne realized that Cameron was simply not ready to take that risk. The Revenue's analysis showed that, while the 50p rate raised next-to-nothing compared to 45p, there was some prospective difference in tax-take between a top rate of 40p and one of 45p. Clegg sought advice from his longtime ally Neil Sherlock, who had left his senior position at KPMG to become his director of government relations. Sherlock, discreet and friendly, had been nicknamed the 'Warlock' by journalists because of his political wizardry (he had, after all, defeated Boris Johnson for the Oxford Union presidency in the Trinity term of 1985). Sherlock advised Clegg on the likely implications for revenue of different rates. He also urged him not to go down to 40p, which had been the top rate for all but one month of New Labour's thirteen years in power. On this matter, Lib Dem differentiation with Labour's past was essential. Thus, by a process of elimination and for different reasons, Cameron, Osborne and Clegg converged upon 45p.

The price exacted by Clegg was a substantial increase in the annual personal tax allowance from £8,105 to £9,205 – a tax cut for twenty-five million people that would also lift two million out of income tax altogether. The sticking point, which led to an uncomfortable exchange and exasperation on both sides, was timing. Clegg felt it was essential that the two tax cuts – 50p rate and personal allowance – should happen simultaneously. Cameron objected: 'Come on, once the 50p cut is announced people will think it's happened.' Clegg stood his ground. 'No,' he said. 'They *have* to happen at the same time.' The atmosphere was one experienced time and again by Coalition ministers in a fix: lifelong habits of courtesy straining under the weight of exasperation, and acrimony hanging in the air like the scent of cordite. In the end, Cameron and Osborne recognized that they needed Clegg's support at a moment of high political vulnerability and let him have his way on timing: both measures would come into force in April 2013.

The Coalition's ruling triumvirate believed that the Budget was risky but necessary and politically balanced. Osborne felt sufficiently well-prepared to accompany Cameron on his trip to Washington. This was a serious works outing: in addition to the Prime Minister, his wife and the Chancellor, the travelling party included Hilton, Llewellyn, Fall, Oliver, Gabby Bertin and Rupert Harrison. The President did everything he could to signal to the wider world that he valued his alliance with Cameron personally, as well as with Britain strategically. The visual highlight of the trip was the image of President and Prime Minister, casually dressed, watching a basketball game together in Dayton, Ohio. The jet-lagged Cameron was even allowed to sleep in the presidential bed on Air Force One on the way back from the outing. Obama was now visibly at ease with his British friend, he and the First Lady quite content to sit chatting with the PM, Osborne and Hague on the terrace of the presidential residence. Cameron's team had come a long way since 2008 when Obama himself had dismissed the Tory leader as a 'lightweight' and US officials reported the view of Mervyn King, Governor of the Bank of England, that Osborne 'lacked depth'.[5] Osborne was now on very good terms with Tim Geithner, Obama's Treasury Secretary, and Robert Zoellick, the president of the World Bank. The Cameron Government had gambled on Obama's re-election and enmeshed itself with his administration.

When Osborne was later pressed on the wisdom of his decision to go to Washington the week before a Budget, he would produce a framed photograph from the trip to the US with undisguised excitement. Though a Roundhead *ex officio*, he was a Cavalier by temperament, determined to experience everything that politics had to offer. He might, for instance, deplore all that Balls stood for, but he thoroughly enjoyed the company of his opposite number – who often said that Osborne was the Tory he would like to have a drink with. For this Chancellor, the choice between going to America to hang out with Obama or lingering in London to monitor Twitter and the blogs in case of Budget leaks was no choice at all.

It is probably true, furthermore, that the unravelling of the Budget would not have been prevented if Osborne had been on duty at his Treasury desk for the whole of the week before his speech on

21 March. Possibly, the media management would have been better if the Chancellor had been around to stop what he was sure were leaks from the Lib Dems. By the time he stood up in the Commons, almost every significant measure had already been pre-announced and the only stories left to be written concerned the smaller measures that were meant to pay for the big ones. Osborne ran through the principal announcements in less than an hour: stamp duty would be charged at 7 per cent on any property bought for more than £2m and at 15 per cent if it was bought through a company. As ever, Number Ten, in a wishlist drafted by Rohan Silva, had requested a big drop in corporation tax – a symbolic fiscal Big Bang – and, as ever, the Treasury had opted for a gradual decrease – from 26 per cent to 24 per cent in this case.

The day after the Budget, Osborne knew instinctively that he was in big trouble, feeling like an Old Testament prophet who suddenly foretells 'six months of anguish'. There were, he saw, two serious errors, one of substance, the other of presentation. First, he had increased too many little taxes to raise the revenue necessary to pay for the higher personal allowance. This meant that he was fighting a whole range of battles simultaneously with aggrieved interest groups, some of them well-represented in the media. It would, he realized, have been easier to pick one revenue-raising measure and take all the political pain in one dose. Second, he had expected the increase in the personal allowance to have greater traction as a moment of political significance – the liberation of two million people, the least affluent in the workforce, from income tax. That ought to have been cause for celebration, evidence of the Government's commitment to those on the bottom rung – or so it had seemed. But nobody wanted to know. The cut from 50p to 45p generated a much greater controversy, stoked by Miliband's instant (and adhesive) judgement that this was a 'millionaire's Budget'.

Even as Osborne was issuing his biblical prophecy, he was being taken to task over the so-called 'granny tax'. In his Budget, he had announced that the century-old 'age-related allowance', which meant that pensioners started paying tax at a higher income level, was to be phased out. The tax break had been worth, on average, £285 a year, to five million older people, who would now pay an extra £3.3bn in income tax over the following four years. This was trespass on terrain notionally treated as sacred by Cameron – pensioners' entitlements. Osborne's claim that the removal of the tax break was a 'simplification' merely exasperated those who saw this as an unconscionable stealth tax.

Also under fire was the Chancellor's proposed cap of £50,000 on tax relief for charitable donations. The justification for such a limit was to stop those on higher incomes making excessive use of this form of relief. But the charities fought back, hard and systematically. John Low, the chief executive of the Charities Aid Foundation, argued that 'tax relief on major donations is not tax avoidance. It is supporting major donations by people who in some cases are donating the proceeds of a lifetime's work to charity.' Universities, which were especially vulnerable to such a cap, joined the clamour. In May, Osborne announced a complete U-turn on this proposal. 'It is clear from our conversations with charities,' he said, 'that any kind of cap could damage donations, and as I said at the Budget that's not what we want at all. So we've listened.' He listened, too, on the so-called 'heritage tax', his plan to raise VAT on building improvements, offering places of worship 100 per cent compensation.

The serious politics of the elderly, of charities, of churches and of their respective treatment was matched by the absurdity of the 'pasty tax'. In a document on VAT anomalies published as part of the Budget, the Government proposed to 'apply VAT at the standard rate to all food which is at a temperature above the ambient air temperature at the time that it is provided to the customer, with the exception of freshly baked bread. This will clarify the rules in this area and ensure that all hot takeaway food is taxed consistently.'[6] Like so many attempts by officialdom to end an anomaly, it seemed to pose more questions than it answered.

Worse, it made Cameron and Osborne seem out of touch with ordinary people and their eating habits. The *Sun* launched a 'Who VAT all the pies?' campaign. The Chancellor, pressed by Labour MPs, could not remember when he last ate a pasty. Cameron claimed he had enjoyed one at Leeds railway station – only to be caught out by the *Sun*, which established that there was nowhere at the station to buy pasties. Osborne was forced into a partial climbdown, exempting products that were left to return to 'ambient temperatures' on shelves in shops and bakeries; food kept warm in hot cabinets would still be liable. The U-turn was estimated to have cost the Treasury £40m. But its real cost was political.

In the great fiscal scheme, the 'pasty tax' was a minor matter. So too was the climbdown on VAT for static caravans – which would now be imposed at 5 per cent rather than 20 per cent. But both episodes chimed awkwardly with the suspicion that the Coalition's most senior figures were hopelessly detached from normal life and seemed at times to be speaking to ordinary people from a phrase book. With nimbler political footwork, the overall capping of tax relief could have been presented as a 'tycoon tax'. Aside from the U-turn on charitable donation, Osborne insisted that anyone seeking to claim more than £50,000 of relief a year would have a cap set at 25 per cent of their income. This measure, championed by Clegg and inspired by Obama, was a riposte to the charge that Osborne had delivered a Budget for the rich. Just as no household could claim more in benefits than the average income, so no wealthy person could slip below the 25 per cent tax rate (Ken Livingstone was badly damaged in the 2012 Mayoral contest by the disclosure that he had paid an effective income tax of only 14.5 per cent – less than a City Hall cleaner). The symmetry between the two caps was there to be explained and proclaimed. But the 'tycoon tax' proposal made little impact upon the political class, let alone the public consciousness. That, in turn, reflected the strong appearance of central malfunction, reinforcing the sorry impression of an administration whose screen had frozen.

Precisely when backbench discipline was most needed, it was lacking. Revolts on financial measures are unusual, as they are generally regarded as issues of confidence. Yet, on 18 April, the Government suffered a series of unsettling revolts over the Budget, as dozens of Coalition MPs rebelled over its various provocations. In the original vote to impose 20 per cent VAT on static caravans, the Government's majority fell from eighty-three to twenty-five.

At PMQs on the same day, Miliband landed a clean left hook: 'On charities, the reality is that the Prime Minister is not making the rich worse off. He is making charities worse off. Over the past month we have seen the charity tax shambles, the churches tax shambles, the caravan tax shambles and the pasty tax shambles, so we are all keen to hear the Prime Minister's view on why he thinks, four weeks on from the Budget, even people within Downing Street are calling it an omnishambles Budget.'

The description stuck. In a piece for Conservative Home the following day, Lord Ashcroft said that the threat of the UK Independence Party 'is linked to what some have unkindly called, sadly correctly, the "omnishambles" of recent weeks'. Ashcroft continued: 'I think Conservative voters will stay with the party – and others will support us – IF they see a competent government with a grip on events, a plan for the economy, an understanding of public services, that knows what it wants to achieve, and can show that it is delivering on its promises on things like crime and immigration. If they cannot see such a government, then yes, some will go to UKIP – and some will go to Labour, or elsewhere, or stay at home. The main problem is not so much that people think the Conservative Party is heading in the wrong direction, it is that they are not sure where it is heading. And that includes me.'[7]

Such language is lethal when it rings true. In a single word, borrowed from a Malcolm Tucker rant, the Coalition had been scorned as a team of incompetents; clueless as to where it was going except that it would lead to a U-turn; undisciplined, demoralized and – perhaps – all washed up. It was now Cameron's urgent task to prove otherwise. If he failed, it might – as he knew – be his last task, too.

Never had David Cameron been so solitary. Sir Jon Cunliffe, the Prime Minister's adviser on Europe and Global Affairs, about to become the UK's man in Brussels, warned him before the EU summit in December 2011: 'It is the one form of negotiation where you will be completely alone.' As Conservative leader and now Prime Minister, he had quickly grown used to the sensation of being surrounded by aides and assistants: even over Christmas, when he embarked on long country walks, his protection officers were always close by, ready to pick him up, wherever he was. But he had taken no entourage into the dinner and talks with his twenty-six fellow EU heads of government on the evening of 8 December. It was a ridiculous way to do business. They ate, each nation had its say, and then the haggling began. The night wore on. Cameron could see that Nicolas Sarkozy was getting impatient and, though Angela Merkel was more sympathetic to the British dilemma, she was not going to back the Prime Minister. Cameron explained that he could not sign up to the proposed deal for the reform of the euro and of the EU's capacity to intervene in national fiscal decisions. Though Britain stood outside the single currency, Cameron regarded the proposed compact, sweeping in its scope, as a threat to the single market generally and the British financial sector specifically. The PM did his best to sound reasonable and accommodating – but firm. After he was finished, as he told aides afterwards, 'Sarkozy went off on one.'

As the French President raged at perfidious Albion, Cameron reflected that the Anglo-French bond forged over Libya had its limits. The pressure continued, the hours passed. It was obvious, the PM explained afterwards, that 'they thought I would cave', and had planned accordingly. In such situations, time, peer pressure and fatigue usually did the trick, forcing the caffeine-soaked summiteers to sign something – anything – so they could go outside, claim victory to the press, and get to bed. But Cameron did not want agreement at any price, and had made clear in a BBC interview with Nick Robinson for the *Six O'Clock News* on the Wednesday that he was more than willing to deploy the British veto if necessary.

'What I'm saying is that if – and Eurozone countries do need to come together, do need to do more things together – if they choose to use the European Treaty to do that, Britain will be insisting on some safeguards too,' he said. 'As long as we get those, then that treaty can go ahead. If we can't get those, it won't.' Evidently, his EU partners thought this was mere sabre-rattling to pacify his truculent Eurosceptic backbenchers. But, on this occasion, it was no such thing. By 2.30 a.m. on 9 December, it was overwhelmingly apparent to him that no acceptable deal was on the table. Cameron was no believer in needless sleep deprivation, and often boasted that he dropped off as soon as his head hit the pillow. Explaining his position, the British Prime Minister walked out.

Eighteen months afterwards, the legal impact of Cameron's veto was still a matter of contention. Could the other twenty-six countries go ahead with a full-blown pact that was implemented by EU institutions? The PM initially appeared to assent to this, but the detail was far from clear. In the so-called 'Pringle' judgment of November 2012, the European Court of Justice ruled that 'the Member States are entitled, in areas which do not fall under the exclusive competence of the Union, to entrust tasks to the institutions, outside the framework of the Union . . . provided that those tasks do not alter the essential character of the powers conferred on those institutions by the EU and FEU [Functioning of the European Union] Treaties'.[1] But whether this constituted legally watertight permission for the EU-minus-Britain to use the Union's institutions as it pleased to enact a save-the-euro fiscal strategy was still hotly contested.

In contrast, the political significance of the veto was evident from the moment Cameron walked out of the room. As a young Special Adviser, he had watched the EU destroy John Major, as it had helped to destroy Margaret Thatcher. After 1989, Europe had filled the Marx-shaped hole in the world-view of the Left. Tony Blair had detected a secular providence and political teleology in the European dream, and, in his 2002 party conference speech, even referred to the euro as 'not just about our economy, but our destiny'. Gordon Brown had saved Blair and Britain from that millennial goal with his 'five tests' for Britain's membership of the single currency.[2] Extraordinarily, however, it was not until Osborne's emergency Budget in June 2010 that the Treasury's 'Euro Preparations Unit' was finally abolished; the last, fossilized remains of the 'prepare and decide' strategy of the New Labour years.

There had been a time when its most fervent advocates spoke of the euro becoming a global currency like the dollar, and warned that Britain would be consigned to irrelevance outside this new currency. Now, as the Eurozone crisis gripped the continent, rather different questions asserted themselves: how great would the impact be upon the recovery of the UK economy and how important was it to the British national interest to prevent the implosion of the single currency?

For Cameron, the fate of the euro and of the EU was not only a geopolitical matter; it was a totemic issue for his tribe. The Conservative Party was now divided only between different kinds of Eurosceptic; between those who wanted to stay in the EU, but on a renegotiated basis, and those, like the MEP and journalist Daniel Hannan and the lucid MP for Clacton, Douglas Carswell, who believed Britain would be better off outside. Like Steve Hilton's case for exit, Carswell's argument was not driven by nostalgia but the very opposite: a conviction that membership of a slow-moving, unaccountable, continent-wide bureaucracy made little sense in a new century, the politics of which would be transformed by networks, transparency and a new form of democracy driven by digital technology.[3] They argued not that the EU was a horribly modern peril to all they held sacred, but that it was not modern enough: a relic of the last century. What mattered (such Tories argued) was the freedom to trade globally and the pursuit not only of wealth but of wealth-per-capita. It was time, they said, to make a break with Britain's obsession with scale and post-colonial reach, and to imagine Britain as a free, prosperous Singapore off the shore of Europe.

Ken Clarke and Michael Heseltine remained keen supporters of the EU ideal, but they were the Last of the Euro-hicans, having failed to persuade a younger cohort of Tories to follow their path. They had, it seemed, no new arguments. In his 2012 conference speech, Cameron spoke of the countries that were on the rise in the new global contest. 'They are lean, fit, obsessed with enterprise,' he declared, contrasting such countries with those in decline: 'Fat, sclerotic, over-regulated, spending money on unaffordable welfare systems, huge pension bills, unreformed public services.' Implicitly, he was detaching Britain's future from the European past.

The problem confronting Cameron was one of disappointment and of emphasis. As Hague's adviser, Daniel Finkelstein had remarked that some Tory Eurosceptics 'wouldn't take "Yes" for an answer'. No matter what the Conservative leader – Major, Hague, Duncan Smith, Howard, and now Cameron – proposed, there would always be a core of irreconcilables, convinced that they were being sold out or stitched up. The objective was always to keep their numbers to a manageable limit, so that the business of Parliament was not entirely at the mercy of a backbench caucus – as it had been during Major's ratification of the Maastricht Treaty. After the 2010 election, Cameron was heard to remark that coalition with Clegg was probably easier than governing with a small majority and being 'in coalition with Bill Cash' – the fervently Eurosceptic veteran MP for Stone. Cash had been known to well up when contemplating the sacrifice which, in his own view, he had made by standing up for Britain's interests in the Commons. 'I could have been in the Cabinet, you know,' he would say in private.

As for emphasis, Cameron knew that the party had suffered electorally because it appeared to be too preoccupied by Europe. Consistently, poll after poll showed that Tory policy on the EU was very much in line with majority opinion. But Europe was not a priority for most voters at the end of 2011. Even more than they had in the years of prosperity, the electorate worried about jobs, the economy, their children's future, their family's security, local health services, housing, crime and the chaotic immigration system. When Hague promised to 'Keep the Pound' in the 2001 election, his pledge chimed with the electorate – but it was nowhere near enough. Cameron knew that the Conservative promise had to be broad and all-encompassing, and that the party could no more appear to be a single-issue pressure group obsessed by Brussels than it could a club of the rich.

This was why the Tory leader warned his party in 2006 to stop 'banging on about Europe'. His point was not that it had to moderate its collective opinion of the EU – that was non-negotiable – but that it had to show it offered the voters more than shrill hostility to Brussels. In this respect, he was quite right. In an Ipsos MORI survey conducted just before the 2010 election, 'Europe/EU' was ranked only sixteenth in a list of 'very important' issues, cited by a mere 3 per cent of those certain to vote. But Cameron's intervention at his first party conference as leader infuriated many Eurosceptic MPs, who felt they had been conned.

Their fury was exacerbated when he announced that there would be no referendum on the Lisbon Treaty once it was part of European law. His 'cast-iron guarantee' to hold a popular vote no longer applied (see Chapter 10). But Cameron had not gone soft on the EU. As promised in the 2005 leadership contest, and to the particular dismay of Angela Merkel, the German Chancellor, he withdrew the Conservative Party from the centre-Right grouping in the European Parliament, the European People's Party. In June 2009, Hague announced the formation of the European Conservatives and Reformists (ECR), 'an anti-federalist' bloc initially composed of fifty-five MEPs. The grouping was mocked as marginal and ideologically dubious. Hague's future Cabinet colleague in the Coalition Ed Davey declared that the Tories had now 'left the mainstream of European politics and joined forces with a rag-bag of parties with extreme views. The Conservatives have opted to throw away influence in Europe in favour of ideological isolationism.' In the second leaders' TV debate in Bristol, Clegg accused Cameron of aligning himself with 'nutters, anti-Semites, people who deny climate change exists, homophobes' – less than three weeks before he aligned himself with Cameron. For the Tory leader, this sort of rhetoric was a small price to pay for the delivery of a promise he had made four years before when looking for ways to draw Eurosceptic votes away from David Davis and Liam Fox. He hoped it would sedate the hard-core backbenchers and keep them onside: a naive expectation, if ever there was one.

In office, Hague had to make clear what he had meant by his cryptic promise that – if the EU Lisbon Treaty were ratified – he would not 'let matters rest there'. In the European Union Bill, he offered part of the answer – legislation that stated explicitly that European law derived its authority solely from Parliament (a rebuff to senior judges who had claimed otherwise). It gave Parliament a greater say in what ministers could and could not agree with Brussels. Above all, it established a framework for referendums on EU measures that would be hard for future governments to repeal. As the Foreign Secretary put it in the *Sunday Telegraph*, it 'will put into the British people's hands a referendum lock on any further changes to the EU's treaties that hand over powers from Britain to the EU, a lock to which only they will hold the key . . . a massive advance for national democracy'.[4] But not massive enough for some Tory backbenchers, who insisted that the Bill was too vague, allowed ministers excessive discretion over the trigger for a referendum, and declared the sovereignty of the Queen-in-Parliament with insufficient clarity. In a wonderful collision of metaphors, Cash protested that one of its clauses was 'a judicial Trojan horse leaping out of Pandora's box'. Brussels, the sceptics complained, was continuing to accrue power – in the extension of the EU arrest warrant, in the Van Rompuy report on economic governance, in its ambitions to regulate the City. The Tory manifesto had explicitly promised that 'key powers over legal rights, criminal justice and social and employment legislation' would be restored to the UK from Brussels. Yet, in November 2010, Clegg had insisted that 'we are not going to reopen this issue of the repatriation of powers. We are not proposing to go backwards.'

There was plenty of legal content to this parliamentary conflict. But, at root, it was about trust. For some MPs, the prospect of future referendums was poor recompense for what they saw as an unforgivable broken promise on the Lisbon Treaty. The presence in the

Cabinet of staunch Eurosceptics such as Iain Duncan Smith, Owen Paterson and (until October 2011) Liam Fox was partly intended to reassure the parliamentary party. But Tory MPs still saw the hand of Clegg at work in everything. They had been denied a referendum on Lisbon – while the Deputy Prime Minister had been granted one on the obscure issue of AV. To the more suspicious Conservatives, the polyglot Clegg, a former MEP and a passionate European, personified everything they dreaded: a charming euro-entryist, quietly nudging Cameron towards a weaker position on Europe. Such is the paranoia bred by coalition. Bruised by the tuition fees debacle and the disaster of the referendum, Clegg wondered if Cameron's backbenchers grasped the reality of his situation and the limits of his influence.

In October, a motion submitted by David Nuttall, the Conservative MP for Bury North, came before the House, thanks to a new system which allotted Commons time to e-petitions that had secured more than 100,000 signatures and then been selected by the Backbench Business Committee. This particular motion called for a referendum on Britain's membership of the EU. Cameron could have treated the whole business as a perfectly legitimate opportunity for backbenchers to vent their frustrations, before a free vote that would not be binding upon the Government.

Instead, he insisted that the debate be brought forward so that he and Hague could be present, and imposed a three-line whip. A parliamentary wheeze had suddenly become a trial of strength between the PM and his increasingly testy backbenchers – quite unnecessarily, in the collective view of the party and of many media commentators. Number Ten made it clear that the vote was not an issue of conscience but of party loyalty, and that each rebel vote would be interpreted unambiguously as a gross discourtesy. Osborne had a technique with recalcitrant MPs which was to praise their bravery. 'Very courageous of you,' he would say icily, 'to put your career in a cul-de-sac because of your principles.' There were times when Cameron and Osborne would play 'good cop, bad cop', but this was not one of them. The parliamentary party felt that it was entitled to vent its frustration and demand a referendum in a non-binding motion. But the PM and Chancellor had a phased EU strategy – not yet made public – which they did not want disrupted by what one senior Cabinet minister called 'student politics'.

The risk was high. There had been bad blood between the leadership and MPs since the expenses scandal. In the Coalition's first month, Cameron had made an ill-advised bid to transform the character of the backbench 1922 Committee by allowing ministers to take part in its deliberations. The ostensible case for the proposal was that, in coalition, a party needs to act cohesively in Parliament and cannot afford strategic division between ministers and MPs. But this was an opportunistic argument. After four and a half years trying to bring the parliamentary party to heel, Cameron saw his chance and seized it. In the first weeks of his partnership with the Lib Dems, it was still possible to talk about the 'new politics' without provoking laughter and the new Prime Minister saw no reason why this supposedly grand realignment should not involve rule changes that would, at last, tame the 1922 Committee. In this instance, arrogance bred misjudgement: Cameron had seriously over-reached himself, infuriating his backbenchers, who recognized the bulldozer of control as it rolled noisily towards them.

A legal challenge organized by Cash forced a face-saving compromise whereby members of the front bench were able to attend but not to vote – a point clarified by Number Ten and the committee's new chairman, Graham Brady.[5] But the ill-feeling lingered, compounded by the shortage of patronage under a Prime Minister at the head of a Coalition who had a temperamental aversion to reshuffles. Time and again, the rebels in October 2011 voiced private fury at the appointment earlier in the month of 29-year-old Chloe Smith as Economic Secretary to the Treasury. Hell hath no fury like a middle-aged male Tory scorned.

As the day of Nuttall's motion approached, the PM's team hoped that George Eustice, formerly his press secretary, now leader of the 'Fresh Start' group of Eurosceptic MPs, could broker a compromise. When that failed, Cameron, his senior colleagues and his aides could only warn MPs that they would be reading the division lists very carefully – with the heavy-handed insinuation that careers were on the line. Patrick McLoughlin, the Chief Whip, was regarded by the

Prime Minister both as a 'Willie Whitelaw figure' (to quote one Number Ten aide) – a source of discreet and reliable guidance – and a trustworthy enforcer, who knew exactly how far to go. In an administration of well-manicured political apparatchiks, McLoughlin was a former miner who was sometimes nicknamed 'Clemenza', after the *Godfather* character, because of his burly frame and absolute intolerance of indiscipline and self-indulgence. He would later urge the sacking of Brooks Newmark, the MP for Braintree, from the whips' office over his supposedly undignified use of Twitter (Newmark frequently tweeted on television and films he had watched). 'This is not the fucking Oxford Union,' the ex-miner was overheard yelling at one rebel. 'This is not some fucking sixth-form debating society. This is the bloody House of Commons.'[6] There were rumours that the defiant would be docked holiday time, blocked for four years from becoming a minister and even deselected. But this did not prevent eighty-one Tories defying the whip. After the vote, they filled the bars, embraced one another and toasted what they considered a moral victory. The Coalition had picked a fight with the Conservative Party, and been given a bloody nose.

Tory discipline had rarely been so poor in Cameron's five years as leader, and even some of his closest allies wondered why he had been so inflexible. The answer lay in the past, and in the future. The PM was ready to risk a bad outcome – which was precisely what he got – to make clear to his MPs that EU policy was too important for parliamentary self-indulgence. He could not, he felt, turn a blind eye to a motion that called for a referendum on Britain's membership. There could be no return to the nineties and the parliamentary mayhem of the Major years. He had no wish to be at odds with his backbenchers and was quick, after the vote, to stretch a hand out to the 'valued Conservative colleagues' who had embarrassed him only a few hours previously. But he wanted them to know that he would not tolerate parliamentary anarchy on European diplomacy. Whether they would back down was another matter. As one Downing Street source put it at the time: 'The question is: have the rebels got a taste for blood?' This episode was the closest Cameron had yet come to saying: 'Back me or sack me.'

He also required a backdrop of party discipline if he was going to enact his broader strategy on Europe. It had always been his intention that Hague should oversee a review of the 'balance of competences' between Britain and the European Union, a process that was formally launched in July 2012.[7] The findings of this investigation would form the basis of a bid for a renegotiation of Britain's membership of the EU. From the first stirrings of the Eurozone crisis, Cameron and Osborne had come to believe that this plan, though fiendishly difficult, was feasible. If the seventeen nations within the troubled currency were to secure the European fiscal structure they needed to give it a chance of surviving, they would require the active assistance of Britain, still the third-biggest net contributor to the EU. As the PM and Chancellor saw it, they had been presented with a once-in-a-generation opportunity to reboot the UK's relationship with Europe. The euro-kaleidoscope had been shaken, and the dynamics of the EU potentially transformed.

On the European stage, Cameron's objective was to show that he wanted Britain to stay in the EU – but not at any cost. His counterparts needed to realize that his demands were serious, not merely a theatrical turn for domestic consumption. The veto, less than two months after the Commons vote, served notice that the British Prime Minister meant what he said. And, as would become clear, he had a lot more to say.

On his return from Brussels after the summit, Cameron was hailed a hero by Tory backbenchers gathered for a dinner at Chequers. Nick Boles sent him a text via Ed Llewellyn telling him that he was now in such a strong position that he could safely announce to the 1922 Committee his intention to make a Christmas present of the Falklands to Argentina's president, Cristina Kirchner.

Meanwhile, Clegg was seething. On hearing the news very early on 9 December, his initial reaction had been one of shocked resignation rather than fury. He saw little option but to distance himself from the Eurosceptic celebrations and hold his fire. But on the Saturday he took soundings and decided to speak out. Richard Reeves, his strategy director, urged him to stand up for what he believed, and for his very clear conviction that the national interest would be damaged by self-indulgent isolation. On Sunday, Clegg told the BBC's Andrew Marr that he was 'bitterly disappointed by the outcome of the summit', adding that there was now a real danger that the UK would be 'marginalized within the EU. I don't think that's good for jobs, in the City or elsewhere, it's not good for growth, and it's not good for families up and down the country.'

Behind the scenes, he complained to his senior Tory colleagues that the lack of consultation had been a disgrace and made a mockery of his position as Deputy Prime Minister. 'I should have been consulted!' was the refrain. Cameron's team, meanwhile, was vexed that Clegg's tantrum was becoming the story and threatening to steal the limelight from the PM's big moment. Llewellyn had warned Jonny Oates before the summit that there might not be a deal, on the basis of what Sarkozy and Merkel were saying. But Clegg insisted that he should have been involved in real-time decision-making, and certainly given a chance to dissuade Cameron from deploying the veto. According to one senior Tory: 'It was like a toddler falling over. You know it could go either way – totally fine, or a complete screaming fit. I think Nick was persuaded to have a hissy fit and once he got going there was no stopping him. It was real pink-cheeked fury.'

If the AV referendum had been a parlour game for politicos, this was the real thing. The Coalition would not break up over a single EU summit, but it was creaking at the joists. Cameron grasped that he had to make his deputy feel valued and respected, more than a human shield between himself and the electorate. The two men talked it through, by phone and in person, always leaving the detail to Llewellyn and Oates, the sleepless *consiglieri* whose task it was to turn broad brush-strokes into detail. Cameron's message to his deputy was sympathetic rather than contrite: 'I had to do this but I don't want to cause you problems.' Though the PM could hardly offer him minute-by-minute consultation, he could promise much more elaborate channels of communication between Cameron's team and Clegg's office during subsequent EU summits. Though the Lib Dem conspicuously declined to attend the PM's statement to the Commons on the Monday, he met Cameron twice on the day to discuss its content. In private, the Prime Minister admitted that he could easily find himself in a second round of coalition negotiations with Clegg after the 2015 election, and had to behave accordingly. A second hung Parliament was a horrible prospect, but a possibility he had to allow for. Abroad, Cameron had been able to cry: 'Very well, alone!' On the home front, parliamentary arithmetic – and the opinion polls – meant that isolation was a luxury he could ill afford.

What he could not conceal from Clegg was his sincere belief that the context was changing rapidly, and that reform of Britain's relationship with Europe – at least – was now essential. The proposition that the country's best interests lay outside the EU was becoming ever more popular and ever more respectable. It had last surfaced as a mainstream idea in the mid-nineties, the twilight of the Major Government. When Norman Lamont, recently sacked as Chancellor, had told the Conservative Philosophy Group that it was time to think seriously about leaving the EU, television crews had gathered outside Jonathan Aitken's home in Lord North Street where the meeting was being held. No less dramatically, the billionaire Sir James Goldsmith had founded the Referendum Party, a movement with a single objective: to force a popular vote on Britain's membership of the EU. This was the backdrop to Major's extraordinary decision in June 1995 to call a leadership contest, urging his Eurosceptic opponents to 'put up or shut up'.

By 2012, the option of exit was once more being dusted off and taken seriously at the highest levels.[8] It was known around Westminster that Hilton – hardly a reactionary – was now firmly against membership of the EU. Cameron joked about 'Steve and Europe' but he knew that his senior adviser, like Oliver Letwin, was responding empirically to the reality of European regulation and its impact upon British competitiveness, enterprise and liberty. Michael Gove was reported by the *Mail on Sunday* to believe it was time to tell Brussels: 'We are ready to quit.' According to the newspaper, the Education Secretary wanted Britain to issue an ultimatum: 'Give us back our sovereignty or we will walk out.'[9] The response to the story was striking. Philip Hammond, the Defence Secretary, told *The Andrew Marr Show* that Gove was simply articulating 'what many of us feel'. Theresa May announced that the UK intended to opt out of

130 crime and policing measures – including the European Arrest Warrant – before selecting which ones to rejoin and on what basis. At the highest levels of the party, the centre of gravity was shifting fast.

Indeed, the Home Secretary had been very publicly pursuing a single deportation case that was oxygenating support for exit. Although the long battle to expel Abu Qatada involved the European Court of Human Rights (ECHR) rather than the European Union, its frustrating twists and turns certainly emboldened those who wanted Britain to sever its connections with continental jurisdictions. Best known as Osama bin Laden's 'ambassador to Europe', Qatada had also been a spiritual guide to the late Abu Musab al-Zarqawi, for several years the head of al-Qaeda's franchise in Iraq and the terrorist responsible for many atrocities, including the video-taped beheading of the Liverpudlian engineer Ken Bigley in 2004. The cleric had also been an associate of Zacarias Moussaoui, the 9/11 conspirator, and of Richard Reid, the so-called 'shoe bomber', and was described by a British immigration court as a 'truly dangerous individual'. Successive Home Secretaries had been struggling since 2005 to deport him to Jordan, where he held citizenship.

In January 2012, Qatada won a famous victory in Strasbourg, where the ECHR upheld his appeal against removal. It did so not because it was persuaded that he himself would be badly treated in Jordan but because – it was alleged – some of the evidence likely to be used against him might have been obtained by torture. The ruling was made not under Article 3 of the European Convention (against torture) but Article 6 (which protects due process). The Strasbourg judges, in other words, were not objecting to what might happen to the cleric but to the possible origins of some of the evidence that might be deployed against him by the Jordanian prosecutors. Qatada's case exemplified a basic question of counter-terrorism strategy: the ability of a state to deport an individual whom it cannot prosecute, cannot detain indefinitely, but believes is a threat to national security. In resisting the state's efforts to resolve that conundrum, a lone Islamist had deftly exploited precisely the Western culture of rights and entitlements that, in other contexts, he so deplored.

Ken Clarke did his best to encourage the forty-seven-member

Council of Europe, the body that oversees Strasbourg and of which
the UK had chairmanship at the time, to keep the ECHR out of
national asylum and immigration cases except in 'exceptional circumstances'. But direct action was clearly required if the stalemate
over Qatada was to be broken. In February, he was released from
Long Lartin top-security jail in Evesham under strict, though
time-limited, bail conditions. In March, May took the exceptional
step of travelling to Jordan to seek undertakings that could end the
deadlock. The following month, the Home Secretary told the Commons that 'the assurances and the information we have gathered will
mean that we can soon put Qatada on a plane and get him out of our
country for good'. But, in November 2012, the Special Immigration
Appeals Commission upheld a fresh appeal, ruling that it was not satisfied by Jordan's undertakings and that May should already have
revoked the deportation order. In December, Cameron discussed the
matter further with King Abdullah of Jordan in Number Ten. The
case was still unresolved the following April when the Home Secretary announced that she had signed a new treaty with Jordan intended
to clear the way for Qatada's deportation.

This courtroom farce prompted Cameron to float the possibility
of a 'deport first, appeal later' arrangement, under which deportees
would only be able to appeal against a decision while still in the
UK – thus suspending their removal – if they faced 'a real risk of serious, irreversible harm'.[10] It was clear that, without such an overhaul,
he was tending towards temporary exit from the ECHR, an option
he had first floated in August 2005. The variable quality of judges
from the forty-seven member states, the backlog of cases snarling up
the court's work, and the vexatious use of the ECHR as, in effect, a
small claims court: all these defects strengthened the argument for
the UK's provisional withdrawal. As long as Clegg was on the ticket,
such dramatic steps were out of the question. But Cameron's exasperation was now such that, whatever the outcome of this absurdly
protracted deportation, a radical realignment of Britain's relationship
with the ECHR seemed certain to feature in the 2015 Conservative
manifesto.

The Qatada case was not just about national security. It had become a test of nationhood. But what kind of nationhood? Economic hardship, the Eurozone crisis, the clustering of the Coalition around the centre ground and the decline of trust in mainstream politics had conspired to create an environment perfect for the UK Independence Party. Its leader, Nigel Farage, cultivated a pub-friendly image that grafted exasperation with the political class on to blokish charm: it was as though Ken Clarke had a naughty Eurosceptic nephew. Increasingly, the party's entire campaign was draped over Farage's personality: his speeches were, as he recalled in his memoirs, 'spontaneous outbursts from the heart – or the spleen – unpolished, unfiltered by sneering comment and captions'.[11]

Ukip still presented itself as a constitutional movement, animated by a lofty desire to restore full sovereignty from Brussels to the Queen-in-Parliament. But its hostility to the EU was only one aspect of a broader quarrel with change and cultural upheaval. The party's trailblazers in blazers regarded Europe as but one threat among many. Its campaign literature and website revealed that, for its angry members, Europe was bad, but immigration was worse, 'a deliberate attempt to water down the British identity'. If it were properly controlled, the party argued, 'large areas of British countryside [would] not be destroyed by house-building'. Instead, 'jobs are lost and services failing under a tide of immigration'. Not even KFC was sacred: the party was inconsolable when some branches of the fast food chain stopped selling pork products to avoid deterring Muslim customers. Officially, the independence demanded in the party's very name referred to freedom from Brussels. But its fixations were overwhelmingly cultural rather than constitutional. It was exploiting the EU's crisis of confidence to make progress as a gentrified anti-immigration movement.

In 2012, Ukip's surge became impossible to ignore. As it started to push Labour into third position in opinion polls, and attract media attention, Michael Fabricant, a Tory vice-chairman, proposed that the two parties form an electoral pact. Farage's response was cleverly destructive. He would consider alliances and pacts – but never with Cameron. In Downing Street, Andrew Cooper cautioned the Prime Minister against treating the emergence of Ukip as a coherent secessionist moment — the simultaneous splitting off of a chunk of traditional Tory voters who must be won back by a new strategy.

Cooper, one of the founding fathers of Conservative modernization (see Chapter 1), was a softly spoken truth-teller, who believed absolutely in the power of research and political judgement based on polling data, 'qualitative analysis' (focus groups) and other forms of empirical work. In this, he was greatly influenced by the Labour strategist Philip Gould — a debt that did not recommend him to tribal Tories.[12] Many underestimated him at their peril. He had joined Cameron's team from Populus, the polling firm he founded in 2003, only on condition that the Tory leader remained true to the modernizing principles that had helped him win in 2005. He had a temper, too. After one election defeat, he had left a series of messages on Ken Clarke's phone, saying: 'This is all your fault.'

For modernizing Conservatives like Cooper, Ukip was a state of mind, not a party: a political Tardis, lurching back in time, with the twist that it was smaller on the inside than it looked on the outside. Its defining characteristic was incorrigibility. The whole point was that it could not be wooed or tamed. If Cameron tore up his strategy and went hurtling off to the Right in search of these voters, he would win few of them back — and lose a great many centrist waverers in the process. It was a statistical fact that Cameron stood no chance in 2015 unless he took votes from Labour and Lib Dems. Tim Bale of Sussex University analysed the likely impact of the Ukip vote in marginal constituencies and concluded that it had been 'vastly exaggerated. At best we're talking about no more than a handful of seats — certainly nowhere near enough to mean the difference between the Tories being the biggest party and a comfortable overall majority.' Most of the PM's advisers urged him to manage the storm of mid-term protest not by appeasement but by governing well.

But, as Cameron often said, 'by-elections cast a long shadow' — and there was no denying the gains that Farage was making. Cameron had been aggrieved to lose Louise Mensch, a rising star, destined for the Cabinet, who resigned as MP for Corby in August 2012 so she could move to New York to live with her husband and family. He regarded Mensch as politically sympathetic to him, media-friendly (if anything, too visible) and definitely worth testing in a ministerial role to see if she was capable of handling a Cabinet portfolio. Number Ten and the whips had gone to great lengths to make her working day compatible with the demands of family life. In the resulting by-election, Labour seized the seat – and Ukip finished third with 14.3 per cent, its highest-ever share of the poll in any such contest. In Rotherham, it came second, hugely helped by the uproar caused by the removal of three children from the care of a local couple because the foster parents were Ukip members. The party repeated the trick in Middlesbrough in November, beating the Lib Dems and Tories into third and fourth respectively. The Prime Minister could not simply avert his gaze. Whatever his own view of Ukip – whose members he had described as 'closet racists' in 2006 – he was concerned about the effect its ascendancy was having on Conservative morale and upon the Tory-inclined media. The cult of Farage – the saloon bar Briton betrayed by an out-of-touch government – was not quite on a par with the cult of Boris. But it was growing all the time, another dramatized critique of the remote public school elite running the Coalition.

Cameron's ambition was not only to win back voters tempted by Ukip but to fashion a new position for Britain in the shifting geometry of Europe. He had invested heavily in personal relationships with the individuals who would shape that geometry. Sarkozy recovered quickly from his detonation in Brussels over Cameron's veto, and the two men remained on friendly terms until the Frenchman's electoral defeat in May 2012. His successor as President, François Hollande, was less immediately engaging, not least because his own blueprint for the EU was unabashedly centre-Left in ideological complexion. As with Sarkozy, it would take military and security imperatives (in Mali and Algeria) to bring the two heads of government together.

Cameron's instinctive courtesy served him well in this respect. One of the lessons that many Tories drew from the Thatcher years was that success is achieved dialectically, by picking fights and winning them. But this was not Cameron's way at all. His negotiating technique was to find common ground, identify difference, and work outwards to maximize the former and minimize the latter. Even after the veto, he did not find it difficult to speak amicably with José Manuel Barroso, the President of the European Commission, and Herman Van Rompuy, the President of the European Council.

But his closest relationship in Europe by far was with Merkel. There was genuine warmth between the two politicians, often compared by observers to the relationship between a fond aunt and her occasionally errant nephew. Merkel loved Chequers, and liked to spend the evening there catching up on *Midsomer Murders*, one of her favourite shows (Cameron's team even tried to arrange a meeting with John Nettles, who played DCI Barnaby). To return the favour, the German Chancellor invited the PM and his family to her own official retreat, Schloss Meseberg, an eighteenth-century Prussian manor house about fifty miles north-west of Berlin. Cameron's wife and children warmed to Merkel, too, which made her visits all the more enjoyable. She also understood that Britain's relationship with the EU was as distinctive as her own country's. In this respect, a visit to John Gummer's constituency, Suffolk Coastal, when they were both Environment Ministers, had opened her eyes to the reality of British Euroscepticism and the domestic context in which Cameron was addressing the European Question. In her conversations with the PM more than a decade later, she would still refer to the stern patriots of Suffolk Coastal 'in terrified tones'. The close relationship between the two helped their respective teams to bond: when Cameron visited Merkel on one occasion, the talks were followed by a group outing to a *Bierkeller* – the underground joints where huge glasses of beer are consumed around wooden tables, often to the sound of oompah bands: serious diplomacy leavened by traditional German hospitality.

When Cameron told Merkel that he intended to make a speech that would define his European strategy, she listened and gave him what counsel she could, making clear how earnestly she hoped that Britain would remain part of the EU. 'Couch the speech in an argument about Europe having to change,' she advised; it was important that he be seen to be arguing for a better Europe, not just a better deal for Britain. Merkel also warned Cameron not to deliver the speech, as he had planned, on 22 January 2013 – the fiftieth anniversary of the Élysée Treaty signed by De Gaulle and Adenauer, to be marked by a grand celebration in Berlin. 'That'll go down very badly,' she said.

Cameron had originally intended to announce his proposals at the Tory conference in Birmingham, but decided that such a setting was too party-political and lacked statesmanship. The fierce negotiations over the EU Budget in the autumn seemed a poor context, too: in October, fifty-three Tory rebels joined forces with Labour to defeat the Government in a vote calling for a real-terms cut in Britain's spending on the MFF (the EU's multi-annual financial framework) for 2014–20. The speech was due to be delivered in Amsterdam on 18 January 2013, but had to be postponed because of a hostage crisis in Algeria: 800 hostages, including many Britons, had been seized by jihadis at the In Amenas gas field. It was inconceivable that Cameron and his team should be out of London, answering questions on the minutiae of the repatriation of powers, the complexity of referendum questions and the internal politics of the Conservative Party, while British citizens were still in mortal danger in the Algerian desert.

As the scale of the attack became clear, Cameron spoke to Obama, who was about to give his own second inaugural address. Much as he wanted Britain to remain part of the EU, the President conceded that he would probably be making the same strategic judgements in the PM's shoes. Finally, after much deliberation, Cameron settled on 23 January 2013, and Bloomberg's London headquarters as the venue for his speech.

The extended wait had prompted the PM to joke that his EU strategy was 'tantric'. But he occasionally lost patience with those who questioned the delay. 'There is a thing called government to get on with, you know,' he said to one such friend; a flash of the petulance that Miliband and Balls were always trying to provoke. The idea at the heart of the speech – a referendum on a renegotiated basis for British membership – had been implicit in Conservative policy for years. But, in the summer of 2012, the detail started to be hammered out by the PM, Osborne, Hague and Llewellyn – the chief of staff also acting as speech-writer and rapporteur. Jeremy

Heywood and Jon Cunliffe, now the UK's Permanent Representative to the EU, were also consulted. Osborne's view was that the referendum 'genie was out of the bottle' and that, as divisive a political issue as Europe could be, the one argument that united almost all the disputants was 'let the people decide'. But decide what? As the core group discussed Llewellyn's drafts, it became clear that the only question that made any sense was: 'In or out?'

As Merkel had advised him, Cameron began his long-awaited statement by praising the EU, but noting its changing significance. 'Today the main, overriding purpose of the European Union is different: not to win peace, but to secure prosperity.' The EU, like its constituent nations, had to confront the reality that 'the challenges come not from within this continent but outside it. From the surging economies in the east and south. Of course a growing world economy benefits us all, but we should be in no doubt that a new global race of nations is under way today.' He wanted 'the European Union to be a success. And I want a relationship between Britain and the EU that keeps us in it.' He also accepted that those nations in the Eurozone would be seeking a new treaty: 'Those of us outside the euro recognize that those in it are likely to need to make some big institutional changes. By the same token, the members of the Eurozone should accept that we, and indeed all member states, will have changes that we need to safeguard our interests and strengthen democratic legitimacy. And we should be able to make these changes too.'

This was the crux of the speech, simultaneously making an offer and issuing a genteel threat. If the EU was to hold together and prosper, its twenty-first-century custodians had to accept that 'flexible, willing co-operation is a much stronger glue than compulsion from the centre'. This entailed a recognition – the heart of the matter for British competitiveness and public service reform – of a simple proposition: 'it is neither right nor necessary to claim that the integrity of the single market, or full membership of the European Union, requires the working hours of British hospital doctors to be set in Brussels irrespective of the views of British parliamentarians and practitioners.' As Europe changed, a referendum would have to be put to the British people. The PM repeated his claim that 'now –

while the EU is in flux, and when we don't know what the future holds and what sort of EU will emerge from this crisis – is not the right time to make such a momentous decision about the future of our country'. It was, he argued, 'wrong to ask people whether to stay or go before we have had a chance to put the relationship right'. Instead, the terms of membership would be renegotiated and the vote held 'within the first half of the next Parliament'.

It is a measure of the declining trust in politicians – even the trust politicians feel for each other – that Cameron still faced so much scepticism on his own side. As he took his seat for the first PMQs after his dramatic intervention, he was cheered to the rafters by his fellow Tories waving their order papers. Yet, even before the speech, a group of 100 MPs, led by John Baron (Basildon and Billericay) had written to the PM calling for legislation that ensured a plebiscite would be held in the next Parliament, on the grounds that 'a commitment on the statute book to hold such a referendum would address the very real lack of public trust when people hear politicians making promises' – a sharp reference to Cameron's 'cast-iron guarantee' on Lisbon.

At the World Economic Forum in Davos, meanwhile, the PM and his entourage bumped into Boris Johnson, sporting a woolly hat, who reassured him that every time he met a senior European politician he was praising the speech: 'Bien joué, David Cameron, n'est-ce pas?' But Europe's elite would take some convincing. Laurent Fabius, the French Foreign Minister, said that 'if Britain wants to leave Europe we will roll out the red carpet for you'. His German counterpart, Guido Westerwelle, declared that 'cherry-picking is not an option', while Lord Mandelson suggested that Europe would not take kindly to being treated as a 'cafeteria service where you bring your own tray and leave with what you want'. Guy Verhofstadt, the former Belgian Prime Minister who had become head of the liberal grouping in the European Parliament, said that 'his speech was full of inconsistencies, displaying a degree of ignorance about how the EU works'.

Cameron, however, was pleased by the speech and the furore it had sparked. He knew perfectly well that repatriation of powers from Brussels was fiendishly difficult. Lord Denning had long ago argued that European law 'is like an incoming tide. It flows into the estuaries and up the rivers. It cannot be held back.' To regain its full fishing rights in 1985, Greenland had to leave the EEC (as it then was). Yet Cameron believed that the old inflexibility was no longer tenable and that there was a decent deal to be hammered out, as British demands and continental crisis converged. Already, he had claimed success in ending Britain's obligation to bail out Eurozone members, staying out of the fiscal compact, negotiating to return certain Home Affairs and Justice powers, and reforming fisheries policy. But it was not enough. In the words of one Cabinet minister, 'we need to get back the right to work as hard as we want to'. Although Britain had a theoretical opt-out from the working-time directive for employees who chose to work for more than forty-eight hours a week, its labour market flexibility was always under fire: the Jaeger ruling by the European Court of Justice in 2003, for instance, meant that time spent sleeping at hospital counted as working hours for doctors. Eustice's Fresh Start group issued a 'Manifesto for Change' that had at its core a demand for 'the complete repatriation of social and employment law'. This was a tall order. But many, perhaps most, Conservatives would be disappointed with anything less.

The risk was as great as the opportunity. Europe would now dominate the skyline for years to come, a second mountain peak alongside the economy. It would be a proxy issue for ill-concealed leadership bids, a means by which Cameron's prospective successors could court party and public opinion. But the greatest test lay in the towering paradox of his own position. To stay in the EU, as he still wished, he must persuade our continental partners that he was prepared to leave; just as he had been prepared, when necessary, to use the veto. His entire career was founded upon his understanding of elites – how to join them, how to turn them to his advantage, how to master them. Was he really willing to lead Britain out of Europe? Did he dare to leave this mighty 'Inner Ring'?

Andy Coulson walked into David Cameron's suite of offices in Norman Shaw South, the annex to Portcullis House. The Tory leader was in a meeting but saw his communications chief, back at last from his grilling by the Commons Culture, Media and Sport Select Committee. He stood, grinning broadly, and embraced him. The two men laughed, evidently enjoying a private joke – as indeed they were.

As part of their preparation for a trip to Afghanistan, the pair had undergone special security training together with SAS instructors. Amongst the unpleasant situations which they were taught how to handle was kidnapping. On one particularly sensitive question the guidance was clear: if a member of their group was raped by the kidnappers, the others were to embrace him on his return from the ordeal as a signal of solidarity. This was Cameron's way of signalling solidarity to Coulson.

On this particular day in July 2009, the storm clouds had once again gathered over the head of the Tory comms chief, as the committee delved into the hacking scandal at the *News of the World*. Cameron was determined that Coulson should not be driven out by the intermittent pressure of parliamentary questions and investigations by the *Guardian*. After two years of collaboration, his loyalty reflected genuine friendship but also political need. Coulson was one of only three colleagues – the other two being Osborne and Hilton – who were capable of changing his mind, to whom he always listened, and upon whom he was truly reliant. 'Indispensable' is not a word often heard in the cut-throat trade of politics, but these three were as close to that status in Cameron's world as was possible.

He believed that Coulson had already paid a heavy price for the hacking scandal, resigning from the editorship of the *News of the World* – a position from which he had been expected to rise to the chair of the

In It Together

Sun. He was also more inclined than some bosses to give people a second chance. More to the point, he recognized that Coulson was being attacked as a way of damaging him and questioning his judgement. As far as he was concerned, every attempt to dig up the scandal and make Coulson's professional life impossible was a coded or explicit attack upon his fitness to be Prime Minister. This strengthened his resolve to stand by his friend and colleague.

Cameron's determination was matched by those pursuing the story: principally, the Labour MPs Tom Watson and Chris Bryant and, for the *Guardian*, Nick Davies.[1] As their inquiries continued, it became less and less plausible to argue that the illegal hacking of mobile phone messages had been the work of a lone reporter, Clive Goodman, and a single private investigator, Glenn Mulcaire, both of whom had been jailed in 2007. In July 2009, the *Guardian* revealed that News International, Rupert Murdoch's newspaper company in the UK, had paid Gordon Taylor, the chief executive of the Professional Footballers' Association, to drop legal action that would have led to other journalists at the *News of the World* being named and dragged into the scandal. In September, Scotland Yard disclosed that it had found suspected victims of hacking in the armed services, police and government – many more than those cited in the Goodman–Mulcaire trial. As much as Cameron wanted Coulson at his side, his comms chief sensed that the pressure might soon become intolerable for both of them.

Throughout 2010, as the team moved into government, more individuals disclosed that they had accepted payments from News International to drop legal actions. In December, Ian Edmonson, number three at the *News of the World*, was suspended and *The New York Times* published a lengthy report on the burgeoning scandal, alleging Coulson's complicity in the industrial-scale interception of phone messages. By this stage, he was already preparing his departure, which he discussed with Cameron, Osborne and Llewellyn. All tried to dissuade him, but to no avail. Coulson was now the subject of a running story which was clearly not going to fade away, and, under those circumstances, he could not function as director of communications in Downing Street. Announcing his resignation on

21 January 2011, he said that 'when the spokesman needs a spokesman it's time to move on'. Five days later, the Met's Deputy Commissioner, Tim Goodwin, launched a fresh inquiry into the hacking scandal to be headed by Sue Akers, the Head of Organized Crime and Criminal Networks, who assembled forty-five officers to work on Operation Weeting.

On 24 March, John Yates, the police officer in charge of the original investigation, made an astonishing admission to the Commons Culture Committee. His team, it transpired, had not gone through Mulcaire's copious records. In effect, Akers was starting from scratch. On 5 April, the Met arrested Edmonson and chief reporter Neville Thurlbeck. Over the summer, Operation Tuleta was set up to investigate computer hacking not covered by Weeting's remit. A third inquiry into police corruption – Operation Elveden – was established by Akers. She now had 11,000 pages of material to process, containing 4,000 names.[2] Watson and Bryant were relentless in every available forum, digging away at a story that was now being followed around the world. Lurking beneath every intervention was a question of dual complicity: how much had Coulson known at the time and what had he later told Cameron? This was not, the two Labour MPs believed, simply a story about a newspaper spinning out of control, or even just the saga of a media mogul's overweening ambition. It was, they hoped to prove, a scandal that revealed a media-political complex at work, in which newspaper support was traded for commercial advantage by the members of an extraordinary elite.

In parallel to the hacking scandal – but soon to collide with it – was Murdoch's £7.8bn bid for BSkyB, now monitored in the Government by Jeremy Hunt rather than Vince Cable (see Chapter 4). In March, News Corporation, Murdoch's parent company, offered to move Sky News into a new company, enshrining its editorial freedom in articles of association enforced by a corporate governance and editorial committee. Two days later, Hunt told the Commons that he was 'minded' to accept News Corp's takeover. On 30 June, the Coalition announced that it was ready to give the green light to Murdoch. Ofcom had originally backed a referral to the Competition Commission, but was now satisfied by News Corp's undertakings. In a written statement, Hunt declared that 'whilst the phone hacking allegations are very serious they were not material to my consideration'.

A further eight-day consultation began, set to end on 8 July. John Bercow, the Speaker, granted a request submitted by Watson for an urgent statement by Hunt. In a thirty-five-minute debate, the Culture Secretary said that he had simply followed the advice of Ofcom and the Office for Fair Trading. Murdoch was now days away from true control of the broadcasting giant he had created and the consolidation of the world's most powerful media company.

That dream was shattered on Monday, 4 July, at 4.29 p.m., when the *Guardian* website posted a deeply shocking story. In March 2002, the report revealed, the *News of the World* had hacked Milly Dowler's phone while the murder victim was still officially missing. John Whittingdale, the chairman of the select committee, still argued that this appalling disclosure remained 'a very separate question' from the BSkyB takeover.[3] Ed Miliband, however, sensed that this was a defining moment, not least for his leadership of the Labour Party, and decided to take a colossal risk. In the first instance, he advised Rebekah Brooks, former editor of the *News of the World* and the *Sun*, now CEO of News International, to 'examine her conscience' and 'consider her position'. Brooks was one of Murdoch's most favoured and valued employees, practically a family member. By taking her on, Miliband was, in practice, declaring war on the most powerful media mogul in the world.

For now, Cameron adhered to the Government's position that the two stories – hacking and BSkyB – were separate. There would have to be an inquiry into what had happened at the *News of the World*; perhaps, indeed, a broader investigation. But the bid was a different matter. 'One is an issue about morality and ethics,' he said, 'and a police investigation that needs to be carried out in the proper way, the other is an issue about plurality and competition which has to act within the law.' Ofcom did not share his certainty: as far as the regulator was concerned, the holder of a broadcasting licence had to be 'fit and proper', a matter that was now open to question.

James Murdoch, the chairman of News International, moved fast, setting up a management and standards committee to hose down the newspaper group – and, in a last-ditch bid to save the BSkyB deal, announcing the closure of the *News of the World* on 7 July. On the following day, Coulson was taken into police custody at Lewisham station in south London, detained on suspicion of conspiring to hack phones and of corrupting the police. Plain clothes officers searched his home in Dulwich and seized a computer. Coulson maintained his composure, but found the experience sickeningly demeaning.

Playing catch-up, Cameron announced that there would be a judge-led inquiry, and accepted his responsibility as Prime Minister to take whatever action proved necessary: 'It is on my watch that the music has stopped.' Had Rebekah Brooks offered him her resignation, he said, he 'would have taken it'. But Coulson had become a friend and remained so; he had received no 'specific information' about his alleged misconduct at the *News of the World*. Inside Number Ten, emotions were very mixed. Coulson had been a popular colleague, often approached for his advice on matters that had little to do with communications. He was egalitarian by temperament, as polite with cleaners as he was with senior colleagues. 'It was difficult to watch a friend being arrested on TV', according to one close ally. Competing with this was a fear that the walls of the temple might be about to come tumbling down. Where would all this end? 'If Andy was being nicked, who was next?' says the same ally. And not all of this quiet anger was aimed at Coulson himself. It was well-known that Cameron had been desperate for his comms chief to follow him into office, and twisted his arm in every way imaginable. Was the whole Government about to pay a terrible price for that insistence?

As BSkyB shed 11.7 per cent of its value in a single week, Hunt asked Ofcom whether News Corp's undertakings could, in fact, be trusted and referred the bid to the Competition Commission. Whittingdale, also shifting his ground, declared that 'the best thing would be if [the deal] could be put on hold'. On 13 July, News Corp announced its withdrawal of the bid, which its deputy chairman, Chase Carey, said was 'too difficult to progress'. On the same day, the PM announced that Lord Justice Leveson would be heading the inquiry. Two days later, Brooks resigned as CEO of News International and was quickly taken into police custody.

The turmoil continued to spread through the nation's institutions as Sir Paul Stephenson, the Met Commissioner, and Assistant Commissioner John Yates announced their respective resignations. On 19 July, Rupert and James Murdoch appeared before the Commons Culture Committee. A mood of heady celebration spread amongst those who had seen the tycoon and his family as a force for ill in the life of the country. Somewhat absurdly, the embarrassment of the Murdochs was described as the 'British Spring': hardly respectful to those who had fought in the Prague Spring of 1968.

Nor, in spite of claims to the contrary, was Murdoch finished. But he had fallen victim to the very cultural transformation he had helped to bring about. Britain was no longer a deferential nation and – aided by digital technology – the British now insisted on seeing the inner wiring of the nation's institutions and professions. The bankers had been first, then the political class with the expenses scandal – and now it was the turn of the media. It was not the morals of redtop reporters that had changed. It was the public's collective taste for transparency, and demand to be shown the warts on the body politic.

The PM's primary objective was not to be swept away in the storm of revelation and retribution. Court cases, he knew, were expected to follow the scandal: Coulson and Brooks were likely to be amongst those charged. Until then, the Leveson Inquiry would be the principal crucible in which his own position and the position of the Government would be scrutinized. The judge himself made clear from the start that he intended to interpret his remit liberally, in the widest sense, and to pursue the truth as far and assiduously as he could without prejudicing pending legal cases. In Robert Jay QC, the joint head of Thirty-Nine Essex Street Chambers, he had a leading counsel who was to become the star of the inquiry: calm, arch and fond of obscure words deployed to keep everyone on their toes ('propinquity', 'pellucidly', 'bailiwick').

What made the inquiry unique, other than its subject matter, was the decision to televise its hearings. The Scott, Hammond, Hutton and Butler Inquiries had all been gripping in different ways. But they had not been seen on plasma screens, on iPads, phones and in the news feed on the walls of shopping malls. This raised the stakes appreciably for the politicians and celebrities delivering testimony. To varying degrees, they became performers as much as witnesses. Leveson cracked down on those he felt were behaving theatrically or unleashing their rhetorical powers inappropriately. Michael Gove, for instance, believed privately that the whole exercise might imperil the freedom of the press and rehearsed his appearance meticulously. In spite of his credentials as an orator, he had sought help with his communication skills from Graham Davies, the presentation coach, a former barrister and President of the Cambridge Union. When the Education Secretary argued under cross-examination against 'any prior restraint' or curtailment of press liberty, the judge snapped that he did 'not need to be told about the importance of free speech, I really don't'.[4] But politicians are like quantum particles: they respond to observation.[5]

For Cameron, the threat was specific and serious. Though not on trial, he faced three unavoidable questions to which he had to supply satisfactory answers. Had he and his colleagues become too close to the press generally and to the Murdoch newspapers specifically? Had there been a deal, explicit or otherwise, to advance News Corp's commercial interests in return for the support of its UK titles, especially the *Sun*? And how much had he known about Coulson?

In the six years of his leadership, his character, judgement and integrity had never been subjected to such scrutiny. It was essential that, at the end of the cross-examination, formal and informal, he be acquitted in the court of public opinion. A Prime Minister trying to kickstart a sluggish economy, reform public services, overhaul the welfare system and repair the social fabric could not afford to be seen as a knave – or a fool.

The first question was the easiest to answer. In private, and soon in public, Cameron freely admitted that he had spent too much time with journalists, something which – with one or two exceptions – he regarded as a political chore rather than a gossipy pleasure. In the first years of his leadership – before Coulson's arrival – he had distanced himself from New Labour by scorning its obsession with the press. Blair and Brown had governed in nervous coalition with the media and he was not about to make the same mistake. Like his subsequent slimming down of the Number Ten policy and political operation and the cap imposed on the number of Special Advisers, this proved to be an over-correction.

To make an impact, an Opposition leader had to cultivate at least a working relationship with the media. Much of this involved saying the same thing over and over, in a time-consuming whirl of lunches, dinners, and meetings with newspapers and their proprietors. It was impractical to think otherwise. One of Coulson's tasks was to improve the party's relationship with broadcasters and to devise a communications strategy focused on television rather than print.

It was no accident that his successor as director of communications was a senior BBC executive, Craig Oliver, who had edited the *Six O'Clock* and *Ten O'Clock News*. Oliver, in turn, regarded the digital sphere – especially Twitter – as the new political battleground, and one on which the Government had to take the initiative rather than simply to respond. His critics regarded him as bland and ill-suited to the street-fighting role he had taken on and wished that Cameron and Osborne had been able to persuade the other lead candidate, Jon Steafel, the *Daily Mail* executive, to sign on the dotted line. Others argued that Oliver was being blamed for the pathologies of the Coalition and the divisions within the Conservative Party, and was, in fact, a solid and assiduous spokesman for the PM, a team-player who was particularly close to Andrew Cooper, Cameron's director of strategy. As one Number Ten insider says: 'Craig had a tough job following Andy. But he wasn't the one who forced the Leveson Inquiry, was he? Some said he was useless but, as often as not, he was simply a lightning conductor for criticism of the boss. He was like a new character in a soap that gets the blame for something that happened in the last series.'

The Prime Minister had prepared meticulously for his appearance at the inquiry on 14 June 2012, with, amongst others, Andrew Feldman, his old friend from Brasenose, now co-chairman of the party, playing the part of Jay. In his five-and-a-half-hour testimony, Cameron accepted that, at one point, he had been 'sort of struggling a bit to get the message across' even to 'Conservative parts of the press'. It had been a political necessity to address this problem, and trying to ensure decent coverage in the Murdoch-owned titles – the *Sun*, *News of the World*, *Times* and *Sunday Times* – was only one part of the campaign.

Murdoch was unimpressed by Cameron's first phase as party leader, his meritocratic hackles rising in response to the smooth Etonian who apparently wanted to 'hug a hoodie'. When asked in July 2006 what he thought of Cameron, the media mogul replied: 'Not much. He's bright. He's quick. He's totally inexperienced.' But the meetings continued: in August 2008, Murdoch's son-in-law, Matthew Freud, arranged for Cameron to visit him aboard his yacht off the Greek island of Santorini. There were drinks on the *Rosehearty*, the Murdochs' yacht, and then a dinner party hosted by Freud on his vessel, *Elisabeth F.* Thereafter, the Camerons were flown on Freud's Gulfstream IV to Dalaman in Turkey, where they joined Sam's family for a sailing holiday to mark the sixtieth birthday of her mother, Lady Astor. The relationship between Tory leader and media tycoon had thawed perceptibly, not least because Rebekah Brooks urged Murdoch to give the young leader a chance. Once Cameron was in office, he continued to see him in Number Ten – using the back-door entrance, at the request of his hosts.

Before his appearance, Cameron had conceded that 'we all did too much cosying up to Rupert Murdoch'. Blair had become a family friend of the News Corp magnate. Brown, too, had forged a bond with him – though one that had disintegrated after the *Sun* had switched allegiance, leaving Brown furious and Murdoch rueful. It was evident that no such affection had arisen between him and Cameron. Much more important in this context was the PM's friendship with Rebekah Brooks. Cameron knew her second husband, Charlie Brooks, a fellow Old Etonian, and the couple lived near the Prime Minister and his wife in Oxfordshire. As Cameron told the inquiry: 'I think as we get closer to the election and the decision of the *Sun* [to back the Conservatives] and also the wedding and she's moved in to Charlie Brooks' house, which is very near where I live in – where we live in the constituency – then the level of contact went up, and we saw each other socially more. Definitely we were – particularly once she started going out with Charlie Brooks, living a couple of miles down the road, I was definitely seeing her more often because my sort of friendship with Charlie and as a neighbour and, you know, we – Charlie and I played tennis together and all sorts of other things, which I'm sure we'll come on to, so that was why I was seeing more of her.' But this was misleading. Cameron knew Charlie Brooks only slightly before his marriage to Rebekah. It was Rebekah who brought him closer to Charlie, not the other way round.

In this instance, the supposed 'Inner Ring' was the so-called 'Chipping Norton Set' – a socially busy group of politicians, celebrities and media figures living near to the market town of Chipping Norton in Oxfordshire. Its members were variously said to include Charlie and Rebekah Brooks, *Top Gear*'s Jeremy Clarkson, Alex James (the journalist and Blur bass-player), Matthew Freud and Elisabeth Murdoch, Charles Dunstone (co-founder of Carphone Warehouse) and Howard Stringer (chairman of the Sony Corporation). The group had no formal status and those mentioned as its members often questioned its existence except in the minds of journalists.

To a great extent, the whole 'Chipping Norton Set' conceit was a way of fleshing out and adding colour to the relationship between the PM and Rebekah. More than the Blairs and the Browns, the Camerons kept the press at bay. There were dinners, invitations to Chequers and beers in the Downing Street flat for journalists. But – generally speaking – there was a clear division between these occasions and their social life. In his submission to Leveson, Cameron listed a small number of journalists who were close friends: Daniel Finkelstein, Sarah Vine and Alice Thomson of *The Times*; Xan Smiley and Christopher Lockwood of *The Economist* (the latter subsequently hired as a member of the policy unit); and Robert Hardman of the *Daily Mail*. All of those he named were longtime friends. Rebekah Brooks was different. She was not a member of the Cameroon gang, the 'Notting Hill Set' or a veteran of the Tory research department. Yet her charm and powers of persuasion had enabled her to break through Cameron's armour. According to one of his allies, 'she was like a Pre-Raphaelite ninja'. Many of the guests at Cameron's forty-fourth birthday party at Chequers in October 2010 were astonished to see her there (Number Ten failed to list her presence at this gathering in its initial submission to Leveson). Yet there she was – as she always was – at the centre of power.

Jay did not spare Cameron in his cross-examination. The PM had already admitted riding a horse, Raisa, loaned to her by the Met. In Court 73, he was subjected to the barrister's cringe-inducing exegesis of her texts to him. He had seen Brooks twice over Christmas 2010, not long after the Cable debacle (James Murdoch also being present at one of the social gatherings in question). In a message sent to Cameron in October 2009, she referred to an issue involving *The Times* and wrote: 'Let's discuss over country supper soon.' This was a humiliating level of detail for a serving Prime Minister. Worse, it implied that the kitchen dinners in Oxfordshire were where the real business got done.

The text had been sent on the eve of Cameron's conference speech: 'But as always Sam was wonderful – (and I thought it was OE's that were charm personified!) I am so rooting for you tomorrow not just as a proud friend but because professionally we're definitely in this together! Speech of your life? Yes he Cam!' In a single SMS, Brooks had managed to refer to Cameron's school background, to blur their friendship with News International's support of his leadership, and to annex his best-known slogan – symbolic of his belief in fairness and shared struggle – and to make it the motto of their private bond, their supposed interdependence as PM and media boss. An inclusive declaration had been turned into an exclusive assertion of oligarchic affinity. We are all in this together – but some more so than others.

Having a top-rank silk rake mercilessly and wittily through private texts was ignominious enough for Cameron – but the political damage was sustainable. Blair had been much closer to Murdoch, and was reported to be godfather to Grace, the second youngest of his six children. In 2008, Brown's wife, Sarah, had hosted a 'slumber party' at Chequers attended by Wendi Deng, Murdoch's wife, Rebekah Brooks and Elisabeth Murdoch. New Labour, scarred by the *Sun*'s brutal treatment of Neil Kinnock in the 1992 election – 'If Kinnock wins today will the last person to leave Britain please turn out the lights' – was much more preoccupied by News International's support than Cameron. Revealed in unprecedented detail by the inquiry, the cosiness between the political class and the press was undignified. But it was not a specifically Tory pathology. To limit the damage further, Cameron had pre-emptively begun publishing details of his contacts with senior media figures.

But that, of course, did not answer the second question: had there been a deal, of any sort, between Cameron and Murdoch, trading the support of the News International stable, or parts of it, for commercial benefit? According to the conspiracy theory, Coulson had been seconded to Team Cameron, notionally as director of communications, but, in reality, as the day-to-day link man between Government and media empire. In an angry speech on 13 July 2011, Brown had levelled the charge pithily, saying that, even when he was still Prime Minister, 'the Opposition invariably reclassified the public interest as the News International interest'. As Jay observed, the influence of the press upon politicians was nothing new. But there was a less palatable possibility: 'that for some the quid pro quo is a higher price, namely the bestowing of commercial favours by government'.

In his own evidence, Coulson resisted Jay's feline invitation to agree that there was something more subtle than 'express trade-offs', but involving an 'unhealthy' cosiness. Cameron had been told by James Murdoch of the *Sun*'s switch of allegiance at George, a club in Mayfair, over a drink on 9 September 2009, and informed Coulson by phone. Naturally, both men were pleased. But the newspaper's declaration was more an attack on Brown than a stirring endorsement of Cameron. Coulson protested that he 'would have preferred them to have done it in a different way. And at a different time' – his point being that there was no bargain between the party and News International, no back-scratchers' timetable. Indeed, Coulson continued, if there was such a deal, it made little sense to put Cable, 'a combative member of the Liberal Democrat party', in charge of the department that oversaw Murdoch's broadcasting empire. It was true, Coulson said, that he had retained shares in News Corporation worth £40,000 while working in Number Ten, an oversight for which he expressed regret in his witness statement: 'Whilst I didn't consider my holding of this stock to represent any kind of conflict of interest, in retrospect I wish I had paid more attention to it.' But since he had not been involved in the BSkyB deal in any way – except, tangentially, after the *Telegraph*'s report on Cable – he had failed to focus on the shares.

Cameron, too, rejected the proposition that 'the relationship [had] become transactional, that although there may not be express deals, there are implied understandings or concordats, because each party well knows what the other wants'. Yes, there were no 'overt deals', the PM said. But neither had there been a 'nod and a wink and some sort of covert agreement'. In all its forms, the allegation, he said, was 'absolute nonsense from start to finish' and 'an entirely specious and unjustified conspiracy theory' that Brown had 'cooked up' to explain the *Sun*'s desertion and 'justify his anger'.

On 12 June 2012, Osborne addressed the charge head-on: 'The claim is, principally by our political opponents but also others, that there is some vast conspiracy, where the Conservative Party knows before the General Election that News International wants to bid for more of Sky, that we sign up to some deal in return for their support as expressed through the endorsement of the *Sun* and then, when we get into office, we hand over BSkyB. That is what the previous person at this Inquiry [Brown] has alleged this morning. It is complete nonsense, and the facts simply don't bear it out. We had no idea that they wanted to bid for Sky before the General Election. When the General Election had happened, Dr Vincent Cable, a Liberal Democrat, is put in charge, and you have to be a real fantasist to believe that come these events, we had knowingly allowed Vince Cable to be secretly recorded, we knowingly allowed the *Telegraph* not to publish that information. That information then emerges in the middle of the afternoon and we then, all as part of this cunning plan, put Mr Hunt in charge. It doesn't stack up.'

Thus expressed, the charge certainly seemed fanciful, a comedy of errors rather than a great media-political plot. Behind the scenes, however, Cameron was fretful about Hunt, whose contact with News Corp had been close and constant. In an interview with *Broadcast* magazine in August 2008, the then Shadow Culture Secretary had declared that 'what we should recognize is that [Rupert Murdoch] has done more to create variety and choice in British TV than any other single person'. The communication between Fred Michel, a senior News Corp lobbyist, and Hunt's department was especially revealing. In one email sent in June 2011, Michel had briefed his colleagues, including Brooks, that 'JH [Jeremy Hunt] is now starting to look into phone-hacking/practices more thoroughly and has asked me to advise him privately in the coming weeks and guide his and No 10's positioning.' Hunt considered issuing a statement immediately, dismissing Michel's claim, and denying categorically that he had spoken to him about the Coalition's response to the hacking scandal. Instead, the Culture Secretary decided to wait for his own appearance to set the record straight. While Michel himself conceded that his use of the letters 'JH' was misleading, Adam Smith, Hunt's Special Adviser, fell on his sword, admitting that 'my activities at times went too far and have, taken together, created the perception that News Corporation had too close a relationship with the department, contrary to the clear requirements set out by Jeremy Hunt and the permanent secretary that this needed to be a fair and scrupulous process'.[6]

When Leveson reported in November 2012, the section that most relieved Cameron concerned Hunt, who was Health Secretary by then with a rising public profile and an essential campaigning role. The judge observed that Hunt had been 'walking a tightrope' as he tried to be even-handed over the BSkyB deal and that the correspondence between Michel and Smith represented 'a serious hidden problem'. But, in all other respects, the bid had been 'commendably handled' and no 'credible evidence of actual bias' had been presented to the inquiry. It was 'not in the least surprising' that the Culture Secretary 'had an opinion upon a major media issue'.[7] This was as good an outcome as Cameron had any right to expect – and he had been braced for worse.

The third question, he knew, would outlive the inquiry and the report and spill into court cases in the latter half of the Parliament: what, precisely, had he known about Coulson's activities at the *News of the World*? The question, he grasped, would be posed again and again before a general election that was certain to be, amongst other things, a contest of character. So often, US presidential elections had become snarled up by questions of 'judgement' and 'integrity' – most recently, the ridiculous but persistent claims that Obama had misled the American people about his birthplace. Cameron knew that he would be asked repeatedly why he had hired Coulson, and why he had stuck with him, dragging the Government into the spectacular distraction of an inquiry into media ethics when it should have been fixing the country.

Cameron's loyalty to his communications chief was in character, and revealed a profoundly entrenched aspect of his personality that was both a strength and a weakness. Though sociable and socially adept, he did not make close friends easily; and when he did admit someone to his inner circle, as he had with Osborne, Coulson and Hilton, he was desperate not to lose them. Even when they departed, he kept in touch – Coulson, for instance, stayed overnight at Chequers two months after his resignation. This character trait meant that Cameron was less capricious as a boss, unwilling to be panicked into sacking colleagues who were in trouble, even when it was the politically expedient thing to do. Those who confidently predicted that he would fire Osborne during 2012, or swap him with William Hague, revealed only their misunderstanding of his political psyche. It is doubtful that Cameron would have accepted either ploy even if Osborne had suggested it. Loyalty within and to this trio was the cement of his political life. Cameron had rarely been as angry or upset as he was when Hilton launched a semi-public attack on the Government's lack of radicalism before his departure to America.

In Coulson's case, the PM could say, with good reason, that his director of communications had done an impressive job in Number Ten and, in marked contrast to previous occupants of that role, generated no controversy or ill feeling as one of Downing Street's most senior officials. His colleagues in Number Ten spoke of his professionalism, calm manner and determination to make the Coalition work by stretching out a hand to *Guardian*-reading Lib Dems who were expecting a merciless redtop right-winger. All the questions – and there were plenty of them – related to his four years as editor of the *News of the World*.

A sub-plot of the drama was that Coulson had not been subjected to 'developed vetting', which is necessary for access to 'Top Secret' material, and was only scheduled for this clearance in November 2010 after a terrorism incident at East Midlands Airport. Much more interesting, however, was the informal vetting carried out by the Tory leader himself. Cameron was notably incurious in his conversations with his former employee about what, precisely, had happened at the newspaper on his watch.

In the spring of 2007, the two men met at Cameron's office in Norman Shaw South at the Commons. As the PM told Jay: 'I asked for the undertaking about what he knew and he said that he had resigned because he did not know.' Coulson then saw Llewellyn and Francis Maude for additional discussions about the job. When Coulson was on holiday in Cornwall shortly before the announcement of his appointment, Cameron spoke to him again on the phone. According to Coulson's clear memory, as he put it in his witness statement for Leveson, the Tory leader had 'asked me about the Clive Goodman case'. Pressed on this by Jay, Coulson was again very specific about this all-important phone call: 'I was able to repeat what I'd said publicly, that I knew nothing about the Clive Goodman and Glenn Mulcaire case in terms of what they did.' Coulson had chosen his words with care.

Cameron later described this specific reassurance as a much more general undertaking. On 13 July 2011, for instance, he told the Commons that 'I hired a tabloid editor. I did so on the basis of assurances he gave me that he did not know about the phone hacking and was not involved in criminality.' But had Coulson really gone that far? In a debate on the scandal a week later, the PM answered questions from 136 MPs, many of them about his former comms chief. Again, he assigned great significance to the phone conversation while Coulson was in Cornwall: 'I have to say, the reason I hired him was above all the assurances that he gave me. That is the key part of the decision and that is what I am prepared to say.' And again: 'He gave me an assurance that he did not know about the hacking scandal, and I took my decision. That is a judgement that I do not hide or run away from. I am totally accountable for it.'

There was a crucial divergence here. Coulson had said one thing, and Cameron had heard – or remembered – quite another. During their three and a half years together, his past as a tabloid journalist came up occasionally. 'I wasn't running a sweet shop, Dave,' he would say. As the scandal gathered pace, 'there was a permanent conversation', as Cameron put it to MPs. Ian Katz, deputy editor of the *Guardian*, had warned Llewellyn of Coulson's past employment of Jonathan Rees as a private investigator; Rees could not be named in the media, as he had been charged with murder (the trial collapsed in 2011), but Katz felt that Cameron's chief of staff should know. He also repeatedly warned Hilton, who was a longtime friend from Oxford. Alan Rusbridger, the newspaper's editor, also warned Cameron's private office. In July 2011, Cameron said that this information 'contained no allegations directly linking Andy Coulson to illegal behaviour, it didn't shed any further light on the issue of phone hacking, so it wasn't drawn to my attention by my office'. This was a slippery answer. Katz might not have had anything new to say about the specific 'issue of phone hacking' but his warning about Coulson's association with Rees was certainly worth a few minutes of the PM's time. It is hard to avoid the conclusion that those around Cameron did not want to be the bearer of bad news, and that Cameron himself did not want to hear it. He had come to rely on Coulson, as had others in Number Ten. He did not want to hear that his media 'genius' (his word) was going to be torn from his circle.

In fact, Coulson himself saw long before Cameron the way the wind was blowing. After the Gordon Taylor story broke in July 2009, he asked Llewellyn if they could speak and told him he understood the political realities of the situation. 'Whatever you and Dave and George decide,' he told the chief of staff, 'you'll get no quarrel from me.' More than once he offered to resign. But Cameron was not letting go of his friend and ally. Even before Coulson had quit, Jeremy Heywood was suggesting that a public inquiry be held (in months to come, Heywood would feel that Gove and other senior ministers blamed him for Leveson, believing that the whole circus was his doing). Still the PM stuck by his communications chief.

There remain legal limits to what can be said about Andy Coulson and the *News of the World*. But his relationship with Cameron was a case study in political friendship. The Tory leader became dependent upon a formidably able colleague. Coulson, his career as an editor ruined, was given a second chance in a completely different career, at the apex of Government. With hindsight, both regretted their respective decisions to offer and to take the job. But such decisions go with the grain of human nature.[8] Coulson told Cameron that he had known nothing of the Goodman–Mulcaire case; Cameron heard a much broader denial of knowledge. It was in this textbook example of 'wilful blindness' that the political trouble began.

The Leveson Report was not, primarily, a political document, but the findings of an unprecedented inquiry into the 'culture, practice and ethics of the press'. The investigation had lasted sixteen months, taken oral evidence and testimony from 378 individuals and 120 organizations, and subjected the political and media class to an extraordinary level of public scrutiny. But now the 2,000-page report was being removed from the respectful setting of Court 73 and sent hurtling into the sweaty political casino. The press, Cameron knew, would not like it one bit. Meanwhile, the campaign group Hacked Off had established itself successfully as the voice of the victims. In his evidence to the inquiry, Cameron had set his own Government what became known as the 'Dowler test'.

As he put it in his evidence to Leveson: 'I will never forget meeting with the Dowler family in Downing Street to run through the terms of this Inquiry with them and to hear what they had been through and how it had redoubled, trebled the pain and agony they'd been through over losing Milly. I'll never forget that, and that's the test of all this. It's not: do the politicians or the press feel happy with what we get? It's: are we really protecting people who have been caught up and absolutely thrown to the wolves by this process? That's what the test is.'[9] As noble as this sounded, it essentially handed the power of veto to Hacked Off. As long as the campaign was unhappy, Cameron would struggle to claim that he had fulfilled his promise.

Number Ten was given the report under embargo twenty-four hours before its publication. The PM deputed a team to parse, analyse and dissect Leveson's findings and recommendations: Craig

Oliver, Llewellyn, Heywood and Oliver Dowden, his senior political adviser. Others stood ready to weigh in with their assessments and reactions. But they had already deduced that the judge was going to recommend some form of statutory regulation. Lord Hunt, the chairman of the Press Complaints Commission, and Lord Black of Brentwood, chairman of the Press Standards Board of Finance, had worked with intelligence and patience to demonstrate how tougher self-regulation might work. But it was clear that Leveson had moved well beyond such a solution.

In urging Tory MPs not to exploit the report as an opportunity to take revenge on the press for the expenses scandal, Cameron was not speaking with the voice of the appeaser. He did not want to be remembered as the Prime Minister who subjected the press to statutory control, putting some of the world's most famous newspapers in chains. As much as the press infuriated him, he was loath to usher in a culture of journalistic caution and blandness, of editors frightened of taking risks and reporters whose sense of the public interest was crushed by fear of a press law.

Equally, he found it hard to answer Kate McCann, mother of the missing Madeleine, when she had asked him why the leaking of her diary – an episode that left her feeling 'mentally raped' – had not already prompted a change of press practice. How was it still possible for the tabloids to print appalling insinuations about the (totally innocent) Christopher Jefferies after the murder of his tenant, Joanna Yeates, in 2010? 'What are the lessons from this?' Kate McCann asked Cameron. It was his unpalatable task to ensure that, on the basis of Leveson's report, they were identified and learned.

As expected, the judge declared that the behaviour of the press, at times, 'can only be described as outrageous' and had caused 'real hardship and, on occasion, wreaked havoc with the lives of innocent people'. The report called for a new regulatory body, independent of current journalists, the government and commercial concerns, empowered to fine media organizations as much as 1 per cent of their turnover up to £1m, and – crucially – underpinned by statute. 'I cannot, and will not, recommend another last chance saloon for the press,' Leveson declared.

Like all prospective reformers of professional ethics, he hoped for 'political consensus'. His reward was precisely the opposite. Just before Cameron's statement in response to the report, he and Miliband had one of their most aggressive confrontations to date in the Commons. The Labour leader challenged the PM furiously over what he knew was coming: at what stage in the proceedings, Miliband asked, had Cameron suddenly become an opponent of all statutory involvement in press regulation? What was the basis for his sudden passion? The two party leaders usually remained civil away from the Despatch Box. But, on this occasion, the air crackled with real anger. Cameron felt, and continued to feel in the negotiations that followed, that Miliband was being insufferably pious and sanctimonious. The PM's argument was simple: that the deployment of statute in this case was a 'Rubicon', more than a technicality or a matter of practicality. Its impact would be momentous and effectively irreversible. Leveson might re-label statutory regulation a 'statutory verification process', but Cameron recognized what was being proposed for what it was.

Once again, the Coalition was split, and, on this occasion, the division between Cameron and Clegg was pushing the Lib Dem leader towards conciliation with Miliband. After one meeting of the party leaders in which the Labour leader had moralized a little too much, Clegg turned to Cameron and said: 'Now you can see why I don't want to go into coalition with him.' Cameron's view was that Clegg's behaviour suggested precisely the opposite. Ed and Nick had come a long way since the days of the AV referendum when Miliband would not share a platform with the Lib Dem leader for the 'Yes' campaign. Cameron could see the risks of a parliamentary vote, especially given the number of Tories who felt the press had it coming. But, by early 2013, he was losing patience with Clegg and his dalliance with Miliband. 'You can go off and do whatever you want with Labour!' he snapped.

Letwin fulfilled what was becoming his expected role in the unwritten constitution by suggesting an ingenious solution. Working with James Harding, the outgoing editor of *The Times*, he proposed that press regulation be overseen by a Royal Charter of the sort that established the BBC and the Bank of England. By raiding the attic of British tradition, Letwin appeared to have breathed life into the Leveson principles. What had not been resolved – and remained a deal-breaker for most newspapers – was the possible role of statute.

Exasperated by the impasse, Cameron decided to pull the plug on inter-party talks. At 9.45 a.m. on 14 March, he called Clegg and Miliband to say that it was time to put the matter before the Commons. Let MPs decide what party leaders apparently could not. Now it was Clegg's turn to be caught off guard by his governing partner and the two men had a conversation that the Lib Dem later described as 'scratchy' – which is to say a 'full-blown domestic'. He had told Cameron not long before that the Government should simply seize the initiative. 'Look,' he said, 'if we had just passed the charter, I guarantee that they [the press] would have grumbled – but within a week would have been wondering what all the fuss was about.' At the Treasury, meanwhile, Danny Alexander made a similar case to Osborne.

By this stage, however, Cameron was concerned about the risk of the Government's parliamentary business being sabotaged by persistent ambush. Already the Defamation Bill and the Enterprise and Regulatory Reform Bill had attracted Leveson-related clauses. Hugh Grant, roving ambassador for Hacked Off, had warned that the Coalition's legislative plan would be obstructed unless he and his fellow campaigners achieved their objectives.

Cameron's counter-punch was to introduce an amendment to the Crime and Courts Bill to force the issue in the Commons. This was precisely what Clegg did not want: a parliamentary free-for-all. But the PM had now reached the point where he believed that the Lib Dem leader and Miliband were privately colluding against him on Leveson – and thoroughly deserved to have the rug pulled out from beneath them.

The day after the talks were cancelled, one of Clegg's staff was in Miliband's office working on a Lib–Lab counter-amendment. By Saturday the 16th, Cameron's team was quoting Dean Rusk's famous line from the Cuba Crisis – 'the other fellow just blinked' – and claiming that Miliband and Clegg had seen sense. The remaining question was whether the PM accepted the so-called 'enshrinement clause': a statutory instrument to ensure the amendment of the Royal Charter would require two-thirds majorities in both Houses. Inter-party talks carried on into the early hours of Monday, 18 March, with Oliver Letwin, in mustard cords, busy in Miliband's office alongside representatives of Hacked Off. As bizarre a scene as this undoubtedly was, Letwin was concerned that the Labour leader was sitting on the proposals and, seeing an opportunity to force the pace, took it. Though it was odd to have a senior minister sitting in the office of the Leader of the Opposition – and was quickly presented in the media as yet another example of Letwin's eccentricity run riot – he feared that Miliband might never make a decision unless he went and wrung one out of him. Meanwhile, Cameron's team joked that it was 'part of the unwritten constitution that Oliver's yellow trousers make an occasional appearance'.

The plans, which involved legislative measures, were summarily dismissed by all but a handful of press titles. Fraser Nelson of *The Spectator* became the first editor to say that the magazine would not sign up to the Royal Charter. In April, the newspaper industry produced its own proposals, close in spirit to the original charter plan, but without 'state-sponsored regulation'. Hacked Off claimed that this blueprint was only 'the latest proof that most of the industry has learned no lessons from the Leveson experience'.

How had the apparently straightforward decision to hire a tabloid editor led to this ignominious point? 'Dave is an optimist,' says one who watched the whole saga from close quarters, 'and he wanted the story of his recruitment of Andy to have a happy ending.' The great irony is that Coulson himself was minded to step down a lot sooner than he did, but was persuaded to stay. If only Cameron had listened to his trusted adviser.

'It was the closest we have come to a Cuban missile crisis': thus did one of Cameron's closest aides characterize the Coalition's brush with catastrophe in July and August 2012. Nobody was paying much attention to the political drama carving through the Government, which was poor competition for the greatest show on Earth unfolding at the Olympic park. When its internal rupture was over, the Coalition's most senior figures rationalized what had happened and insisted that normal service had been resumed. Cameron and Clegg were now practised in explaining to the neighbours what the sound of smashing crockery and raised voices had been the night before. But – for a few days – even the Prime Minister and his deputy were uncertain about the future of their partnership.

The cause of hostilities was Lords reform, but other grievances had played their part in the collapse of diplomacy. After the triple ordeal of tuition fees, the NHS rebellion and the AV referendum, Clegg had struggled to maintain unity in his party ranks and to maintain the morale of his MPs and activists, who feared a wipeout at the next election. By the spring of 2012, Ukip was pulling ahead of the Lib Dems in opinion polls, as Clegg's party routinely fell below 10 per cent. The Deputy PM declared himself 'really sad' after the local elections on 3 May, in which the Lib Dems lost 336 seats and Labour continued its march through the party's strongholds. Lord Oakeshott, a Lib Dem peer and close ally of Cable, warned that the movement's viability as a competitive electoral force was now at stake: 'For me, what matters is whether we can fight the next election as a nationwide, powerful, independent force, and if we have another year like this, we won't be able to.'[1]

Even under fire, Clegg missed no opportunity to assert his commitment to the Coalition. Privately, he was aggrieved by what he regarded as Tory treachery on environmental policy. In Opposition, Cameron had defined himself to a considerable extent by his commitment to greenery – 'Vote Blue, Go Green'. On a visit to Chris Huhne's department in the first days of the Coalition, the new Prime Minister had said that he wanted to lead 'the greenest government ever'. The commitment had not been entirely abandoned: the Green Investment Bank had gone ahead, as had subsidies for electric vehicles, domestic renewable energy and (most contentiously) high-speed rail. But sluggish growth had focused Tory minds and put Cameron under growing pressure – not least from Boris Johnson – to make his priorities clear. The Tory leader's pledge to rule out a third runway at Heathrow had been a milestone for green campaigners. But now the PM was reviewing his options, a 'reset' that would lead, in September 2012, to the establishment of an aviation inquiry under Sir Howard Davies, the former chairman of the FSA and director of the London School of Economics. Even this was branded by the London Mayor as a 'fudge-orama'. As for wind power: when John Hayes, the Tory Energy Minister, attacked the imposition of turbines upon communities in 'our green and pleasant land' and said 'enough is enough', Cameron hedged his bets, saying that, while existing commitments would be respected, 'all parties are going to have to have a debate about what happens once those targets are met'. Ed Davey, by then Lib Dem Energy Secretary in succession to Huhne, took the extraordinary step of querying the legality of his own junior minister's remarks. Perhaps inevitably, Hayes was moved in the next reshuffle. But the trend away from greenery was clear throughout 2012.

Clegg was dismayed by what he described to aides as 'a flagrant reversal of a totemic commitment'. The Lib Dem leader complained: 'When I raise it with Osborne he just says: "I don't believe in this agenda. Of course we had to say all this stuff in Opposition."' The Chancellor denied taking such a crass position. But he had always been sceptical about eco-politics and had been much encouraged, yet again, by Nigel Lawson, whose book on global warming made the case for caution in response to 'the new religion of eco-fundamentalism'.[2] Osborne's experience as a finance minister in an era of economic crisis had made him more dubious than ever about the practicality of globally co-ordinated action. His 2011 party conference speech clarified his position. 'We're not going to save the planet by putting our country out of business,' he said. 'So let's at the very least resolve that we're going to cut our carbon emissions no slower but also no faster than our fellow countries in Europe.' As far as this Chancellor was concerned, the decarbonization of Britain's fuel economy was a luxury it could not afford.

To Lib Dem ears, this was heretical. It also prompted Clegg to ask himself: 'Am I still in coalition with the same party?' He knew full well that a Conservative leader – like any political chieftain – is managing his own internal coalition, and that Cameron had to fend off daily criticism from the Right and online anger in the Tory 'digi-verse'. Just as Ukip was supplanting the Lib Dems as the party of protest, it was winning over many traditional Tory voters who saw the Coalition as a metropolitan stitch-up that did nothing for them. But Clegg drew a distinction between necessary gestures and substantial changes.

In this context, he depended upon Cameron to be a reliable parliamentary manager, and to stop his party from sabotaging a measure that mattered deeply to the Lib Dems. One such reform was the long-delayed overhaul of the House of Lords, which like electoral reform, to an extent just shy of comedy, had been repeatedly kicked into the long grass during the New Labour era. The Royal Commission under Lord Wakeham, white papers and numerous consultations had failed to settle the question of the second chamber's future – a constitutional project that, according to Asquith in 1911, 'brooked no delay'. A century later, Cameron was reported to consider it a 'third-term issue'. But for his partners in government it had acquired grave significance: the Lib Dems had always been strongly in favour of constitutional reform, and their collective sense of self-worth depended on bringing this long saga of false starts and evaded responsibilities to a satisfactory conclusion. More to the point, they needed something of this character to justify the gamble of coalition and to compensate for their devastating defeat in the AV referendum.

Cameron knew how much Lords reform mattered to Clegg's

party. What he had failed to see was how much it mattered to his own. The proposals before the Commons in the summer of 2012 were yet another variant on a solution proposed in various forms for decades. The Upper House would be transformed in phases, its membership halved to 450 peers – or another agreed title – 80 per cent of whom would be elected. An appointments commission would select the remaining ninety members, who, like their elected counterparts, would serve a non-renewable fifteen-year term.

To the surprise of Cameron and Clegg, these proposals stirred formidable controversy on the Tory benches – and not only among the Cameron-bashers and angry reactionaries. The PM was partly out of touch because so much of his time was taken up by Coalition management. But that was not sufficient excuse. In the words of one close aide: 'I think Dave would admit now that his lines of communication with the parliamentary party had declined. There was a history of tension – expenses and so on. He had become too dependent upon Patrick [McLoughlin, Chief Whip] and not spent enough quality time with the troops. And I don't just mean a glass of warm white wine with ten other MPs every six months. That sort of token gesture was worse than nothing.' The consequence of this neglect was a dangerous degree of ignorance about the extent of Conservative opposition to Lords reform.

Most startling of all, perhaps, was the identity of the leading Tory rebel. Jesse Norman, the MP for Hereford and South Herefordshire, had helped to define Cameronism – if there was such a thing – in a book on the 'Big Society' and as co-author with Janan Ganesh of a pamphlet on 'Compassionate Conservatism'. Already a member of the Treasury Select Committee, and highly rated by Cameron and Osborne, he was obviously destined for rapid promotion. He had never voted against Government legislation before. Yet, on examining the planned reform of the Lords, he concluded that it was 'a very serious threat to the constitution', and, after making inquiries, quickly realized that 'there was a body within the centre of the party' that agreed with his diagnosis of the proposed tinkering.[3] The reforms, he believed, were an unholy mess, and one that would undermine the very specific role played by the Upper House in the life of the nation. As presently constituted, it was less a legislative chamber in its own right than a feisty advisory annex to the Commons, a storehouse of experience, expertise and political wisdom, and a highly effective scrutineer. The election of 80 per cent of its members would necessarily transform its status and its legitimacy. In 1963, Labour's Richard Crossman had put the argument thus: 'An indefensible anachronism is preferable to a second chamber with any real authority.' Whatever the Coalition insisted to the contrary, the scope for clashes between the two chambers would increase dramatically – and, with it, the possibility of US-style legislative gridlock, breakable only by the Supreme Court. This, Norman felt, was too important a change to nod through in the interests of time-limited unity.

Though he did not seek nomination as shop steward of the rebels, this is what he quickly became. Number Ten was amazed, appalled and finally furious. As the potential scale of the revolt became clear, pressure mounted on those thinking of defying the three-line whip. According to Norman: 'The whipping operation was formidable. It included ministers and colleagues on the backbenches, people were [subject to] multiple conversations designed to change their mind. It says a lot for the people who voted the way they did that they weren't swayed by that.' The whips themselves were at the forefront of the battle – McLoughlin drily describing his office as the 'human resources department of the parliamentary party'. Every day, half an hour before the start of business in the Commons, he and his colleagues would meet – the Conservatives alone for the first fifteen minutes, to be joined by the Lib Dems for the second half (with the Lib Dem Alistair Carmichael and Tory John Randall as joint Deputy Chief Whips). As to their daily work: Andrew Mitchell, who would go on to succeed McLoughlin, albeit briefly, as Chief Whip and was a veteran whip from the Maastricht era, said that 'whipping, like stripping, is best done in private'. This was because every whip had to carry a carrot and a stick. In a time of coalition, under a Prime Minister who hated reshuffles, there were fewer carrots – that is to say, frontbench jobs – to go round. The stick had to be applied sparingly to retain its rarity value and frightening mystique. When the whips failed, they would often call on Osborne to issue a warning. One backbench rebel, penalized in the 2012 reshuffle, ran into the Chancellor not long after the murderous game of musical chairs was complete. 'Well,' said Osborne, 'at least you know why.'

But, over Lords reform, the whole system failed, and on 10 July Cameron paid the price. At 3.58 p.m., under intense pressure, the Government withdrew its programme motion – a timetabling measure – to avoid defeat on that vote. Just after 10 p.m., the results of the vote on second reading were read out to a packed House: ninety-one Conservative MPs had voted against the bill, including forty-six from the 2010 intake. Among the rebels, in addition to Norman, were Penny Mordaunt, Charlotte Leslie, Nadhim Zahawi and Louise Mensch, all of whom were being groomed for senior ministerial posts. Many, like Norman, had never voted against the Coalition before. This was not a standard-issue revolt by the usual suspects: the disenfranchised, the has-beens and the ideologically exiled. It was the worst kind of uprising that a self-proclaimed modernizing party leader can face: an uprising by the new breed.

Cameron, who had been busy during the day meeting François Hollande, was unnerved and angry in equal measure. He confronted Norman furiously after the vote and was overheard calling the MP's honour into question. The Tory whips, too, had been humiliated by the incident, and Randall, their second-in-command, was said to have taken the result especially badly. Hearing of this, Norman thought it best to call it a night and headed home.

Though the rebellion was first and foremost a row within the Conservative family, its implications for the Coalition were much greater. Clegg felt that Cameron had not done enough to prevent the rebellion and to save the legislation. One of the Tories he liked and trusted most was Mark Harper, the Conservative Minister for Political and Constitutional Reform at the Cabinet Office, with whom he had worked closely on the Parliamentary Voting System and Constituencies (PVSC) Act 2011. Clegg knew Harper well enough to see that he was struggling to get Lords reform past his own party. He had told Cameron that, while Harper was fighting to get the job done like a character 'out of a superhero cartoon', it was clear that the proposals were in real trouble. Cameron had waved away his concerns: 'Mark's handling it.'

After the Lords vote, Clegg knew only that he would have to act, and to take action that showed his own party, the Tories and the public that Conservative MPs could not wreck Lib Dem measures with impunity. This brought him to the question of the boundary review as mandated by the Parliamentary Voting System and Constituencies Act. The proposed reform would reduce the number of parliamentary constituencies from 650 to 600 and redraw their boundaries according to new rules that were expected to favour the Tories. Under the reformed system, the Conservatives would need a 7.6 per cent rather than a 10.5 per cent lead to win a majority. By common consent, the proposed reorganization was expected to be worth fifteen to twenty seats to Cameron's party. The Chancellor had been known to count from one to twenty to colleagues who doubted that the review was as important as the party's high command insisted – 'One, two, three . . .' and so on, impressing upon them that the new boundaries might make the difference between victory and defeat.

As far as Clegg was concerned, the implementation of the review was a legitimate target for retaliation. As the Tories soon protested, the relevant paragraph on page 27 of the Coalition *Programme for Government* established a linkage between boundary organization and the referendum, not with Lords reform: 'We will bring forward a Referendum Bill on electoral reform, which includes provision for the introduction of the Alternative Vote in the event of a positive result in the referendum, as well as for the creation of fewer and more equal sized constituencies.' This was the twofold purpose of the PVSC Act. Clegg was not impressed by this logic, arguing that the political reforms listed in Section 24 of the Programme were an indivisible programme. If Lords reform fell, so too could the boundaries plan.

Over supper with Osborne, he said that the Tories were demanding too much of the Lib Dems. The referendum had failed, then Lords reform – and now he and Cameron were asking his party to implement a boundary review that would damage their own chances at the next election and improve Tory prospects. 'You can't expect my MPs to commit hara-kiri,' he said. Urgent and repeated discussions followed, one-to-one and round-table meetings involving Llewellyn, Oates, Letwin and Alexander, as well as Cameron, Osborne and Clegg. The Lib Dem leader was increasingly forthright about the consequence of Lords reform failing: 'Be clear about what will happen if you can't deliver this. As far as we're concerned, if we lose this as well, we will regard it as a breach of the Coalition agreement.'

The Tories disagreed fundamentally with the linkage Clegg had proposed. But they understood that this was a political problem, rather than a textual debate. At a meeting in Cameron's flat, Osborne suggested a compromise: 'Can't you say that you will withdraw your support from boundary changes, but you won't vote against?' Clegg tried to get across to them what he thought was at stake: not only his own position, but the future of his party as a serious electoral force. 'The one thing I'm not prepared to do is to be the last leader of the Lib Dems,' he explained.

On 6 August, Clegg made a statement announcing that Lords reform would be ditched and blaming the Tories for the collapse of the proposals. Cameron and co. had seen the statement and requested some changes of tone. But the substance was unaltered. Even after these amendments, Clegg's language displayed an edge of bitterness that had not been apparent in his complaints about the AV referendum or the EU veto: 'The Liberal Democrats are proving ourselves to be a mature and competent party of government. And I am proud that we have met our obligations. But the Conservative Party is not honouring the commitment to Lords reform. And, as a result, part of our contract has now been broken.' He would not, he said, permit the Tories to cherry-pick the measures they liked and discard those they did not. With this in mind, he had 'told the Prime Minister that when Parliament votes on boundary changes for the 2015 election, Liberal Democrats in Parliament will oppose them'.

In a single sentence, Clegg had cost the Conservatives up to twenty seats, and perhaps victory at the next general election. The impression of Coalition disunity would probably take an electoral toll, too. Tim Montgomerie of Conservative Home concluded that the Tory Party had 'suffered its worst electoral setback since Black Wednesday' – encapsulating a mood of deep gloom on the Tory benches matched by fury at Clegg's supposed vindictiveness.

The Fixed Term Parliaments Act had made it harder to bring down a Government except in a general election. There were now only two ways of forcing an early dissolution: if a traditional vote of confidence was lost by simple majority, and a Government could not be formed within fourteen days, Parliament would be dissolved. Alternatively, if two thirds of the House of Commons demanded it, a mid-term general election would follow. The crisis of July–August 2012 had not brought the Coalition close to such straits. But, for the first time, as one senior Cameroon puts it, 'we weren't sure what was going on, and what they were really thinking'. They were right to be alarmed. In private, the Lib Dem leader told aides that 'this is war'. Some of his senior colleagues – including the notionally belligerent Huhne – suggested that he find a way to climb down. But his mind was made up. Let justice be done, though the heavens fall.

For his part, Cameron was taken aback by Clegg's determination to see his threat through. When the Labour peer Lord Hart of Chilton put down an amendment to the Electoral Registration and Administration Bill, delaying the boundary changes and cut in number of MPs until 2018, the Deputy PM offered his support, and Conservatives and Lib Dems were whipped to vote in opposite lobbies – a depressing moment for Cameron. 'This goes beyond the pale,' he told Clegg. 'Well,' Clegg replied, 'then I'm afraid it goes beyond the pale.' There was talk on the Conservative side of keeping the boundary changes alive with a different deal, whereby the Tories would make concessions on state funding of political parties in return for the new constituency map. But the Lib Dem leader was by now immovable. 'I can't, under any circumstances, allow these boundary changes to take place before the next election,' he said. 'This is an existential threat. Sorry, you should have thought of this before the AV referendum.'

While risking disaster, Clegg was also trying to avert it. His view was that, paradoxically, he had taken the only action that could save the Coalition. As he had warned his Tory colleagues, he was not the only Lib Dem worrying that the next election might be an Extinction Level Event. The party needed to be reminded that it still had muscles to flex, that it was in government, not in captivity. More immediately, he believed that his party would have kicked him out of the leader's office if he had not taken substantial retaliatory action for the collapse of Lords reform. 'If I had not done it,' he told colleagues afterwards, 'I don't think I would have survived another three months.'

But he had survived. What to do next? Clegg was a reflective man, more so than Cameron, whose intellect was directed towards practicality and away from emotion. The Lib Dem's chosen book on *Desert Island Discs* was Lampedusa's *The Leopard*, a novel set in Sicily during the *Risorgimento* that puts political action, the force of tradition and the yearning for change in a grand historical context. Like Cameron, Clegg was able to step aside from politics and see beyond it – not least because of his deeply happy marriage. His wife, Miriam, was content to host dinners with him at Chevening and to make occasional appearances at official functions. But she thought the traditional role of the adoring wife at party conferences was ridiculously old-fashioned, and laughed at the idea that a career woman would have time for such nonsense. It was apparent to those who knew the couple best that they had found a way of making Clegg's political career compatible with family life – not least because that career was not going to last for ever. Cameron, Osborne and Clegg represented a generational shift in political demography that had begun with Blair and Brown. In a culture that valued newness, youth and virility more than experience and wisdom, the highest offices of state were increasingly going to be occupied by men and women in their forties and early fifties. The rule was not absolute – Clarke was still attending Cabinet aged seventy-two, and Vince Cable, at sixty-nine, continued to fancy his chances as Clegg's successor. But the trend was clear. As Blair and Clinton had already demonstrated, the new breed of young statesmen needed a plan for their fifties, sixties – and beyond.

Clegg did not require that plan quite yet. He believed that his party still needed him, and that his responsibility to the movement involved more than asserting himself occasionally against Cameron. The longer he considered the Lib Dem predicament, the more clearly he grasped that the wound had been dealt by the tuition fees debacle. According to one senior source: 'Nick looked into the eyes of the party and saw that they felt sullied by it, that they'd done something wrong. Lib Dems are earnest people who care about policy and are meticulous about it. They hated what had happened over tuition fees. It was killing morale in the party.'

In Asturias over the summer, he talked to his wife about this problem of collective psychology and concluded that he should give the party an opportunity to clear its conscience and voters a spur to think again about the Lib Dems. He also discussed the idea with Pippa Harris, Sam Mendes's business partner, a university friend whom he regarded as a surrogate sister. Harris saw the germ of a broadcast and helped him with the text. The instantly famous 'Sorry' speech was broadcast to coincide with the Lib Dem conference. Looking directly into the camera, Clegg apologized to the electorate for the tuition fees affair. 'We shouldn't have made a promise we weren't absolutely sure we could deliver,' he said. 'There's no easy way to say this: we made a pledge, we didn't stick to it – and for that I am sorry. When you've made a mistake you should apologize. But more importantly – most important of all – you've got to learn from your mistakes.'

Clegg knew full well that the broadcast would invite mockery – but, since his intention was to reframe the way in which the voters perceived the Lib Dems, he was not fussy about the way in which its message got across. Within hours, it was being set to music and posted on YouTube as a dance remix. The track, 'Nick Clegg Says I'm Sorry' by The Poke & Alex Ross, was released on iTunes as a charity record and peaked at 104 in the Singles Chart. He thought the stunt was funny, as close to digital chic as a Lib Dem leader was likely to get. The political impact of the apology was unquantifiable. But – to an extent he could not have predicted – it had gone viral.

As the Deputy PM prepared to say sorry, Cameron reshuffled his Cabinet. The Prime Minister hated these cavalcades of jubilation, misery and intrigue – with good reason. They disrupted continuity of reform; they upset more people than they pleased, especially in a coalition; and they absorbed far too much of the most precious resource that a senior politician has – time. Working with a white board in his office, Llewellyn applied himself to the pitiless task, moving round the names as the parameters shifted. In this case, the most prolonged debate concerned the fate of Iain Duncan Smith. Cameron and Osborne had grown worried about Ken Clarke's liberalism at the Justice Department and feared that the Tories would lose credibility on law and order. The great veteran, who said the reshuffle had caused the 'usual comic shambles', was shifted to a roving brief: 'minister for anecdotes', as one Cameroon put it mischievously. Duncan Smith, a believer in rehabilitation, but a man of the Right, was a natural candidate to replace him. In addition, Osborne remained worried about IDS's capacity to implement the fiendishly complex Universal Credit. The plan, therefore, was to move Chris Grayling up a notch to replace Duncan Smith as Secretary of State for Work and Pensions.

Instead of simply announcing all this to IDS, however, Cameron gave him the choice – to stay where he was or to go to Justice. Duncan Smith had seen Daniel Finkelstein, the *Times* commentator and a close friend of Osborne, on *Newsnight* suggesting that he might be moved. In fact, Finkelstein was simply commenting on a rumour which had just been reported by Nick Robinson on the news. But Duncan Smith assumed – quite wrongly – that Osborne had briefed his journalist friend and was trying to sew up the move in advance. This mistaken impression strengthened his mulish determination to stay where he was. IDS told the Prime Minister that he would prefer to see through the enactment of his welfare reforms – or 'life transformation' as he now liked to describe his strategy. 'Years from now,' he told Cameron, 'I'd like to think you'll look back and say: "He was the man to do it."'

Instead, Grayling was moved to Justice and Owen Paterson to Environment – a good result for the Tory Right. The party's electoral prospects were improved by the appointment of Grant Shapps as Conservative chairman, as Sayeeda Warsi, to her great disappointment, was given the consolation title of 'Senior Minister of State' at the Foreign Office, with specific responsibility for Faith and Communities. Warsi felt that, as the first Muslim woman to serve in the Cabinet, she had broken barriers and did not deserve to be (as she saw it) discarded. The grand title – invented to appease her – cushioned the blow. But nothing could disguise the fact that she was on her way down.

But the Lib Dems had cause for celebration, too, as David Laws returned to a combined role at the Cabinet Office and Education Department. The junior governing party also strengthened its day-to-day influence over domestic policy as Jeremy Browne was shifted from the Foreign Office to become a Minister of State at the Home Office, and Norman Lamb, one of Clegg's closest allies, moved to Health.

After the reshuffle Clegg warned Cameron: 'Be careful. If you lurch to the Right, you'll change what holds this Coalition together.' The Lib Dem leader's warning was correct as a general principle, but his analysis of the new ministerial line-up was mistaken. The real shift in the reshuffle was not so much ideological as psychological. Cameron wanted to raise the Coalition's visible energy levels and to push forward kinetic ministers with a capacity to inspire confidence: Shapps, Grayling, Nick Boles as Planning Minister, and the Tiggerish Michael Fallon, now a robust Tory sidekick for Cable at the Business Department. Craig Oliver, Cameron's communications director, had requested that each department have at least one practised communicator in its team. It had also been agreed that Jeremy Hunt could not still be at the Department of Culture, Media and Sport when Leveson reported – just in case. Instead, in a signal of high confidence in his talents, Cameron promoted him to Health, where an epic political task awaited him. Hunt was an unusual figure in the Coalition – politically similar to Cameron, a moderate Tory who, as the phrase had it, was so ambitious he squeaked when he moved. But he was not part of the Cameroon gang and had never sought membership. Like the other emerging contenders for the leadership, May and Hammond, he preferred to plough his own furrow, loyal but not one of the PM's cronies. Hunt had the political wreckage of the Lansley strategy to clear, the reforms themselves to implement and the public inquiry into the Mid Staffordshire NHS Trust scandal to handle.[4] It was a challenge that might destroy him, or propel him to the party's leadership.

The reshuffle was striking for two other reasons. First, it marked the entry to Government of the next generation of Tories: Matthew Hancock, Sajid Javid, Esther McVey. Second, the new line-up showed that, even after a ghastly year, Osborne remained a mighty force in the Coalition. Thwarted in his bid to move IDS, he got his way in every other respect. At the Treasury, he had first-class ministers in Javid and Greg Clark, and one of his closest allies, Matthew Hancock, dividing his time between Business and Education. With new Secretaries of State at Health and International Development (Justine Greening) he finally had the scope at least to consider removing the budget ring-fences from these two departments – not immediately but as part of his mid-term fiscal strategy.

Greening was displeased by her move to Development. According to one account, she told the PM: 'I did not bloody well come into politics to distribute money to people in poor countries.' Although Number Ten officials disputed this precise phrasing, her sentiment was clear enough. Boris Johnson was almost equally angry about her move. Quite correctly, the Mayor deduced that she had been shifted to prepare the ground for Howard Davies's report on aviation capacity and a possible U-turn on Heathrow's third runway – an idea to which Greening was bitterly opposed. Johnson consulted allies to see whether he should rain on the reshuffle parade, and decided to risk it. 'There can only be one reason to move her and that is to expand Heathrow airport,' Johnson said. 'We will fight this all the way.'

Andrew Mitchell was shocked to learn that Greening had expressed disappointment and anger about her move to the portfolio he had relished in Opposition and office for more than seven years. As the replacement for Patrick McLoughlin, who was heading off to Transport, Mitchell had been appointed Chief Whip, with a brief to bring unity, purpose and discipline to the parliamentary party in the difficult years ahead. Cameron and Osborne were sure he was the man for the job. Mitchell was sorry to leave Development behind. But he knew there was a job to be done.

Two weeks later, he was leaving Downing Street and asked the duty police officer to open the gate so he could exit on his bicycle. The conversation that ensued was to plunge the Government into its strangest crisis yet.

16. 'Plebs'

There was little to console Andrew Mitchell as he headed back from Chequers, reflecting on his ruined Cabinet career. But he realized, with a chuckle, that he was almost certainly the first Cabinet minister to have included the word 'fuck', or one of its many derivatives, in his official resignation letter. Truly, this was the unexpected face of Conservative modernization.

In the four and a half weeks since the verbal exchange in Downing Street that had cost him his job as Chief Whip, it was gallows humour of this sort that had kept him going. In all other respects, the experience had been unpleasant and surreal in equal measure. Granted stay after stay of execution, and daring to hope intermittently for a full reprieve, Mitchell had learned how grim it was to pace in a cell on Westminster's Death Row. In the end, his fate had been decided by clamour and the persistence of his accusers, rather than a forensic investigation of what had happened.

On Wednesday, 19 September, he had emerged from 9 Downing Street, the Chief Whip's official address, approached the exit with his bicycle and asked a police officer to let him out. 'Would you be so kind as to open the gate?' he recalled saying. The request was declined. 'Look,' Mitchell went on, 'I'm the Chief Whip, I work at Number 9.' That didn't work, either. Mitchell then said, in earshot, 'You guys are supposed to fucking help us.' This was Mitchell's clear recollection, which I reported in the *Sunday Telegraph* on 23 September.[1]

Two days before, the *Sun* had splashed a very different version of the story across its front page. According to the paper, Mitchell had said: 'Best you learn your fucking place. You don't run this fucking government. You're fucking plebs.' This was much more than rudeness, requiring an apology. It was an allegation of despicable social snobbery that pithily confirmed the caricature of the Tory-led Government as a gang of arrogant amateurs who considered themselves born to rule and intrinsically superior even to those in uniform protecting them. It also chimed with the image of Mitchell as 'Thrasher' (his school nickname at Rugby), the merciless whip of the Maastricht era, upper-crust member of David Davis's gang, a bruiser in a pin-striped suit. This did poor service to Mitchell's 'One Nation' politics, his old-fashioned belief in the debt that the strong owe the weak and his essential courtesy. But political crises are mediated by caricature more than nuanced reality.

Nor could the timing have been worse: on the day before the incident, two police officers, PCs Fiona Bone and Nicola Hughes, had been shot dead while investigating a suspected burglary in Mottram, Greater Manchester. As an officer in the Royal Tank Regiment, who had served in Cyprus as a UN peacekeeper, Mitchell had always taken very seriously the debt owed to the Armed Forces and the police. In the days that followed, the Chief Whip told his confidants that (after his family's misery) the allegation that he was dismissive of that debt to men and women in uniform was the most purgatorial aspect of the whole episode.

After speaking to the officer involved in the case, John Tully, chairman of the Metropolitan Police Federation, called for the Chief Whip to go: 'He should resign. As a Cabinet Minister it's unacceptable for someone of his standing to use such disrespectful and abusive language to a police constable let alone anyone else.'[2] The story spread like wildfire on Twitter, with the hashtags #gategate and #plebgate. Mitchell was reprimanded by the PM, who expressed public and private disapproval of the Chief Whip's conduct. The conversation between Cameron and Mitchell had been brusque and businesslike. The PM did not want to lose a minister whom he felt was perfectly suited to his new role; but he was undoubtedly angry that a recently promoted Tory should have apparently fuelled the 'Flashman' myth: that this was a Government of public schoolboys bullying their supposed 'social inferiors'. He and Osborne doubted that Mitchell had used the word 'plebs', but the swearing – not disputed – was bad enough. On a visit to Greater Manchester Police headquarters, the

Prime Minister added that Mitchell had apologized to him and 'thoroughly to the police, and that needed to be done'.

This was an obvious opportunity for Lib Dems, awaiting the public response to Clegg's 'Sorry' at their conference in Brighton, to demand much deeper contrition from a senior Tory. Tim Farron, the party's president and a potential leadership candidate, kept up the attack. Boris Johnson, whom Mitchell had helped when he was an aspiring parliamentary candidate, said that it would have been 'wholly common-sensical' for the police to consider arresting the Chief Whip. Mitchell was taken aback. 'I got Boris on the candidates' list!' he exclaimed to an ally. Once again, the Mayor was leaping on the bandwagon of a headline-generating story to signal his own priorities. In this case, he was letting the world know that he sided with the Metropolitan Police (for which he was responsible) rather than a Conservative member of the Cabinet (for which he hoped to be responsible in due course).

Returning to work on the Monday, Mitchell made a brief appearance on the pavement of Whitehall to deny that he had used the words 'attributed' to him. Dressed sombrely in dark suit, white shirt and navy blue tie, he approached the huddle of hacks and cameras, his hands clasped like a doctor giving an update on a famous patient, doing his best not to look flustered. He had apologized, he said, and hoped 'very much that we can draw a line under it there'. In fact, his troubles were just beginning. On Tuesday, 25 September, the *Daily Telegraph* published in full the 442-word police log of the incident. This record supported the *Sun*'s account, and supplied further details. 'After several refusals Mr Mitchell got off his bike and walked to the pedestrian gate with me after I again offered to open that for him. There were several members of the public present as is the norm opposite the pedestrian gate.' The log then recorded Mitchell's alleged tirade exactly as the *Sun* had reported, including his use of the word 'plebs'. The officer noted that members of the public looked 'visibly shocked' and that Mitchell had been warned that if he did not stop swearing he would be arrested under the Public Order Act. The log continued: 'Mr Mitchell was then silent and left saying "you haven't heard the last of this" as he cycled off.'

This presented a dire conundrum for Cameron and Osborne. The story was clearly not going to go away, and, as the Chancellor pointed out, its implication was serious whatever the outcome: either a senior Cabinet minister or the police protecting the occupants of Downing Street had told a systematic lie. Decent people, it was true, said vile and snobbish things, and Mitchell certainly had a temper. But Osborne knew the Chief Whip well, having opened a line of communication with him in 2005 when he was running Cameron's leadership campaign and Mitchell was managing David Davis's. Knowing his basic decency and habits of courtesy, he did not believe that the Chief Whip would have uttered the word 'plebs' – or that it was a word that was really used any more. What he had to impress upon Mitchell was that the stakes were now vertiginously high: 'We will stand behind you – but you have to understand that if you have lied, the world will come down on you.'

That moment very nearly arrived after an email was sent to the Deputy Chief Whip, John Randall, supposedly from a tourist claiming to have seen the incident. The author of the semi-literate message said: 'Imagine to our horror when we heard Mr Mitchell shout very loudly at the police officers guarding "YOU _____ PLEBES!!" and "YOU THINK YOU RUN THE _____ COUNTRY" and just continued to shout obscenities at the poor police officers. My nephew, as was I, totally taken aback bu his, MR MITCHELLS' behaviour and the gutter language he used, especially it appeared directed at the police officers.' According to one senior source: 'At this point, Andrew was very close to being sacked.' Instead, Sir Jeremy Heywood was asked to conduct an inquiry; he quickly concluded that there was no evidence to justify the Chief Whip's resignation.

The PM and Osborne hoped they could ride the story out. To this end, Mitchell stayed away from the Tory conference in Birmingham – but his story did not. In the Chief Whip's absence, the party's oligarchy – his Cabinet colleagues – stoked the fires, encouraging activists, MPs and reporters to prepare the tumbrils. It wasn't that Mitchell was especially unpopular: he extended hospitality to many of his ministerial colleagues, inviting them to a play at the Almeida Theatre in Islington or dinner at his north London home to sample

his famous cellar (his family had founded El Vino, the wine mer-
chants and owners of the Fleet Street bar referred to by Beaverbrook
as 'El Vino's public house'). There was institutional resentment of his
department and its ring-fenced budget, but the sums involved were
comparatively tiny – £7.9bn. If anyone was blamed for the ring-fence,
in any case, it was Cameron rather than Mitchell.

This was business, not personal. When a colleague is perceived to
be doomed, only the most steadfast friends stick by him or her. In
Mitchell's case, Philip Hammond was not among them: the Defence
Secretary said that the story had been 'very damaging', while MPs
were reported to have approached Graham Brady, the chairman of
the 1922 Committee, to express their concerns. At a meeting of the
committee on 17 October, it became clear that Mitchell was losing
the support of his own side: Osborne, waiting outside, watched the
clock and realized that things were not proceeding happily for the
Chief Whip. Asked afterwards if the grilling had gone well for him,
Mitchell replied ruefully: '-ish'. He was audibly shaken.

Piling on the pressure, Labour tabled a Commons motion that
called upon Mitchell to forfeit £1,000 of his salary as a symbolic fine:
roughly the penalty he would have faced if prosecuted before a
magistrate. Miliband taunted the Chief Whip as 'toast' and pressed
for a vote on his conduct. On the Thursday night, Mitchell decided
that he had to go. Not least in his calculations was the impact the protracted story was having upon his family, and how distressing it was
for his wife to learn that local people were speaking out anonymously
against them to the press (poor reward for the out-of-hours emergency treatment she had been known, as a popular doctor, to offer
those living nearby). Mitchell also saw that Labour's 'punching of the
bruise' – going back to the story again and again – was distracting
attention from good economic news (unemployment and inflation
down) and favourable crime figures. Irked by this victory for political
noise over natural justice, Cameron reluctantly accepted his resignation and appointed Sir George Young to succeed him.

Cameron's position had not changed: Mitchell had sworn at a
police officer, which he felt merited a reprimand, an apology and
all the attendant media attention. But, for all his or her claims to the

contrary – 'I won't let the media tell me who I have in my Cabinet!' – a Prime Minister is not a free agent when it comes to such decisions. Though a political resignation looks like a solitary act, it is usually a group effort, a collective phenomenon. It is a tribal expulsion in which the elders express the wishes of the clan. The media provide the forum, and amplify the voice of anger. In this case, the Conservative Party staged a minor uprising against its new Chief Whip. According to Philip Cowley, professor of politics at Nottingham University and longtime analyst of MPs' revolts, Tory backbenchers in this Parliament had shown themselves particularly ready to rebel. As Cowley observed: 'the Chief Whip was facing major problems whoever it was'. As a veteran ex-whip of the Maastricht era, Mitchell knew the ropes. But he also had foes-in-waiting who remembered his conduct as a whip in the Maastricht years, when the very survival of the Major Government depended upon the whim of the sceptics, and the whips' office was all that stood between the PM and oblivion. After Mitchell appeared to deny Miliband's charge in the Commons that he had sworn, Michael Fabricant, straw-thatched MP for Lichfield, tweeted with relish that the Chief Whip had 'managed to re-ignite [the story] himself. Self-ignition?'

In fact, the Mitchell story was far from over. In December, the police version of events began to unravel in an extraordinary way, as *Dispatches* and Channel 4 News revealed CCTV footage of the incident. Although the recording lacked an audio track, there was no indication of an altercation: Mitchell and the police officer had only a brief exchange, with no indication in their body language of a serious confrontation. Crucially, there was no sign of the 'several members of the public' watching the scene as recorded in the police log: the pavement outside the pedestrian gate to Downing Street was deserted. Most shocking of all was the separate disclosure that the author of the email that had backed up the log's account was not a civilian at all, but a police officer.

Mitchell, now simply the backbench MP for Sutton Coldfield, was furious that Heywood had not pursued any of this in his inquiry, the implications of which had been quickly deduced by Michael Crick and a team at Channel 4. As he told friends: 'It's like being sent out to buy some eggs and seeing a murder on the way – and just coming back with the eggs.' Heywood simply did not feel it was his job to dig too deep, or to do the work of investigating officers – though, in so doing, he had left Mitchell in an unpleasant limbo. Some of his allies, including Davis, considered a full-scale parliamentary onslaught on Heywood. But Mitchell himself was reluctant to see the 'dogs of war' unleashed on the Cabinet Secretary, conscious that this would cause collateral damage to Number Ten and to Cameron. Cross-examined by the Commons Public Administration Committee, Heywood conceded the limitations of his inquiry. 'We accepted there were unanswered questions including the possibility of a gigantic conspiracy, or a small conspiracy, but we decided on balance to leave things as they were,' he told MPs. The committee's chairman, Bernard Jenkin, told Heywood: 'You lost a minister because of false allegations about him that were not properly investigated.'[3] Heywood did not consider his role in such a situation to be as extensive as the committee did. The real problem, as Osborne had pointed out at the time, was that the nature of the case made it impossible in practice to ask the police to look into the matter. Mitchell was left seething with fury at Heywood's nonchalance and the mandarin's decision 'on balance' not to make inquiries that might have saved his Cabinet career. He could not even console himself that the Cabinet Secretary had a personal animus against him: Heywood simply couldn't be bothered.

Now, however, a full police inquiry – Operation Alice – was underway, led by Deputy Assistant Commissioner Patricia Gallan, with thirty officers at her disposal. By March, one civilian and ten police officers from four different forces were under investigation (at the time of writing, DAC Gallan's inquiry was still open). Mitchell launched libel proceedings against the *Sun* and lodged a further complaint with the Independent Police Complaints Commission over the apparent leaking of its report into the affair. In a letter to the IPCC deputy chairman, Deborah Glass, he wrote: 'We are deeply dismayed that the Metropolitan police appear to have leaked part of their report prepared for the Crown Prosecution Service (CPS) to certain members of the press and spun it to the advantage of the police officers involved. This was an enquiry into a dishonest and illicit attempt to blacken my name and destroy my career. It would appear that this police enquiry continues precisely that process.'[4]

Rarely had a senior politician been so thoroughly or so quickly vindicated in popular perception after the ordeal of resignation: the path was now clear for Mitchell to return to frontline politics. Inescapably, his case reflected appallingly upon some police officers, their apparent capacity for fabrication and their readiness to see a man's career ruined – perhaps, it was speculated, in protest at redundancies and cuts. But would the truth have emerged without Channel 4's persistence? Once again, incuriosity had taken its toll. Why had nobody in Downing Street chased the (very clear) video evidence or the phony email?

The Conservative Party had lost its nerve, too – over a single word, which Mitchell had not even used. At the heart of the whole story lay the Cameron Government's neuralgic relationship with class: its public insistence that social background did not matter and its private anxiety that, to the electorate, it might matter very much indeed. The word 'plebs' was loaded with symbolic aggression. As alarming as it was to Downing Street that Mitchell stood accused of using such a word, it was even more alarming that the allegation might ring true to the electorate; that it confirmed every ghastly suspicion that the Tory Party was led by people who really *did* believe themselves born to rule and therefore regarded the police as no more than proletarian shock-troops at their beck and call.

Publicly, Cameron confronted this with his most banal mantra: 'It's not where you come from, it's where you're going.' It had been a reasonable thing for him to say during the leadership contest when he was fighting inverse snobbery about his Etonian education. Why on earth should he apologize or be penalized for his background? But as a description of how society worked, the slogan was plainly ridiculous: parents would not spend more than £30,000 a year on public school fees if it did not make a difference 'where you come from'. The idea of the 'classless society' championed by John Major was a decent man's aspiration – a shining city on a hill, not a destination that had already been reached. Social caste was no longer all that mattered, or even what mattered most: aspiration competed more

aggressively with background to determine destiny. The Thatcher
Government did more than any of its immediate predecessor administrations to spread opportunity and to urge individuals and families
to break the mind-forged manacles of class. But the idea that those
manacles had gone was risible.

In private, Cameron worried about this constantly. He consulted
Coulson all the time about the social character of his initiatives and
how they would be perceived. Some senior Tories dismissed all discussion of class as 'chippiness', as if that were the end of the argument.
They took comfort from the conspicuous failure in May 2008 of
Labour's by-election campaign in Crewe and Nantwich, which
sought to portray the Tory candidate, Edward Timpson, as a 'toff'
with no understanding of ordinary voters: Timpson was elected,
with a swing away from Labour of 17.6 per cent, the first Conservative gain in a by-election since 1982. Hilton, in particular, was
dismayed by the conclusion drawn by many Conservatives that class
was now dead as a political issue. Cameron did not believe that for a
moment. He knew that, in politics, a background such as his own
could be a hindrance as well as a help. Osborne had long worried that
perceived privilege might be a stumbling block to public service
reform – along the lines of 'What would you lot know about *that*?'

This was why Cameron encouraged Annunziata Rees-Mogg, the
Conservative candidate for Somerset and Frome in 2010, to call herself 'Nancy Mogg' in her campaigns. It was also why some Cameroons
were so concerned by the disclosure in 2009 that Zac Goldsmith, the
candidate for Richmond Park, had claimed non-domicile tax status.
In fact, Goldsmith, who went on to win the seat, had already
instructed his accountants to relinquish his non-dom advantages (he
also went on to discuss offering his seat to Boris Johnson, should the
Mayor need instant entry to the House of Commons). But, throughout the 2010 campaign, Cameron fretted about the impression that
the party was a rich man's club. The expenses scandal, with its duck
house, moat-cleaning and servicing of Aga stoves, had strengthened
the stereotype of the Conservatives as a social sect rather than a One
Nation movement. He also knew that the controversial 'A list' of
candidates had increased the number of women and people from

ethnic minorities standing as Tories, but done much too little to change the socio-economic background of the new parliamentary party. Where were the new Joe Lamptons, the young people from modest backgrounds looking for room at the top?

In times of austerity, resentment of privilege naturally increases, and is not confined to the indigent. Today's gilded young leader could easily become tomorrow's despised toff; a new and talented team could fast attract loathing as a feckless oligarchy. Cameron wanted to be remembered as a social reformer and to make the Conservative Party a force for social renewal as well as economic growth. But he knew that it was hard for someone born into affluence to claim kinship in adversity with those born in tower blocks, into multi-generational worklessness, who were going in ever greater numbers to food banks: more than 350,000 in 2012, according to one charity, almost triple the total for the year before.[5] As Cameron's cousin Ferdinand Mount – a former head of the Downing Street policy unit – put it in a lucid analysis of modern British oligarchy: 'The unchecked growth of inequality has begun to corrode our sense of belonging. George Osborne continues to proclaim that, in tackling the deficit, "We are all in this together." This mantra is increasingly met amongst the less well off with a resounding raspberry. It is so clearly the case that, proportionately, they are afflicted by the crisis and the cuts far more than the well-to-do, who are protected by their professional cartels and the *omertà* of the boardroom.'[6] While Cameron might take issue with the letter of his cousin's argument, he often indicated in private that he grasped the potential strength of class-based politics, dormant not dead: not old-fashioned organized labour versus the state and the bosses, but a more insidious conflict between haves and have-nots, between privilege and the excluded. This was especially likely if the wealthy were seen to be ignoring or scorning the basic tenets of fairness.

One of the Tory leader's strengths had always been an ability to see the difference between formal rules and the public's visceral sense of right. It had served him well in 2008 during the expenses scandal. 'Politicians have done things that are unethical and wrong,' he said. 'I don't care if they were within the rules. They were wrong.' A similar case arose in early 2012, over the bonus payable to Stephen Hester, the chief executive of the state-controlled Royal Bank of Scotland. On top of his £1.2m salary, Hester had been awarded shares worth only slightly less than £1m – the limit set by the Prime Minister. Was Hester 'in it together' with everyone else, or not? In the face of mounting public fury, senior Government sources said that this was 'what happens when reality and populism clash'. The danger was spelt out thus: if Hester quit, as he might, so too would the chairman of the board, Sir Philip Hampton, along with several of the bank's directors. The resulting turmoil at RBS would be profoundly hostile to the deeper public interest. Number Ten and the Treasury concluded that Hester had to have his bonus – modest by his own standards, no doubt, but still thirty-eight times the median salary (£26,000). Clegg took issue with this, arguing that the bonus was not settled, and that such bonanzas should not even be considered until RBS – 83 per cent of which was publicly owned – was safely back in private hands. The Lib Dems mischievously reminded the PM of his own decree in a recent interview with *The House* magazine: 'You need moral markets because you need people to make moral choices, you want businesses to make moral choices.' He had also told the *Sunday Telegraph* that 'the market for top people isn't working, it needs to be sorted out'.

A dangerous impression had arisen of a plutocracy that demanded help from the public sector when its casino debt became unpayable – but refused to behave with humility thereafter. RBS was indeed a plc, listed on the Stock Exchange. Yet it was in no meaningful sense a bank like any other; and Hester and his colleagues were not performing the role of regular bankers. Narrowly saved from total failure in 2009, its journey back to something approaching viability was a dramatization of something broader: the rescue of the financial sector not only from commercial disaster, but also from the stain of shame. In the eyes of the taxpayer, Hester was a public servant, on a public mission that should be governed by a public-spirited ethos. Angela Knight, the chief executive of the British Bankers' Association, said that he should be paid the 'going rate'. But there was no 'going rate' for such a job.

In his successful quest for public support over the proposed benefits cap, the PM appealed not to populism or vindictiveness, but to the deep-seated human notion of orderliness. He understood that it offended a collective sense of fairness and social cohesion that some households might be able to claim more in state handouts than the take-home pay of a person earning more than £35,000 p.a. gross of tax. Precisely the same concept of decorum inspired disbelief that the senior repairman at a state-controlled bank should be granted nearly £1m *in addition* to a salary that was in itself beyond the imaginings of the vast majority of voters. Hester's bonus contravened a culture of decency that was not part of the law of contract or the mechanics of the market. It was much stronger than that.

The risk for Cameron was that, having taken on Gaddafi, vetoed an EU treaty and imposed cuts across Whitehall, he might be faced down by the bankers. It was only when Labour decided to put Hester's bonus to a Commons vote that the CEO decided to waive the reward. It was a narrow escape for RBS and, indirectly, for Cameron. But little had really changed. In spite of the £390m fine imposed on the bank for Libor rigging, and losses of £5.2bn in 2012, RBS paid out bonuses of £607m for the year – including £215m for the division behind the Libor scandal.

Irony is never far from political life, and so it was with Cameron and class. He was the first Conservative Prime Minister who explicitly and sincerely regarded 'social justice' as a Tory priority – not as an old-fashioned paternalist, putting a price-tag on social order, but as a believer in 'spreading privilege' and in broadening opportunity. The sneers of the Left that he was spreading only poverty and taking benefits away from the vulnerable simply made him more determined to stake out this terrain – in education, welfare policy and localism.

Yet he struggled to shake the political stigma of privilege. His reorganization of the Number Ten policy unit in April 2013 was marred by a furore over the social background of his advisers. The unit's new head, Jo Johnson, was another Old Etonian, as was Jesse Norman, brought back from his brief exile over Lords reform and recruited to the policy board. In an interview with the BBC's *World at One*, Cameron reverted to his usual (and inevitable) formula: 'I appoint people because they are good enough to do the job, and they are the right person for that job. I have people around me who have all sorts of different backgrounds, and all sorts of different schooling. The question is: are you going to be good enough to do the job?'[7]

But class was to Cameron what the zipwire was to Boris – with the difference that he was unable to make light of it or turn it to his advantage. Norman tried to explain Eton's dominance with reference to its exceptional 'commitment to public service'. In his defence, the MP protested that he was simply trying to explain that the privilege of a world-class education entailed a responsibility to serve society – as, to be fair, Norman himself did in numerous charitable activities. But the remark was interpreted as straightforward Etonian arrogance. This latest burst of recruitment of talent to Number Ten and the Cabinet Office was seen as a victory for the old school tie; not an enhancement of the human capital at the Government's disposal – Johnson, Norman and the others were an impressive team – but as a narrowing of its social base. John Harris, the *Guardian* columnist, expressed the perception thus: 'If you want to bang on about hard work, aspiration and opportunity, it might be an idea to find people with experience of what they actually mean. In other words, even if a degree of "modernization" was imperative, was it the wisest move to select a public-school clique to do it?'[8] Downing Street's answer to such questions was always and invariably that Cameron recruited on the basis of talent, rather than background. He was a meritocrat and would not insult anyone by hiring them simply to fill a quota.

But the issue here was not social philosophy. It was news management and political common sense. A good story – the strengthening of Number Ten's policy-making capacity – had been overshadowed by yet another row about public schoolboys and the importance of being Etonian. In spite of his general anxieties about class-based politics, Cameron was willing to take a hit in order to surround himself with those he regarded as the right people. None of his advisers sought to prevent him. It is probable that Coulson would have done so (he had felt no compunction about telling the PM where he could or could not go on holiday – imposing a ban on further OEs in

Number Ten would have been the work of a moment). This is why Cameron was so incurious about Coulson's past, so desperate not to lose him. He knew, instinctively, that he was one of the very few who would speak truth to power. According to one Cameroon: 'I can hear Andy saying it: "Come on – all these Etonians? You're having a laugh, aren't you? The tabs [tabloids] will kill us." That's what Dave doesn't have any more.'

Well into his eighth year as Conservative leader, Cameron doubted that he would ever be able to shrug off his image as a son of privilege. What mattered, as he looked ahead to the last two years of the Parliament, was whether he would pay a price for this perception. In an article for the *Daily Telegraph* after the party's poor showing in the May local elections, David Davis was quite explicit about what his former rival for the leadership needed: 'more conventional Tory policies, not because they are Tory, but because they work: less pandering to metropolitan interest groups: and please, please, no more Old Etonian advisers'.[9]

The great failure of Cameron's modernizing strategy had been the failure to break free of the party's social moorings and persuade less-affluent working people, as well as entrepreneurs and businessmen, that it was on their side. Lord Ashcroft's mega-polls – such as his survey of 8,000 people in November 2012 – revealed that the public believed the Tories were willing to take tough decisions, that Labour had not yet learned the lessons of defeat, and that Cameron was considerably more 'prime ministerial' than Miliband. Yet in one area – understanding 'ordinary people' – the Labour leader enjoyed a 26-point advantage over the PM, and his party was 25 ahead of the Tories when compared according to the same criterion.[10] More than thirteen years after Blair had declared that the class war was over, social perception was still at the heart of Cameron's electoral problems. No wonder Miliband claimed so brazenly to be a 'One Nation' leader. There were no 'toffs' or 'plebs' in polling booths: only voters.

'What they don't want is to roll up to a church and find Derek and Clive having their wedding': thus, in a conversation early in the New Year, did the Prime Minister explain to his advisers the resistance of Tory Party members to same-sex marriage. The image of Dudley Moore getting married to Peter Cook – the original, awesomely profane Derek and Clive – was an arresting one, and not quite what Cameron had meant. His point was that Conservative activists were generally opposed to gay marriage only if it meant change in their places of worship. A secular reform could be managed, he believed. As he would later admit to the same colleagues, he had radically underestimated the scale and depth of the hostility in his party to same-sex unions.

After the storm, it was easy to forget that the two governing parties had originally competed for ownership of this legislation. Andrew Cooper, Cameron's director of strategy, had not lost sight of the modernizing principles he had done so much to establish as a pollster and senior adviser. When he spoke of 'modernity', Cooper was not talking about metropolitan liberalism or a licentious free-for-all but contemporary life in all its variety. As Michael Portillo had spelt out in 1997, a Conservative leader who hoped to win had 'to deal with the world as it now is'.[1] This meant toughness on law and order – tougher, certainly, than Ken Clarke had been at the Justice Department. It meant accepting and addressing popular anxieties about immigration, while acknowledging the benefits of labour mobility in a globalized economy and celebrating the pluralism of twenty-first-century urban life. It meant rigorous candour about the challenge of the 'global race' – coupled with a reassurance that the Government was 'on your side' in that contest. And it meant, Cameron now believed, extending the institution of marriage to same-sex couples. The Lib Dems had wanted to pilot the reform, but Cooper made sure that the Home Office consultation announced in September 2011 had Tory fingerprints all over it and was seen to have been 'personally pushed through by DC'. The strategy director was delighted. 'Modern compassionate Conservatism lives!' he texted allies.

In the months that followed, the proposals that became the Marriage (Same Sex Couples) Bill were sometimes perceived as a bolt from the blue, or a crass attempt by Cameron to rebrand his party as it approached mid-term. But the bill was neither of these things. More than any other single reform enacted by the Coalition, it symbolized Cameron's politics and the continuity of his beliefs: what Blair described, in his own case, as an 'irreducible core'. As the child of a successful marriage (his beloved father, Ian, had died in 2010), and the beneficiary of another, he believed in the institution heart and soul. But he recognized that it was imperilled in an age of instant gratification rather than lifelong commitment. Although the proportion of marriages that ended in divorce in England and Wales had fallen slightly between 2005 and 2011, it still stood at 42 per cent.[2] In the Prime Minister's eyes, matrimony was an institution in dire need of restoration and renewal. Unlike Osborne, he believed that there should be some recognition of its significance, however small and symbolic, in the fiscal thickets of incentives, tax breaks and benefit triggers.[3]

The PM's support for same-sex marriage reflected, of course, a belief that the lifelong commitment of two men or of two women was worthy not only of civil recognition but also of the same kind of civil recognition as the marriage of a man and a woman. Civil partnerships, as far as he was concerned, were only a transitional measure. But Cameron also saw his reform as a means of strengthening an ailing institution. Gay people who married would not only be exercising a new right; they would be recruited to, and thereby reinforce, an ancient system of social organization. Whereas opponents of the measure saw it as the weakening of the most basic social unit, Cameron believed not only that human happiness would be enhanced, but that marriage itself would be strengthened. Whether or not this reform should be a priority was, of course, a matter of opinion – although many who claimed to be calling for the postponement of the measure were really seeking its abandonment. Peter Bone, the Conservative MP for Wellingborough, even suggested that it be delayed until 2017, and a question about gay marriage tacked on to the planned referendum on EU membership. Such interventions implied that the issue was a frivolous distraction at a time of economic challenge. But Cameron did not regard the issue as a frivolity or a sideshow. In fact, it encapsulated his social philosophy more precisely than any other measure or initiative.

Those who said he had sprung this on his party – a typical stunt by the panicked metropolitan elite – had simply not been paying attention. As far back as the 2006 Tory conference, the new Tory leader had made a passionate defence of marriage, paused theatrically and added: 'And by the way, it means something whether you're a man and a woman, a woman and a woman or a man and another man.' Cameron was not jumping on a bandwagon, or suddenly yielding to liberal pressure, but acting upon a belief he had made clear seven years before. He was taking the nation in precisely the direction he had promised in the 2005 leadership contest: towards openness, equality of treatment and what, in a *Newsnight* appearance in 2013, Francis Maude called 'the centre of gravity of social attitudes'.

In an article for *The Times* in November 2012, Osborne wrote that 'I am proud to be part of a Government that will introduce a Bill to allow gay marriage. It is worth reflecting that in Britain, as America, a clear majority of the public support gay marriage, and an even bigger majority of women support it. That majority support is just as high in the North as it is in the South, and it is equally high among all socio-economic groups.' Responding to Obama's re-election, Osborne was warning his own party not to declare war on contemporary society as the Republican 'Tea Party' had: 'President Obama's high-profile endorsement of equal marriage for gay couples also enthused younger voters. But polls found that a majority of all Americans supported him on the issue and voted for it in all four states that held ballots.'[4] Osborne could not resist reminding his readers what Obama had tweeted as his victory was declared: 'We are all in this together.'

In February, the Chancellor, William Hague and Theresa May wrote a letter to the *Daily Telegraph* affirming their support for the measure: 'Civil partnerships for gay couples were a great step forward, but the question now is whether it is any longer acceptable to exclude people from marriage simply because they love someone of the same sex. Marriage has evolved over time. We believe that opening it up to same-sex couples will strengthen, not weaken, the institution. Attitudes towards gay people have changed. A substantial majority of the public now favour allowing same-sex couples to marry, and support has increased rapidly. This is the right thing to do at the right time.'[5] In the bitter aftermath of the vote on gay marriage, some Tories insisted that Cameron should be replaced at once by Boris Johnson. This reflected only the determination of disgruntled Conservatives to project all their hopes on to the Mayor and the façade of City Hall. He differed from Cameron in many respects. But he was not, and had never been, a social conservative. As Peter Tatchell put it in the *Evening Standard*: 'Boris's backing for same-sex marriage was a game-changer.' No less than the Prime Minister, he grasped that his party must make peace with modern life, both because it was the right thing to do and because all other paths led to electoral disaster.

It helped that the Cabinet minister steering the reform through the Commons was Maria Miller, a mainstream Conservative rather than an ultra-modernizer, who presented the measure as a sensible and modest change, rather than a generational moment in the history of civil rights (which it was). Educated at a comprehensive and the LSE, Miller looked and sounded like a true Tory, and had graduated to the Cabinet after two years working for Duncan Smith on welfare reform. She was good at reassuring Tory backbenchers that the reform was not a covert bid to make Soho the nation's capital or to subvert the established Church. Quite the opposite, she explained: this was an attempt to reinforce marriage, a fundamentally conservative institution, by extending its scope to same-sex couples. Repeatedly, Miller expressed respect for those who opposed or had anxieties about the bill, especially MPs who felt that their religious beliefs were being disregarded. She and Cameron made much of the so-called 'quadruple lock' in the proposals, which protected religious institutions and faith groups from litigation over gay marriage, and ensured that, in practice, no priest, rabbi or imam would ever have to officiate unwillingly at a same-sex wedding. The Church of England and the Church in Wales were explicitly exempted from the new system: a disappointment to many Anglicans, it transpired, but an absolutely essential provision. By strategically delegating the question to the Church itself – relocating it in a separate legal silo, so to speak – Cameron had ensured that the legislative debate would not degenerate into a blazing row about religious freedom. In return, he asked only that the churches render unto Cameron that which was Cameron's.

This did not stop religious sensibilities being mentioned in the Commons debate on 5 February, which was essentially an argument between two forms of conservatism: the preservative and the liberal. Cameron, of course, believed that his measure was both – protecting marriage, while enhancing freedom. But for others it represented a choice. Declaring that she would positively abstain, Andrea Leadsom, the Tory MP for South Northamptonshire, said that, for those who saw marriage as a sacrament, such a change was bound to have consequences: 'I have deep sympathy with the hundreds of my constituents who fear that legislation for same-sex marriage will profoundly encroach – although this may be unintended – on their right to live according to their faith. For many, the conviction that marriage can take place only between a man and a woman means that they feel that their own marriage is undermined by what they see as a profound change to the biblical definition.'[6] This was the crux of the opposition.

Ian Paisley Jr of the DUP went further: 'Whether members care to admit it or not, there is a natural, a biological, and indeed a scriptural order to life. Marriage begat children, by and large, children begat family, by and large, and families are the root of society; they form society. It's a simple observation of life, a timeline, but it goes right to the root of what we are discussing today in debating in this House.' Another Tory MP, Stewart Jackson, warned of a clash between different kinds of freedom. 'This is a Pandora's box, for endless litigation, for division in society setting one group against another, and we must for that reason, for community cohesion, resist this bill.' In a perplexing reference to the pioneering black civil rights activist of the 1950s, he added: 'Rosa Parks did not give up her seat to send me to the back of the bus as a Christian.'[7]

On the other side of the argument, Margot James, the MP for Stourbridge, said that 'we may have gone two steps forward, but I fear we may have gone one step backwards. The modernisation of the Conservative Party is not yet complete. Having been different for most of my life, I can assure you that being treated equal is very welcome indeed and we still have some way to go, not just in the area of gay people but in other areas. I believe my party should never flinch from the requirement that we must continue this progression.' Brooks Newmark, the Conservative MP for Braintree, correctly diagnosed the generational dimension to the row: 'I have five children, and if any of them thought I was going to oppose this Bill, they would think I was bonkers. The vast majority of people under 40 support this Bill.'[8] Sir Peter Bottomley argued that the measure's mandate flowed not from manifestos, but from the duty of the Commons to respect and to respond wisely to the tide of social change. Opinion polls suggested that the electorate was indeed broadly supportive of the measure – 45 per cent versus 36 per cent in a *Sunday Telegraph* survey in March – though unable to see why it was a priority for Cameron.[9] A *Guardian*/ICM poll in December had shown even stronger support – 62 per cent for the reform versus 31 per cent against.[10]

In essence, this measure concerned the status of marriage as a secular social institution rather than as a sacred rite. It identified commitment, rather than procreation, as the essential purpose of such unions. It also, naturally, addressed the status of gay people: no longer treated as a tolerated minority, but as fully fledged citizens, enjoying the same rights and opportunities as their heterosexual neighbours. The symbolism was immense: if society applauded and honoured a same-sex marriage as it would the marriage of a man and a woman then – emphatically – it was no longer treating homosexuality as an affliction, a condition of inferiority or a pathology.

Much as Cameron and Miller presented the bill as an exercise in incremental reform it was much more than that – radically enshrining the principle of equality of worth. Each generation, the PM knew, was given the chance to conduct an audit of its inner social wiring. True equality could not be granted, only recognized. The introduction of civil partnerships in 2004 had been an important step forward but posed a fundamental question: why was it necessary for same-sex couples to have a separate procedure to formalize their life-long commitment to one another? As one gay Tory MP put it at the time: 'It still told me where I could sit on the bus.' The sheer absurdity of separate treatment paved the way to further reform, and the secular state's removal of this final segregation. In this sense, Miller's proposals drilled deep into the collective psyche, bringing close to completion a process that was launched by the Wolfenden Report in 1957 and the decriminalization of homosexual acts: it had taken gay people fifty-five years to make the journey from prison cell to the altar.

The Commons voted overwhelmingly for change, by 400 to 175 – a majority of 225. As a statesman, Cameron could feel richly satisfied by a measure that would still be remembered when Leveson, 'pleb-gate' and the turf wars in Number Ten competed for space in the footnotes. As party leader, however, he had little to celebrate. In spite of his own appeals, the emollience of Miller, and the arguments made by Osborne, Hague and May, no fewer than 136 Conservatives had opposed the bill – including two Cabinet ministers (Owen Paterson and David Jones, the Welsh Secretary). Just 127 Tories had supported the measure, which was carried by a heavy margin thanks only to overwhelming backing by Labour and the Lib Dems.

Behind the scenes, Cameron would later concede that his political antennae had failed him in this instance; he had lost contact with his own tribe. A party that is serious about power cannot surrender policy or strategy formulation to its membership. But, if they feel unloved or traduced, those members can cause a leader very considerable problems. Months after the vote, he was still writing dozens of letters to activists and constituents seeking to allay their fears and to reassure them that what he was doing was authentically Conservative, and not a betrayal of the party's most sacred beliefs. 'I want this sorted out by

July,' he told his advisers. But it was clear that the ill-feeling the reform had sown in the Conservative Party would endure long after that.

Light relief in this fraught debate was provided by the actor and memoirist Rupert Everett, who said that the last thing his fellow homosexuals should do is sign up to a failing institution: 'It's just hideous. The wedding cake, the party, the champagne, the inevitable divorce two years later. It's just a waste of time in the heterosexual world, and in the homosexual world I find it personally beyond tragic that we want to ape this institution that is so clearly a disaster.'[11] And, as it happened, the Coalition had indeed spawned an epic example of this disaster in the downfall of Chris Huhne and the unsparing detail in which his failed marriage to the economist Vicky Pryce was held up to the light.

A few weeks after the 2010 election, it emerged that Huhne was involved in a 'serious relationship' with Carina Trimingham, his former press adviser, and was leaving Pryce, his wife of twenty-six years, with whom he had three children. This would have remained a personal misfortune with no political ramifications if not for the persistence of a journalist and the determination of a scorned wife. Isabel Oakeshott, the political editor of the *Sunday Times*, befriended Pryce and quickly gathered that 'she was out to get Chris Huhne'. The weapon of choice was the disclosure that Huhne had pressured her into taking driving licence penalty points in 2003 while he was seeking selection as Lib Dem candidate in Eastleigh. This was a criminal offence, which, when disclosed, would certainly force Huhne's resignation. But the revelation would also put Pryce at risk of punishment.

According to Oakeshott's absorbing account of the saga – the reporting of which helped her win the Political Journalist of the Year Award – Pryce was explicit about her desire to destroy Huhne's political career. ' "He can't be leader," she said. "He shouldn't even be in the cabinet. People should know what he's really like." So there it was: she wanted to bring him down. I made sure I had understood her correctly.'[12] Pryce said that she 'would need some reassurance that it would indeed bring CH down'. She even considered telling Clegg's wife, Miriam. Having consulted her paper's lawyers, Oakeshott warned

Pryce that 'the bottom line is that, however the story is done, there is some risk to you. It would be dishonest of me to pretend otherwise ... At the end of the day, it's a question of whether you're prepared to take the risk or not, but one thing you can be sure of is that once the story is out, CH would be forced to resign and his career would be in tatters.' With the journalist's help, Pryce tried to get Huhne to admit what he had done – and to record him saying so. An initial version of the story appeared in May 2011, and was pursued by the *Mail on Sunday* – with Pryce's help – the following weekend. Questioned by police, Pryce declined to comment. Huhne and his office denied all the allegations.

Initially, the story was framed by Huhne's supporters as a smear campaign against the Energy Secretary, who had lost to Clegg in the 2007 leadership contest but was well-positioned, along with Cable, to replace him if Clegg's position became untenable. Yet Huhne's real enemy was not his former leadership rival but his former wife. Pryce had not only been humiliated by Huhne. She had also quit her job as chief economist at the Business Department, lest there be any perceived conflict of interest now that her husband was in the Cabinet.

In February 2012, Keir Starmer, the Director of Public Prosecutions, announced that both Huhne and Pryce would be charged with perverting the course of justice. The Energy Secretary had no option but to resign – replaced by Ed Davey, a Clegg loyalist but also a potential contender for the leadership when the succession next became an issue (Cameron and his deputy had agreed in advance that the job would be his if the incumbent was charged).

For a year, Huhne fought to get the case thrown out. The trial forced the story of the family's collapse to be made public in appalling detail. Texts that were never meant to be disclosed were read out in court. Peter Huhne's heart-breaking messages to his father were an inventory of pain, and showed how his youngest son, aged eighteen, had paid for the horribly public break-up of his parents' marriage and subsequent traumas played out in the national media. 'I don't want to speak to you, you disgust me,' he said in one. Then: 'You are the most ghastly man I have ever known. Does it give you pleasure that you have lost most of your friends?' And again: 'Leave me alone, you have no place in my life and no right to be proud. It's irritating that you don't seem to take the point. You are such an autistic piece of shit. Don't contact me again you make me feel sick.'[13] For those who saw politics as a great game, this was a humbling taste of the real price of all the ambition and vengeance.

On 4 February 2013, Huhne shocked Westminster by pleading guilty on re-arraignment and resigning his seat in the Commons – triggering a by-election in Eastleigh that Clegg had been desperate to avoid. On 11 March, Huhne and Pryce were each sentenced to eight months' imprisonment. Clegg described the case as a 'personal tragedy', while Cameron said that Huhne's fate was 'a reminder that no one, however high and mighty, is out of the reach of the justice system'.

Less than three years had passed between Huhne's elevation to the Cabinet and his first night in a cell at HM Prison Wandsworth. If nothing else, this said something about the extraordinary pace of modern politics, the brutal speed with which a potential party leader could become an inmate. By the time Jonathan Aitken and Jeffrey Archer were charged with their respective offences, the Conservatives had long left office. In contrast, *R. v Huhne* reached court well before the Coalition's Mid-Term Review was published. For other senior ministers, the case was a *memento mori*, a frightening reminder of the proximity of political mortality. All Governments suffered what Bill Clinton called 'cellular degeneration'. Now, inexorably, the process seemed to be speeding up.

It was not what the Coalition wanted to be known for: a story about which everyone had an opinion, a criminal soap opera involving a scorned wife, a Cabinet minister, a mistress and a revenge worthy of Jacobean tragedy. Orthodoxy had it that most of Huhne's colleagues were glad to see the back of him. For Clegg, it marked the end of the theatricals that were Huhne's speciality – his brandishing of the AV leaflets in Cabinet being the most obvious example. The Tories were weary of Huhne using his ministerial position as a springboard to the Lib Dem leadership and believed that many of Clegg's problems – and therefore the Coalition's – were his doing, or at least encouraged by him. But this was not the whole story. His spikiness, ambition and dramatic flourishes had made him intermittently unpopular; as one colleague put it: 'Chris's ideal would be to carry a red box, but enjoy the freedom of Opposition.' But he was regarded as good company, too, intellectually adventurous and socially ecumenical. Andrew Mitchell had been to the theatre with Huhne and his girlfriend, and was not the only Cabinet minister who had grown to like him. As Huhne's release drew closer, Clegg said that he still had 'a lot of respect for' him and hoped to see him when he left prison.

The Lib Dem leader and Cameron had grown weary of explaining that their own relationship was not like a marriage at all. But they had been, and remained, mutually interdependent, relying on one another to survive politically. In its own lurid, occasionally unwatchable way, the fall of Huhne and Pryce had shown how vulnerable anyone could be to the people he or she trusted and depended upon. You didn't have to be in the dock to pay a price. And as the court cases involving the hacking scandal drew closer, Cameron feared, with reason, that it was his turn next.

18. Eastleigh ever after

'A fucking disaster': thus did Andrew Cooper, Cameron's strategy chief, describe the appointment as Conservative campaign director of Lynton Crosby. It had taken a while to seal the deal, but the Tories and their new signing were ready to announce it by November 2012. The Australian political consultant, often described as the 'Wizard of Oz', an 'evil genius' or an electoral 'Darth Vader', had been hired by Cameron because he was a winner: four election victories for John Howard, the second-longest-serving Australian Prime Minister in history, and two mayoral triumphs for Boris Johnson.[1] His record was not unblemished. He hadn't been able to pull it off for the Tories in 2005. But he believed he could do a lot better a decade on, in the 2015 general election, against Ed Miliband rather than Tony Blair, campaigning on behalf of the incumbent David Cameron, who already had 304 seats, rather than Michael Howard, the Opposition leader, who had started out with fewer than 170. Crosby was a bull of a man, bespectacled, mild on first encounter but evidently fizzing with barely suppressed energy. He despised complacency and would tell his visitors only that the election was 'winnable'. That much was clear from his decision to take the job: Lynton Crosby did not make a habit of working for losers.

Steve Hilton, who was good friends with Crosby and his wife, Dawn, nonetheless assumed that the hiring meant there 'won't really be a campaign job for me in 2015'. It encouraged Hilton to think laterally and to pursue his ambition to become a mayor when he returned to the UK. 'Next time, I want to be a political practitioner, not just an adviser,' he told friends: he had learned the hard way that, beyond a certain point, you could not live out your political dreams through others. If he wanted 'Hiltonism' to be implemented, he would have to do it himself, perhaps in an English city or borough:

disappointingly, only one of the ten urban areas (Bristol) given a referendum in May 2012 had voted to adopt a mayoral system. Even so, there were now sixteen such directly elected chief executives in England, including Boris. Why should he not be one, too? Better that than the same old rows about what went in the manifesto, where Dave was going that morning, what to make the theme of the day and how closely to stick to the campaign 'war book'. As the months passed agreeably in northern California, Hilton became increasingly convinced that his true destiny was to enter politics as a candidate for office rather than to remain a consultant; to be a change-maker rather than just a frustrated agitator for change.

Cooper's anxiety, however, was not only about the number of cooks working on the Tory broth, a problem that had certainly cost the party seats in 2010. It was also the prospective flavour of the broth that bothered him. Though not the ultra-metropolitan liberal of caricature, Cooper was undoubtedly a modernizer who wanted the Conservative Party to look like a movement responding to the real world rather than a sect trying to escape it, or marooned in nostalgia and yearning for a lost way of life. In the past few months, he and Craig Oliver had developed what they believed was a simple and persuasive narrative – the idea of the 'global race' in which the Tories would be 'on your side' – and had reached the point where their colleagues were starting to use this idiom voluntarily and subconsciously. Crosby was a man who spoke his mind, and his mind was usually filled with robust, no-nonsense conservative ideas. He had reportedly used the phrase 'fucking Muslims' at a meeting when working for Johnson's campaign. Neither he nor Boris could remember him saying this – and they were not words one would forget in a hurry – but for Tory mods, Crosby was the equivalent of Jack Nicholson breaking the door down with an axe in *The Shining*: 'Little pigs, little pigs, let me come in . . .'

Cameron was well aware of this, and was amused by the trepidation that Crosby seemed to inspire. He could afford to laugh about it as he had already pre-empted the problem, retaining the Australian to bring order, discipline and generalship to the campaign, rather than to rewrite its content. As it turned out, Crosby thought the

Cooper–Oliver themes were good and was not chafing at the bit to tear them up and start again. Cooper was especially relieved and went out of his way to correct the opinion he had originally voiced. True, there was a long way to go until polling day 2015. But Cameron believed that, with Crosby *and* Cooper, he would have a campaign that could carry him over the line, even without the lamented boundary review.

Much less welcome was the Eastleigh by-election prompted by Huhne's guilty plea. It was almost certain that one of the Coalition parties would prevail on 28 February: the constituency might be held by the Lib Dems' Mike Thornton, an outcome which Clegg badly needed, as he continued to live hand-to-mouth politically; or it could fall to the Tories, who believed they had found a strong, Ukip-immune candidate in Maria Hutchings. Nigel Farage was still defying the main parties with an ascent that showed no sign of slowing down. However the Tories rationalized the Ukip phenomenon – mid-term, slow recovery, the compromises of coalition, disillusionment with mainstream parties, the related appetite for 'none of the above', Farage's honing of his tribune-in-a-trilby act – it rattled them. Protest parties came and went, but it looked like Ukip had come and was staying – for the foreseeable future, at any rate. In the guts of the Tory Party, there was a bacillus of suspicion that the rise of Farage was a direct consequence of Cameron's flaws, and that if he were to retire to Chipping Norton, the threat would instantly recede. The Ukip leader encouraged this by suggesting that he might be willing to do business with the Conservative Party if it were led by 'a Boris or a Michael Gove' – the indefinite article implying there was no shortage of such candidates – but not while it was held hostage by Cameron: the Etonian Captivity, so to speak.

Farage, like Boris, was hailed as an antidote to Coalition culture. Cameron and Clegg had to tread with care, speak diplomatically and decide daily what outrage, great or small, they were willing to visit upon their respective parties in the name of keeping the show on the road. For Farage, the only show in town was his relentless campaign to make the Prime Minister look ridiculous, over-privileged and out of touch. Cameron's promise of a referendum on Britain's membership of the EU ought to have put Ukip out of business overnight. But it did no such thing. That was because, as seen in Chapter 13, Ukip was no longer a movement driven by the urge to get out of Europe. What the party stood for in early 2013 was not only independence of the EU, but independence of all politicians, bureaucrats and meddlers: Farage's mission was not to persuade the voters of his fitness to pass laws or to govern, but to question the fitness of everybody else. His gift was to pursue an utterly destructive plan, its only objective the democratic sabotage of the main parties, but to do so with infectious cheerfulness. Farage showed that fury could be fun.

Cameron believed that there were two possible ripostes to the threat. One was to chase Ukip off to the demotic Right, lurching precisely as Labour wanted him to, and as his predecessors since Major had done. Hague was at hand to remind him of how that movie ended, and he did so with impressive regularity, urging the Prime Minister not to emulate the mistakes that had helped Blair win his second landslide in 2001. The other response was to treat Ukip as no more than a chirpy complaints department, and to deal with its attack in deeds rather than words; by governing well.

The Mid-Term Review, it must be said, was barely noticed by the voters. But it was a psychologically necessary process to remind the PM's colleagues in both governing parties that they were in office, active on many fronts, and not trapped, as it sometimes seemed, in the stocks as Farage and others hurled rotten fruit at them. In a New Year interview with the *Sunday Telegraph*, he spoke strategically of the exercise as an incentive to think in years, rather than months. 'What the review is about,' he said, 'is what new areas [need] long-term reform to equip our country for the modern challenges, like making sure we have a new method of paying for road building. Because roads, the arteries of our economy, are becoming furred up by traffic jams and lack of new road capacity. Making sure we have a simple pension system so that it really pays you to save during your working life – that's a big long-term change.'[2] In similar spirit, he mentioned care for the elderly and those suffering from dementia, 'another big, chunky long-term reform – these sorts of things we're grouping together in a mid-term review to say, "Here are big challenges, some of them go way into the next parliament."'

It sounded like an affirmation, for his own benefit, rather than rhetoric, for everyone else's. As he and I talked in an otherwise deserted function room in a Manchester hotel where he had just addressed Tory activists, he spoke (for the first time on the record) about his career plans. The idea had somehow got about that, having been leader since 2005, and Prime Minister since 2010, he hoped to win the next election and then, in the manner of Blair, step aside halfway through the Parliament. I knew from previous conversations that he did not want to go 'on and on', to borrow Margaret Thatcher's fate-tempting phrase. So I asked him if his premiership was starting to have the feel of the finite. Was he thinking about life after Downing Street? Not a bit of it, it transpired. Normally, he declined to answer this question, or address the matter of his own future. But he was in a different mood that January evening.

'There are so many things we need to do that need to get properly done. I feel the road map in front of me has got so much on it that needs to get fixed that I don't think of it like that . . . I feel I have plenty on my plate, in terms of delivering the Gove school reforms, the Duncan Smith welfare reforms, massive change to our foreign policy that William Hague and I have been putting in place, the whole trade agenda, the deficit – I feel there is so much.'

I pressed him. When he came to tell voters in 2015 that, if they elected him, he would serve a second 'full term', would he mean those two words absolutely literally (not, as Blair had in 2005, to connote 'a couple more years')? 'Yes. Look, I want to fight the next election, win the next election and serve – that is what I want to do. I often say to Conservatives, stop complaining about the things we haven't done, look at the things we have done and are doing. This is an enormous reform agenda and that's enough to keep us all busy, so that's how it stands.'

Did he mean it? His aides certainly seemed to think so. As one of his closest advisers put it: 'It's a realization not only that he wants his strategy to be implemented, but that he wants to be the one to implement it.' The personal, it seemed, had been grafted on to the strategic. Thanks to the Fixed Term Parliaments Act, this translated into Cameron staying in Number Ten until at least 2020 – voters permitting, of course. It was a ploy in character. He thrived on adversity, on the smell of paint as he huddled in the corner: his finest speech had been his conference address without a formal text in 2007, a performance that helped to dissuade Brown from calling an election the Tories believed he would win. Not for the first time, Cameron's leadership was under assault from several directions – and his bold response was to announce his aspiration to match Blair's period in office (ten years), draw close to Thatcher's (eleven years) and match her tenure of the leadership (fifteen years). Staying till 2020 would make him one of the longest-serving Prime Ministers of modern times, ahead of Asquith, Churchill and Wilson. Of course, all this presupposed Tory victory in 2015, or a hung Parliament yielding another coalition headed by Cameron: an outcome that, in early 2013, was still far from his grasp.

To my ears, his remarks signalled the end of Cameron the Pragmatist, an incarnation that had long been struggling, and suggested that he had succumbed to the radicalism required by his times. This did not mean he would succeed, or be re-elected. His definition of 'radicalism' was not the same as Steve Hilton's. But he had apparently clarified his thinking. His mission now was not only to clear up Labour's mess, but to prepare Britain for the 'global race', a task that would take him, and the country, many years to accomplish. It was the closest a person of Cameron's temperament comes to an epiphany.

Surrounded by tacticians threatening his position, he busied himself increasingly with the strategic. He accepted, for instance, that the arithmetic in the Commons meant that a second hung Parliament was entirely possible. From time to time, he would raise the question of a second coalition with Clegg. 'If we did it again,' he mused to the Deputy Prime Minister, 'I'd have to seek collective permission.' Cameron realized that Clegg would need similar authorization. It was an unlikely outcome. How far would the elastic of Conservative patience stretch? Would the Lib Dem membership even consider it?

Yet it was in the nature of the turbulent political landscape, so different from the New Labour era, to think about long shots.

After a year of Boris-mania, Cameron's own position was still questioned. Bizarrely, in late January, it emerged that Adam Afriyie, the wealthy but politically undistinguished MP for Windsor since 2005, was preparing for a leadership contest – whenever one was held. Osborne joked that he seemed to believe that the top job in the party could be won with a good PowerPoint presentation. In the same brutal spirit, a Number Ten source quipped that Afriyie was so untalented that the only way he could get a job was to become Tory leader. This was harsh, but essentially fair. The proto-candidate, drearily and absurdly described as the 'British Obama' simply because of his ethnicity, gathered around himself a small gang: Jonathan Djanogly, Mark Field, Bill Wiggin and a handful of other MPs. Taken aback by the coverage of his ambitions, Afriyie promised nervously that he would 'never stand against David Cameron'. This was a meaningless pledge, since the party's rules had long outlawed the old-fashioned leadership challenge of the sort launched by Sir Anthony Meyer against Thatcher in 1989, by Michael Heseltine the following year, and by John Redwood against John Major in 1995. An incumbent leader could only be tested in a vote of no confidence – triggered if 15 per cent of the parliamentary party (forty-six, in this case) wrote to the chairman of the 1922 Committee, Graham Brady. Only if the incumbent lost that vote – as Iain Duncan Smith did in 2003 – would a contest be held, in which the deposed leader could not stand. If Afriyie or anyone else wanted the top job before Cameron was ready to go, he would have to engineer his sacking by the parliamentary party. This was not inconceivable, but plainly at the margins of probability. For a start, Cameron's fall would probably cause the Coalition to collapse – and neither governing party was remotely interested in an early election.

What the curious case of Adam Afriyie did do was to force the party to consider all this – to go through the motions and assess its options. At this stage of the Parliament, it was Ed Miliband whom the Tories had expected to be facing a leadership crisis. Instead, it was the Prime Minister himself who was being undermined by such talk, the work of a garrulous minority apparently more consumed by internal party intrigue than by the governance of the country. It was psychologically convenient to present Cameron as a loser holding back a team of winners. It was also the default position for Tories in trouble. The party had long been in the grip of the delusion that everything flows from leadership. The trouble with this misapprehension was that it encouraged mutinous instability as much as deep loyalty. One of the greatest misconceptions to afflict Conservatives was that all problems could be overcome by a change of leader.

The Eastleigh by-election nurtured such speculation even more. Labour simply hoped to improve its position and selected a celebrity candidate, the author and broadcaster John O'Farrell. The Lib Dems, meanwhile, were facing electoral punishment for Chris Huhne's disgrace, a problem compounded by the allegations of sexual misconduct against their former chief executive, Chris Rennard. Defeat would certainly nourish predictions that Clegg was courting a national wipeout.

In addition to their visible lack of confidence, the Tories had to answer for the loss of the UK's triple-A credit rating, a global kite-mark by which Osborne had originally set great store. They had put up a candidate who talked like a member of Ukip. So the peril was clear: if the Conservative Party could not seize a target Lib Dem seat in which the ex-MP was facing jail, while his party was mired in a sex and cover-up scandal, then what hope did it have on the national stage? By-elections of this importance always attracted a flying squad of senior politicians and grandees pestering voters for weeks before polling day. But Eastleigh was of a different order. It was as though the Westminster village had moved en bloc to Hampshire for the month.

At 3 a.m. on the morning after the by-election, Ed Llewellyn sent a comradely text to Shapps, the relatively new party chairman, to let him know how well he was doing in hellish circumstances. The Lib Dems had held on to the seat: Clegg lived to fight another day, and Cameron quickly reasoned that this was probably essential to the health of the Coalition. What he could have done without was being pushed into third place by Ukip. The Farage surge had gathered pace, fuelling the notion of an 'organic split' on the Right to match the comparable division between Labour and Lib Dems that had done so much damage to the former party's electoral prospects between 1979 and the rise of Tony Blair. There had been pop-up parties on the Right before, fringe movements and groupuscules harrying the Conservatives: Sir James Goldsmith's Referendum Party, Robert Kilroy-Silk's 'Veritas' and the Anti-Federalist League. But only Ukip under Farage had achieved the critical mass to interest the electorate as well as the media.

According to Stewart Jackson, MP for Peterborough, the Prime Minister had paid in Eastleigh for his supposed deference to 'the liberal metropolitan elite'. It was true that Cameron had stirred controversy with his proposals for gay marriage. But in other respects he was doing precisely what the Tory Right said that it wanted. He had promised an In—Out referendum on Europe, the first since 1975. He had introduced tougher border controls that lay behind the fall in net migration by a third announced recently by the Office for National Statistics. Where was this wicked elite when Chris Grayling announced plans to build a super-prison or to prepare for withdrawal from the European Court of Human Rights? Or when the welfare cap and benefits freeze was announced, or when Gove promised to restore rigour and discipline to the nation's classrooms, or when Osborne planned the next round of spending cuts? The deafening silence was the roar of a paper tiger.

The rise of Ukip reflected not neglect of traditional Tory terrain by Cameron but a much deeper anger at the hectic pace of the contemporary world. As I wrote at the time: 'This is a bad era in which to live if you like uniformity, continuity and predictability. Ukip is the tiny figure in a blazer waving a fist at the unstoppable cyber-titan of modernity.'[3]

If anything, the by-election established that the Tories could not trump Ukip at its own game. They were perhaps punished for trying to do so, even, feebly, borrowing the party's distinctive purple and yellow colour scheme in Conservative campaign literature. As real as its impact was, Ukip had yet to make the big leap to parliamentary viability. In a snap survey of 760 Eastleigh residents on polling day,

Lord Ashcroft established that Ukip's share of the vote would fall radically in a general election. Of those who had voted for the party, 75 per cent said that they had done so as 'a general protest' against mainstream politics. Farage had yet to persuade voters that he deserved their support in a national contest.

Yet time was undoubtedly on his side. He had more than two years to make the next gear change – long enough, but not too long. Eastleigh had been a thoroughly traumatic experience for the Tories, pregnant with the sense that there was more to come. When Cameron had walked into Number Ten, Britain had three parties that deserved serious attention. Now, beyond doubt, it had four.

19. Jeffrey's revenge

Cameron was the first to spot it, and he tried, on each occasion, to correct the error. But how do you tell the most powerful man on the planet that he is calling your own closest lieutenant the wrong name? 'Well, Jeffrey . . .' President Obama continued. 'It's *George*,' whispered the Prime Minister. There was indeed a Jeffrey Osborne, a funk and soul legend, whose duet with Dionne Warwick, 'Love Power', had stood the test of time especially well. But he was not the Chancellor of the Exchequer.

This particular session of the G8 summit at the Lough Erne resort, County Fermanagh, was on camera and monitored by aides in the so-called 'listening room'. The Prime Minister had hoped that the gathering would be remembered for the three Ts: tax, trade and transparency. But as soon as his communications director, Craig Oliver, heard what was happening he realized that this would be the story: 'President doesn't know Osborne's name.' It was bound to sting, not least because the Chancellor was such an enthusiastic Atlanticist, a collector of US political memorabilia and a man never happier than when discussing what Doris Kearns Goodwin's masterly book, *Team of Rivals*, had to say about contemporary politics as well as about Lincoln himself ('I think I *got* Lincoln for the first time').[1] Fortunately, Osborne had a capacity to see the funny side of politics, even when the joke was at his expense. During the Deripaska scandal in 2008 – which nearly finished him off – he admitted, with a chuckle, that the story 'had the lot': a yacht, a Russian plutocrat, Bullingdon boys bearing a grudge and Peter Mandelson. Andy Coulson – who, with Cameron, saved Osborne's skin on that occasion – did not see the lighter side. As one visitor noted: 'You could hear Andy shouting two doors down.'

So, demeaning as it was to be called 'Jeffrey' by the Commander-in-Chief with the global media looking on, it was no more than a distraction from a high-stakes strategy in domestic policy that was nearing completion. Osborne had long ago conceded that he would not achieve his original ambition of wiping out the structural deficit in a single Parliament. After the 'omnishambles' triggered by the 2012 Budget, his urgent priority was to exude competence, restore public confidence and persuade the voters, in deed as well as word, that what they had seen was no more than an ugly blip: a tall order in itself. Next – and even more ambitiously – he had to convince them that the trajectory was still correct, and that, borrowing Bill Clinton's pitch for Obama's second term, Cameron and his team needed and deserved more time.[2]

The strategy remained fiscal conservatism matched by 'monetary activism' (jargon for the use of interest rates to encourage prosperity) – the latter to be pursued in collaboration with the new Governor of the Bank of England, Mark Carney, the former boss of the Bank of Canada, who took over at Threadneedle Street in July 2013. The core political message had become as familiar as the click of a metronome. 'It is a hard road, but we're getting there,' said Osborne in his Autumn Statement in December 2012. 'Turning back now would be a disaster.' What this meant, in practice, was that the period of austerity would last until at least 2017/18. Ten days before Osborne's speech, he and his senior colleagues gathered to sign off the principal announcements. The key, from Clegg's point of view, was that the agreed £3.5bn of welfare cuts should be matched by pressure on the wealthy: Osborne announced that benefits would rise by only 1 per cent a year until 2015, but was also as robust as he had ever been on tax evasion and avoidance, insisting that even the gnomes of Zurich were not beyond his grasp.

Clegg was still concerned by the increasingly caustic rhetoric deployed on benefits by Osborne and other Tories. He could see that, in preparation for the election, the Chancellor was painting a vivid dividing line between the Conservatives and Labour, and wanted there to be no misunderstanding between the two governing parties. 'There's a limit to how far I'm going to follow you on this,' he told Osborne. On more than one occasion, Clegg insisted that 'people care about motive' – meaning that voters who were rationally persuaded of the case for cuts still did not like the idea that the Conservative Party was somehow having fun kicking the vulnerable. In the months that followed, he and the Chancellor continued to tussle over benefit reform.

Clegg felt that Osborne was trying to bounce him into radical cuts, springing ideas on him without warning. At one meeting of the Quad, the Chancellor, looking as innocent as he could manage, produced a sheaf of material. 'These are just some welfare ideas!' he said cheerfully. Clegg was not amused. 'Look,' he said, 'if you're prepared to reopen your red lines on wealthy retirees, then I am prepared to look at mine [on welfare]. Otherwise – no.' Cameron shook his head. He would not countenance any U-turn on pensioner benefits. 'It would be my tuition fees,' he said to Clegg – a tart reference to the Deputy PM's most painful experience in government. 'I'm not going to look at these bits of paper any more,' Clegg announced. In the Commons, he would occasionally lean over and quietly warn Cameron and Osborne that they were 'over-egging' the demotic attacks on skivers and benefit frauds. There was an aggression in their language with which the DPM did not feel at all comfortable (neither, for that matter, did Duncan Smith, who preferred to speak of redemption and recovery rather than to stigmatize the workshy).

The Chancellor did not relent, urging Danny Alexander to put pressure on the Lib Dem leader. 'We're going to take Labour apart on welfare,' the Chancellor told his Chief Secretary. 'Do you want to be in the same place?' This was a barely coded warning: welfare was going to be central to the Tory election campaign, and the Lib Dems had to decide which side they were on. Clegg did not take kindly to the form or content of the message. This was the aspect of the job that annoyed him most.

The local elections in May were humbling for the Lib Dems, who fell to a 14 per cent share of the vote, well behind Ukip on 23 per cent. Yet, in private at least, Clegg declared himself more content than he had ever been as Deputy PM, engaged in the delivery of policies and the implementation of measures which his party had either initiated or co-piloted. He was also pleasantly surprised by the durability of his relationship with Cameron. Looking back, he wondered whether their initial bond would have been possible without the shared assumption that they were addressing a national economic crisis. He sometimes mused that the Coalition would have been unworkable in a time of prosperity. But the origins of their political friendship meant that – for all the problems along the way – there remained a core of understanding. In one discussion in July, he remarked to Cameron that there were about fifteen issues they had to resolve in an hour: 'We could bicker about each of these or we could just come to a good arrangement.' Their capacity to do so, most of the time, remained the sturdiest foundation of this unexpectedly long-lasting Government.

What annoyed Clegg most was being caricatured by Tories as obstructive or unreasonable – as when he vetoed plans to relax child-to-staff ratios for childcare. 'I don't like being accused of U-turns,' he told colleagues. 'I'm totally pissed off that every time I reasonably respond to something I'm accused of treachery.' When the chips were down – when the media were on the attack, his party angry, the Tories scheming – Miriam's advice was consistent: 'The only way to get back at them is to show that coalition can work.'

The politics of welfare cuts were multi-dimensional, and the tension between the Deputy Prime Minister and Osborne was only one facet of this fissile political brew. In his 2012 Budget speech, the Chancellor had quite openly pitted Iain Duncan Smith against his Cabinet colleagues. 'The welfare budget is set to rise to consume one third of all public spending,' the Chancellor said. 'If nothing is done to curb welfare bills further, then the full weight of the spending restraint will fall on departmental budgets.' In an interview with the *Daily Telegraph* in March 2013, Philip Hammond echoed this sentiment and claimed that there was a 'body of opinion within Cabinet that believes that we have to look at the welfare budget again'.[3] That was certainly true: the Defence Secretary was not the only departmental minister convinced that there must be more savings to find in the £200bn welfare bill. In Cabinet that week, Alexander reproached Hammond for airing the Coalition's 'dirty laundry' in public. In truth, however, it was the Treasury that had kicked off the row by encouraging Duncan Smith's colleagues to gang up on him.

There was indeed a loose-knit group of departmental Cabinet ministers – the self-styled 'National Union of Ministers' – who objected with ever-greater confidence to paying for the ring-fenced budgets, or to the failure to cut welfare faster, or to both. Vince Cable, for instance, objected strongly to the protection of health, schools and international development, which meant that his own department had to cut more deeply. Hammond wanted more welfare cuts, as did Theresa May. But the Lib Dems stood in their way, determined not to go beyond the cuts agreed in the autumn.

Duncan Smith, too, was fed up with the constant insinuation that, were he only to try a little harder, the cuts in the welfare budget would be swift and straightforward. To a group of Tory MPs demanding that he wield the butcher's knife more ferociously, he said: 'Will you do me a favour? Tell me which bit exactly you want me to cut.' He often found that Tory colleagues who called for tough measures in general were the most squeamish about specific savings. It was one thing to call for IDS to slash the overall bill. But many Tory MPs were unnerved by (for instance) the new under-occupancy penalty – or 'bedroom tax' – that took effect from April 2013 and filled surgeries with troubled constituents, fearful that they would have to move house because they had a spare room and could not afford the extra payment. The case of Stephanie Bottrill, a Solihull grandmother, who had committed suicide in May and left a note blaming the bedroom tax, sent a shiver through the ranks of every party.

Aware that the Chancellor thought he was dragging his feet, Duncan Smith pointed out to Cabinet colleagues that his department would have saved £30bn in working-age benefits by the end of the Parliament. A benefit cap of £26,000 per household was in place. Most welfare payments were falling in real terms. Ken Clarke, whom Duncan Smith had defeated in the 2001 Tory leadership race, cheerily remarked that the measures enacted by the Cameron Government were the toughest of their sort he had ever witnessed. But Duncan Smith still felt besieged, fighting to enact a reform programme that was controversial enough but scorned by the Treasury (and several Cabinet colleagues) for its supposed fiscal timidity. When Clegg's team read reports that IDS had unilaterally offered to make additional specific cuts to assist Hammond and May, they were dismissive. 'Iain knows perfectly well that can't happen,' said one source close to the Deputy PM. 'That's why he can make the offer safely.' The Treasury was even more curt: 'It's the sort of totally hopeless, well-meaning thing Iain does. You can't have parallel negotiations.' Full stop.

Congratulated by one friend on the comparatively successful 2013 Budget, Osborne replied: 'It bloody well had to be.' After the political fiasco of 2012, nothing else would do. This, his fourth Budget, was his most brazenly populist to date, aimed squarely at working voters who 'do the right thing'. Petrol duty was frozen and the beer duty scrapped. He ordered his Cabinet colleagues to come up with an additional £2.5bn in cuts to fund projected capital spending, reduced corporation tax by a penny and cut national insurance. Yet, as ever, Coalition policy was a tie-dye of blue and yellow. The Chancellor spoke of tax not as an evil necessity but as 'part of the glue that holds society together'. At the very least, the experience of coalition had taught the Cameroons that visible fairness was essential for a Government seeking to make radical changes. Whether the voters perceived this Government's reforms to be fair had yet to be tested; but the lesson had been learned.

The centrepiece of the Budget was Osborne's 'Help to Buy' scheme, a clear nod to Margaret Thatcher's 'Right to Buy' and the older Conservative ideal of the 'property-owning democracy'. As a scheme offering equity to borrowers purchasing new-build homes, it naturally attracted criticism as 'sub-prime politics' and the basis of a new housing bubble. Osborne anticipated this, but believed the risk was minimal and more than justified by the potential political dividend: as he saw it, this was what modern Conservatism should be about.

There was no concealing the grim growth and borrowing figures. Yet the more the Chancellor was urged by his opponents in the Conservative movement (and some of his friends) to pump in the rocket fuel of emergency tax cuts, the more stubborn he became in his insistence that economic stability was the prerequisite of all else; that in an age of global uncertainty, fiscal conservatism was the only sound path to follow and the only reliable basis of prosperity and a 'compassionate society'.

As he prepared the 2010 spending review, Osborne had expressed the firm hope that he would not have to 'come back' – that is to say, to make a fresh series of demands. But in 2013 that is precisely what he did, setting out his plans for 2015/16 and cutting a further £11.5bn. Although the review encompassed only a year, it proved more complex than Osborne's team had anticipated. At the MoD, the impasse was ended by the patience of Jeremy Heywood, who oversaw a series of meetings to break the deadlock over mostly technical issues. The so-called 'Asterix' department – the last to yield to HM Treasury – was Vince Cable's. Sharp words were exchanged between the Business Secretary and Danny Alexander, even after Cable had seen off the draft 'list of horrors' of proposed cuts.

The tension was exacerbated by Osborne's statement to the Commons on 26 June. Cable's team was furious that the Treasury team had shifted the baseline against which the cuts would be measured, apparently to make it appear that the Business Secretary was a bigger loser than he had expected. This struck the Business Secretary as petty vindictiveness, the chest-beating of Treasury silverbacks.

But he also knew why he was being punished. Cable was now openly critical of the Coalition's fiscal strategy, demanding 'greatly expanded' capital spending in a pre-Budget *New Statesman* essay and claiming, even more heretically, that the 'balance of risks' might have shifted sufficiently since 2010 to justify higher public borrowing.[4] He felt the Government had not done enough to reform banking, a task he had wanted to supervise himself, and that the casino of the financial sector, though better regulated, had not truly ditched all the bad habits of the past. The banks were still not lending sufficiently to small and medium-sized enterprises. In Cable's opinion, the job had not been properly done. In June, Stephen Hester announced that he was stepping down as the chief executive of the Royal Bank of Scotland (81 per cent of which was owned by the taxpayer). 'There's no doubt that Hester was pushed', according to one senior source. 'George wants to get a new face in for the privatization.' But the future of the bank was consigned to a review. The sell-off of the Lloyds Banking Group could begin. But the fate of RBS remained uncertain.

By the time Osborne unveiled his second spending review, Cable was more convinced than ever that the election campaign had already begun and that, as polite and businesslike as the Tories usually were, the marriage was now completely loveless. He and Michael Fallon could collaborate perfectly amicably on the sell-off of the Royal Mail. But they did so as business colleagues, not collaborators in a great political realignment. Cable had always believed that the partnership between the two parties was an arrangement of convenience rather than of emotional attachment or ideological convergence and joked to his allies that 'everybody else in the Coalition seems to have ended up where I started'.

With Huhne no longer a contender, he was in prime position to lead the party should Clegg fall. In Cable's view, there would have been a full-blown leadership crisis if the Lib Dems had lost Eastleigh. But the seat was saved, and so was Clegg – for now. Even so, the party, still fearful of a wipeout in 2015, was keeping its options open. So was Cable. He kept up his Friday dancing lessons – an enjoyable way of staying trim – and waited to see what tunes the political band would strike up next.

The most jealously guarded secret of the spending review was its blueprint of welfare measures, the fruits of months of work by Neil O'Brien, Osborne's Special Adviser and a former director of Policy Exchange. At the think-tank, O'Brien had specialized in poverty, welfare and North–South attitudes, and imported some of the ideas pioneered by the US writers Reihan Salam and Ross Douthat in their book *Grand New Party*, which explored ways in which the Republican Party could extend its appeal to the working class.[5] O'Brien, who had taken a First in PPE at Oxford, instinctively understood the need to woo blue-collar voters to the Conservative standard. Osborne's review imposed a new cap on welfare spending for four years; it required job seekers to come to the job centre once a week rather than once a fortnight; there would be a new seven-day wait until benefits could be claimed; and if claimants could not speak English they would have to attend language classes.

Yet again, all this had caused friction with Clegg. On the Saturday evening before the review's announcement, the Deputy PM and Chancellor talked it through. Clegg believed the Tories, for all their talk of 'fairness', were contaminating welfare reform. 'I don't have a problem with the policy in anyone else's hands, George,' he said. 'It's the way you present it.' The next day Clegg and his family were in Hampshire to see one of Miriam's colleagues. The Lib Dem leader was trying to handle detailed discussions while having a normal family weekend, with no officials listening in to a series of mobile phone conversations with his senior colleagues which became, he later told aides, 'pretty acrimonious'. Clegg got in touch with Steve Webb, the Lib Dem Minister of State at the DWP, to see if he understood the detail correctly. Meanwhile, he was furious that the Chancellor was apparently up to his old tricks, putting pressure on Alexander. Osborne texted the Chief Secretary: 'Nick is trying to re-open this deal.' Alexander forwarded the message to Clegg who was, once again, angry at what he regarded as crass arm-twisting. He instinctively warmed to Osborne, with whom he had a lot in common. But this was, in the DPM's view, an abuse of Alexander's strong loyalty to both men, reducing politics to a great game.

To which Osborne's response was, in effect – absolutely, and watch me win it. In early June, Ed Miliband and Ed Balls had made carefully choreographed speeches that their handlers described euphemistically as a 'recalibration' of Labour's fiscal strategy. The Shadow Chancellor had asked for more time before making the shift, but been over-ruled by his party leader, who believed he would not make progress until he clarified his spending plans. Bruised by an interview with Martha Kearney on *World at One* in April, Miliband had concluded that he had to embrace the reality of what he was likely to confront if he became Prime Minister in 2015 and to acknowledge the constraints to which he would be subject. He and Balls therefore accepted the spending envelope for 2015/16 that they would inherit from the Coalition and proposed a three-year cap on welfare expenditure.

The Labour leader and Shadow Chancellor believed they could still win the argument on borrowing for capital expenditure, if not for current spending. They claimed that the election would now be about spending priorities: 'the language of priorities is the religion of socialism', Nye Bevan had famously said, and the two Eds believed they could make the battle against the Tories a contest of values. Even so, this shuffle off Keynesian home turf towards the economics of austerity was a huge concession for Miliband and Balls to make, and perhaps Osborne's greatest victory to date. At Labour's National Policy Forum on 22 June, Miliband described his mission in these terms: 'Only if we have the discipline that the challenge of our times demands can we credibly change the direction of our country.' The nature of this discipline and the basis of that hypothetical credibility had been defined by the Chancellor.

Osborne, of course, had missed his own targets and been mocked for doing so. But he had defined the rules of the game, the terms of the debate. If, as was frequently asserted, Margaret Thatcher regarded her finest achievement to be 'Tony Blair', then the Chancellor's equivalent might yet prove to be the partial conversion of the two Eds. Miliband despised Osborne's gamesmanship and stratagems – as the Labour leader saw it, a deplorable way of reducing statesmanship to a poker night. The Chancellor saw no shame in his style of politics and regarded Miliband as insufferably sanctimonious – ill-equipped for the rough and tumble of real politics. Nobody had set as much store by 'dividing lines' in politics as the Labour leader's own former mentor, Gordon Brown: the notion that electoral contests depended upon absolutely clear contrasts had been at the heart of Labour's three successive victories, two of them, in 1997 and 2001, by a landslide. Now it was the Tories defining the dividing lines, and Miliband did not like it one bit. This struck Osborne as prim hypocrisy.

He had, in any case, another such line he wanted to paint in garish blue between himself and Labour. From the start, it had been a principle of Osbornomics that, broadly speaking, 80 per cent of deficit reduction should be financed by spending cuts and only 20 per cent by tax rises. In an appearance before the Treasury Select Committee in July, he upped the ante. 'The further consolidation after 2015/16 is built into the tables as a spending reduction,' he said. 'I am clear that tax increases are not required to achieve this. It can be achieved with spending reductions.' At a lunch organized by the Parliamentary Press Gallery, he was no less categorical: 'I think this can be delivered through spending and savings both in welfare and in departments, and there is no need for tax rises to contribute to that fiscal consolidation.'

This was an electoral gamble. Voters knew, in general if not in detail, that the precedents were bad. When a politician promised that he would not have to raise taxes – 'read my lips', 'I have no plans . . .' – one could usually assume that this is precisely what would happen. Osborne was placing a wager on the public's trust in his capacity to deliver. He was also, specifically, pinning his party's electoral prospects on an assessment of the voters' priorities. In a few, all-important sentences, he was declaring his belief that, in one particular sphere, the Coalition had won the argument: if they had to choose, the public would prefer spending cuts to tax rises.

The Government's public diplomacy (as distinct from routine communications and spin) had often been weak, sometimes catastrophically so: witness the NHS reform debacle. But, on the particular question of the deficit, it had managed to introduce a financial abstraction to kitchen table debate – 'the Deficit' as a mysterious but scary national bogeyman – by sheer force of repetition and confident assertion. As long ago as April 2009 – when Cameron still hoped for a Tory majority – he had warned his party's Spring Conference that an 'Age of Austerity' was at hand. Four years on, Osborne's message in the 2013 spending review was threefold: that, as he had already conceded in the 2011 Autumn Statement, the deficit was a tougher nut to crack than he had hoped; that austerity would continue to force 'tough decisions' upon the Government for years to come; but that – crucially – the quality of public service need not suffer.

The problem had never been the identification of prospective cuts. It had been the practical question of how to make this or that saving politically manageable. Slowly, but perceptibly, the terrain of the manageable had been extended and colonized. Too often, the debate in the Tory movement was no more than an argument over what was statistically conceivable, when it needed to be a more sophisticated discussion about political practicality and the handling of public anxiety. Osborne knew that many in his own party considered the cuts much too timid and wimpish. This he could live with. What mattered was that the public not equate cuts with declining service: austerity had to be a prompt for public service reform, not an excuse for shoddiness.

In this respect, the crux of Osborne's spending review speech was a taunt directed at Labour. Look at the Home Office's performance, he said: 'What was the prediction from the Opposition three years ago? Crime would rise. And what has happened instead? Crime has fallen by more than 10 per cent.' The incremental approach adopted by Cameron and Osborne – gradual habituation, repeated explanation – had worked and made it possible for them to proceed with the cuts; or so they believed.

It was for precisely this reason that a new, extended timetable for the Universal Credit was unveiled in July. The original plan, devised in 2011, had entailed a rapid national roll-out from autumn 2013. But Duncan Smith announced that only six more job centres would now adopt the scheme in October, and that those involved in the pilot would remain, in the first instance, single Jobseeker's Allowance claimants. 'We are trying to land this at the right time and not according to an artificial timetable,' IDS told the Work and Pensions Select Committee – while insisting that the new system would still be fully introduced by the end of 2017.

That was comfortably beyond the 2015 election, to Osborne's relief. The outcome of that contest, he knew, would depend to a great extent upon the economy – or at least its perceived trajectory. Was the country heading in the right direction? That was the question that would be asked, along with the related issue of national leadership: should the reins be left in Cameron's hands or passed on to Miliband?

Though still slow and fragile, the recovery seemed to be gathering pace – a little. It was possible to speak of growth in the services sector and healthier levels of construction – tentatively. Osborne and his lieutenants were close to superstitious in their fear of a false dawn or misleading blip. Talk of 'green shoots' was strictly forbidden, lest the growth of the sapling be jinxed. The only thing worse than recession was complacency followed by recession.

They were no less disciplined when asked about another, related question: was Osborne still a contender to succeed Cameron? In the summer of 2012, that question invited only scornful guffaws in Tory circles. But, in politics, scorn can be as ephemeral as praise. In the wake of his second spending review, as the economy began to perk up, so did MPs' interest in Osborne. If he could secure a stable recovery and mastermind a Tory majority in 2015, his place in political legend would be safe and his prospects excellent. The comeback is one of the most basic and treasured stories in political myth – and the Chancellor's sheer stamina and resilience encouraged the thought that he should, at least, be a candidate when the moment came.

Osborne's own view was this: that no student of New Labour could possibly see any good coming, ever, from a Chancellor angling for the top job. 'I would never want to be the beneficiary of David Cameron's misfortune,' he told friends – sincerely, in their view. He also felt that Brown had dishonoured a great office of state by behaving as if it were a wretched wooden spoon in the political race rather than an extraordinary privilege. Again, Nigel Lawson was the role model: Osborne regarded him as a true statesman who had made a huge impact upon his times and never craved the top job. Was he – or any other successful Chancellor – to be judged a failure simply because he had not become Prime Minister? Osborne saw it as part of his mission to restore dignity to a role that Brown had associated with thwarted ambition, faction-fighting and a decade of personal hysteria.

All the same: he believed he had what it took to be Prime Minister one day, that he would be good at it. He knew that his ease of manner in private did not survive the journey to a plasma screen, and that this was a problem in the modern age: any prospective party leader must be good on television. But nobody fully acquainted with his other political skills was ready to rule him out. If Boris personified the Conservative Party's yearning to live life as one long Mexican Wave, Osborne might yet appeal to its collective self-image as the party of national rescue, getting the job done, clearing up Labour's mess. The decision was hardly imminent. He had much work to do at the Treasury. But the man Obama called Jeffrey was still in the game.

20. Farewell to the Lady

The music of Parry, Elgar and Vaughan Williams curled through the aisles and transepts of St Paul's Cathedral, as the congregation waited. Pockets of history could be seen throughout the church: craggy US statesmen, carved from the rock of Rushmore, former Prime Ministers, giants of British business, representatives of every aspect of a life lived to the hilt; the mourners had gathered from every continent, faith and generation.

At 10.45 a.m., the Queen and Duke of Edinburgh arrived at the Cathedral's West Steps, received by the Lord Mayor, who, carrying the Mourning Sword, went ahead of the Queen. The Archbishop of Canterbury, Justin Welby, and the Bishop of London, Richard Chartres, joined the procession at the Great West Door, moving towards their seats under the Dome. The Cathedral clock struck the hour and the coffin, draped in the Union Flag, was carried into St Paul's and placed upon the Bier. Michael Thatcher and Amanda Thatcher, her grandchildren, carried cushions bearing the Insignia of the Order of the Garter and the Order of Merit, laid on the Dome altar.

The funeral of Baroness Thatcher of Kesteven on Wednesday, 17 April 2013, was an occasion freighted with history and national introspection. The Iron Lady was the most significant peacetime Prime Minister of the twentieth century, a defining figure in her era, and a global protagonist as much as a British statesman. Confronted with the triple challenge of economic ruin, untamed union power and what turned out to be the final chapter of the Cold War, she had risen to the task, transforming the political landscape as she did so. 'New Labour' would never have happened without her enduring influence. Idolized and vilified long after she left office, Margaret Thatcher towered over all who succeeded her.[1]

The service was decorously apolitical, a strictly religious occasion rather than an ideological rally. By convention, normal politics is adjourned at such moments in national life: Ed Miliband and Nick Clegg both paid solemn tribute to the former Prime Minister, acknowledging her impact upon the country in which they had grown up. Yet, precisely because of that, there had never been the slightest chance of a quiet farewell. Thatcher had become the stuff of legend long before the end of her life on 8 April, in the Ritz Hotel. Myth claimed her as its own decades before mortality. This happens so rarely in politics that the response to her death was always fated to be intense, all-consuming and seething with political energy.

Cameron was in Madrid at the Moncloa Palace when he heard the news. Craig Oliver got a message through to him while he was having lunch with Mariano Rajoy, the Spanish Prime Minister. The PM called a few minutes later, seeking an update. 'It's a sad moment,' Cameron reflected – and then discussed with his communications chief how quickly he could get back to London to make a statement outside Number Ten. Oliver and other members of the inner team drafted some thoughts for him, while Cameron himself jotted down his own ideas on the plane. The final version was honed when he got back to Downing Street, ready for live delivery on the 6 p.m. bulletins.

The country, he said, had lost a 'great leader, a great Prime Minister and a great Briton'. He continued: 'Margaret Thatcher didn't just lead our country – she saved our country. And we should never forget that the odds were stacked against her. She was the shopkeeper's daughter from Grantham who made it to the highest office in the land.' The binding principle of her life, he said, 'was her lionhearted love for this country. She was the patriot Prime Minister and she fought for Britain's interests every single step of the way.'

In the days that followed, the PM would be criticized for over-reacting to Lady Thatcher's death, and, in particular, for the recall of the Commons to pay its tributes on Wednesday, 10 April. But the PM had weighed his options carefully. On his return from Madrid, he, Oliver and Ed Llewellyn sat down to consider how they should handle this and related questions. The Easter recess ended on Monday, 15 April: the Commons could conceivably wait until then. But Cameron quickly concluded that many people would take great offence if MPs waited a full week to honour the former PM.

The political class had not forgotten the extraordinary week that followed the death of Diana. The two moments were scarcely comparable – except in one vital respect. Thatcher, like the princess, had inspired, and continued to inspire, very strong emotions. Cameron was all too conscious that, like Blair in the days after Diana's death, he would be under close scrutiny. This was no time for the trembling lower lip, or a eulogy to the 'People's Premier'. Sentimentality had no part to play in this particular pageant. But a pageant it most certainly had to be: a tribute on an appropriately grand scale to a historic figure. In the days that followed, Oliver and Llewellyn made it their mantra not to 'under-cook' the moment.

There was initial concern in Number Ten as stories began to circulate about parties to celebrate Thatcher's death and other tasteless stunts. Some protesters announced their plan to turn their backs on the coffin as it passed by on its journey from the Chapel of St Mary Undercroft to St Paul's (and did so on the day of the funeral, though greatly outnumbered by respectful mourners lining the pavements). Less than two years after the riots, there was concern that the revived row about Thatcherism and its significance might provide a pretext for fresh disturbances. But Cameron soon realized that the flashes of loathing and retro-rage were a part of the commemoration, the flipside of the homage and tributes that he had led. For all the talk of her 'divisiveness', part of the pugnacious British psyche missed the rancour and the rows of the eighties, the decade when Britain awoke and decided not to be a second-rate power. It was also a time of sudden privation in many communities, in which the postwar consensus collapsed and a long (and continuing) debate had been launched about the proper extent of state services and benefits, the nature of social responsibility, and the difference between the two.

Before her death, a Conservative Cabinet minister told me that his party was still 'a long way off recovering from the 22nd of November 1990' – the date of her defenestration from office. What he meant was that a part of the Tory movement felt that the clocks had stopped on that day, and waited still for business as usual to be resumed. In the most obvious sense, she remained the gold standard for Conservatives against which all else was measured. Cameron and George Osborne (who shed a tear at her funeral) cited her fiscal conservatism to vindicate their own deficit reduction strategy and refusal to change course ('you turn if you want to'). Though he had always honoured her legacy and hosted events for her at Number Ten, Cameron was not remotely Thatcheresque in style or, in his own view, truly Thatcherite in ideology. When the *Sunday Times* interviewed him days after her death, he squirmed under cross-examination:

Q: Do you regard yourself as a Thatcherite?

DC: I would say I was a big Thatcher supporter . . . I joined the party when she was in the ascendant.

Q: Are you a Thatcherite?

DC: No. Other people might call me that. I think the label's now . . . it's slightly become . . . labels don't quite mean what they did then.[2]

Cameron could have done himself a favour within his own party by embracing the label and describing himself as her political heir. But that was in no sense his intention. As far as the PM was concerned, the last thing the Conservative Party needed in 2013 was to be perceived as a restorationist sect, taking Britain back to the eighties. Some Tories – many, in fact – could think of nothing more appealing than a return to the pinstriped brashness and swagger of that decade. ('There's nothing wrong with the eighties!' says Phil, the Conservative aide in *The Thick of It*. 'I mean, a lot of good things came out of the eighties! *Miami Vice*. Deregulation of the Stock Exchange. Us being in power.') There were certainly some Conservatives who believed that Boris Johnson would pick up where she had left off. This was a serious misunderstanding of his location on the ideological spectrum. But the Mayor's larger-than-life persona was what encouraged the comparison. He, too, his champions claimed, could be a global cheerleader for Britain.

The peril for Cameron was that his party might slip from collective homage into a cult of nostalgia. To reduce politics to a branch of the heritage industry, of course, was to miss the whole point of Thatcher and Thatcherism. She grasped that politics was not about the veneration of an inherited consensus but the particular needs of the time. The Tory radicals with whom she surrounded herself, especially in the late seventies and early eighties, were iconoclasts, determined not to let Britain tumble into economic oblivion, certain that their party had to change completely to acknowledge the task it faced. She presented herself not as a custodian, but as a liberator and disruptor. Those who had turned her beliefs into an immutable doctrinal orthodoxy had learned the wrong lessons.

The practice of politics was not, in any case, about doctrinal conservation but Darwinian adaptation. In the eighties, it was enough for the Tories to be seen as 'cruel but competent' – but no longer. It fell to Michael Gove to make this point in a *Times* article. As the Education Secretary wrote: 'time has underlined how crucial it is to ensure that we also applaud the values of care, nurture and solidarity that protect the vulnerable at times of change'. His point was not to disown the Thatcher era but to remind his fellow Tories, even as they mourned, that the culture and texture of everyday life had changed profoundly since 1990. There was no future in karaoke Thatcherism, the forlorn impersonation of a former leader.

Yet the controversy was about much more than the future strategy of a single party. In a *Newsnight* discussion, Norman Lamont observed that the nation was acting as if she had died in power rather than twenty-three years after she left office. The debate that followed her death felt like a punch-up about the day's news rather than a calm historical audit of events long past. The argument crackled with life, energy and contemporary relevance. Even the motley celebrations of her death were a form of victory for the Iron Lady. It was remarkable to watch these minor acts of rebellion mounted by young people who were not even born when she left office. Like Diana, Thatcher unleashed passions that were usually corseted by the twin forces of British reserve and the more recent pressure never to give offence to anyone, ever. Like her socialist enemies, she was a dialectician who believed that bad arguments had to be confronted and defeated, not ignored or appeased. Candour of this sort had been swept away by the age of spin. The return of impassioned straight talk in April 2013 – if only briefly – was invigorating.

For the Left, there was no shortage of evidence that the order she did so much to create was collapsing: the financial crash, the emergence of the underclass, the tribulations of the Murdoch press, the housing crisis. For the Right, there was unfinished business, work that could never be accomplished by a coalition. The 2010 Tory intake of MPs – many of them still at school when she left Number Ten – identified strongly with her governing ethos and supply-side revolution. Already, they had collected their radical opinions in a short book entitled *Britannia Unchained*, which was a generational battle-plan as well as a vision of what might be possible under a fully Conservative government.[3] Indeed, it was quite plausible that the next Tory leader would be one of 'Thatcher's grandchildren': Priti Patel, Liz Truss, Kwasi Kwarteng, Dominic Raab, Chris Skidmore or one of their talented comrades.

The passion faded as the period of mourning passed. But – subliminally – the memory of Thatcher helped to shape the contours of political life long after her funeral. One of the most furiously contested arguments in the week after her death had concerned her contribution to women's rights and feminism – or its absence. Nobody could deny her achievement as the first female Prime Minister. But had she made it any easier for there to be a second?

Once again, the spotlight fell on Theresa May, who, in her own cautious fashion, was testing the water for a future run at the leadership no less clearly than Boris or Gove.[4] A month before Lady Thatcher's death, she had made a speech at Conservative Home's Victory 2015 conference that ranged far beyond the operational parameters of her department and amounted to a personal manifesto. Scrupulously loyal – 'getting a majority Conservative government, led by David Cameron, is vital in 2015' – her address was nonetheless a robust pitch to be the modernizing candidate in the next leadership race, whenever it happened. 'We're at our best when we don't try to re-create the past,' the Home Secretary declared, 'but adapt our policies to the needs of the day – while continuing to root those policies in our values. We're at our strongest when anyone and everyone can feel the Conservative Party is for them – when we're the party for all.' No terrain was off limits: she called for bolder public service reform, a more robustly strategic economic policy and 'a different vision for the role of the state'.

Not all of May's colleagues were relaxed about her intervention. At a political Cabinet the week after her speech, Michael Gove declared himself 'shocked' that some of his colleagues were stoking leadership speculation. The Education Secretary did not name May – but did not have to. In June, she was at it again, this time under the auspices of the Reform think-tank. Once again, she declared herself utterly loyal to Cameron – and then set out her own vision of government, concentrating this time on the long haul of public service reform. In private, there was a masculine snort of the kind usually reserved for the staircase at the Garrick. 'Theresa is a jolly nice girl with a terrific team,' said one Tory grandee. 'But she'll never be leader. Not a chance.' This, paradoxically, was May's best hope: to be underestimated at first, as Thatcher was in 1975. Even the patronizing language was the same, thirty-eight years on. The much cannier Gove grasped the precedent and spotted the strategy, even if his less historically minded colleagues did not.

The after-shock of Thatcher's death was also felt in the parliamentary party, which was still at odds with its leader for all the familiar reasons. A fortnight of press tributes and television programmes about the Iron Lady had exacerbated the sense that something had been lost, that the cable connecting the Tory benches to the leader's office had been severed. In his bleaker private moments, Cameron was becoming savagely self-critical about his misreading of the party on gay marriage. 'This is down to me,' he told one ally. 'If I'd known what it was going to be like, I wouldn't have done it.' But he was stuck with the measure now.

In June, Lord Dear, a crossbench peer, tried to sabotage the Marriage (Same Sex Couples) Bill with an amendment that would reject the proposals outright at second reading. It was clear from the speeches made by Conservatives that the fate of the bill had become disastrously entangled with a broader perception that Cameron's team positively loathed the party rank-and-file. In May, Lord Feldman,

Tory co-chairman and a friend of the PM, had allegedly referred to Conservative activists as 'swivel-eyed loons'. Though Feldman denied he had spoken the words attributed to him, they chimed with the worst fears of the grassroots.

In the debate on the Dear amendment, Lord Mawhinney, a former party chairman himself, identified an explicit linkage between the bill and Feldman's supposed remarks. 'For forty years,' he said, 'my life has been driven by Christian and Conservative convictions, and now I am led to believe that because I continue to hold those values and principles I am a swivel-eyed loon.' Other Tory veterans took a more relaxed approach. 'Last year, my wife and I celebrated our diamond wedding,' said Lord Jenkin of Roding, a Cabinet minister in the Thatcher era, 'and I have to say that it has been a marriage with mutual comfort and support. Is this bill going to redefine that marriage? I cannot see how that could possibly happen.'

The Dear amendment was decisively defeated by 390 votes to 148, and the bill became law in July. But the animosity lingered after the showdown in the Lords. Over Europe, Cameron's offer of a referendum on membership had conspicuously failed to satisfy the backbenchers who yearned once more to hear that familiar voice say: 'No, no, no.' In May, an amendment was tabled by John Baron and Peter Bone regretting the absence of an EU referendum bill from the Queen's Speech – a bill that would never be tolerated by the Lib Dems. Number Ten briefed that this parliamentary gambit was a 'mouse in the room' and that the PM was not about to jump on the table. The rebels were defeated, by 277 votes to 130. But Cameron was annoyed that 114 Conservative MPs had seen fit to embarrass him publicly, behaving as though the Coalition did not exist or the Lib Dems could be safely ignored. Worse, his own backbenchers, by voting for the amendment, were telling the world that they did not really trust the Prime Minister: they had heard his promise of a referendum but still wanted it written into law, by parliamentary sabotage if necessary.

In one ear Cameron had the self-appointed heirs of Thatcher, accusing him of going soft on Europe. In the other was Clegg, who believed that the PM's plan could not possibly succeed. In the wake of the amendment vote, he told Cameron that he did not believe Merkel and Hollande were as biddable as the Prime Minister hoped, or presently disposed to embark upon an elaborate Treaty negotiation leading to a realigned, reformed EU. 'David,' he said, 'you do realize that you are going to be flying from one capital to another seeking crumbs from the table-top to present to Peter Bone and the rest of them? And it won't work.' Cameron nodded politely. 'Maybe,' he said. 'But I have to do it.'

The PM accepted Clegg's point in one central respect. Before he renegotiated Britain's relationship with Europe, he had to renegotiate his relationship with his own party. He had come of age politically in the Major years; his Foreign Secretary had led the party at its lowest ebb. He knew that the electoral cost of disunity, or even perceived disunity, was grievous. So – at the very least – he needed a truce with his own tribe. 'My strategy,' he told one senior ally, 'is clearing the battlefield.'

As a first step, senior ministers had to stop showing a bit of ankle to the Eurosceptics. Yes, Michael Gove and Philip Hammond had already declared that, in a referendum held there and then, they would vote for Britain's exit from the EU.[5] But William Hague spoke for the PM when he told the *Sunday Telegraph* that there would be no more freelancing: 'The rest of the Cabinet will not be answering hypothetical questions.'[6] Second, Cameron threw the weight of the Government – or at least its Conservative component – behind a private member's bill demanding an EU referendum. Having topped the ballot of members that allowed him to introduce his own legislation, James Wharton, Tory MP for Stockton South, adopted the draft bill already prepared by Downing Street. The leadership obliged with a three-line whip.

This was political theatre rather than lawmaking: denied Government time, the bill could be debated only on Fridays and was vulnerable to filibuster. The Lib Dems missed no opportunity to scorn what Danny Alexander loftily called a 'parliamentary stunt'. Though Clegg's party had proposed an in–out vote in their 2010 manifesto, this pledge was to be triggered only when Britain 'signs up for fundamental change in the relationship between the UK and the EU'. The Lib Dem leader was convinced that no such treaty was on the cards. So his position was at least internally consistent.

Even so, the process itself served a substantial purpose, as a confidence-building measure within the Tory Party and a signal by Cameron that he took his MPs seriously and shared their enthusiasm for a referendum. On the eve of the division – in which 304 MPs voted for the Wharton bill and none against – the PM hosted a barbecue for the parliamentary party, flipping burgers in the July heat as his fellow Tories downed pints of bitter and chatted, in better spirits than for many months. Three days after the cook-out, Abu Qatada was finally deported to Jordan on a plane from RAF Northolt. It had taken eleven years to expel him, from his arrest in 2002 to his departure on 7 July 2013. No saga had better dramatized what the Tory Party believed was wrong with 'Europe' – manifested in the EU or, as in this case, the ECHR. Though Dominic Grieve, the Attorney General, opposed withdrawal from the court, his was a lonely voice at the party's top table. May and her team argued that exit from the ECHR should be a prominent pledge in the 2015 Conservative manifesto.

Cameron knew that he and his colicky backbenchers would fall out again: management of MPs was simply not his forte, and they themselves had grown used to thinking ill of him, confusing the constraints of coalition for personal indifference. But he had survived a rancorous six months in which Government and party had been leading separate lives. The death of Thatcher had shed light on that fissure and – to a certain extent – compounded it. It had reminded the Tory movement of what it missed, or thought it missed. It had made the arguments sharper, the ordnance heavier. It had been a celebration of the past, as well as an unflinching assessment of the present.

After Diana's death, the nation indulged in a fiesta of emotion. In this instance, it had paid its respects in a very different fashion: with an outpouring of honesty. As all politicians knew, honesty can be painful stuff if you are on the receiving end. But Cameron had withstood the parliamentary battles over gay marriage and the referendum, a pincer movement of social conservatism and weapons-grade Euroscepticism. He was scarred but still standing. Though he knew that the Iron Lady disapproved of coalitions, he was also sure that she had understood the realities and practicalities of office much better than many of her latter-day disciples. She remained an inspiration to him, still the magnetic north of British politics. The question for Cameron as Parliament entered the recess for summer 2013 was whether he could turn this hard-won stability into a winning proposition: to carry on – if not on and on.

21. A new England?

William Hague listened patiently on the secure line to John Kerry, the US Secretary of State, as they discussed strategy in Syria. 'Tomorrow, I'm going to the White House,' Kerry said, 'and I'm going to tell them all this! Tomorrow!' The Foreign Secretary liked his US opposite number, who had succeeded Hillary Clinton in February 2013. Kerry, a former Democrat presidential nominee, had got to know Hague when he was chairman of the Senate Committee on Foreign Relations.

The two men were of a common mind on Syria to the extent that they agreed the bloodstained status quo was not an option: the brutal regime of President Bashar al-Assad was neither stable nor yet doomed. But the famously enthusiastic Kerry, who sometimes resembled a Basset hound experiencing a sugar rush, was promising more than he could deliver. President Obama had shown no inclination at all to plunge his hands into the Syrian furnace. Cameron had helped to coax him into a strictly limited engagement in Libya (see Chapter 9). But the Commander-in-Chief was not minded to listen on this occasion.

The late Christopher Hitchens observed that Obama 'thinks that a lot of important disagreements arise out of misunderstanding' and could be resolved by protracted cerebration.[1] Much as he liked him and valued his friendship, Cameron feared that Obama's natural caution was now a serious, structural problem on the geopolitical stage.[2] For months, he had been urging the President and other heads of government to focus upon the Syrian crisis. At home, he sought a wide range of advice, consulting the Damascus-born businessman and philanthropist Wafic Said, who understood Assad's personality well, and General Sir David Richards, the outgoing Chief of the Defence Staff, who warned him that a no-fly zone would be insufficient and that a clear political objective was essential before any military operation was considered.

In May, Hague and the French Foreign Minister, Laurent Fabius, persuaded the EU not to renew its arms embargo on Syria. The message to Assad was clear: get to the negotiating table or we will arm the rebels. Russia, which had already thwarted action by the UN Security Council, announced that it would proceed with a consignment of anti-aircraft missiles to the Syrian regime. These weapons, according to Sergei Ryabkov, Russia's Deputy Foreign Minister, would 'go a long way to restraining some hotheads' from meddling in the country's civil war.

As Hague explained, the best argument for the new EU position was that the moderate rebels led by Salim Idris had thus far been the only group struggling to receive weapons. The Assad regime and the jihadis – particularly Jabhat al-Nusra, an Islamist front officially affiliated with al-Qaeda – had established strong supply lines, in sharp contrast to the struggling Free Syrian Army (FSA). The weakest, least plausible force in the conflict, therefore, was the only one that promised a tolerable, pluralist future for the war-torn country.

To their great frustration, Cameron and Hague found themselves increasingly isolated at home and abroad. John Redwood spoke for many, perhaps most, Tories, when he said that 'the last thing you need is to tip more weapons into this cauldron'. There was force in the argument that arms intended to reach the FSA might easily end up in the hands of the Syrian Islamists, who were already imposing sharia justice in their strongholds. Only a few days before the arms embargo was lifted, Drummer Lee Rigby had been hacked to death in Woolwich, south-east London, allegedly by British jihadis. British public opinion recoiled at the prospect of their doctrinal comrades in Syria being sent more weapons, albeit inadvertently.

Alongside this could be heard an older argument, expressed most pithily by Douglas Hurd when, as Foreign Secretary, he opposed the arming of Bosnian Muslims on the grounds that it would only create 'a level killing field'. Cameron now held the seat – Witney – that Hurd had represented for fourteen years. Like Hurd, the PM disliked ideological approaches to foreign policy and had no time for 'neo-conservatism'.

Yet he parted company radically with the former Foreign Secretary –

and with Obama, for that matter – when it came to the limits of global responsibility and the duty to intervene. Though he had never been a Tory isolationist, he certainly entered Number Ten determined not to be distracted by foreign escapades. But office had changed him and altered his horizons. It had hardwired him into the grid of global power, and awakened him to the radical difference that action – or inaction – by a handful of men and women could make to the fate of millions. For a politician determined to take everything in his stride, this had been a violent awakening.

At the G8 meeting in Lough Erne, Cameron was determined to make progress on Syria. In Number Ten before the summit, Putin had aggressively opposed any measures to arm the rebels. 'One should hardly back those who kill their enemies and eat their organs,' he said – referring to film of a rebel fighter apparently chewing the liver torn from a dead soldier. Cameron found the Russian President much more approachable at the G8 gathering and planned to press him on Syria again at the working dinner on Monday, 17 June. The PM, Llewellyn, Oliver and Liz Sugg, Cameron's indispensable head of operations, looked at the seating arrangement and reset it so that it would not feel confrontational: Putin against the rest.

The eight heads of government, joined by the respective presidents of the European Commission and Council, José Manuel Barroso and Herman van Rompuy, feasted on Kilkeel crab, prawn and avocado salad, roast fillet and braised shin of Kettyle beef, with artichokes and Comber new potatoes, followed by apple crumble with Bushmills whiskey custard. Putin struck Cameron as firm, but not aggressive, happy to talk and keen to make clear that he did not regard Assad as a friend. But he wanted to protect Russian interests; and he also disliked the idea that the group gathered at the table could go around the world picking off regimes.

Overall, the summit burnished Cameron's reputation. After the dinner, he sat down with Llewellyn, Oliver and John Casson, his private secretary on foreign affairs, to review what had been achieved, and was not displeased by the progress on tax and trade. There was no rancour over Syria. But, in a sense, that was the problem. None of Cameron's fellow leaders felt as strongly as he did about the conflict and their capacity to prevent the bloodshed. In this respect, for now, he stood alone.

This was a case study of a much broader phenomenon. The Coalition had been forged on the anvil of economic crisis. But it had become a laboratory for much else: public service reform, the voting system, social mobility, gay marriage, a radical overhaul of welfare, preserving social cohesion, defining 'fairness' and an argument about Britain's place in the world. Against expectation, Cameron had come to believe that his country still had a limited but substantial role preventing atrocity where it could. He might not be a neo-con but he was certainly a Gladstonian. His preoccupation with Syria startled even those who knew him best. It verged on a fixation, a personal test. 'He talks about it *all the time*,' one aide mused in the spring of 2013. 'Brings it up when you least expect it.'

Every Prime Minister conducts a conversation with the public about the nature of his (or her) country; but he (or she) also conducts a conversation with himself (or herself). 'The whole map of Europe has been changed,' said Churchill, as Secretary of State for the Colonies, in 1922, 'but as the deluge subsides and the waters fall short we see the dreary steeples of Fermanagh and Tyrone emerging once again.' He meant that the sectarian plight of Ulster was immutable and intractable. But he was wrong. The fact that, nine decades later, a G8 summit could be held safely in Co. Fermanagh showed that a nation can, and must, change.

It was one of the many surprises of the Coalition that Cameron should preside over a period not only of economic repair but – potentially – fundamental change to the nature of the United Kingdom. The very existence of that entity would be contested on 18 September 2014, when the Scots answered the question: 'Should Scotland be an independent country?' By the middle of 2013, the two campaigns – 'Yes Scotland' for independence and 'Better Together' for the Union – were already digging in for a bitter contest. Huge questions were posed by the possibility of independence.[3] What percentage of the UK's debt would be inherited by Scotland? How would its monetary policy be decided? What would happen to the nuclear weapons depot at Coulport and the naval base at Faslane?

Broadly speaking, the polls suggested that the Scots would vote to stay in the United Kingdom. But the early surveys of opinion had also suggested that Britain would vote 'No' in the EEC referendum of 1975 and 'Yes' to AV in 2011. Alex Salmond, the SNP leader and Scotland's First Minister, was a ferocious political street-fighter and an opponent to be feared. Glasgow's hosting of the 2014 Commonwealth Games shortly before the referendum was bound to have an impact upon its outcome. Nothing could be taken for granted about this vote, any more than the separate plebiscite Cameron had offered on EU membership. 'Yes' in 2014 and 'Out' in the European referendum: it was at least conceivable that, by the end of 2017, a new nation composed of England, Wales and Northern Ireland would have voted to leave the European Union and be pondering its place in the global landscape. Would such a nation still have a permanent seat on the UN Security Council? Or be welcome in the G8? These and other questions about the nation's future could no longer be dismissed as the stuff of political fantasy. Cameron, the supposed pragmatist, had held the door open to extraordinary radicalism. There were times when it seemed that not even he had grasped how transformative the possibilities now were.

For the time being, he and Clegg continued to tend and train the dog that had not barked: the survival of the Coalition was their greatest achievement, so obviously so that it attracted almost no comment. 'If the economy doesn't recover,' the Lib Dem mused to friends, 'Labour will win anyway.' But – win or lose – it mattered to both of them that they go the distance, the full twelve rounds. That act of endurance would be part of their shared legacy.

All regimes, wrote the ancient historian Ronald Syme, are oligarchies. Was the Coalition just a fresh alignment of an old elite, or something genuinely new? Only posterity could deliver a reliable verdict on that one. But it was lazy to dismiss the bipartisan government as an expedient, just as it was stating the obvious to say that Cameron and Clegg had confronted limited options in May 2010. Much more striking was the political will that had held the arrangement together – the insistence upon its survival that trumped all the disagreements, dips and disasters.

The Lib Dem leader had not only dared to form the first peacetime coalition since the National Government in the thirties, or, arguably, Churchill's caretaker administration of 1945. He had done so with the Conservatives: a strategic risk of colossal proportions. Clegg believed that the partnership depended too heavily upon their personal relationship and that Whitehall had not risen to the challenge with new structures and procedures. All the same: the mechanism endured, and he had made that possible. Even as he risked personal and collective extinction, he had shown that the Lib Dems could be a party of power, 'keeping the Tories honest', as he put it, and – if the need arose in future – ensuring that Labour were fiscally responsible. His movement had proved it could govern. As he said to senior colleagues: 'They now have to decide whether that's what they want.'

As for Cameron, he was a cluster of paradoxes: a pragmatist at the helm of a radical government; a foreign policy realist demanding intervention; the ultimate Tory insider insisting that his mission was to spread privilege; a tribalist who had formed a coalition. His enemies longed to dismiss him as a lightweight, but that was not consistent with the sheer heft of the measures undertaken by his Government. Easy as it was to mock his most familiar slogan, everyone wanted a slice of it. 'I like his constant repetition of "we're all in this together",' said Boris; 'indeed, I am vain enough to have a feeling that he nicked it from me.'[4] Even Bill Clinton annexed the line, embracing the 'we're-all-in-this-together society'. In this respect, at least, Cameron was on to something.

No party leader – Conservative or otherwise – had faced real-time internal dissent on such a scale. This was a technological development rather than a personal slight. The digital revolution had subjected him to a permanent acupuncture of criticism: even when he gave the punters what he thought they wanted, notably the promise of an EU referendum, Twitter and the blogs were reliable delivery systems of round-the-clock dissatisfaction. Before he had finished his speech making that particular pledge, the blogosphere was crackling with objections, scepticism and queries, real and vexatious – all from the PM's own side, that is.

Disagreeable as this might be for Cameron, it was part of the job description. Dissent and awkwardness remained the vital life signs of a democracy. Enoch Powell famously said that for a politician to complain about the press is like a ship's captain complaining about the sea. For his twenty-first-century counterpart to object to the impatience and ferocity of digital media would have been no less hypocritical.

That said, it was important to register the change. This techno-logical shift had altered the nature of political leadership – not just in the obvious sense that all politicians now had at their disposal a range of new and extremely powerful campaigning tools, but in ways more elemental and basic. The emerging digital world favoured the shrill comment over the considered sentence. It rewarded wit, showman-ship, authenticity and surprise more than it acknowledged the long haul, political stamina or the hard-won agreement. Boris, though far from shrill, was the conspicuous beneficiary of this new culture, unfazed as he was by its extraordinary demands. He was the Roman tribune reborn in the Google era, Zaphod Beeblebrox with a classical education.

In his book *Together* the philosopher Richard Sennett argues that 'modernity's brutal simplifiers' have not erased our capacity for col-laboration.[5] What made Cameron most intriguing as a Prime Minister was precisely this: that he was the first modern Conservative leader to take seriously the challenge identified by Sennett, and to look for forms of co-operation that involved more than spending money the country had not yet earned. He was the first Conservative Prime Minister who claimed to put 'We' before 'Me'. This was still greeted with hollow laughter in some quarters, and it certainly prompted a question that would not go away: whether the voters would ever take such a claim seriously when made by a Tory, especially a Tory from Cameron's background.

Like so much else, that would not be tested until the 2015 election. Cameron and his senior colleagues knew that the hardest trials lay ahead. Like runes, the pitiless graphs of the global economy would do much to settle their fate. So would the feelings of the voters, dis-tinct from statistics: the imponderable patterns of hope and anxiety that nourish politics and determine its path. The PM and his deputy could be certain of adversity, and of little else. But that had always been, and would remain, the binding force of the Coalition, the rough, essential thread that ran through its improbable fabric, its twists of blue and yellow. And it was that, for now, that kept them, their parties and the rest of us in it together.

22. The recovery position

'We're going to have a tax rebellion.' In more than three years of coalition, George Osborne's most senior colleagues had grown used to his refusal to panic (a disinclination which his foes – and some of his friends – regarded as complacency); he was supposed to be the Coalition's chess-player who had thought four moves ahead to fox the enemy. So his categorical warning commanded attention. 'If we keep adding things to people's energy bills, there *will* be a rebellion.'

The words 'poll tax' hung in the air, unspoken but understood by all to whom the Chancellor addressed this refrain. Osborne had been impressed by the energetic campaign against fuel duty increases led by the Harlow MP, Robert Halfon, and, in his 2013 conference speech, signalled his intention to freeze this tax for the rest of the Parliament. But it was not only as motorists that voters were feeling the pinch. As he looked at the political horizon – which was meant to be his greatest talent – Osborne saw a 'perfect storm' of energy levies coalescing to cause the Government serious trauma, a hurricane of electoral fury that would sweep away all the early gains of the recovery.

Cameron was reaching similar conclusions. When he weighed up Ed Miliband's abilities and shortcomings in private, he would claim that the Labour leader specialized in 'observations not policies'. In the PM's opinion, 'One Nation Labour' was a diagnostic campaign rather than a serious blueprint for change. But Miliband had confounded him politically at the party's annual conference in Brighton with a strong attack on the 'cost of living crisis' and a promise to freeze gas and electricity prices 'until the start of 2017'. Whether or not Labour could, as its leader promised, 'reset the market' was beside the point. The pledge resonated with voters, an old-fashioned 'retail offer' on the political doorstep, and one that addressed the gap between statistical recovery and personal experience. Nothing was more vexing to families still struggling to make ends meet, fretful under a grey sky of job insecurity, debt and high prices, than to be assured that the sun of prosperity had broken through the clouds. Miliband's speech in September addressed this resentment directly and made the political weather well into the autumn.

As late as November, a Populus survey found that 38 per cent of voters agreed that the national recovery was underway but that only 11 per cent felt part of it. The cost of energy was becoming symbolic of a deeper sense of grievance, as Labour's insistence that this was a recovery 'for the few' continued to gain traction. As he prepared his Autumn Statement, the Chancellor confronted a primarily political challenge. It was not enough to blame Gordon Brown for the downturn; it was positively dangerous to declare 'Plan A' a success, and pause for applause. In post-Crash politics, growth alone was no longer sufficient. The distribution of prosperity was as much an issue as prosperity itself. What the voters wanted was not triumphalist rhetoric but a recognition of their hardship and practical help with household budgets.

Clegg's advice, as in the past, was not 'to play on Miliband's side of the course'. Lynton Crosby was wary of anything that complicated the Tory message and threatened the clarity which he believed was central to the party's prospects. But Osborne was insistent that the peril could not be wished away: 'There is a problem, and we have to deal with it.' He and Cameron felt no compunction about pinching Labour ideas if they were good – 'take the steak and leave the gristle' was a natural slogan for this most eclectic of governments. More to the point, they knew that Miliband had chosen his terrain with good reason. The average price of electricity and gas had risen, in real terms, by 20 per cent and 41 per cent since 2007, and 15 per cent of that increase was the consequence of energy and climate change policies imposed by Whitehall or Brussels.[1] Osborne – who made little secret of his scepticism about climate change – was impatient to strip out as many of these green levies as possible.[2] Clegg, once again, was dismayed by the Chancellor's approach to the Coalition's environmental strategy. Cameron, once again, had to arbitrate between the two.

'For me, the green agenda is important,' the PM told his aides.

'For Nick, it's existential.' This was accurate in both the planetary and the political senses. Clegg truly believed in the orthodox science of global warming and was aghast that civilized politicians could (as he saw it) put political self-interest ahead of species survival. When the *Sun* reported that Cameron had instructed his staff to 'get rid of all the green crap' from energy bills, or when, during the floods of January and February, Owen Paterson, the Environment Secretary, signalled his scepticism about climate change, the DPM squirmed: at such moments, it was hideously difficult to persuade his own high-minded party that the Coalition remained viable. That said, his own position was also governed by electoral calculation. In seeking a new electoral base for his party, Clegg was desperate not to lose the 'eco-vote' to the Green Party (Cameron, ever the computer game enthusiast, compared local battles between Lib Dem and Green activists to 'Pacman versus Pacman, each trying to eat the other').

Sympathetic as he was to the Deputy Prime Minister's dilemma, the PM agreed with Osborne that the Coalition faced a challenge it could not evade. 'I told you that this was going to be a problem,' he reminded Clegg in one of their many conversations about rising energy bills. 'It's too much.' As he complained to his advisers: 'The Lib Dems want to subsidize every last windmill in the world!' It was his job, as he saw it, to contain these ambitions and to temper Lib Dem idealism with Tory pragmatism.

Clegg believed that Cameron had lost his nerve – not because of Miliband's speech but because of remarks made by Sir John Major at a lunch for the parliamentary press gallery in October. Out of the blue, the former Prime Minister had called for a windfall tax on profiteering energy companies to 'claw that money back to the Exchequer where their primary job is to get the economy working and back to work'. In Number Ten, Cameron made no secret of his fury: here was Major being a back-seat driver, precisely as Thatcher had been to him. Wearily, he told Osborne: 'I have got to break this impasse.'

The DPM, meanwhile, reported to aides that Major's intervention had had 'an electric effect on David and made him panic'. Mindful of this, he told Cameron and Osborne that he would sign up to the package 'as long as the carbon saved is the same as it would have been'.

Accordingly, the Autumn Statement on 5 December fleshed out a promise already made by the PM to 'roll back' the mounting green levies, and to cut household energy bills by £50 a year. Was it enough?

Osborne's broader strategic purpose was to present Labour as the greatest threat to a recovery still in its infancy. Though he was able to announce upgraded growth forecasts for 2013 and 2014, and a steady reduction in the deficit, his paradoxical objective was to emphasize how fragile the Coalition's achievement still was. After all this fiscal heavy lifting, he did not want the electorate to conclude that it was safe to relax and vote for Miliband. It was a nasty political paradox: if the voters believed the job was done, they might also believe that the Conservative-led Coalition had fulfilled its purpose and could be quietly euthanized.

Cameron also insisted upon the announcement of the long-promised £1,000 transferable tax allowance for married couples – a measure for which, as we have seen, the socially liberal Osborne had never felt much enthusiasm and which Clegg dismissed as the 'unmarried tax penalty'.[3] After the controversy over same-sex marriage, the Tory leader needed a traditionalist measure to reassure his tribe. He also believed strongly that the institution of marriage deserved recognition in the fiscal thicket.[4] For the PM, politics and principle converged in this case.

Knowing how much this meant to Cameron, Clegg decided to exact a price. 'If you want *your* tax cut,' he said, tartly, 'you're going to have to pay for it.' The price was £600m – to be spent on free school meals for all infant school pupils in England. Unexpectedly, this quid pro quo – announced at the Lib Dem conference in Glasgow – was to play a part in one of the most personal battles in the lifetime of the Coalition.

Though Clegg had always disagreed with Michael Gove ideologically, it was not until late 2013 that the tension between the two men became a problem for the Government. In private, Cameron speculated that the Lib Dems attacked the Education Secretary – 'bitching up Michael' – as a proxy target, a surrogate for the PM himself. The daily business of the Coalition made it hard for senior Lib Dems to vilify Cameron or Osborne, half of the ruling 'Quad' in which two of their own number sat. But Gove – a close ally of both men – was fair game, already caricatured by grass-roots Lib Dems as an implacable neo-Thatcherite determined to tear down the state education system. This was true in the sense that Gove wanted radical reform of a structure that he believed had failed generations of children. He was no gradualist, either. Like Hilton, he believed that a government – any government – should proceed on the basis that it had only one Parliament in which to do its work and prosecute its principal objectives with unremitting urgency. Its reforms must be fast, sweeping and – most important of all – immune to instant overthrow by successor administrations. As far as Gove was concerned, he had five years in which to revolutionize the school system. More intellectually eclectic than his detractors claimed and an early enthusiast for coalition, he was nonetheless determined that the Lib Dems would not stand in his way.

In a speech in October at Morpeth School in Tower Hamlets, Clegg attacked several core aspects of Gove's reforms – notably, the right of free schools and academies to hire staff without formal Qualified Teacher Status (QTS). 'Diversity amongst schools, yes,' said the DPM. 'But good universal standards all parents can rely on too. And, frankly, it makes no sense to me to have qualified teacher status if only a few schools have to employ qualified teachers.'[5] This directly contradicted the support for unqualified teachers in free schools given the week before in the Commons by David Laws, the Lib Dem schools minister and one of Clegg's closest allies. Gove, who was in America, was angry but also confused. He had known that the speech was coming – but not that the Lib Dems would brief the media on this particular line. Julian Astle, Clegg's senior policy adviser, tried to mend fences, arguing that the objective had been to get the story out of the way. Gove was not impressed by this rationalization.

As he explained to allies, the Education Secretary understood perfectly well that 'being anti-Gove is totemic' for those who believed the status quo in the public sector should be defended from Tory revolution. Clegg needed their votes, and Gove was relaxed about that. What he would not countenance was a land-grab or a serious Lib Dem campaign to dilute his reforms. The powers devolved to free schools and academies were the very essence of his blueprint. To insist, as Clegg had, that all teachers should have QTS was not a technicality but a point of principle, symbolic of the battle between uniformity and diversity, between the power of the 'Blob' and the power of individual schools. It infuriated Gove that the Lib Dems should be playing fast and loose in this way. As the Education Secretary put it to one friend, Clegg's appeasement of public sector unions was no more honourable than a central-casting Tory 'resisting reform of hedge funds'.

The briefing and counter-briefing escalated. It was widely reported that Gove's team considered the free-school-meals pledge no more than a ham-fisted stunt, believed it would be hard to deliver, and resented the £150m raid on schools' capital budget to pay for new kitchens where necessary. After his departure from the Education Department, Dominic Cummings (Gove's adviser[6]) made his views public on Twitter ('Clegg/Quad=origin of problem') and the BBC's *World at One* programme: 'Officials in DfE were unanimous that it was a bad gimmick and introduced in a way that makes it hard to avoid implementation chaos. Officials were obviously right.'[7]

The Lib Dems firmly believed that Cummings had been Gove's attack dog, feeding the media with headline-friendly lines – though the ever-contentious adviser insisted that his spinning days were behind him. Clegg was annoyed by the contrast between what he read in the press and Gove's civility when they met, which he regarded as profoundly disingenuous. He was especially furious that his wife, who had helped him launch the policy, had been dragged into the controversy. As Clegg saw it, the Education Secretary's response was to shrug innocently as if to say: 'Aw, shucks – not me.' Gove claimed to be a 'great devotee of free school meals'. The Deputy Prime Minister continued to fume, now persuaded that his ostensibly friendly colleague had crossed the line from social radical to rogue ideologue. 'He can't unilaterally decide all these things, like on qualified teachers,' Clegg complained. Gove's attitude was that he could, did, and would continue to do so, as long as he remained in post.

Two Lib Dems stood in the midst of all this, buffeted by the political winds. One was Danny Alexander, the Lib Dem Chief Secretary, whose job it was to find money for everything, and to persuade his party that the Autumn Statement or Budget they had just heard described on the *Today* programme as a victory for Conservatism was in fact a thoroughly Liberal Democrat package. It was Alexander who would receive a hastily scribbled note from Osborne in Cabinet or on the front bench when Clegg spoke too soon, or was about to pledge the Coalition to a spending proposal it could not afford. Alexander was scarcely a charismatic figure, but his steely composure at the Treasury and calm performances on television and radio had persuaded a growing number of Lib Dems that, if the party suffered grievous losses in 2015, he (rather than Tim Farron or Vince Cable) might be the man to succeed Clegg.

The other figure caught in the crossfire was Laws, briefly Alexander's predecessor at the Treasury, now performing a combined role at Education and the Cabinet Office and busily working on the Lib Dem manifesto. Even when appointing him to this hybrid job in 2012, Cameron had fretted privately that he and Gove might butt brainy heads. More than once, Laws felt he was kept out of the loop – but especially so when Gove declined to reappoint Baroness (Sally) Morgan as Chair of the schools inspectorate, Ofsted. Gove explained to her in person that, having appointed her in 2011, he did not intend to retain her services after 2014. It was necessary, he said, to refresh the leadership of any team from time to time. Privately, he had also reached the conclusion that this particular role should not be performed by an individual who 'wore a political badge' – as Morgan, formerly Blair's director of government relations, undoubtedly did. Though composed when told of her imminent ejection, she did not disguise her view that Gove was making a grave misjudgement. When the story broke, she declared herself to be only 'the latest of a fairly long list of people now who are non-Conservative supporters who are not being reappointed'. Gove countered that his priority was to enhance operational efficiency rather than to purge the ranks of the nation's quangos. Laws was enraged by his exclusion from the final decision on Morgan's future – an issue which he believed was still open to discussion – and did not hide his anger.

In the first days of the Coalition, this particular Lib Dem had been

identified as a 'total sweetie' by Cameron's team – a cuddly team mas-
cot for the new alliance. His dyspeptic response to Morgan's sacking
was no less symbolic of the accelerated ageing process to which the
alliance was succumbing. The youthful promise of the Rose Garden
was a distant memory. As an entity, the Coalition often seemed crot-
chety, arthritic and hard of hearing. The enchantment had gone, and
with it the benefit of the doubt. Political rust conspired with the
prospect of the general election to make the two parties more suspicious of one another and more distinct in their operations.

The Tory party, in particular, longed to have its independence
back: some senior Conservatives lobbied Cameron to rule out a
second coalition in the party's general election manifesto. The PM
tantalized the readers of *The Spectator* with the promise that 'there's a
good list of things I have put in my little black book that I haven't
been able to do which will form the next Tory manifesto'.[8] Graham
Brady, the chairman of the 1922 Committee, revealed that Cameron
had indeed agreed that MPs would take part in 'a definitive consultation with a vote' if another deal were struck between the two
parties.[9]

All the more striking, then, that the Coalition held together at all;
that Labour's poll lead no longer looked impregnable; that the main
political issue of the day was no longer the viability of Osborne's
'Plan A' for the pace and form of the recovery. There was no shortage
of MPs on both sides urging their respective leaders to start winding
down the partnership in 2014, perhaps by moving from full coalition
to a 'confidence and supply' option, whereby the smaller party supported the larger solely on finance bills and votes of no confidence.
But there was no taste for this at the top. For all the disagreements
and often bitter compromise, a disentanglement by stages held no
appeal for either Cameron or Clegg.

The Fixed-term Parliaments Act made the dissolution of the
Commons before 2015 extremely difficult. Neither party, in any case,
had the slightest interest in an early election: Clegg believed (because
he had to) that the passage of time would habituate the electorate to
the idea of the Lib Dems as a party of government rather than a party
of protest. Cameron, meanwhile, needed the statistical recovery to

translate into an appreciable reality and – perhaps – political credit to his party. Osborne reassured his colleagues that at some point in 2014 there would be a political shift. 'When inflation is overtaken by the increase in people's earnings,' he said, 'that's when the change will come.'

Even as Cameron publicly looked forward to stretches of clear blue water and the freedom to enact the measures in his little black book, those around him prepared mentally for the possibility of a second coalition. As one very senior source put it to me in early 2014: 'A victory? That I can't see. It's a stretch, even with the recovery. But *Coalition 2: The Sequel* – that's entirely possible.' Such musings could not be uttered on the record, of course. Electoral etiquette precluded candid discussion of anything other than victory. The Tory tribe and right-of-centre commentariat craved single-party government and recoiled with horror from the prospect of a second deal with the Lib Dems. Part of Boris's appeal to his party undoubtedly lay in the licence he enjoyed outside the Coalition: unlike the other contenders to succeed Cameron, he could publicly mock the Lib Dem leader as the 'great yellow albatross'.

Clegg found some of the Mayor's public utterances crass beyond belief. In November, Boris had provoked controversy with his Margaret Thatcher Lecture and its position on the nature of inequality ('Whatever you may think of the value of IQ tests, it is surely relevant to a conversation about equality that as many as 16 per cent of our species have an IQ below 85 . . . The harder you shake the pack, the easier it will be for some cornflakes to get to the top'[10]). The Deputy Prime Minister accused the Mayor of 'unpleasant, careless elitism' and objected with especial vehemence to the use of the word 'species'.

Yet, asked in December whether he could envisage himself as Boris's deputy in a different coalition, he replied without qualm: 'Yes, of course. I'm quite un-precious about the idea that someone who has a much stronger democratic mandate than me but hasn't got an outright mandate has every right to be a prime minister, and for me to be a deputy. I want my party to punch above its weight, and indeed we do.'[11]

This was now the essence of Lib Dem strategy, as conceived by Clegg: an unprecedented mix of desperation and high ambition. On the one hand, he was scrambling for every vote, fretful that the threat of extinction still loomed over his party, clinging to polls which showed that a reasonable percentage of the electorate *might* opt for the Lib Dems in 2015. On the other, he hoped and believed that the party – assuming it still existed as a serious parliamentary force – had a rich future in office.

This was the Clegg offer for 2015: the claim that the party of protest led by Charles Kennedy (which had won sixty-two seats in 2005, principally by opposing the Iraq War) had morphed into a party of government, permanently available to the British public to invigilate and moderate the worst impulses of the other parties. The Lib Dems would, Clegg claimed, bring fiscal credibility to a mostly Labour administration and compassion to the Tory table. 'I want the Liberal Democrats to be in government,' he said in the same interview. 'I can't predict which combination, whether it be the Conservatives or Labour [but] I think both [for] myself individually, personally, and the party, that we're good at governing now – we are good at governing from the Liberal centre ground. We fight tenaciously where we think there's a danger of the Government lurching off in the wrong direction.'

This sometimes involved decisions which were hard to decode except with reference to the internal politics of Clegg's party. The sacking of Jeremy Browne from the Home Office in October, and his replacement by the maverick Norman Baker, was inexplicable as a step to improve the Coalition's efficiency. Rather, it marked the DPM's determination that Lib Dems should be inside government doing liberal things and making their mark – which he felt Browne had not been doing. He wanted a party that was neither limited to protest nor boringly Tory-lite. In Baker's case, Clegg had chosen a media-friendly renegade who could bash Theresa May on immigration with varying degrees of subtlety as the election approached.

Browne would eventually fight back, publishing a book that enabled him to flex his governing muscles before the media mirror and to show the Coalition what it was missing.[12] The Lib Dems, the ex-minister suggested, had lost their identity as 'a bold, ambitious liberal party' and become 'an ill-defined, moderating centrist party that believed its primary purpose was to dilute the policies of other political parties'. It was a shame, Browne observed laconically, that Clegg 'makes a virtue of being the brake within the government rather than the accelerator' and 'thinks he has to meet his detractors halfway in political no man's land'.[13]

This struck Clegg as the splutter of a meteor that had fizzled out. But Browne was right that it was impossible to please both sides in an argument. In January 2014, the Lib Dems' internal inquiry conducted by Alistair Webster into allegations of sexual misconduct against Lord Rennard, the party's former chief executive, delivered its final report. Webster declared it 'unlikely that it could be established beyond reasonable doubt that Lord Rennard had intended to act in an indecent or sexually inappropriate way' but 'an apology would be appropriate, as would a commitment to change his behaviour in future'. Rennard refused to apologize and was suspended from the party he had taught to campaign and to practise brutal 'pavement politics'. The five women who had brought the allegations felt the door of officialdom slam in their faces. Those who supported Rennard objected that the presumption of innocence had been battered by a media witch-hunt and that an inconclusive inquiry had resulted in demands for a wholly unnecessary statement of contrition. Everybody, in other words, was angry. For days at a time, Clegg's energies were dominated by this emotive case. 'You're the first person for ages who hasn't bent my ear about Rennard,' the Lib Dem leader told one visitor to his Commons office.

Even so, he was as confident as the facts would allow about the party's trajectory. At its 2013 conference, he believed, it had completed its complex and painful metamorphosis – an exaggeration but no longer a completely absurd claim. 'We said: We're going to change our traditional theological opposition to nuclear [power], we're not going to snap back to our original populist position on tuition fees, we're not even going to advocate restoring the upper rate [of income tax] at 50 [per cent], we'll keep it at 45, and in addition to that, we continue to commit ourselves to the fiscal plan.' Even Vince Cable, having let his scepticism about 'Help to Buy' and fears about rising house prices be known, voted with Clegg in the economy debate.

This metamorphosis meant taking ownership of the pain but also expecting some credit for the success: the political stability which the Coalition had bequeathed to economic policy was clearly dependent upon the Lib Dems' participation. They were also especially proud of the steady rise in the income tax personal allowance, which Osborne increased to £10,500 in his fifth Budget; and grateful for the polls which showed the public emphatically regarded this progressive measure as yellow rather than blue. Still, it rankled that their Coalition partners should suddenly claim it as their own, a measure delivered by a Conservative Chancellor. 'It's amazing!' one of Clegg's inner circle raged to me at the time. 'The Tories resisted this for so long, and now, all of a sudden, it's their idea!'

There was much speculation before this Budget that Osborne would address the problem of 'fiscal drag' – specifically, the growing number of people now paying the 40p tax higher rate of income tax. The Treasury had certainly encouraged speculation that he would have good news for 'Middle Britain'. But the nature of that news was kept under wraps (the lessons of the 2012 'omnishambles' for media management had not been forgotten). Indeed, the group given foreknowledge of the plan to reform the pensions system – in particular, to scrap the requirement for those with a defined contribution scheme to buy an annuity when they retired – was remarkably small. Outside the Treasury, only Cameron, Clegg, Iain Duncan Smith, Steve Webb (the Lib Dem pensions minister), David Willetts, Oliver Letwin and Nigel Lawson were given advance notice of this top secret, market-sensitive blueprint. Yet again, Lawson was performing the role of mentor to Osborne, and offered his unequivocal support for the reform. 'Yes, long overdue,' he said. 'Everyone will tell you it can't be done.' This was true: the Chancellor encountered considerable resistance to his plan at the Treasury but was heartened by the support of his experienced Permanent Secretary, Sir Nicholas Macpherson.

On 19 March, Osborne went ahead and announced the reform – fulfilling, it transpired, a forgotten promise he had made in 2011, that 2014 would be the 'Year of the Saver'. Gove was overheard remarking that his friend and ally had made the best possible practical challenge to Ukip 'without mentioning the party by name'. It was no secret that Nigel Farage's movement tended to appeal to older voters, former Tories dismayed by the Coalition and Cameronism. Farage might object that Ukip was taking votes away from all parties and none, which was true. But, as Peter Kellner of YouGov argued persuasively, 45 per cent of its supporters had voted Tory in 2010, compared to only 11 per cent who had backed Labour.[14] The Chancellor was seeking – amongst other things – to woo back defectors to Ukip without launching an ideological arms race that the Conservative Party could never win.

No less politically important was the welfare cap imposed by Osborne in the Budget – set at £119.5bn in 2015–16. The ceiling did not affect spending on the Jobseeker's Allowance, the state pension and some other benefits. But it was a potentially momentous punctuation mark in the history of the post-war state, all the more remarkable for being inscribed in the bipartisan ink of coalition. A welfare cap had already been set for individual households: £26,000 a year for couples or lone parents. Now, a limit was being set upon what government itself could spend. This was not a quasi-constitutional bar: no Parliament may bind its successor. But if ministers in this or subsequent administrations intended to breach the cap, they would have to seek explicit parliamentary approval. Osborne's rationale was liberal in the classic sense of the word: namely that, left to itself, government will spend more. His intention was to recruit representative democracy as a brake upon this tendency and encourage Parliament to be a force for fiscal stability. The cap was but one feature of his Charter for Budget Responsibility, which set out the Government's fiscal and debt management objectives. His less lofty ambition was to force Labour to sign up to his charter in the ensuing Commons vote on the cap. Much as Miliband condemned Osborne's 'gamesmanship' – evidence, the Labour leader believed, that politics was just another field sport for the Cameroons – he and Ed Balls declined to walk into the sucker punch. The Opposition front bench backed the measure, confining the Labour rebellion to thirteen MPs.

The cap also marked an end to one of the Coalition's longest-running feuds – or, at the very least, a truce. The hardback edition of this book revealed, in the Tory conference week of 2013, the sheer extent of Osborne's intermittent contempt for Duncan Smith, and the depth of IDS's resentment at the way in which the Chancellor treated him. By early 2014, however, the feud seemed to have played itself out, or, at the very least, to have been suspended. Osborne began to speak of the Work and Pensions Secretary in quite different terms, concluding, as the Coalition's fourth birthday approached, that he 'could not have done' what he had done to the benefits system without the moral vision of Duncan Smith.

This was no small compliment. Welfare reform was full of political peril and, while Osborne was confident of broad public support for the Government's strategy, he was keenly aware of the pitfalls awaiting any minister who strode on this terrain. In March, Atos – the French firm which had been mired in controversy over its Work Capability Assessments of benefit claimants – withdrew early from its £500m contract, which had been due to last until August 2015. One third of its decisions had been overturned on appeal, a dismal record. There had been well-publicized instances of suicide after claimants had failed the tests. It was with great relief – and financial compensation to the taxpayer – that ministers bade farewell to Atos. In this and other respects, Osborne conceded, IDS's moral authority had prevented political disaster.

As for Duncan Smith, his aides referred, euphemistically, to the unexpectedly high levels of 'cross-government support' in the months leading up to the Budget. What they meant was that they and their boss had been spared the usual Treasury punishment beating. Would the peace hold? Only the two men themselves could answer that question. But the truce was welcome.

This was more than a diverting development in the Westminster soap opera (although it was most certainly that). As a student of the New Labour years, Cameron knew how seriously the work of a government could be disfigured by personality clashes and matters of temperament rather than differences of ideology or policy. Much of his time was devoted to management of high-maintenance individuals, which is another way of saying to leadership. This was not a fashionable approach to understanding politics: the waning of the Blair–Brown era, the defining moment of the Crash and the frustrations of coalition had turned the eyes of the Tory commentariat towards big-ticket policy events and battles for the soul of modern Conservatism, and away from what King Lear calls 'court news': the study, as he puts it to Cordelia, of 'who loses and who wins, who's in, who's out'.[15]

Yet it was impossible to understand one without the other. The Coalition's conduct – its successes and failures – was inexplicable without a grasp of its functioning and failure as an experimental form of oligarchy. Every party leader has to maintain a certain level of public and private unity. Uniquely among modern prime ministers, Cameron depended upon this within and between *two* parties. His greatest, rarely acknowledged success had simply been to keep the show on the road and – with some spectacular exceptions –to keep the peace. With a year to go until the election that would define his place in the history books, he depended more than ever upon the preservation of that hard-won peace.

23. One foot on the drawbridge: Syria and Ukraine

Unlike his boss, Ed Llewellyn was in Number Ten when news of the Ghouta massacre of 21 August 2013 reached the UK Government. The Prime Minister's chief of staff had been expecting this terrible moment to come – a chemical attack in Syria – but that did not diminish its impact. The images emerging from the suburb of Damascus, not least of tiny corpses packed in ice, were the stuff of nightmares, and for those, like Llewellyn, with young children especially intolerable.

The scale of the atrocity was, and remained, unclear: intelligence estimates of the number of fatalities ranged from 250 to more than 1,500. But, as Llewellyn knew, the real issue was not one of numbers, but of military conduct. By deploying the chemical agent sarin, Assad (assuming, as the British Government did, that it was Assad) had violated one of the clearest principles of international warfare. As long ago as the Hague Declaration of 1899, the nations of the world had promised 'to abstain from the use of projectiles the object of which is the diffusion of asphyxiating or deleterious gases'. The moral force of this and subsequent prohibitions was horrifically compounded by memory of the Holocaust and of Zyklon B. Those responsible for the attack on Ghouta had shown precisely what they thought of this commitment and those memories.

Cameron was on holiday in the Cornish resort of Polzeath when the news broke. He and Llewellyn agreed that something 'bloody well needed to happen'. Over the summer, the PM had fretted that President Obama's innate caution might be an insuperable obstacle to the action that needed to be taken.[1] In the days that followed, it would often be suggested in the media that Cameron was urging the US Commander-in-Chief to stiffen his sinews and confront his responsibilities, as leader of the free world, in a test-case involving strictly outlawed WMD. It was orthodox to claim that the President still needed to be persuaded of the need for military intervention.

In fact, Obama's opinion about Assad and what needed to be done had hardened dramatically over the summer. In a secure call with Cameron on Saturday, 23 August, the President made clear that his patience had run out and that – as important as it was to take account of public war-weariness – the time had come for an unambiguous, multilateral response to the Syrian dictator's repeated provocations. 'Obama wanted to go more or less immediately', according to one involved in the transatlantic talks. 'He was pushing Dave to go quickly. This time, he really was decisive.' The President also insisted upon a deadline: the strike would take place on or just before Monday, 2 September.

Obama and Cameron discussed some of the operational detail for the proposed air-strikes and, specifically, the need to get one of the UK's Trafalgar class of submarine (armed with Tomahawk missiles) into the region as soon as possible. The two heads of government would have to take account of parliamentary and congressional opinion respectively, and listen respectfully to the UN Security Council. But – barely forty-eight hours after the original attack – it seemed all but certain that the United States and Britain were about to take military action against Assad. What followed, therefore, was an embarrassment to Cameron and one which was to sour his relations with Ed Miliband permanently.

It was the end of August, and many of the Coalition's leading figures were still scattered around the world on holiday or speeding back to London. In the days that followed his first conversation with Obama, Cameron formed a virtual war cabinet with William Hague, Osborne and Clegg, in constant touch with one another to plan the difficult weeks ahead. As over Libya, the Deputy Prime Minister was both deeply involved and strongly supportive: when it came to chemical weapons deployed against children, the liberal interventionist and the liberal Conservative reached more or less identical conclusions.

The role of Parliament in times of conflict remained unclear. Since the Iraq War, there had been a series of attempts to give statutory force to the convention that only the Commons could authorize military action. In fact, this rule had been dropped from Gordon Brown's Constitutional Reform and Governance Act in the abject final months of his premiership. But the political reality was not in doubt: a government intending to go into battle, however briefly, needed the support of the Commons – which, in this instance, meant recalling Parliament.

From the start, Sir George Young, the Chief Whip, warned the Prime Minister that he could not take Tory backbench opinion for granted: Cameron might need to look elsewhere for support. The PM called Miliband for an exploratory chat and then invited him to Number Ten for a more extensive conversation. He acknowledged that any Opposition leader in time of conflict was in a 'difficult position'. He or she could not afford to be seen as a pushover, rubber-stamping decisions taken by HMG. Cameron understood that, if he wanted Miliband's help, he would have to help him, too. The Labour leader had to be able to persuade his own parliamentary party that he was not merely cheering on Cameron from the sidelines; that the Opposition was scrutinizing the plan effectively and that Miliband himself was a participant in an international humanitarian endeavour, rather than a passive observer of a Coalition war.

In his initial conversations with Cameron, Miliband returned repeatedly to the need for UN involvement – a reasonable request, as far as the PM was concerned, as long as it did not hand Putin a veto over every act of British foreign policy. The intention, Cameron insisted, was not to embroil the West in all-out war but to shock Assad with a moment of fiery resolve, and to force him to the negotiating table in order to plan the new Syria as the Serbs, Croatians and Bosnians had mapped out the future of the former Yugoslavia in Dayton, Ohio, in 1995.

In their first and second meetings at Number Ten, Cameron felt that Miliband was being 'helpful and responsible', voicing concerns but signalling as clearly as he could that the operation was politically 'doable'. In retrospect, the Prime Minister could not decide whether the Labour leader's subsequent withdrawal of support was a straightforward act of sabotage, or the consequence of Miliband's own miscalculation of Labour opinion: he didn't deliver his own party's vote, because, as it turned out, he couldn't.

A bit of both, perhaps. As Coalition and Labour draftsmen set about wording a motion that Miliband could support, it became increasingly clear to Cameron that the negotiations were not going to end well. As he complained to NSC colleagues, he had 'bent over backwards' to accommodate Labour, publishing an intelligence document and a summary ruling by the Attorney General. Osborne warned that Miliband might not be able to unite his Shadow Cabinet, let alone the Labour parliamentary party, behind some form of intervention. In the debate, Miliband claimed that the intelligence disclosed so far was 'important' but that 'we need to gather further evidence over the coming days'. Labour looked forward in a leisurely way to a 'sequential road map' as if discussing a conference agenda rather than an imminent military operation. The final motion was not even an explicit endorsement of military action, but called instead for an appropriate response once the investigations of UN weapons inspectors were complete. Determined to exhaust every possibility, Osborne made an eleventh-hour appeal to Labour on ethical grounds: 'It's not going to happen [UK involvement in a strike] but just vote for this!' But even the new wording was too much for MPs, who voted the motion down on 29 August by 285 votes to 272.

To Miliband's surprise, Cameron pulled the plug there and then. It was clear, the PM said, that Parliament wanted no part in a strike against Assad, and, whatever his own opinion, 'the government will act accordingly'. The visible delight of some on the Labour side, including Jim Murphy, then Shadow Defence Secretary, inflamed emotions further on the Coalition front bench. Michael Gove, usually the most civil member of the Cabinet, shouted: 'You're a disgrace!' at the MPs who had stopped UK military action in its tracks.

Clegg and his team were appalled by what they saw as Miliband's opportunism. What might it be like to govern in coalition with this man after the 2015 general election? The Lib Dem leader said it was essential that the party rule nothing out: its future depended upon an open-minded capacity to govern with the larger parties, and to work alongside their leaders. But – months after the vote on Syria – some of Clegg's team were still wondering aloud if they would be able to work alongside Miliband or to trust him.

Similar thoughts crossed the mind of President Obama when he read a newspaper cutting explaining what Miliband had done. The Commander-in-Chief was furious, as President Bush had been with Michael Howard when he questioned aspects of the Iraq War. If Miliband became Prime Minister in May 2015, he would have to work with Obama for a year and a half until the latter completed his second term. This was not an auspicious omen for the Labour leader – a reminder that inaction, like action, has consequences. He might be able to secure the consulting services of David Axelrod, Obama's campaign guru in the 2008 and 2012 elections, as he did in April 2014.[2] But winning the full confidence of the President himself would be a different matter entirely. When Jim Messina, one of Obama's most valued strategists, later told him that he had been hired by the Conservative Party and would be advising Cameron on how to beat Miliband, the Commander-in-Chief responded enthusiastically. 'Do whatever it takes,' he replied. 'I like that guy.' Getting the PM re-elected had become a presidential objective.

Cameron and Osborne were furious with Miliband, naturally. But they were also chastened. The PM's parliamentary intelligence had been faulty and the Government's whipping operation lacklustre. But the vote was a lucid decision by Parliament, not just a managerial error by the PM. He believed that the UK should be at America's side and hoped that Obama would be able to go to Congress with the endorsement of the British Parliament in his back pocket. What he had underestimated was the deep impact that Iraq had had upon his backbench colleagues. He knew, of course, that the war on Saddam had made Tory MPs deeply suspicious of foreign entanglements and military adventures. He himself, after all, had drawn a sharp distinction in the first year of his leadership between neo-conservative foreign policy and his own liberal Conservatism. He was suspicious of Jeffersonian blueprints, or 'one-size-fits-all' projects to spread democracy by drone.

But Iraq had disfigured Tory opinion much more thoroughly than he fully realized until the Syrian debacle. Osborne reflected that countries take many years, sometimes decades, to recover from military trauma. In America, he pointed out, the scars of Vietnam did not heal until the Reagan years and the invasion of Grenada. The pain of Suez lingered until the unexpected triumph of the Falklands War. As Cameron met MPs before the vote, it became clear that many of them were simply unwilling to repeat what they regarded as the catastrophic consequences of the motion authorizing war on Saddam in 2003. 'It doesn't matter what you say,' David Amess, the MP for Southend West, told him. 'I won't vote for it because of Iraq.' Jesse Norman was obliged to resign from the Downing Street policy board after abstaining in the vote. He, too, drew explicit parallels with the war to topple Saddam. 'Is it any wonder,' he wrote, 'that the British people, and British parliamentarians, have found themselves pausing at the last-minute publication of excerpts from intelligence sources, including the JIC [Joint Intelligence Committee]?'[3]

Part of the resistance reflected the more familiar and prosaic charge that Cameron was always being distracted from his central economic mission – by same-sex marriage, Lords reform, Libya and now the atrocities of the Assad regime. But the roots were deeper than resentment of the current Prime Minister (compounded by lingering resentment of Blair). The vote was, as Cameron told his advisers afterwards, 'pretty big potatoes', with potentially huge ramifications for British foreign policy. On the morning after the motion's defeat, Osborne said on the *Today* programme that there would be much 'national soul-searching' as its implications sunk in.

The greater risk was that there would be hardly any such reflection. Hours after the vote, British officers were already being excluded from key meetings at US Central Command in Tampa, Florida. There was a time when this would have been seen as a national humiliation: but no longer, it seemed. Cameron and his Chancellor detected with alarm an increased yearning to pull up the drawbridge and to liberate Britain from the cares of the world. This was partly a response to the Crash, a vague sense that the recession was a foreign toxin that could be drained from the system by – somehow – reducing the UK's interdependence with the rest of the world.

As children of the eighties, a political decade launched by the Falklands War and wrapped in the Union Flag, the PM and Chancellor were strong believers in nationhood and instinctive Eurosceptics. But they knew that Britain could not have globalization à la carte. In their world-view, the UK still had strong strategic interests around the globe, a humanitarian responsibility in its most poverty-stricken zones, and a pivotal role in the opening up of markets. The PM wanted to maintain the 'essential relationship' with America and – after renegotiation of its membership and an In–Out referendum – to keep Britain in the European Union.

Osborne felt a greater kinship than Cameron with US neo-cons. But both agreed that the world was more than a big marketplace and that the pathologies of a globalized planet (cross-border crime, terrorism, the traffic in WMD, the international influence of rogue states) respected no borders and no limits. One of the great questions of the post-9/11 age was whether the new polities in the regions that spawned Islamist terror could be stable, democratic and free of WMD. In this context, Syria was more than an opportunity to make amends for Iraq, or a dress rehearsal for Iran. It was extremely important in and of itself. Britain's confused response had signalled to Assad that bureaucracy dressed up as democracy was the West's most resilient cultural feature. Suddenly, the UK Parliament looked like a weak link in the chain. As the UN declared Syria the 'humanitarian calamity' of the century, many MPs wished they could have a second vote: but Cameron was not interested in further posturing and positioning, or another carnival of inaction.

The PM spoke to Obama from Chequers after the vote and the President assured him: 'We're still going ahead.' So it was a great surprise to Cameron and his team when, on 31 August, the Commander-in-Chief put the strike plans on hold and referred the matter to Congress. In an unexpected announcement in the White House's Rose Garden, he declared himself ready to order the attack but 'having made my decision as Commander-in-Chief based on what I am convinced is our national security interests, I'm also mindful that I'm the President of the world's oldest constitutional democracy'.[4]

The extent to which the UK's withdrawal from the operation triggered or contributed to Obama's decision remains deeply contentious.[5] What is certain is that Parliament's embarrassment of Cameron drained much of the momentum from the process and all but isolated the President on the world stage. The only thing more risky than unilateral action is an initially multilateral plan from which your allies start to back out.

Mortified as he was, Cameron decided to make the best of a bad hand at the G20 summit in St Petersburg the following week. After Britain was reportedly dismissed as a 'small island' by a Russian official, the PM grabbed the steering wheel and sped off to prepare his reply. Normally, for security reasons, prime ministers are not supposed to drive. But at the summit there were electric cars to ferry the participants from one location to another, and Cameron, commandeering one such buggy, gave his officials, Craig Oliver, Liz Sugg and Helen Bower, an occasionally hair-raising lift. En route, the team helped their chauffeur draw up an inventory of British accomplishments, which he duly rattled off to the media when they arrived. The PM ended his list with a quip: 'If I start talking about this "blessed plot, this sceptred isle, this England", I might have to put it to music, so I think I'll leave it there.' From the ashes of the Commons vote, Cameron sought to extract at least some wit – and perspective. Over dinner, President Kirchner of Argentina delivered a twenty-five-minute anti-war speech, prompting Angela Merkel and Cameron to roll their eyes at one another. In the end, the PM removed his translation earpiece: everyone has his limits.

Cameron and Obama had a chat before dinner at the summit hotel and compared notes. Neither man was inclined to brood on past failure but both were concerned that the pressure on Syria to decommission its WMD should not be relaxed, even if the option of military strikes was off the table for the foreseeable future. Their host at the G20, President Putin, had opposed them over Syria, and was now struggling to contain his smugness at the unravelling of the Anglo-American strategy. But Cameron and Obama did not want him to feel he could now do as he pleased, an authoritarian imperialist unafraid of the West's decadent democracies.

That anxiety was tested all too soon. In February, the President of Ukraine, Viktor Yanukovych, fled Kiev after five days of unrest in the capital. By the end of the month, Russian units were in the Crimean Peninsula, installing a puppet regional Prime Minister. Putin was determined not to lose a major territory in his sphere of influence and one that was home to so many ethnic Russians. Though his rhetoric celebrated the principle of self-determination, the strategic imperative was to maintain control of Sevastopol, home to Russia's Black Sea Fleet and its new Mediterranean Task Force; to burnish his domestic reputation as a strong defender of Russia and its interests; and to maintain the pressure upon the new regime in Kiev. As one of the most astute observers of Russian affairs, Anne Applebaum, observed: 'Putin invaded Crimea because Putin needs a war.'[6]

It was a sobering thought for Cameron and his advisers that if Ukraine had succeeded in joining Nato in 2008, British troops would be facing war against Russia even as the US Sixth Fleet ploughed across the Black Sea towards Crimea. Article 5 of the North Atlantic Treaty requires member states to come to the aid of all others under military attack. In this case, such assistance could feasibly have escalated into a full-blown West–East conflict, terror of which loomed over the twentieth century. But the Cold War was over, Ukraine was not in Nato and Putin was acting without reference to global opinion.

Cameron was confronted with political confusion and strategic disarray. He came to refer to the Ukrainian crisis as the 'disappointing chapter' in his own story – a mark not of self-obsession but of the bleak recognition that some knots could not be untied. One of Osborne's mantras was that 'a politician must be able to think as his opponent does' (and even to sympathize with him: for all their public antipathy, the Chancellor liked Ed Balls and was delighted to have a drink with him or to sponsor him in the London Marathon). Cameron agreed with this as a guiding principle, and tried to grasp the weakness underpinning Putin's bellicose stance by putting himself in Vlad's boots – the humiliation that the Ukrainian revolt against Russian influence had visited upon him, the yearning of so many

Ukrainians to align with the EU rather than Russia, and the dilemma posed by Yanukovych's flight.

All the same, Cameron stuck to his basic position that the Russian President could not behave like this with impunity. As he told his aides: 'Russia is going to suffer. It will suffer a lot.' In Hague's office, there were those who believed that Putin's actions were 'as big a strategic shock as 9/11'. While the Foreign Secretary and Cameron did not go that far – at least publicly – they knew that the crisis was a test of the West's resolve in general, and that much more depended upon its outcome than the fate of Ukraine (important as that was). Such capricious military aggression on the EU's doorstep was not something that could be dismissed. Regional instability, neo-imperialism and preparations for civil war: all these imperilled Western investments and trashed the international law underpinning global trade.

The US–EU strategy, quickly agreed, was one of phased sanctions. Dozens of individuals had their assets seized and right to travel withdrawn; talks on a US–Russia investment treaty were suspended; and the G8 meeting due to be held in Sochi in June was scrapped. Obama and Merkel warned Putin of certain escalation if he did not pull out his forces. Cameron spoke four times to the Russian President in the weeks immediately after the invasion, and was dismayed by his state of mind. Four years into the job, after many meetings on the summit circuit, the PM had a sufficiently cordial relationship with Putin to dispense with the pleasantries and diplomatic euphemisms, and to get down to business. But – even as conveyed by a polite translator – the Russian's thoughts were very clear and did not, at this stage, tend towards any form of compromise or face-saving solution.

Cameron's hope was that, over time, the realities of twenty-first-century trade and geopolitical pressure would do their work. Putin was indeed a figure from the past, a KGB kingpin who regretted the fall of the Soviet empire, a shirtless czar on horseback, calling the primeval forces of Russian might back to the battlefield. But – away from this historical fantasy – he also governed a country dependent upon the capitalist system that the Soviet Union failed to topple. The question was whether the rogue bear could be lured away from atavism, with all its ancestral appeal and sinew, and back to the top table of the global club with its rule book and required standards of behaviour.

Yet Russia was not the only nation facing questions about the future – and the recent past. Some senior Tories explicitly blamed Labour's mischief over the Syrian vote for Putin's audacity in Crimea. Sajid Javid, the Financial Secretary to the Treasury, identified a 'direct link between Miliband's cynical vote against [the] Syria motion and Russia's actions on Ukraine', while Nick Boles declared that Cameron had been 'right to urge Parliament to stand up to Putin and punish Assad's use of chemical weapons. Look where Miliband's weakness has led us.'[7]

Once again, however, there was a counter-argument that had nothing to do with partisan allegiance. It was made most eloquently by Douglas Carswell, the MP for Clacton, who suggested that 'sometimes boundaries do need to be redrawn – and the world is a better place for it'. This was the cerebral end of a spectrum at whose other end was the pub-ready opinion of Nigel Farage that such conflicts were simply 'none of our business'. The Ukip leader went too far when he expressed admiration for Putin as 'an operator . . . The way he played the whole Syria thing – brilliant.' But his call for the UK not to meddle beyond its borders gave voice to a pinched and petty sentiment that, if not quite the spirit of the age, was certainly spreading. After Iraq, in an age of austerity and economic anxiety, as the great engine of digital dissent vaporized what little trust remained in governments, this was the slogan to which people were signing up.

The notion of global interdependence might have logic, economic reality and enlightened self-interest on its side. But it was trickier to explain on the stump than 'none of our business'. In this context, Cameron remarked to one friend: 'It's going to take a long time to exorcise the ghost of Iraq.' As long as he was Prime Minister, Cameron would keep his foot firmly on the drawbridge. But it was getting harder.

24. Stuck in the middle

Nick Boles awaited his fate. Lynton Crosby had decided that enough was enough: it was time to make an example of one of these Oxbridge loudmouths, these Tory boys who loved the sound of their own voices more than the sound of a returning officer announcing victory. The papers and political websites were full of it: the speech Boles had given to Bright Blue, the liberal Conservative think tank, on 19 November, had triggered a vigorous controversy about the direction of the party, as it was surely meant to. As far as Crosby was concerned, the party had to choose – between self-indulgent chatter and self-discipline – if it was serious about winning the election in eighteen months. Nick would have to go.[1]

Ostensibly, Boles's speech was an offer of contrition. As an arch-modernizer, he had suggested in 2010 that the two governing parties might reach an electoral pact or 'coupon' arrangement for 2015, to maximize the number of seats won by Lib Dems and Conservatives and ensure that the Coalition's grip upon the Commons was even greater in its second Parliament. Boles's purpose, he said, was to withdraw that proposal and offer an analysis based on experience rather than hope alone.

Liberals should vote Conservative in 2015, he said, not because of a pact, but because the modern Tory party was the true protector of freedom. Linking George Osborne's economic liberalism and the institutional liberalism of Michael Gove's school reforms to the social liberalism of same-sex marriage, he argued that Conservatives were now the authentic trustees of liberty. Though framed as an admission that he had exaggerated the scope for a lasting alliance with the Lib Dems, the speech was really addressed to his fellow Tories and urging them not 'to play up to the caricature' of those who would 'paint us as heartless extremists'. As clearly as any senior Conservative, Boles had always grasped that too many voters 'don't like us and they don't like our motives'. The task was what it had always been: to convince the electorate that the Tories 'are not aliens from another planet'.

Boles knew he was the beneficiary of Cameron's loyalty. Crosby wanted a ministerial head on a spike where all senior Tories could see it. But the PM was not going to sack a loyal ally for repeating the modernizing message with which he had won the leadership in 2005. Indeed, he was so used to being criticized from the Right that it was salutary to be reminded occasionally of his centrist origins. When a deputation of moderate and green Tory MPs, including Laura Sandys, Greg Barker and Zac Goldsmith, met the Prime Minister to urge him not to abandon the environmentalist agenda or to lurch to the Right, he remarked that it made a nice change to be lobbied by centrist Tories, so used had he become to the fury of right-wing MPs and commentators encouraging him to chase the voters who had defected to Ukip.[2]

The latter pressure – the yearning to match or even trump Nigel Farage – increased as the radical Right improved its record in by-elections. In Wythenshawe and Sale East in February, the Tories were denied second place yet again, prompting yet another bout of introspection and drum-beating. Ukip still lacked the scale to fight a truly national campaign in a general election but its nimble opportunism was well-suited to the fetid, febrile atmosphere of by-elections and the simplicity of its objective. It suited Farage to be seen as the enemy of all the Establishment parties and not as Ed Miliband's best friend, inadvertently helping Labour win office. But what Ukip did best was to rattle Conservative politicians and, like Sirens wearing blazers, tempt them to make a strategic shift which would absolutely ensure Tory disaster in 2015.

Days before the Wythenshawe by-election, Tim Yeo, the de-selected Conservative MP for South Suffolk, told the *Daily Telegraph*'s Benedict Brogan: 'If we allow Ukip and our fear of Ukip to be what drives our policy that will lead us undoubtedly to defeat.'[3] Cameron had not yet made that mistake. But too much time was still dedicated to soothing those who might defect, appeasing the furious, and halting the seepage of votes to Farage. As I observed at the time, the consequence was a sort of reticence. The PM, so often accused of being ruled by Clegg, sometimes resembled a captive of the Right – and never more so than when the subject under discussion was immigration.

In a conference interview with Andrew Marr, Cameron memorably described migration policy, education and welfare as the faces of a 'three-sided coin'. The solecism reflected a worthy approach. The PM's ambition was to drain the poison from the issue, and to address it as a responsible policymaker rather than a protector of blood and soil. Mindful of the pressure imposed by immigration upon public services and housing, he undertook to overhaul the malfunctioning procedures of the border control system in legislation. Less wisely, he had pledged to limit net immigration to 'tens of thousands' a year – a demotic promise quite at odds with the technocratic means he was proposing.

It was an impulse that seized every Prime Minister – as it had Gordon Brown when he promised 'British jobs for British workers'. Such rhetoric did not so much play the race card as misrepresent the global race. It suggested, quite misleadingly, that Britain could afford to turn away migrant labour to make life easier for less-motivated, less-qualified indigenous workers. It overstated what any government could do to keep out those who came to Britain from around the ever-expanding EU to fill the jobs that British citizens turned down or could do less well. In eight years of party leadership, Cameron's handling of immigration had been mostly deft, pragmatic and mature. But the occasional lapse raised expectations that he could not meet and played into Ukip's eager hands. In the summer of 2013, the Home Office sent vans into six London boroughs, urging illegal immigrants to leave the country with the slogan: 'GO HOME OR FACE ARREST.' This was precisely the sort of measure that was bound to look like a crass, redneck stunt to the very centre-ground voters whom Cameron had always claimed were his principal electoral quarry. Not surprisingly, Danny Alexander condemned the vans as 'ghastly'.

In a pre-conference interview with the *Sunday Telegraph* in September, Cameron said that Miliband's supposed lurch to the Left had left many voters who had backed Blair without a home. 'There must be quite a lot of people who believe in a free-market economy, who want a compassionate society, who support properly run public services, who used to have a home in Labour and don't any more. I think it is a good time to say to those people, you can have a home in the Conservative Party.' Did he, therefore, regret the vans? 'No, not a bit, I don't at all.'[4]

Which was the real Cameron? In this confusion, as Crosby well understood, lay the PM's deepest political problem. Strategic integrity – broad consistency on the big issues – was one of the principal signs of leadership. It was quite possible to admire and even to vote for the party of a politician without approving of every policy he proposed, every action he had taken. What counted was his bearing: the capacity to turn competence into statesmanship.

Nobody was more struck by Crosby's emphasis – discipline, discipline, discipline – than Andrew Cooper, Cameron's director of strategy. He had vigorously questioned Crosby's appointment and asked the PM whether it would be possible to have 'Lynton without Lyntonism'.[5] What Cooper meant was: could the party have Crosby's campaigning methods without his right-wing campaigning message? Did Cameron want a repetition of the 2005 election, which Michael Howard had lost handily? Cameron's reply was twofold. 'The main difference is that my judgement is better than Michael Howard's,' he told Cooper. Second, Crosby had no intention of 'lurching to the Right'. He simply wanted to win.

Cooper was pleasantly surprised by Crosby's determination to stamp on any suggestion that the party was heading rightwards. When newspaper reports appeared that Cooper intended to leave, Crosby was deeply concerned that the story would metastasize into a media row about the trajectory of the party. Cooper, who had always intended to return to his polling company, Populus, found himself in the surreal position of debating with his colleagues when he could leave without creating the impression that he was flouncing out for ideological reasons – which he was not. He had found Crosby a reassuringly professional colleague. When he did finally leave, it was Lynton who rushed to his assistance in a minor dispute over money with the party's co-chairman, Lord Feldman.

Crosby was not alone in his concerns about the Tory message: its consistency and comprehensibility. Cameron himself was increasingly consumed by memories of 2010 and the Tory campaign's lack of clarity. He was determined not to make the same mistake again. But intention and reality are rarely identical.

Theresa May's Immigration Bill was primarily an attack upon illegal entry to Britain and consequent abuse of the welfare system and public services, rather than a draconian programme that might endanger Britain's economic interests by its severity. It obliged landlords to check whether tenants were authorized to be in the UK, banks to ensure the same before offering accounts to migrants, and registrars to notify the Home Office of planned weddings of UK citizens to people outside the EU. It made deportation easier and reduced the rights of appeal against such a decision unless deportees faced an authentic risk of 'serious irreversible harm'. It introduced new controls upon access to the NHS, to combat 'health tourism'. It was also the platform upon which Theresa May hoped to burnish her claim to the leadership – as a successful, if unexciting, manager of a notoriously dysfunctional department of state, and an instinctive modernizer who could nonetheless do business with the Right.

Clegg was struck by the number of senior Tories letting him know privately how grateful they were for the presence of the Lib Dems in the Government, restraining the harsher instincts of the Tory tribe. But the Bill was not enough for a significant percentage of the Conservative parliamentary party that had been schooled by three and a half years of coalition to sniff treachery and compromise everywhere. What might have been a showcase for practical Coalition policymaking became a patchwork of confusion and ignominy. The sharpest thorn was the amendment to the Bill proposed by Dominic Raab, the Conservative MP for Esher and Walton, to make the deportation of foreign criminals mandatory, except in the most exceptional circumstances: a radical curtailment of judicial discretion, intended to stop the abuse of Article 8 of the European Convention on Human Rights (which protects family life) to thwart expulsions from the UK.

Though sympathetic to the spirit in which Raab had drafted his amendment, Cameron was firmly advised that this would breach the UK's obligations as a signatory of the ECHR. To avoid a confrontation, he instructed ministers to abstain and gambled that Labour and the Lib Dems would vote down the Raab plan. Out of the blue, May suddenly proposed powers to strip foreign-born terror suspects of British citizenship, a fairly transparent bid to buy off the rebels. Unimpressed, eighty-five Tory MPs voted for the Raab amendment, a revolt that robbed the Bill of much of its sheen.

This was an inglorious moment for the PM. Where did he really stand? Was he – as he suddenly seemed to suggest – a muscular Tory constrained only by the rules of coalition and longing for the liberty to be as right-wing as he wished? Or was he a practical statesman, acknowledging that Britain's membership of the ECHR could not be resolved in a single amendment to a bill about migration policy? And – if the latter – was he too scared to face down his rebels? The most dangerous feature of the debacle was the uncertainty that it had deepened. It was no accident that Lord Howard, Cameron's predecessor as Tory leader, chose this particular moment to make a rare intervention. 'What is needed in this stage of the Parliament,' he declared, 'is a degree of self-discipline by Conservative backbenchers.' Howard did not need to spell out the fact that his warning was addressed to Cameron, too: if the party was to unite, he had to lead it. Unity was more than self-restraint; it was a collective response to authority. A functioning democracy needed those who would speak truth to power. But it also needed leaders brave enough to speak truth to dissent.

The problem, as one Cabinet minister put it, was that Conservatives 'don't really think their party is in power right now' – as if coalition didn't really count. The Tory movement had grown brittle and moody, and resented Cameron with the same fervour with which it had embraced him in 2005. It resented him for being necessary, for making the Coalition work to a surprising extent, and for much else besides.

The shambles at Westminster over the Immigration Bill was a gift to Ukip: a dramatization of all that Farage claimed about the Westminster elite, its introspection and its supposed detachment from the day-to-day concerns of the electorate. No longer a fringe party, Ukip oscillated from absurdity to serious threat. On the one hand, Godfrey Bloom, MEP for Yorkshire and North Lincolnshire, made himself and his movement look ridiculous in August when he described the international development budget as 'giving £1bn a month . . . to Bongo Bongo Land'. This was crass xenophobia thinly disguised as pub banter, the kind of language that would ensure that Ukip never attracted more than a small coalition of the outraged, the empurpled and anti-Cameron defectors. And Farage wanted much more than that. He was determined to establish his party as a serious force in UK politics, vying with the Lib Dems for the bronze medal behind Labour and the Tories: a position on the podium, in other words.

As Ukip chipped away, Cameron pursued his EU strategy with dogged determination. In February, Merkel visited London, and was as helpful as she could be about his renegotiation strategy, declaring that 'I firmly believe that what we are discussing here is feasible, is doable.' She was the first German Chancellor to approach mainstream British Euroscepticism with an open mind – not with disdain as an island pathology, a ludicrous barbarism. It was hard to imagine any of her predecessors making such a statement about a Tory plan to reorganize the EU. Cameron also counted Fredrik Reinfeldt, the Swedish Prime Minister, as a close ally, and was no less impressed by the Italian PM, Matteo Renzi, when he welcomed him to Number Ten in April.

Multi-dimensional diplomacy of this sort was not glamorous, often failed and rarely delivered clear-cut victory. Farage, with his abrasive rhetoric, flash slogans and saloon bar politics, had an easier message to sell. In fact, almost any message was easier to sell than what Cameron had to get across to his party and the public if his EU plan was to work: 'Trust me.'

As it turned out, the next two rounds were fought by Clegg, rather than the PM. Cameron had no intention of debating with Farage on Europe, or any other subject: he could not possibly concede parity of esteem to the Ukip leader. The Deputy Prime Minister, however, had less to lose. Urged on by Ryan Coetzee, his South African political strategist, Clegg believed there was something to be said for publicizing the Lib Dems' unequivocal championship of Britain's continued membership. There were, he calculated, moderate Tories and disillusioned New Labour supporters, unsettled by the sudden possibility of a British exit, whose votes were waiting to be harvested in the May European elections and in 2015. He and Farage were not necessarily bidding for the same custom: the two debates, hosted by LBC and the BBC on 26 March and 2 April respectively, need not be a zero-sum game.

Clegg prepared with Tim Farron, president of the Lib Dems, playing the part of Farage. He was smooth and confident, briskly in command of his brief. But the Ukip leader was playing a different game, raising the temperature and appealing to emotion rather than statistics. Only when his evident admiration for Putin became an issue did Farage falter. The post-debate polls suggested clear victories for the Ukip leader at both events.

Cameron was glad not to be involved. He was concerned about leadership debates before the general election, anxious that they should not suck the oxygen out of the broader campaign as they undoubtedly had in 2010. This time, the PM wanted these head-to-head contests spread over a longer period – perhaps six months – and to encompass a broader range of formats. At least one debate, he felt, should be between those party leaders with a realistic chance of becoming or remaining Prime Minister after the general election: Cameron versus Miliband, in other words. He wanted to exclude Farage entirely – though, as Downing Street aides conceded, this would prove politically difficult if Ukip topped the polls in the European elections.

No less important than the Clegg–Farage debates themselves were the scenes in the spin room, and the noises off on Twitter and broadcast panels that followed. At the LBC event, Andrew Mitchell, the victim of the 'Plebgate' scandal and former Chief Whip and, at the time, a serious candidate to become Britain's next commissioner in Brussels, was to be heard arguing that the only way for the electorate to secure a referendum was to vote Conservative in the general election. John Redwood prowled the spin room, too, blogging that 'Mr Clegg bombed badly in the debate last night.' Peter Bone, Eurosceptic

Tory MP for Wellingborough, was also on hand, complaining that Cameron should have been there making the Conservative case. All of this was a taste of the fervour that would grip the Tory party – and split it – if a referendum on EU membership were to be called. If Cameron won with a Commons majority of any sort in 2015, or negotiated a second coalition that included the fulfilment of his pledge to hold an In–Out vote before the end of 2017, the Conservative Party's energies would be utterly absorbed by Europe, as never before, for up to eighteen months. The Clegg–Farage debates were only a polite throat-clearing exercise compared to what might lie ahead.

The chosen Tory slogan for 2015 was 'security, stability and peace of mind' – or small variations thereupon. Crosby calculated that, for all the Coalition's radical successes, what the public wanted was reassurance and stability. This was no time for introspection or for revolution. The Conservative promise for a putative second term was that only Cameron and his team could finish the job and nurture the recovery to fruition. The PM had a natural inclination to optimism ('let sunshine win the day') but that had to be tempered by a serious recognition that the task was not complete.

Cameron spoke with pleasure of the 'Lyntonization' of the party as code for discipline. He told MPs that there was a distinction between the 'blue-on-red' (Tories versus Labour) strand of the campaign and the 'blue-on-purple' (Tories versus Ukip) battle. He regarded the fight with Miliband as his responsibility alone, a straightforward contest to prove which of them had what it took to become or remain Prime Minister. But against Ukip he needed the active help of his backbenchers, especially the more prominent men and women of the Right who agreed with much of what Farage said. In this context, winning the support of Stewart Jackson, the strongly Eurosceptic and traditionalist MP for Peterborough, was something worth boasting about.

In a ramshackle way, meanwhile, the party was still preparing itself for all eventualities – including a change of leader in 2015. Inevitably, the fortunes of Boris Johnson became the prism through which this question was considered, though it was obvious that there would be other candidates when Cameron finally stood down. The disclosure in the hardback edition of this book that aviation was the area of policy that made the Mayor 'want to drive a T54 into Number Ten' raised the political stakes, especially when the interim report of Sir Howard Davies's Airports Commission was published in December.[6] It was no secret that Davies was baffled by Boris's enthusiasm for a hub airport in the Thames estuary, but he obliged the Mayor by keeping his proposal in play and encouraging him to persuade the commission before the delivery of its final recommendations in the summer of 2015. The Mayor shared with his mentor, Michael Heseltine, a swashbuckling taste for the *grand projet*. He wanted to be remembered for an airport rather than a bike.

Cameron was privately relieved by Davies's decision, which enabled the Mayor to say that his plan was still in contention. He continued to hug Boris close, and to insist that true leadership involved the cultivation of talent, rather than its selective suppression. The PM was also too seasoned a political operator to march into the trap of resentment. As he told Osborne: 'I am not going to be the person who didn't want Boris back.'

The Chancellor, for his part, was pleased by the co-operative spirit in which Johnson approached the 2014 Budget – which, as ever, included a number of decisions relevant to London. In 2010, the Mayor had signalled his readiness to resign over the funding of Crossrail, the new commuter service that required twenty-six miles of new tunnels, and had often chosen the prelude to a Budget to fire off a shell or two from his T54. Not this time: all was sweetness and light between the two men – for now.

Meanwhile, Osborne's closest Cabinet ally, Gove, was candid when asked at a dinner hosted by Rupert Murdoch at his Mayfair home about Boris's credentials as a future Prime Minister – or lack of them. In answer to a specific question, the Education Secretary said that 'the job is very difficult, and David Cameron does it exceedingly well'. Only William Hague and Osborne, Gove continued, had the necessary calm and resolve to be plausible successors in Number Ten. Naturally, he was asked after the dinner (held in December) about what exactly he had said. Gove insisted that his intention had not been to sabotage Boris at the media tycoon's table – only to give an honest answer to a tricky question. But he did not seek to correct the consequent impression around Westminster that he believed Johnson was not up to the top job. There had been rumours of a Boris–Gove axis quietly cementing itself in preparation for 2015, as the canny Education Secretary transferred his allegiance from the Chancellor to the Mayor: these rumours were clearly, as one aide to Gove put it, 'total bollocks'.

The fixation of the media with Boris was also a distraction from the passage of time and the impatient demand of new political cohorts for recognition and their hour in the sun. On the Labour side, the antics of the two Eds sometimes seemed no more than a prelude to the era of the generation to follow: Chuka Umunna, Rachel Reeves and others. On the Tory side, the elevation of Sajid Javid to the Cabinet as Culture Secretary on 9 April was a similar break with the past.

Javid replaced Maria Miller, whose departure was a parable of much broader political dysfunctions and tensions. Instructed to pay back £5,800 in wrongly claimed expenses, she had compounded the error by making an insultingly brief apology in the Commons. Cameron, insistent as never before that he was not going to be told whom to hire and fire by the media, was as stubborn as he had ever been in defending a colleague. But the press would not let up and, in the end, its coverage, rather than the original wrongdoing, became the issue. Miller could not stay in post because she had become, as she said in her resignation letter, a 'distraction'.

Cameron's supporters said that his backing for Miller reflected his innate loyalty. The counter-argument was that the PM, in refusing to sack her quickly, had been doing Farage's work for him: exemplifying the arrogant disdain of the political elite for the taxpayers who subsidized MPs' expenses. Miller had steered same-sex marriage through the Commons, which meant that many traditionalist Tory MPs resented her. She had also managed the Leveson reforms, which had won her no friends in the print media. The Cameron government had not yet marked its fourth birthday. But it had been in power long enough to have chickens coming home to roost – squawking and panicking, a chaos of political feathers.

What would come next? Aged forty-four, Javid fell into the same

In It Together

generational bracket as Cameron, Osborne, Johnson et al. But he represented a quite different cohort, an acolyte of the Chancellor but unblemished by the factional wars of 2001–6 over modernization versus traditionalism. Nor was he a product of Eton and Oxford (or a close variable), a Bullingdon boy with half an eye on Number Ten in his undergraduate days. The son of a British-Pakistani bus driver, Javid was the incarnation of Toryism-as-aspiration, having pursued a highly successful career in banking, culminating in a board position at Deutsche Bank International Limited. His elevation was widely reported as a triumph for Osborne, but it was clearly much more than that. Like Howard's appointment in 2005 of Cameron and Osborne as Shadow Education Secretary and Shadow Chancellor respectively, it felt like the start of a new chapter. Behind Javid was a group of true-blue Tories, mostly neo-Thatcherite in their prescriptions, waiting to stake their claim: Kwasi Kwarteng, Priti Patel, Dominic Raab, Chris Skidmore and others. There were also young modernizers like Gavin Barwell, now a government whip, rising through the ranks.

Javid was the first Asian male Tory to achieve Cabinet rank. But the social composition of his colleagues around the table was such that it seemed more significant that he had not been to Oxford or Cambridge and that he had been educated at a comprehensive school. When Gove had remarked in a *Financial Times* interview that the number of Etonians in the Government was 'preposterous', he emphasized that he liked the individuals concerned and was making a point about the failures of state education, not the evil influence of one particular school.[7] Cameron was furious with the Education Secretary and let him know, directly. 'He was not delighted,' Gove was heard to mutter – like someone who had just been to see the headmaster.

Javid's appointment might be a false dawn, a flash in the pan. But – at the time, at least – it felt like the beginning of a different phase in Conservative politics, and a drama enacted by a new cast of players. The curtain had yet to fall on Cameron, of course. He urged his manifesto team to think about a second term plan fizzing with the modern Conservative virtues of prosperity, home ownership and school independence. He dealt with Clegg as often as ever, holding the Coalition together with gaffer tape and patience. He awaited the triple test of the European elections, Scottish referendum and the grand battle of 2015, with – what?

Trepidation, certainly. But also with the confidence born of confounding those who had said the Coalition would collapse after six months, or two years, or four; that there would be a triple-dip recession; that he himself would be deposed by his own regicidal party. In his private moments, this Prime Minister always appealed to political logic and the irresistible force of English common sense. It was, he knew, a risky approach, since politics so often defied common sense. But it meshed with his character and his core beliefs. Deploying this method, he simply could not see Miliband as Prime Minister – a failure of imagination that might, in the end, cost him dearly. Yet that was how he felt, and there was no point in pretending otherwise. In any case, he was not ready to leave. Caught between Left and Right, confined by coalition, besieged by Ukip and already a veteran party leader, David Cameron remained, at heart, a village cricketer who was not yet willing to draw stumps, still certain that he could get that elusive century.

Acknowledgements

A book of this sort bears one name on the cover but reflects the collaboration, assistance, patience, friendship and love of many. If it takes a village to raise a child, then it certainly takes a newsroom to train a hack.

I owe a huge debt to Caroline Michel, my wonderful agent, for believing in me and in this book, for her friendship and for her wise counsel.

Thank you to all at Penguin who guided me from idea to publication: Will Hammond, Mark Handsley, Anna Ridley, Victoria Philpott, Chantal Noel, Keith Taylor, Nicola Evans, David Hirst, Dave Cradduck and Cat Hillerton. As I was finishing off this book, Tom Weldon was appointed CEO of Penguin Random House UK. I doubt the two facts are related but I am still grateful for his energetic support.

Above all, my heartfelt thanks to Venetia Butterfield. People say she is the best editor in the business, for the simple reason that she is. It has been a delight and a privilege to work with her.

I was thrilled, too, to be reunited with my former *Times* and *Spectator* comrade, Peter Brookes. He is an incomparable political artist and I am honoured that he agreed to provide the cartoon for the cover.

Gold medals for patience go to the three editors for whom I write columns: Ian MacGregor at the *Sunday Telegraph*; Sarah Sands at the *Evening Standard*; and Dylan Jones at GQ. I thank them all for tolerating the distraction of this book and the encouragement and friendship they gave me.

Thanks to the Sex Pistols, Joy Division and Richard Wagner for providing the soundtrack, and Diet Coke and Starbucks for always being there.

Many friends cheered me on, up or both: in particular, Sarah and Johnnie Standing (and all the Hugh Street gang), Melissa Kite, Ann

Scott, D.-J. Collins, John Gray, Simon Mason, Pete Hoskin, Marcus Kiggell, Anya Hindmarch, Jane Miles, Patrick Hennessy, Simone Finn, Kate Maltby, Lisa Hilton and Tessa Jowell. Caroline Dalmeny provided wondrous hospitality and a beautiful place to work. Thank you to each and every one.

Bryan Forbes and Nanette Newman were always generous in their support. It is a measure of Bryan's influence and achievement that his death has left so many feeling bereft. But his inspiration, which I salute, survives: rich and strong.

Above all, I send love and thanks to my family: my two brothers, Pad and Mick, and *their* families. My great good fortune has been to find myself poised between two vintage generations of d'Anconas. My beloved sons, Zac and Teddy, are the heart of my life, and the best of it. Their paternal grandparents – my mother and father – have given me more over the years than I can possibly express. They are my hero and heroine. This book is for them.

M. d'A.

References

Preface: In it together

1 The modern quest for a rhetoric and politics of collaboration is beauti-
fully charted in Richard Sennett, *Together: The Rituals, Pleasures and
Politics of Cooperation* (Penguin Books, 2013).

2 As Alan Macfarlane showed in his *The Origins of English Individualism:
Family, Property and Social Transition* (Wiley, 1978).

3 See, for instance, Polly Toynbee and David Walker, *Dogma and Disarray:
Cameron at Half-Time* (Granta Publications, 2012).

1. 'How the hell did this happen?'

1 'David Cameron: My credo for my country', *Daily Telegraph*, 2 April 2010.

2 I first encountered him when we were briefly colleagues at *The Times*.
The next time I had a conversation with him he was already Political
Secretary to William Hague.

3 Interview, Cabinet minister.

4 Conversation, Brown adviser.

5 Private information.

6 Interview, Conservative adviser.

7 See Nick Boles, *Which Way's Up? The Future for Coalition Britain and How
to Get There* (Biteback Publishing, 2010), p. 131: 'I want to conclude this
book by urging David Cameron and Nick Clegg to announce this
autumn that they want their parties to agree to an electoral pact for the
general election due on 7 May 2015.' Such a proposal did yet seem out-
landish when the book was published in September 2010.

8 See Peter Snowdon, *Back from the Brink: The Inside Story of the Tory Resurrection* (HarperPress, 2010); Simon Walters, *Tory Wars: Conservatives in
Crisis* (Politico's Publishing Limited, 2001); for a fuller account of the
history of the modernizers, see Matthew d'Ancona, 'Last Chance

Saloon: The History and Future of Tory Modernisation', in Ryan Short-house and Guy Stagg (eds), *Tory Modernisation 2:0 – The Future of the Conservative Party* (Bright Blue, 2010).

9 M. Portillo, 'The Ghost of Toryism Past: Spirit of Conservatism Future' (CPS, 1997).

10 The best account of the election-that-never-was is to be found on the blog of Damian McBride, Brown's communications chief: http://dpmcbride. tumblr.com.

11 See Dennis Kavanagh and Philip Cowley, *The British General Election of 2010* (Palgrave Macmillan, 2010); Michael Ashcroft, *Minority Verdict: The Conservative Party, the Voters and the 2010 Election* (Biteback Publishing, 2010), especially pp. 112–24. Tim Bale's magnificent *The Conservative Party from Thatcher to Cameron* (Polity Press, 2010) is indispensable on this failure and much else besides. Even before polling day, Bale had iden-tified the core problem that would deny Cameron outright victory: Tim Bale, 'The Tories: a contaminated brand', *Guardian*, 22 April 2010. See also, d'Ancona, 'Last Chance Saloon'.

12 Interview, senior Conservative.

13 See Paddy Ashdown, *The Ashdown Diaries: Volume One. 1988–1997* (Allen Lane, 2000) and *Volume Two. 1997–1999* (Allen Lane, 2001). The talks continued long after the first New Labour landslide, reflecting Blair's early enthusiasm for a centre-Left realignment that would thwart the Conservative Party's recovery indefinitely.

14 Isabel Oakeshott, Jonathan Oliver and Marie Woolf, 'Nick Clegg: I will not prop up Gordon Brown', *Sunday Times*, 25 April 2010.

15 Interview, senior Liberal Democrat.

16 The best account of Labour's negotiations with Clegg is to be found in Andrew Adonis, *5 Days in May: The Coalition and Beyond* (Biteback Pub-lishing, 2013).

17 The substance of the talks is covered in Adonis, *5 Days in May*; Rob Wilson, *5 Days to Power: The Journey to Coalition* (Biteback Publishing, 2010); David Laws, *22 Days in May: The Birth of the Lib Dem-Conservative Coalition* (Biteback Publishing, 2010); Adam Boulton and Joey Jones, *Hung Together: The 2010 Election and the Coalition Government* (Simon & Schuster, 2010); and Jasper Gerard, *The Clegg Coup: Britain's First Coalition Government Since Lloyd George* (Gibson Square, 2011).

18 Simon Hattenstone interview, *Guardian*, 29 April 2013.

19 Cyril Connolly, *Enemies of Promise* (André Deutsch,1996), pp. 271, 274.

2. *Rose Garden: one plan, two guv'nors*

1 Steve Hilton and Giles Gibbons, *Good Business: Your World Needs You* (Texere Publishing, 2002).

2 *The Spectator*, 18 March 2006.

3 *Sun*, 14 January 2009.

4 See Ben Yong, 'Formation of the Coalition', in Robert Hazell and Ben Yong (eds), *The Politics of Coalition: How the Conservative–Liberal Democrat Government Works* (Hart Publishing, 2012).

5 Interview, Department for Business, Innovation and Skills source.

6 These boasts were to get Cable into hot water, in a *Daily Telegraph* sting operation that had profound consequences for the Government – see pp. 65–70.

7 This caricature is based on a partial reading of the excellent updated biography of the PM by Francis Elliott and James Hanning, *Cameron: Practically a Conservative* (Fourth Estate, 2012), p. 437.

8 Interview, senior Cameron ally.

9 Interview, Number Ten official. See also Robert Hazell, 'How the Coalition Works at the Centre', in Hazell and Yong (eds), *Politics of Coalition*, pp. 49–70.

10 See Jonathan Powell, *The New Machiavelli: How to Wield Power in the Modern World* (Bodley Head, 2010).

11 Interview, Whitehall source.

12 The programme is most easily found online at http://www.cabinet office.gov.uk.

13 Hazell, 'How the Coalition Works at the Centre', p. 55.

3. *Attention deficit*

1 For a fine account of Osborne's first days as Chancellor, and much else, see Janan Ganesh, *George Osborne: The Austerity Chancellor* (Biteback Publishing, 2012); for the fascinating testimony of one of the key protagonists, see David Laws, *22 Days in May: The Birth of the Lib Dem–Conservative Coalition* (Biteback Publishing, 2010), pp. 202–61.

2 Ibid. See also Peter Mandelson, *The Third Man: Life at the Heart of New Labour* (HarperPress, 2010), pp. 462–3.

3 Laws, *22 Days in May*, p. 232.

4 According to one well-sourced account, Huhne tried to warn Clegg off the whole project. See Jasper Gerard, *The Clegg Coup: Britain's First Coalition Government since Lloyd George* (Gibson Square, 2011), p. 185.

5 Laws, *22 Days in May*, p. 237.

6 Ibid., p. 239.

7 For the Tory leader's pre-election thinking on the NHS ring-fence, and much else besides, see the indispensable interviews recorded in *Cameron on Cameron: Conversations with Dylan Jones* (Fourth Estate, 2010).

8 Fraser Nelson, 'They wish we all could be Californian', *The Spectator*, 27 February 2009.

9 Conversation, senior Cameroon.

10 See Richard H. Thaler and Cass R. Sunstein, *Nudge: Improving Decisions about Health, Wealth and Happiness* (Penguin Books, 2009); Robert B. Cialdini, *Influence: The Psychology of Persuasion* (HarperBusiness, 2007); Mark Earls, *Herd: How to Change Mass Behaviour by Harnessing Our True Nature* (John Wiley & Sons, 2009).

11 See Joshua Foer, *Moonwalking With Einstein: The Art and Science of Remembering Everything* (Allen Lane, 2011).

4. 'I wasn't really leading'

1 Interview, senior Lib Dem source.

2 For a useful account of the tuition fees row, see Chris Bowers, *Nick Clegg: The Biography* (Biteback Publishing, 2012), pp. 206–10, 264–75. Also: Peter Waller and Ben Yong, 'Case Studies II: Tuition Fees, NHS Reform, and Nuclear Policy', in Robert Hazell and Ben Yong (eds), *The Politics of Coalition: How the Conservative–Liberal Democrat Government Works* (Hart Publishing, 2012), pp. 173–6.

3 Quoted in Waller and Yong, 'Case Studies II', p. 175.

4 *Daily Telegraph*, 21, 22 and 23 December 2010. In May 2011, the Press Complaints Commission reprimanded the newspaper over the sting, declaring itself 'not convinced that the public interest was such as to justify proportionately this level of subterfuge'. This is a matter of

opinion: the story provided fresh insight into what Lib Dem ministers really thought about their Conservative partners, and – as a consequence – the true strength of the Coalition.

5 See 'The Peace in the Feud', in Max Gluckman, *Custom and Conflict in Africa* (Blackwell, 1956), pp. 1–26.

6 Conversation, senior Lib Dem.

7 'Exclusive – News Corp executive suspected of "orchestrating" leak', Reuters, 22 July 2011. Even at the Leveson Inquiry, Lewis declined to comment on the allegation that he had been involved in the leak to Peston.

8 *Guardian*, November 2010.

9 Conversation, senior Cameroon.

10 See 'Electoral Reform and the Alternative Vote', in Vernon Bogdanor, *The Coalition and the Constitution* (Hart Publishing, 2011), pp. 81–105. Tim Montgomerie's superb account of the referendum campaign can be found at http://conservativehome.blogs.com/avstory.

11 Quoted in Bogdanor, *Coalition and the Constitution*, p. 101.

12 See ibid., p. 96.

13 David Sanders, Harold D. Clarke, Marianne C. Stewart and Paul Whiteley, 'Simulating the Effects of the Alternative Vote in the 2010 General Election', *Parliamentary Affairs* (2010), pp. 1–19.

14 Quoted in Bogdanor, *Coalition and the Constitution*, p. 105.

15 http://ukelectiontrend.blogspot.co.uk/2010/07/how-is-av-polling-trending.html.

16 As did the present author. See 'By choosing Ed Miliband, Labour has handed David Cameron the next election', *Sunday Telegraph*, 26 September 2010. Miliband's success in maintaining party unity caused me and other commentators to revise our opinions of him.

17 The author, the journalist Melissa Kite, unmasked herself in June 2010, after a long controversy over Tamzin's true identity – suspects including both Camerons, Toby Young, Boris Johnson and many others. When the magazine produced T-shirts for young female Tory researchers declaring 'It's Not Me!', they were snapped up quickly.

18 Patrick Wintour, 'Chris Huhne accuses cabinet colleague of Nazi tactics over AV referendum', *Guardian*, 30 May 2011.

19 http://conservativehome.blogs.com/avstory.

20 Matt Chorley, 'Nick Clegg: Deputy PM rages against Cameron "lies" ', *Independent on Sunday*, 24 April 2011.

21 Interview, senior Lib Dem.

22 Interview, Number Ten official.

5. *Political benefits: the fraught politics of welfare*

1 http://www.britishpoliticalspeech.org/speech-archive.htm?speech=315. The first leadership contender to make prominent use of the phrase 'broken society' was Liam Fox in an interview with the *Sunday Telegraph* on 12 June 2005.

2 Boris Johnson, 'What on earth has come over our aimless, feckless, hopeless youth?', *Daily Telegraph*, 19 August 2008.

3 Nicholas Timmins, *The Five Giants: A Biography of the Welfare State* (rev. edn, HarperCollins, 2001), p. 360.

4 Matthew d'Ancona, 'The row over child benefit obscures the radicalism of David Cameron's plans', *Sunday Telegraph*, 9 October 2010.

5 Simon Walters and Brendan Carlin, 'Revealed: the blazing row between Iain Duncan Smith and George Osborne . . . and the tough-talking woman at the centre of it', *Mail on Sunday*, 22 August 2010.

6 Nigel Lawson, *The View from No. 11: Memoirs of a Tory Radical* (Corgi, 1993), p. 383.

7 Speech to the Resolution Foundation, 26 January 2012, accessible on libdems.org.uk.

8 Richard Wachman and Oliver Wright, 'Fear of fitness to work tests driving disabled patients to suicide, say 6% of GPs', *Independent*, 4 October 2012.

9 'Reviewer of fitness-to-work benefit tests to stand down', *BBC News*, 30 July 2012.

10 Rajeev Syal, 'DWP to blame for fitness-to-work tests fiasco, MPs say', *Guardian*, 8 February 2013.

11 Nicholas Watt, Patrick Wintour and Shiv Malik, 'Government U-turn on work scheme', *Guardian*, 29 February 2012.

6. 'So big, you can see it from space'

1 A gripping account of Lansley's policy programme and its fortunes is to be found in Nicholas Timmins, *Never Again? The Story of the Health and Social Care Act 2012* (The King's Fund/The Institute for Government, 2012). See also Peter Waller and Ben Yong, 'Case Studies II: Tuition Fees, NHS Reform, and Nuclear Policy', in Robert Hazell and Ben Yong (eds), *The Politics of Coalition: How the Conservative–Liberal Democrat Government Works* (Hart Publishing, 2012).

2 And of *The Spectator*, which I edited at the time. The magazine took the view that grammar schools were one of the very few proven engines of social mobility.

3 Timmins, *Never Again?*, p. 38.

4 'David Cameron: There is such a thing as society . . . and we must start to value it', *Yorkshire Post*, 13 May 2008.

5 http://www.conservatives.com/News/Speeches/2009/05/David_Cameron_Speech_to_the_Royal_College_of_Nursing.aspx.

6 'Invitation to Join the Government of Britain', The Conservative Manifesto 2010, p. 45.

7 Waller and Yong, *Politics of Coalition*, p. 179.

8 Nigel Lawson, *The View from No. 11: Memoirs of a Tory Radical* (Corgi, 1993), p. 613.

9 Timmins, *Never Again?*, p. 55.

10 *The Times*, 28 February 2011.

11 See Chris Bowers, *Nick Clegg: The Biography* (Biteback Publishing, 2012), p. 275.

12 Timmins, *Never Again?*, p. 87.

13 Owen, a cross-bencher in the Lords, had been, like Williams, one of the original 'Gang of Four' founders of the SDP. He also strongly opposed the bill, which he considered 'fatally flawed'.

14 *Daily Telegraph*, 15 June 2011.

15 To declare an interest: I founded 'Coffee House' as Editor of *The Spectator*, drawing inspiration from the eighteenth-century founders of the magazine and the intellectual, gossipy milieu from which they had arisen.

7. Civil action: the Gove revolution

1 Rosa Prince, 'Michael Gove: wasteful school building programme to be axed', *Daily Telegraph*, 5 July 2010.

2 See, for example, William J. Bennett and others, *The Educated Child: A Parent's Guide from Preschool through Eighth Grade* (Free Press, 2000).

3 Matthew d'Ancona, 'I will be the one, and the Conservatives will be the party, offering genuine change . . . Do you want to hand the keys back to the people who crashed the car?', *Sunday Telegraph*, 6 January 2013.

4 See Michael Gove, *Celsius 7/7* (Weidenfeld & Nicolson, 2006).

5 Especially in the monstrous figure of Nicholas Pratt: 'Sometimes it was great festivals of privilege, and at other times it was the cringing and envy of others that confirmed one's sense of being at the top. Sometimes it was the seduction of a pretty girl that accomplished this important task and at other times it was down to one's swanky cufflinks.' Edward St Aubyn, *Never Mind* (Picador, 2012), p. 151.

6 For an explanation by another Etonian, see Charles Moore, 'The Spectator's Notes', *The Spectator*, 10 May 2008: 'Just because Collegers and Oppidans are both Etonians, it should not be supposed that there is a natural alliance between the two. David Cameron is a typical Oppidan of the top class. Boris Johnson is a typical Colleger ditto.'

7 See Cherie Booth and Cate Haste, *The Goldfish Bowl: Married to the Prime Minister 1955–1997* (Chatto and Windus, 1994).

8 See Melissa Benn, *School Wars: The Battle for Britain's Education* (Verso, 2011), and Millar's blog http://www.thetruthaboutourschools.com/.

9 Tim Shipman, 'Return of the O-Level: Gove announces radical plan to scrap GCSEs "to ensure UK has a world-class education system" but lack of consultation angers Lib Dems', *Daily Mail*, 21 June 2012.

10 Peter Walker, 'Gove's schools vision: back-to-basics with "a thorough grounding for life"', *Guardian*, 7 February 2013.

11 Jonathan Rose, *The Intellectual Life of the British Working Classes* (Yale University Press, 2001).

12 See Toby Young, *How to Set Up a Free School* (Penguin Books, 2011).

13 A battle well described in Andrew Adonis, *Education, Education, Education: Reforming England's Schools* (Biteback Publishing, 2012).

14 http://www.bbc.co.uk/news/uk-politics-11156963.

15 Fraser Nelson, 'Pay attention in class! Michael Gove is teaching the art of politics', *Daily Telegraph*, 16 November 2012.

16 James Cusick, '"Dump f***ing everyone": the inside story of how Michael Gove's vicious attack dogs are terrorising the DfE', *Independent*, 15 February 2013.

17 http://www.mirror.co.uk/news/uk-news/tim-loughton-sacked-minister-in-astonishing-1538388.

18 Toby Helm, 'Are dark arts spinning out of control in Michael Gove's department?', *Observer*, 3 February 2013.

8. 'A huge event in the life of the nation'

1 In Michael Cockerell's BBC film, *Boris Johnson: The Irresistible Rise*.

2 For analysis of the riots, their roots and their consequences, see: Daniel Briggs (ed.), *The English Riots of 2011: A Summer of Discontent* (Waterside Press, 2012); David Lammy, *Out of the Ashes: Britain after the Riots* (Guardian Books, 2011); Dan Roberts (ed.), *Reading the Riots: Investigating England's Summer of Disorder* (Guardian Shorts, 2011); Kieran Yates and Nikesh Shukla, *Generation Vexed: What the English Riots Don't Tell Us about Our Nation's Youth* (Vintage Digital, 2011).

3 See Sonia Purnell, *Just Boris: A Tale of Blond Ambition* (Aurum, 2011), pp. 430ff.

4 See Roberts (ed.), *Reading the Riots*, p. 85.

5 House of Commons Home Affairs Committee, *Policing Large Scale Disorder: Lessons from the Disturbances of August 2011*, Sixteenth Report of Session 2010–12, 19 December 2011, pp. 28–9.

6 John-Paul Ford Rojas, 'UK riots: Sir Hugh Orde says politicians were "irrelevance" in quelling violence', *Daily Telegraph*, 12 August 2011.

7 Matthew d'Ancona, 'UK riots: zero tolerance promises Cameron – but will this be his finest hour?', *Sunday Telegraph*, 14 August 2011.

8 See, for example, Melissa Kite, 'The ambivalence of Theresa May', *GQ*, April 2011.

9 See *TLQ* interview with Bratton, reprinted in *Sunday Telegraph* (www.tlqmedia.com).

10 See Kunal Dutta et al., 'Exclusive: PM's plan to import US adviser angers police chiefs', *Independent on Sunday*, 14 August 2011.

11 Ibid.

12 Before he worked for Nick Clegg, Richard Reeves wrote an excellent scholarly exploration of Cameron's philosophical roots: 'This is David Cameron', *Public Policy Research*, June–August 2008, pp. 63–7.

13 Roberts (ed.), *Reading the Riots*, pp. 39–40.

14 For a brilliant analysis of viral rioting in Sydney in December 2005, see Mark Earls, *Herd: How to Change Mass Behaviour by Harnessing Our True Nature* (John Wiley & Sons, 2007).

15 Roberts (ed.), *Reading the Riots*, pp. 72–3.

16 Ibid., p. 60.

17 Lammy, *Out of the Ashes*, p. 54.

18 See Richard H. Thaler and Cass R. Sunstein, *Nudge: Improving Decisions about Health, Wealth and Happiness* (Yale University Press, 2008), and Robert B. Cialdini, *Influence: The Psychology of Persuasion* (HarperBusiness, 2007). For Cameron's dilemma, see Matthew d'Ancona, 'David Cameron's love of marriage faces its greatest test', *Evening Standard*, 18 January 2010.

19 'Tackling Troubled Families: New Plans Unveiled', available at www.number10.gov.uk/news/tackling-troubled-families-new-plans-unveiled.

20 Roberts (ed.), *After the Riots*, p. 7.

21 Ibid., p. 8.

22 Ibid.

23 Ibid., p. 13.

24 Vikram Dodd, '2011 riots inquiry recommendations ignored by government, says Lammy', *Guardian*, 29 March 2013.

9. Gamble in the desert: the war against Gaddafi

1 Michael Gove, *Celsius 7/7* (Weidenfeld & Nicolson, 2006).

2 See, for example, Sandy Gall, *War Against the Taliban: Why It All Went Wrong in Afghanistan* (Bloomsbury, 2012); Sherard Cowper-Coles, *Cables From Kabul: The Inside Story of the West's Afghanistan* (HarperPress, 2011); Toby Harnden, *Dead Men Risen: The Welsh Guards and the Defining Story of Britain's War in Afghanistan* (Quercus, 2011); Bob Woodward, *Obama's*

Wars: The Inside Story (Simon & Schuster, 2010); Jonathan Alter, *The Promise: President Obama Year One* (Simon & Schuster, 2010).

3 Rachel Sylvester, 'Liam Fox, new Defence Secretary, flies flag for our boys and Eurosceptics', *The Times*, 21 May 2010.

4 William Hague, 'The Arab Spring is more important than 9/11', *The Times*, 23 March 2011.

5 For an incisive guide to the changing tactics and strategy of the Libyan dictator, see Daniel Kawczynski, *Seeking Gaddafi* (Dialogue, 2010).

6 Nicholas Watt and Patrick Wintour, 'Libya no-fly zone call by France fails to get David Cameron's backing', *Guardian*, 23 February 2011.

7 'Libya: David Cameron warns Col Gaddafi of "consequences"', *Daily Telegraph*, 24 February 2011.

8 For a sense of the horror Cameron's team did not wish to be repeated in Libya, see David Rohde, *A Safe Area: Srebrenica: Europe's Worst Massacre since the Second World War* (Pocket Books, 1997).

9 Patrick Wintour and Aida Edemariam, 'Libyan crisis: Kenneth Clarke warns UK at risk of new Lockerbie', *Guardian*, 25 March 2011.

10 Sam Coates and Roland Watson, 'Tories split as Gove demands tougher line on tackling dictators', *The Times*, 3 March 2011.

11 Chris McGreal and Patrick Wintour, 'William Hague on back foot over "James Bond" Libya mission', *Guardian*, 7 March 2011.

12 Patrick Hennessy, 'Missing my mojo? Of course not', *Sunday Telegraph*, 13 March 2011.

13 Samantha Power, 'Bystanders to Genocide', *The Atlantic*, September 2001.

14 Helene Cooper and Steven Lee Myers, 'Obama takes hard line with Libya after shift by Clinton', *The New York Times*, 18 March 2011.

15 See Patrick Wintour and Nicholas Watt, 'David Cameron's Libyan war: why the PM felt Gaddafi had to be stopped', *Guardian*, 2 October 2011.

16 See Francis Elliott and James Hanning, *Cameron: Practically a Conservative* (Fourth Estate, 2012), pp. 471–3.

17 http://www.publications.parliament.uk/pa/cm201012/cmselect/cmfaff/881/11031601.htm.

18 Rupert Smith, *The Utility of Force: The Art of War in the Modern World* (Penguin Books, 2006).

19 Wintour and Watt, 'David Cameron's Libyan war'.

20 Barack Obama and David Cameron, 'Not just special, but an essential relationship', *The Times*, 24 May 2011.

21 James Chapman and James White, 'Fox admits friend Adam Werritty was present during 18 trips overseas and visited him at MoD 22 times', *Daily Mail*, 10 October 2011.

10. The ballad of Steve and Jeremy

1 Walter Isaacson, *Steve Jobs* (Little, Brown, 2011), p. 405.

2 Interview, Cabinet minister.

3 For a more balanced profile of Hilton, see Melissa Kite, 'Mr Blue Sky', *GQ*, December 2011. Also Patrick Wintour and Tania Branigan, ' "David's brain" transforms Tory brand', *Guardian*, 2 December 2006.

4 See Jesse Norman, *The Big Society: The Anatomy of the New Politics* (University of Buckingham Press, 2010).

5 *Daily Telegraph*, 4 December 2006.

6 Conversation, Number Ten official.

7 Conversation, Department for Communities and Local Government source.

8 See Ferdinand Mount, *The New Few or, A Very British Oligarchy* (Simon & Schuster, 2012), p. 245.

9 *Daily Telegraph*, 23 May 2012.

10 For a summary of the long-raging arguments, see Hugo Young, *This Blessed Plot: Britain and Europe from Churchill to Blair* (Macmillan, 1998), and David Charter, *Au Revoir, Europe: What If Britain Left the EU?* (Biteback Publishing, 2012).

11 George Parker and Jim Pickard, 'Hilton wants to abolish maternity leave', *Financial Times*, 27 July 2011.

12 Tamara Cohen, 'Don't block our reforms, Francis Maude tells civil servants', *Daily Mail*, 2 October 2012.

13 Sue Cameron, 'Civil servants "hacked off" by Cameron', *Financial Times*, 14 March 2011.

14 Conversation, senior Conservative source.

15 Chris Bowlby, 'Profile: Jeremy Heywood – the next Cabinet Secretary', bbc.co.uk/news, 21 October 2011. For extended profiles, see Quentin Letts, 'I am in charge', *The Spectator*, 17 March 2012; Amelia

Gentleman, 'Sir Jeremy Heywood: the civil servant propping up the government', *Guardian*, 6 December 2012.

16 http://www.levesoninquiry.org.uk/wp-content/uploads/2012/06/Transcript-of-Afternoon-Hearing-11-June-2012.txt.

17 See Matthew d'Ancona, 'All the policies are in place: now it's time for delivery', *Sunday Telegraph*, 3 March 2012.

18 Sam Coates, 'Four men with four plans for growth . . . Cabinet Secretary reveals tension at top', *The Times*, 22 April 2013.

11. The Boris Situation

1 For Johnson's own account of the Games, see his prologue to *The Spirit of London* (HarperPress, 2011), pp. ix–xxxiii. For biographical details, see Andrew Gimson, *Boris: The Rise of Boris Johnson* (Simon & Schuster, 2012); Sonia Purnell, *Just Boris: A Tale of Blond Ambition* (Aurum, 2011). For an insider's account of Johnson's electoral success in London, see Alex Crowley, *Victory in London: The Inside Story of the Boris Campaign* (Bretwalda Books, 2012).

2 Johnson, *Spirit of London*, p. xxviii.

3 Peter Ackroyd, *London: The Biography* (Vintage, 2001), p. 779.

4 Matthew d'Ancona, 'London 2012 Olympics: The Games can be a beacon of aspiration amid the gloom', *Sunday Telegraph*, 22 July 2012.

5 Johnson, *Spirit of London*, p. xxiv.

6 Hélène Mulholland, 'Boris Johnson gets stuck on a zip-wire celebrating Olympic gold', *Guardian*, 1 August 2012.

7 On which, see Peter Oborne's masterpiece of modern sociology, *The Triumph of the Political Class* (Simon & Schuster, 2007). In 2009, Toby Young, a comprehensive boy who went to the same Oxford college as Cameron (Brasenose), co-wrote and co-produced a Channel 4 docu-drama, *When Boris Met Dave*, initially broadcast on More4. Young characterized Cameron as the 'smooth operator' and Johnson 'the silverback gorilla, the alpha male'.

8 Boris Johnson, 'What on earth has come over our aimless, feckless, hopeless youth?', *Daily Telegraph*, 19 August 2008.

9 Boris Johnson, 'Britain needs immigrants, but it also needs tough border controls', *Daily Telegraph*, 13 September 2010.

10 http://nymag.com/news/intelligencer/encounter/boris-johnson-2012-6/index1.html

11 Crowley, *Victory in London*, p. 30.

12. Omnishambles

1 Matthew d'Ancona, 'Everything you thought you knew about Ed Balls is wrong (ok, almost everything)', *GQ*, October 2011.

2 HM Revenue & Customs, 'The Exchequer effect of the 50 per cent additional rate of income tax', March 2012.

3 At the heart of this scandal lurked the suggestion that members of the Brown Government were encouraging Barclays to submit misleadingly low figures for the Libor – the rate at which banks claim that they borrow from each other. The mismanagement of interest rates during the crisis accounted for a substantial part of the £290m fine imposed on the bank by the Financial Services Authority. In a remarkable *Spectator* interview, Osborne claimed that Brown's circle 'were clearly involved, and we just haven't heard the full facts yet'.

4 For one such survey, see http://conservativehome.blogs.com/thetorydiary/2012/10/nearly-everything-youve-ever-read-about-the-tory-brand-problem-is-wrong.html.

5 Robert Winnett, 'WikiLeaks: Barack Obama regarded David Cameron as "lightweight"', *Daily Telegraph*, 30 November 2010.

6 HM Revenue & Customs, *VAT:* 'Addressing borderline anomalies: Consultation document', March 2012.

7 http://conservativehome.blogs.com/platform/2012/04/maathe-real-ukip-threat.html

13. Banging on

1 http://www.publications.parliament.uk/pa/cm201213/cmselect/cmfaff/writev/futunion/m15a.htm.

2 For a riveting account of the tests and Blair's frustration at their results, see Robert Peston, *Brown's Britain* (Short Books, 2005).

3 See Douglas Carswell, *The End of Politics and the Birth of iDemocracy* (Biteback Publishing, 2012).

4 William Hague, 'No more powers should be moved from Britain to the EU', *Sunday Telegraph*, 9 January 2011.

5 Isabel Hardman, 'The court threat that stopped David Cameron from abolishing the 1922 Committee', *Coffee House*, 25 April 2013.

6 The best account of the whips' office – albeit in a different era – is to be found in Gyles Brandreth, *Breaking the Code: The Brandreth Diaries: Westminster Diaries, 1992–97* (Phoenix, 2000).

7 'Review of the Balance of Competences between the United Kingdom and the European Union', presented to Parliament by the Secretary of State for Foreign and Commonwealth Affairs, July 2012.

8 For a thoughtful account of this development and its implications, see David Charter, *Au Revoir, Europe: What If Britain Left the EU?* (Biteback Publishing, 2012).

9 Simon Walters, '"We're ready to walk out on Europe": Prime Minister's closest ally Michael Gove sparks EU furore with dramatic admission', *Mail on Sunday*, 14 October 2012.

10 David Cameron interview, *Sunday Telegraph*, 6 January 2013.

11 Nigel Farage, *Flying Free* (Biteback Publishing, 2011).

12 See Andrew Cooper, 'How Philip Gould Helped to Save the Conservative Party', in Dennis Kavanagh (ed.), *Philip Gould: An Unfinished Life* (Palgrave Macmillan, 2012), pp. 132–51.

14. Paper value: hacking and Leveson

1 The chronology of the case and the inquiry that followed are well covered in two Guardian Shorts – e-books on *Phone Hacking* and *The Leveson Inquiry*. Even Watson's political enemies made copious use of his engrossing book, co-authored with Martin Hickman, *Dial M for Murdoch: News Corporation and the Corruption of Britain* (Allen Lane, 2012).

2 Full disclosure: my own mobile phone was apparently hacked. My account of the experience appeared in *GQ*, June 2012.

3 See Watson and Hickman, *Dial M for Murdoch*, p. 193.

4 http://www.bbc.co.uk/news/uk-18245965.

5 Every political era yields an inquiry that is a historical record of a Government's life and times. The Hutton Report was a boring document, but the inquiry that lay behind it is an unequalled treasure trove of

information about the Blair regime. The Leveson Inquiry's website is essential reading (and viewing) for anyone interested in the Coalition: http://www.levesoninquiry.org.uk/.

6 http://www.telegraph.co.uk/news/uknews/9225862/Leveson-Inquiry-Adam-Smith-resigns-as-aide-to-Jeremy-Hunt.html.

7 http://www.guardian.co.uk/media/2012/nov/29/leveson-winners-and-losers.

8 For this aspect of human behaviour, see Margaret Heffernan, *Wilful Blindness: Why We Ignore the Obvious at Our Peril* (Simon & Schuster, 2011).

9 http://hackinginquiry.org/news/milly-dowlers-parents-issue-a-statement-ahead-of-mondays-leveson-vote/.

15. 'The last leader of the Lib Dems'

1 http://www.telegraph.co.uk/news/politics/liberaldemocrats/9246527/Local-elections-Liberal-Democrats-might-not-be-able-to-fight-2015-election-as-independent-force.html.

2 Nigel Lawson, *An Appeal to Reason: A Cool Look at Global Warming* (updated edn, Duckworth Overlook, 2012), p. 104.

3 Interview, *GQ*, May 2013.

4 The inquiry, under Robert Francis QC, into the unusually high mortality rates at the Stafford Hospital had been commissioned by Lansley in June 2010.

16. 'Plebs'

1 Matthew d'Ancona, 'I don't believe that Andrew Mitchell let loose the explosive P-word', *Sunday Telegraph*, 23 September 2012.

2 http://www.thesun.co.uk/sol/homepage/news/politics/4549265/Andrew-Mitchell-insults-police-at-Downing-Street-by-calling-them-fing-plebs.html.

3 http://www.telegraph.co.uk/news/politics/9794120/Sir-Jeremy-Heywood-under-fire-over-Andrew-Mitchell-pleb-gate-investigation.html

4 http://www.guardian.co.uk/politics/2013/mar/31/plebgate-andrew-mitchell-police-leaking.

5 http://www.guardian.co.uk/society/2013/apr/24/number-people-food-banks-triples.

6 Ferdinand Mount, *The New Few, or A Very British Oligarchy* (Simon & Schuster, 2012), p. 261.

7 http://www.guardian.co.uk/politics/2013/may/01/cameron-defends-downing-street-appointments.

8 John Harris, 'If Boris is the answer, you're asking the wrong question', *Guardian*, 6 May 2013, p. 24.

9 http://www.telegraph.co.uk/news/politics/local-elections/10037021/Tories-must-start-listening-to-ordinary-voters-not-their-old-school-chums.html.

10 http://www.guardian.co.uk/commentisfree/2012/nov/21/david-cameron-beats-odds-lord-ashcroft-poll.

17. Trouble and strife

1 See p. 336, n. 9.

2 http://www.guardian.co.uk/lifeandstyle/2012/dec/20/divorces-down-2percent-england-wales.

3 See pp. 153–5.

4 http://www.thetimes.co.uk/tto/opinion/columnists/article3598171.ece.

5 http://www.telegraph.co.uk/news/politics/conservative/9848824/High-ranking-Conservatives-back-gay-marriage-amid-Cabinet-split.html.

6 http://www.publications.parliament.uk/pa/cm201213/cmhansrd/cm130205/debtext/130205-0004.htm.

7 http://www.bbc.co.uk/news/uk-politics-21343387.

8 http://www.publications.parliament.uk/pa/cm201213/cmhansrd/cm130205/debtext/130205-0003.htm#13020551001442.

9 http://www.telegraph.co.uk/news/politics/9136017/Dont-make-gay-marriage-a-priority-say-voters.html.

10 http://www.guardian.co.uk/society/2012/dec/26/voters-back-gay-marriage-poll.

11 http://www.guardian.co.uk/film/2012/sep/28/rupert-everett-memoir-vanished-years.

12 Isabel Oakeshott, 'A broken woman', *Sunday Times*, 10 March 2013.

13 http://www.guardian.co.uk/uk/2013/feb/04/messages-toll-chris-huhne-relationship-son.

18. Eastleigh ever after

1 Hugh Muir, 'Lynton Crosby: the "evil genius" taking Cameron into bare-knuckle politics', *Guardian*, 23 November 2012.

2 Matthew d'Ancona, 'I will be the one, and the Conservatives will be the party, offering genuine change . . . Do you want to hand the keys back to the people who crashed the car?' *Sunday Telegraph*, 6 January 2013.

3 'The PM can still win, but it might have to get personal', *Sunday Telegraph*, 3 March 2013.

19. Jeffrey's revenge

1. Osborne found time in 2009 to review this 900-page doorstopper for *The Spectator* (which I was then editing) when he was Shadow Chancellor *and* preparing for the election. Like Gordon Brown, Michael Gove, William Hague and a tiny handful of others, he manages to combine the practice of politics with voracious bookishness. http://www.spectator.co.uk/books/3520976/lincolns-legacy/.

2. See p. 228.

3. http://www.telegraph.co.uk/news/politics/9903718/Philip-Hammond-interview-The-Defence-Secretarys-cold-war-on-further-military-cuts.html.

4. http://www.newstatesman.com/politics/2013/03/exclusive-vince-cable-calls-osborne-change-direction.

5. Ross Douthat and Reihan Salam, *Grand New Party: How Republicans Can Win the Working Class and Save the American Dream* (Anchor, 2009).

20. Farewell to the Lady

1. On this, and much else, no book rivals, or is likely to rival, Charles Moore's superb authorized biography, the first volume of which, *Not For Turning*, was published in 2013 by Allen Lane.

2. *Sunday Times,* 28 April 2013; see also http://blogs.telegraph.co.uk/news/jameskirkup/100214185/is-david-cameron-a-thatcherite-a-simple-question-with-a-complicated-answer/.

3. Kwasi Kwarteng, Priti Patel, Dominic Raab, Chris Skidmore and Elizabeth Truss, *Britannia Unchained: Global Lessons for Growth and Prosperity* (Palgrave Macmillan, 2012).

4. See p. 148.

5. See pp. 248–9.

6. *Sunday Telegraph,* 19 May 2013.

21. A new England?

1. Charlie Rose, interview, 13 August 2010.

2. See p. 170.

3. See Iain McLean, Jim Gallagher and Guy Lodge, *Scotland's Choices: The Referendum and What Happens Afterwards* (Edinburgh University Press, 2013). See also Jason Cowley's interview with Alex Salmond in the *New Statesman* in June 2013: http://www.newstatesman.com/2013/06/phoney-war-not-campaign.

4. *Daily Telegraph,* 6 October 2005.

5. Richard Sennett, *Together: The Rituals, Pleasures and Politics of Cooperation* (Penguin Books, 2013), p. 280.

22. The recovery position

1 See http://www.bbc.co.uk/news/uk-§politics-24646527 for a breakdown of the costs.

2 For Osborne's scepticism about climate change, see Chapter 15.

3 Interview, *Sunday Telegraph,* 8 December 2013.

4 See Chapter 8.

5 http://www.libdems.org.uk/nick_clegg_speech_at_morpeth_school.

6 For Cummings and his impact, see Chapter 7.

7 http://www.theguardian.com/politics/2014/mar/11/dfe-clegg-free-school-meals-utter-balls-minister.

8 http://blogs.spectator.co.uk/coffeehouse/2013/12/david-cameron-interview-tax-coalition-green-crap-and-team-nigella/.

9 For the rolling conversation between Cameron and Clegg on a putative second coalition, see Chapter 18.

10 http://www.cps.org.uk/events/q/date/2013/11/27/the-2013-margaret-thatcher-lecture-boris-johnson/.

11 See note 3.

12 Jeremy Browne, *Race Plan: An Authentic Liberal Plan to Get Britain Fit for 'The Global Race'* (Reform, 2014).

13 Interview with Rachel Sylvester: http://www.thetimes.co.uk/tto/news/politics/article4061350.ece.

14 http://yougov.co.uk/news/2014/02/24/where-ukip-gets-its-support/.

15 *King Lear*, Act V, Scene 3.

23. One foot on the drawbridge: Syria and Ukraine

1 See Chapter 21 for the first phase of the Syrian crisis.

2 http://www.theguardian.com/politics/2014/apr/17/ed-miliband-david-axelrod-adviser-2015-election.

3 For Norman's brief return to the Cameroon fold, see Chapter 16. For his resignation: http://www.telegraph.co.uk/news/worldnews/middleeast/syria/10287483/Downing-Street-adviser-Jesse-Norman-sacked-over-Syria-vote.html.

4 http://www.nytimes.com/2013/09/01/world/middleeast/syria.html?_r=0.

5 For a more conspiratorial analysis of the President's decision, see this essay by Seymour M. Hersh in the *London Review of Books*, 17 April 2014: http://www.lrb.co.uk/v36/n08/seymour-m-hersh/the-red-line-and-the-rat-line.

6 http://fullcomment.nationalpost.com/2014/03/21/anne-applebaum-putin-invaded-crimea-because-putin-needs-a-war/.

7 http://www.theguardian.com/politics/2014/mar/02/ed-miliband-tories-syria-vote-ukraine.

24. Stuck in the middle

1 http://www.brightblueonline.com/index.php/medias/speeches/item/241-speech-by-nick-boles. Full disclosure: at the time of writing, I was on the Advisory Board of Bright Blue.

2 The rise and nature of the UK Independence Party is explored in Robert Ford and Matthew Goodwin, *Revolt on the Right: Explaining Support for the Radical Right in Britain* (Routledge, 2014).

3 http://www.telegraph.co.uk/news/politics/conservative/10625690/Tim-Yeo-interview-Fear-of-Ukip-will-drive-the-Tories-to-defeat.html.

4 http://www.telegraph.co.uk/news/politics/david-cameron/10341422/David-Cameron-a-Prime-Minister-in-a-hurry.html.

5 See Chapter 18.

6 See Chapter 11.

7 *Financial Times* interview: http://www.ft.com/cms/s/2/ebe8018c-aa45-11e3-8497-00144feab7de.html#axzz2w1tfjVmh.

Index

He just wanted a decent book to read ...

Not too much to ask, is it? It was in 1935 when Allen Lane, Managing Director of Bodley Head Publishers, stood on a platform at Exeter railway station looking for something good to read on his journey back to London. His choice was limited to popular magazines and poor-quality paperbacks – the same choice faced every day by the vast majority of readers, few of whom could afford hardbacks. Lane's disappointment and subsequent anger at the range of books generally available led him to found a company – and change the world.

'We believed in the existence in this country of a vast reading public for intelligent books at a low price, and staked everything on it'
Sir Allen Lane, 1902–1970, founder of Penguin Books

The quality paperback had arrived – and not just in bookshops. Lane was adamant that his Penguins should appear in chain stores and tobacconists, and should cost no more than a packet of cigarettes.

Reading habits (and cigarette prices) have changed since 1935, but Penguin still believes in publishing the best books for everybody to enjoy. We still believe that good design costs no more than bad design, and we still believe that quality books published passionately and responsibly make the world a better place.

So wherever you see the little bird – whether it's on a piece of prize-winning literary fiction or a celebrity autobiography, political tour de force or historical masterpiece, a serial-killer thriller, reference book, world classic or a piece of pure escapism – you can bet that it represents the very best that the genre has to offer.

Whatever you like to read – trust Penguin.